REWAR
ENCOUN

Islam and the
Comparative Theologies of
Kenneth Cragg
and
Wilfred Cantwell Smith

Bård Mæland

MELISENDE
LONDON

REWARDING ENCOUNTERS
Islam and the Comparative Theologies of
Kenneth Cragg and Wilfred Cantwell Smith
by
Bård Mæland

First published 2003 by
Melisende
39 Chelmsford Road
London E18 2PW
Tel. +44 (0)20 8498 9768
Fax +44 (0)20 8504 2558
E mail: melisende@btinternet.com
www.melisende.com
ISBN 1 901764 24 9

Editor: Leonard Harrow
Printed at the Cromwell Press, Trowbridge, England

CONTENTS

PREFACE

Rewarding Encounters was first submitted for the degree of *Doctor theologiae* at the Norwegian Lutheran School of Theology (1991, as *Self-Relating and Self-Change*). I am most grateful for the comprehensive attention my *Doktorvater,* Peder Gravem generously paid to the entire process. His numerous and accurate depictions of the *status quo* as well as the way forward has taught me a lot of scholarly inquiry and virtues. Thanks also to my real *Vater,* Jens Olav Mæland, who, if I am not wrong, was the first to direct my attention to the general field of theology of religions, which he in the early 90s regarded 'the currently most important theological challenge'. This statement is certainly less disputable in our century.

In 1999-2000 the Chaplain in Chief and the Army Staff, Norwegian Armed Forces, provided me with a sabbatical in Oxford for which I am most thankful. This stay enabled me to meet people in UK who in various ways contributed to the development of the study: Gavin D'Costa, Hugh Goddard, David Kerr, Christopher Lamb, Anthony O'Mahony, David Thomas, Keith Ward, and Trevor Williams.

Regarding some of the theoretical and analytical parts of the thesis (especially Chapter 6) I am also indebted to my sustained e-mail mate: Andreas Grünschloß, University of Mainz, for responding constructively to my use of his model in my examination of Smith and Cragg.

I was also lucky to get in touch with the persons behind my material. In fact, I did not succeed in meeting Prof. Wilfred Cantwell Smith because of his worsening health and finally his death in February 2000, in spite of an attempt in 1998 after which I received a most generous invitation. Bishop Kenneth Cragg, however, I met in 1997 and several times in 2000 and 2001. I also heard him teaching and preaching. The way he received me and the active interest he took in my inquiries has shown me that his 'open and hospitable faith' is something beyond a mere construct within his writing. My sympathy for his interreligious approach may be recognized throughout my 'reconstruction' of his comparative theology.

I am also indebted to several people who provided me with *sine quae non* resources: The library at the Norwegian Lutheran School of

Theology (Oslo), the Bodleian Library, the Theology Faculty Library, and the Oriental Institute Library (Oxford).

Finally, I want to thank the Norwegian Military Academy and the Chief Chaplain for providing me with a most helpful working situation throughout the time of my studies. Despite my primary theological interests, my military affiliation may be seen as a sign of changing times in the armed forces worldwide, where cross-cultural and cross-religious understanding are regarded as far from peripheral to military operations. The publication of this book also received funding from the Norwegian MoD.

The thesis is dedicated to Leni, my lovable wife and mother of our two beautiful and crazy children, Andrea and Jakob. Leni has been a support and inspiration without which the book would have been quite different. She was often asking me what I 'precisely was doing for the moment.' This rare question helped me, probably more than I am aware of, to make the study more precise and, hopefully, also more intriguing. At the end of the day, this might turn out as my primary hermeneutical education.

Bård Mæland
Oslo, July 2002

1

INTRODUCTION

1.1 The Fly and the Goldfish Bowl: an Inducement

What is the relation between the '*engagé* participant' of a religious community or religious[1] tradition, on the one hand, and the 'serious student' of other religious communities or complexes, on the other?[2] This question highlights the very core of the present study, at the intersection between understanding Islam and doing so as a Christian theologian.

---

[1] 'Religion(s)' and 'religious tradition(s)' are used with equal meaning. As will be shown later in the study (Chapter 2.4), Wilfred Cantwell Smith has suggested a termination of the concept 'religion' in *The Meaning and End of Religion (ME)*. I agree with Smith that 'religion' and 'religions' historically and to a large extent refer to constructed (in Smith's vocabulary: 'reified') entities. Not least the '-isms' clearly indicate that these are tags being added to by external forces (the exception, semantically, to be *Islam*). Yet, how they correspond to an internal self-understanding has to be judged from case to case, not least on the background of how the believers of the various traditions interpret themselves in relation to corporate entities. I do not think that Smith solves this problem by talking of 'cumulative traditions' as opposed to 'personal faith'. See Küng 1986 on this. See also Peter Slater who in his criticism of what he calls Smith's 'suspect philosophy of language' (i.e. his focus on single words and their supposedly single referents) asserts that 'we need the word 'religion' to refer to *whole sets of interactions* with ultimate truth and value in changing cultures,' Slater 1982, 100, my emphasis. When I (against Smith) continue to make use of the traditional concept of 'religion' in both singular and plural, it is done in the specific meaning of *traditions for individual and collective interpretation of life—with reference to some kind of ultimate reality*. This definition comes close to one of Hans Küng, namely that 'religion is a living socio-individuated realisation ... of a relationship with something that goes beyond or enfolds human beings and their world and that prolongs itself into a tradition and in a community,' Küng 1986, xiv. For use in this specific study it could have been considerably narrowed as the study only concerns two Semitic religions. Yet, a definition of religion(s) should also embrace non-Semitic religions as well as modern, popular religiosity, cf. Grünschloß 1994b, 298, perhaps also secular ideologies which refer to 'ultimates' (cf. the notion of 'quasi-religions', Tillich 1963b, 291-300). In this respect I think Paul Tillich's concept of 'ultimate reality' is viable. Although in my study it might appear to be a curiosity, we may note that Buddhism—the famous test case for definitions of religion—may be regarded as included in the definition adopted here. In Buddhism the ultimate is among other things related to the understanding of *anatta*, what Tillich in his distinctive language calls 'absolute non-being,' Tillich 1963b, 309-317, 314 quoted.

[2] See Smith, *The Meaning and End of Religion (ME)*, 13, for the pair of these notions.

Wilfred Cantwell Smith makes an illuminating analogy of the study of religion in a passage in *The Meaning and End of Religion* when he refers to a fly that is walking on the outside of a goldfish bowl.[3] To take advantage of the same analogy, my aim is to ponder the problem of the self-understanding of the fly given the fact that the goldfish is there. One may ask in a theoretical way: What kind of contact or relationship might be possible to develop between the two: penetration, conceptual distance, approximation, perception of isolated worlds of life? Another question to pose is whether the life of the goldfish has any impact on how the fly perceives itself? It may also be inquired, on the other hand, how the present and previous life of the fly contributes to, or determines its perception of the goldfish? Imaginative, yes, but hopefully also illuminating for the matter of what follows.

1.2   Problems, Aims and Theses

This study addresses the question of how a person steeped in Christian theology develops relations with Islam[4] and Muslims. As material for the explorative parts (Chapter 2-5), I have chosen the works of (Albert) Kenneth Cragg (1913-) and Wilfred Cantwell Smith (1916-2000).[5] Throughout the analysis of these works I will be looking to see how they develop relations to Islam, as *they* understand it to be, from the point of their normative Christian self-understanding. My main question follows from this:

1. How are the systematic relations between the interpretations of Islam of Kenneth Cragg and Wilfred Cantwell Smith and their self-understandings to be conceived?

By *systematic relations* I mean 'the systematic-theological and conceptional efforts' Smith and Cragg make in order to relate their Christian faith to Islam and Muslims. By the notion of *self-understandings* I mean the 'normative theological frameworks' of Smith and Cragg respectively. Lastly, the comprehensive answers to the question above that I aim to find and identify in Smith and Cragg, I will denote their 'comparative theologies'.

I must, however, stress that the study does *not* attempt to give an analysis of what the relation between Islam and Christian theology is

---

[3]   *ME*, 7.

[4]   I agree with most of the criticism performed by Smith against perceptions of Islam as a static, systematic entity, cf. Chapter 3.2 and 3.3. Hence, I will use the term 'Islam' more flexibly, as the pair of 'Islam and Muslims'.

[5]   For an outline of *some* biographical data of Cragg and Smith, see the Biography and References at the end of the study.

per se. The problem of the study is an *intra-Christian* problem in the sense of how the same person relates something external (*relatum/ interpretandum*), and to some extent alien (Islam), to something 'of his own' (his self-understanding/*interpretans*).[6] Or stated the other way around: the *self-referential* [7] *process* of developing *theological relations to Islam.* It can be argued that as far as understanding of Islam is a *self-responsible* act of interpretation, any interpretation of Islam will imply a *positioning of oneself,* at least as long as other interpretations of Islam are disallowed.[8] Christian theological relations to Islam are only possible as far as Christian theology implies openness on its own premises.[9] For this I will use the following concept: *self-relating.*[10] The study thus

---

[6] See D'Costa 1986a, 5, for an example of a 'Christian theology of religions' that is understood as an 'activity of *self-understanding* ... the explanatory, continually renewed effort *within* the Christian tradition to examine the implications of that tradition where it is continually *being interrogated* by conjectures of historical change' (my emphases), the 'entrance of world religions' representing one series of such changes or 'diversification of human experience.' Gavin D'Costa refers at this place to Cornelius Ernst, *Multiple Echo,* 1979, 30. By this, the matters of both 'intensification' and 'extensification' are made themes. See below for these concepts. What is vaguely described here, becomes more clearly perceived later in D'Costa's work, e.g., p. 93 where he speaks about the dialectical structure between 'self-understanding' and 'understanding the other', a Christian's 'self-discovery' in dialogue, and p. 122 where 'indigenization' and 'mutual self-transformation' in dialogue can be said to represent two sides of the same coin.

[7] I use 'self-reference' in a system-theoretical meaning, that is: 'basing itself on its own code, utilizing feedback-mechanisms, which maintains the system during its evolutionary interaction with other systems in the surroundings,' Gregersen 1991, 8, my transl. Thus, this understanding resonates with the core-concepts of our study: *self-relating and self-change.*

[8] Cf. Hammerschmidt 1997, 241: 'Meine Interpretationsleistung ist mir nicht äußerlich. In dem Netz möglicher interpretativer Verweisungen positioniere ich mich selbst. *Ich bin es, die sich zu verstehen gibt*', emphasis original.

[9] Gregersen 1991, 9: 'Self-reference is a prerequisite for a system-productive ability to make connections. Only the one who is emotionally stable is, as we know, able to bear the pressure of exposing himself to new challenges and having the surplus to integrate them,' my translation. Thus, for a system to be apparently *enclosed* is the prerequisite for any *openness* to its surroundings.

[10] 'Self-relating' does here not denote the other possible meaning of this notion, provided a genitive relation between the terms, namely as 'an extreme case of relation in which its two terms coincide,' or 'the relation that any object can and must have to itself in order for it to be what it is,' in short: an object-genitive, Gasché 1999, 8. Viewed in the light of the hypotheses induced by the exploration of Smith and Cragg, Chapter 6.5, this meaning is however not entirely absent in the study.

attempts to enter into a discussion of theological understandings of Islam.[11] In this activity, the hermeneutical issue of attuning external perspectives (relations) to internal (the normative theological framework) will be of particular interest.

A well documented problem of perceiving something 'alien', is, especially since Martin Heidegger and Hans-Georg Gadamer, how one's pre-understandings, axioms, prejudices, foremeanings, forestructure, etc., play a significant and inescapable role in the understanding of the 'issue' of an Other'[12], be it as a text, a person, a tradition, or whatever.[13] A less noticed issue, at least in regard of interreligious hermeneutics, is how one's self-understanding is formed, influenced, affected, interrogated, etc., by the encounter with this 'other'. This is denoted self-change in

---

[11] For a discussion of such approaches to Islam, see Hock 1986, 3-8. I share both his criticism of Willem A. Bijlefeld's dichotomic understanding of the relation between religious studies and theology, and his awareness of the not very honourable history of Christian encounter with the 'Orient', e.g., in the fashion of 'Orientalism'. His criticism of Bijlefeld is also an implicit critique of Edward W. Said's position of prohibiting non-Muslims to interpret Islam (cf. Said 1978/1995). However, Said's position is not so much apodictic, as a reckoning with inescapable Orientalist 'misrepresentations' of, and 'interventions' in Islam, caused by racial, ideological, and imperialist stereotypes, which are 'embedded first in the language and then in the culture, institutions, and political ambience of the presenter' and thus serve certain purposes other than the 'truth' of its object, ibid. 272f and 328. What Said primarily asks for is political and historical awareness, as well as an awareness of human experience, ibid. 328. This leads him for example, most interestingly, because much of this might be applied to Smith and Cragg, to a considerable appreciation of the dynamic Catholic Orientalist Louis Massignon (1883-1962), whom he saw as extending the confines of the discipline (Orientalism). On the other hand, Massignon was also to be seen as offering 'a kind of system for producing certain kinds of statements, disseminated into the large mass of discursive formations that together make up the archive, or cultural material, of his time,' ibid. 274. What I see as applying to Smith and Cragg is precisely their historical awareness, as well as awareness of experiences and beliefs/faith of Muslims, though at least Cragg is likely to be criticized for a degree of 'doctrinal preconceptions,' which leads me to suspect Said for too easily emphasizing critical scrutiny over the importance of, e.g., 'precondition' for understanding the 'other'. More on this below.

[12] For Gadamer's use of 'other', which also discloses the relevance of Gadamer for the matter of our study, see e.g. his late text in Gadamer 1994, x: 'Now, instead, there is an Other, who is not an object for the subject but someone to whom we are bound in the reciprocations of language and life. So, too, understanding is no method but rather a form of community among those who understand each other.'
Regarding 'other' and '(one)self, the study attempts to use capitalization when 'other' and '(one)self' denote *epistemic locations* which encounter each other, and lower-case letters when they denote 'other' and '(one)self' in a *concrete* way, of ordinary language, cf. Hammerschmidt 1997, 13. The distinction between the two is however not complete in the study.

[13] Harvey 1987, 284.

this study. Adopting this perspective, Oneself cannot anymore be conceived as a fixed and detached Self because of its participation in the otherness of the Other. If so, this makes self-understanding and understanding of the Other interdependent.[14]

If we apply these insights to our material and the problem of our study, it will be reasonable to pose the following questions as sub-questions to the one presented above:

2. How do the self-understandings of Cragg and of Smith allow, affect and determine their interpretations of Islam (self-relating)? And on the other hand:

3. How do their interpretations of Islam affect and modify their self-understandings (self-change)?

It is the aim of this study to explore, identify and interpret the issues of 'self-relating' and 'self-change' in the writings of Smith and Cragg. Using the terminology of Andreas Feldkeller,[15] self-relating' is denoted as *extensification,* that is, how one's own faith extends itself/is extended by its own resources in order to interpret, relate to, or even include (materially), another faith or religious tradition. The latter, 'self-change', I will call *intensification,* that is: how the awareness of, contact with, and pondering of another faith forms one's own faith.

Most interestingly, it is primarily this latter meaning that resembles the basic meaning of the Latin term corresponding to relation and relating: *relatio.* This term, both in its verbal (*refero*) and derived noun, denotes a 'carrying, bringing, or throwing back,' and even 'represent, set forth anew, and reproduce.'[16] This applies also partly to a possible Greek etymology

---

[14] Hammerschmidt 1997, 12f. It is her aim to avoid a notion of 'understanding' that sees perception of the Other merely as dependent on 'contingent acts of self-understanding'. According to Hammerschmidt, understanding the Other needs also to be self-critically aware of one's motives and fundamental suppositions, as well as ethically and politically engaged in the other through participation in the 'act of understanding' in an 'intersubjective, dialogical room,' ibid.

[15] See Chapter 6.2 related to the discussion of Andreas Grünschloß' heuristic interreligious model.

[16] See 'relatio' in Lewis and Short 1879/1955, 1544f and 1554f. Also the other meanings of *relatio*, e.g. 'report,' 'intelligence,' etc., become understandable given this general meaning of *refero* and *relatio*. This does, however, not mean that 'intensification' is the only possible rendering of the terms with regards to the problem of our study. Also 'relate' (!) is included as one possible meaning, see 1545, II.B.3. Cf. also the (presumably) first logical use of *relatio* by Quintilian as 'relatione ad aliquid', Gasché 1999, 1f and 347, n1. In respect of this study I will assert that it might be feasible to think of two kinds of 'throwing back', namely a) as 'throwing the Muslim faith back to Muslims after being interpreted in the light of the Christian faith', and b) as 'throwing back of the Christian faith to Christians after having attempted to relate it to the Other (Muslim), in order to rethink its

of 'hermeneutics' (cf. *hermeneuein*).[17] Thus, relations are not only to be considered as self-referential but also as *self-constitutive*.[18] A possible term for this is 'reflexive relation', insofar as one's self-understanding, or identity, entails a relation (extensification) that aims at characterizing and constituting itself (intensification of one's self-understanding).[19]

If this hermeneutic circle is seen as a temporal process, a correlated problem that occurs is how to discern between the self-understanding 'before' and an eventual change 'after' encountering Islam in order to understand it. Yet, the alternative is to think of the self-understanding as immune and unresponsive to the understanding of Islam. That, I regard as both unthinkable and naive.[20] In any case, it is neither

---

shape and expressions'. Nevertheless, the astonishing insight for a modern reader is how the reciprocal element has been included in most of the classical meanings of *relatio*. Rodolphe Gasché purports to return to this classical understanding of relation as essentially 'being-toward-another' (Gr *pros ti*), and not 'being-toward-the One' (*pros en*), leaving out the Scholastic/Aristotelian formal concept of relation as a 'diminished being' (Aquinas), 'tiny being' (Scotus), that is: as accident, attribute, a 'thing' to a more perfect entity, Gasché 1999, 1-13 and *passim*. Though Gasché acknowledges the medieval notion of relations as extramental and real, his suggestion is, drawing on Julius Jakob Shaaf, that 'relation' is 'minimal' in another sense, namely as being 'more elemental than all the things that are of explicit philosophical concern' precisely because it is an 'issue at the limit,' that is: because 'as the least possible it marks a limit beyond which no quantity obtains anymore,' ibid. 5f. This limit and 'simple complex' is, most interestingly for our study, furthermore understood as 'a threshold that communicates between entities, or domains, that are all in the position of others among each other,' *ibid.*, 11. Hence relations tie 'others' together in specific and singular configurations. Consequently, Gasché's theory of relations is an argument for *particularity*. See also Anette C. Hammerschmidt's notion of 'the Between as positive place' (Ger. *das Zwischen als positiver Ort*) and 'the Between as the place of understanding' (*das Zwischen als Ort des Verstehens*), Hammerschmidt 1997, ch. 5 and 6 respectively.

[17] I am thinking of the god Hermes in Greek mythology who, *inter alia*, was the deity of the *boundaries* (cf. 'Alien', 'Other') as well as the *messenger* of the gods (cf. relations, mediations), Harvey 1987, 279.

[18] Cf. Gasché 1999. See also Hammerschmidt 1997, 241: 'Jedes Verstehen [impliziert] einen sinnko[n]stitutiven Akt, in dem das Allgemeine der sprachlichen Sinnfixierung seine Bedeutung nur über die Gleichzeitigkeit von Identität und Differenz erhält.'

[19] *CDPh*, 'relation,' article signed S.J. Wagner, 689. This correlates also to the concept of a hermeneutic circle (Heidegger), see Hammerschmidt 1997, 19, who sees 'das Zwischen' as constitutive and constructive as far as it '[durchkreuzt] das Subjekt' by 'der reflexiven Bewegung des (Selbst-)Bewußtseins.'

[20] Cf. David Tracy who in his entry in *EncRel(E)* on 'Comparative theology' maintains, in respect of the importance of *applicatio,* and not only *intelligentia* and *explicatio* as the 'classical Western hermeneutical terms', that 'an application of the interpretation to its context ... is at the same time a precondition to any understanding and interpretation,' Tracy 1987, 453.

possible to identify either of the two ('pre-' and 'post-' self-understandings) exactly, nor to separate them. Rather the opposite: the self-understanding based on theological and other presuppositions colours and determines the interpretation of Islam, as also the study of Islam does the other way around, and hence implies certain degrees of reconceptualization and rethinking of the 'original' self-understanding. To use the words of *Nostra Aetate*, this is a *comprehensio mutua*[21] that not only implies an attempt to comprehend Islam, but also is itself comprehended during the process of understanding Islam.

Along these lines, and related to the problem of the study, I thus suggest that the systematic relations between the self-understandings of Smith and Cragg and their interpretations of Islam are mutually determined and affected by their self-understandings (Oneself) and their interpretations of Islam (the Other). A corresponding way of stating this,

---

[21] *Nostra Aetate*, paragraph 3, Denzinger 1991, § 4197. Though the very notion is evocative, the way this term has its implicit interpretation in, e.g., the *Guidelines for Dialogue between Christians and Muslims* of the Pontifical Council for Interreligious Dialogue (1981/1990) is directed more towards 'understanding each other' and, consequently, does not emphasize so much the *intensification* matter ('itself being comprehended'). The main objective in this study seems to be (by love) to overcome the gap between 'interpretation by another [i.e. the Christian]' and 'self-interpretation of the other [i.e. of Muslims],' 1. Yet, in its 'Paths and Ways' for the dialogue with Muslims (31-34), one might find the point that 'receiving others decisively into one's experience' and 'taking their distinctive nature into account' *provide an opportunity for self-renewal and enrichment*. In this chapter the emphasis within 'mutual understanding', is put on living alongside each other, sharing, venturing and running risks together. Nevertheless, this is seen as *a constant process of personal spiritual growth*, 31. The intensification matter is however well emphasized in one of the other Vatican II documents: *Gaudium et Spes,* as demonstrated by G. D'Costa, D'Costa 2000, 111. *Gaudium et Spes* acknowledges in §40 elements of truth and goodness within Western modernity, which may be both a preparation for the Gospel and, on the other hand, serve 'revealed truth' (i.e. the Christian faith) to be 'more deeply penetrated, better challenged, and set forth to greater advantage ... understand it more penetratingly, express it better, and adjust it more successfully to our times,' Denzinger 1991, § 4344 ('The help that the Church receives from the present world'). *Gaudium et Spes* sees this under the heading of *exchange (Lat. commercium)*, which combines 'relation' and 'change' in mercantile language. In the *Dominus Iesus* from the Congregation for the Doctrine of the Faith in 2000 (16 June), *Nostra Aetate,* the *Guidelines for Dialogue* and *Gaudium et Spes* are resonated in terms like 'considering the values which these religions witness to and offer humanity', 'an attitude of understanding', 'a relationship of mutual knowledge' and 'reciprocal enrichment' (paragraph 2). The restoration (e.g. paragraph 3: 'recall to ... certain indispensable elements of Christian doctrine') of exclusive language is nevertheless obvious (e.g.) (paragraph 15; 'unicity', 'unique', 'singular', 'universality', 'absoluteness', 'exclusive').

which takes the relations as such as the focal points for self-understanding and identity formation, is that the theological self-understandings of Smith and Cragg are dependent upon the relations that are developed towards Islam. That is: their relations to Islam are theologically constitutive.

1.3 Self-Relating and Self-Change in Previous Works on Smith and Cragg

During the 1990s there has been a significant increase of scholarly works on Smith.[22] A similar picture can be seen in relation to the works on Cragg.[23] There are also many works in which Smith *and* Cragg are compared, or where they are represented as two among other authors whose works are analyzed in relation to a common issue.[24] The interest demonstrated in the last three footnotes is only meant to point to the considerable interest

---

[22] This can be illustrated briefly with reference to Andreas Grünschloß who in his dissertation on Smith (Grünschloß 1994a) notes the following findings in the period from 1969-1991/1992: 10 Ph.Ds on Smith alone or as one among other authors, and one M.A. diss. Since that time (1991) there has appeared at least six Ph.Ds (Anderson 1991, Stetson 1993, Grünschloß 1994a, Rokhsefat 1994, Cameron 1997, Bae 1998), Grünschloß' own included, further two that he missed in his biography (Bollinger 1981, Fernhout 1986), two E.D.D. diss., which are very dependent upon the theories of Smith and thus represent the width of the reception of Smith (Christiano 1986, Brown 1997), four M.A. theses (Stevens 1986, Stephens 1988, Van Orman 1994, Mitchell 1994), and two smalller A.B. theses (Psychas 1986 and Gardner 1989; on this level it is likely that there exists more theses on Smith which are not recorded).

[23] Whereas several dissertations were produced in the period 1962-1980 (McCulloch 1962, Virgint 1970, Hambrick-Stowe 1972, D'Souza 1980), there has been a remarkable production, and on a higher level later, especially in the 90s (Richards 1993, Wilson 1995, Wood 1996, Lamb 1997, Tebbe 1998). Given Cragg's sustained production and the lack of comprehension of certain areas of his writings, more theses are awaited.

[24] Not surprisingly, almost all of these works have as one of their concerns the relation and approach to Islam of Cragg and Smith (Ipema 1971, Milne 1975, Hock 1985, Jones 1988, Aydin 1998). One of these also includes a Muslim response, examining the implications for dialogue with Muslims that the works of Cragg and Smith has contributed to (Aydin 1998). Only one work does not primarily deal with a question related to their approach to Islam but instead with their relation to inter-faith dialogue as a method for the scientific study of religion. Yet, in this study the two play only a minor role (Wallace 1994). This fact is, as already mentioned, not surprising given that the intersection between the works of Cragg and Smith has to be somehow located to their understanding of Islam and Muslims, despite the fact that whereas the relation to Islam plays a major role in the authorship of Cragg, it is limited both in time and quantity in Smith.

scholars still pay to the writings of Smith and Cragg, as well as to the vast literature that exists on the ideas of these authors.

The works of interest span various aspects of this study (a. the understanding of Islam, b. the authorships of Cragg/Smith, and c. their normative theology), and include also the most comprehensive/systematical works within these areas of interest. A selection of the following works may give a sufficient picture of the value of the approach in connection with the over-complex situation of secondary literature: Ipema 1971, Hock 1985, Grünschloß 1994a, and Lamb 1997. It should be noted that my emphasis here is not on particular interpretations of Smith and Cragg *per se,* but on how the subject of my study ('self-relating' and 'self-change') is made a theme in these studies. Additional matters will be considered throughout the study where it is appropriate to consider them. Thus, works on Smith and Cragg other than the four mentioned above will be consulted.

I start with two works which treat both Smith and Cragg. Regarding the rather old[25] dissertation of Ipema from 1971, the major aim is to analyze and evaluate how 'four Christian interpreters of Islam' have interpreted Islam during the 19th and 20th century.[26] What seems to be central in Ipema's approach is what he identifies as an aim or criterion for any interpretation of Islam, namely 'that the phenomenon studied be reconstructed in accordance with its essential reality in terms comprehensible to those to whom the report of the findings is to be made' (15). My response to that criterion can be briefly put thus: This criterion corresponds partly to the material he treats. Yet, Ipema seems to leave out the possibilities of theological interpretation of Islam, as well as the issue of reciprocity in hermeneutical processes, to which also any interpretation of Islam belongs. It seems, moreover, that his criterion assumes that it is possible to discover Islam in its essence, and that the Christian understanding of Islam is a matter of a mere 'comprehensible transfer' of the result gained in the studies of Islam. As far as it goes, this is good, but I doubt that this can be the entire case, which will be demonstrated throughout the study. Given his ultimate end for the interpretations, 'a sympathetic understanding of, and feeling for that religion' (7), his approach seems—hermeneutically speaking—too naive.[27]

---

[25] The 70s onwards was a very productive period for both Smith and Cragg. Ipema therefore lacks important material from both of them.

[26] Ipema 1971. The four are: Duncan B. Macdonald, Samuel M. Zwemer, Cragg and Smith. Subsequent parenthetical references refer to this study.

[27] Cf. also his conclusion about how the interpretation of Islam is best facilitated by an interpreter that defines his 'faith-allegiance ..., who yet claims some kinship to men of other faiths and respects the worth of their faith and its expression' (235). Needless to say, this is another approach to the Islam interpretations of Smith and Cragg than mine.

What is lacking in the work of Ipema compared to my hermeneutic perspective, is more present in the 1985 dissertation of Klaus Hock.[28] Against the background of the request for a humble attitude towards the criticism raised against Oriental studies in the last century, the main purposes for Hock are: a) to show how theological interpretations of Islam are based on certain theological presuppositions, criteria and categories, and b) to analyze how the changes of the theological interpretations of Islam relate to the changes in theology in other respects (6).

Hock explicitly establishes his approach in opposition to the dichotomy between theology and interpretation of Islam by Willem A. Bijlefeld in his *De Islam als na-christelikje Religie* (4-6).[29] According to Hock, it is a legitimate task to make a theological interpretation of Islam. Moreover, Hock tries to find a theological level within the general limits of a theology of religion based on 'die *zentralen* Inhalte des christlichen Glaubens' (350), which can enable 'eine theologische Beurteilung und Evaluierung des Islams' (7). Hock finds this related to 'die Struktur des Kerygmas' which is primarily characterized by 'das Scheitern der unmittelbaren Selbstmacht und Selbständigkeit Gottes' (357).[30] One of the implications of this 'begrifflich-kategorialen Struktur' of the *Kerygma* reads as follows:

> Darum muß die christliche Theologie der Religionen bemüht sein, die anderen Religionen *in sich* zu erfassen, und sie dann auf ihre mögliche Bedeutung für den christlichen Glauben befragen, ohne ihre Andersartigkeit zu ignorieren ... Christliche Theologie der Religionen ist offen für den anderen Glauben! (361)

This statement comes very close to the aspects of 'self-relating' and 'self-change' in the present study. Together with the search for 'criteria and categories' of several Christian theological Islam interpreters, this constitutes a hermeneutical perspective: On the one hand Hock discloses the, more or less, implicit presuppositions that constitute the approach towards Islam. On the other hand, after the attempt to interpret a religion

---

[28] Hock 1986. The works of Cragg and Smith are only two of many (i.e. Samuel M. Zwemer, Gottfried Simon, Emmanuel Kellerhals, Hendrik Kraemer, Johan Bouman). In addition to analyzing the works of particular scholars, Hock also tries to make a general survey of diverse epochs and attitudes in the approach to Islam among Western Christian theologians. Subsequent parenthetical remarks refer to this work.

[29] Leiden 1959. See also note 11, p. 3.

[30] Hock quotes at this place Falk Wagner, Systematisch-theologische und sozialethische Erwägungen zu Frieden und Gewalt, in: *Friedenserziehung als Problem von Theologie und Religionspädagogik*, München 1981 (ed. not mentioned).

'in sich', he draws the attention to the significance this will have on the Christian faith.

However, some studies that concentrate on writings of either Smith or Cragg develop more thorough hermeneutical perspectives. An important study in this respect is Andreas Grünschloß' comprehensive dissertation on Smith and his interreligious hermeneutics (Grünschloß 1994). At the end of his dissertation, he considers the *reconstruction and attuning of internal and external perspectives* ('die Rekonstruktion und Abstimmung von Innen- und Außenperspektiven') in explicit connection with Hock's emphasis on a theology of religions that should be developed 'aus der Mitte ihre eigenen Glaubens.'[31] Grünschloß launches here the notion of *Strukturerhaltung* denoting the maintenance of one's own world-view, and *Perspektivenvermittelung,* denoting the process of understanding in relation to 'external' world-views.[32] His point is that those two aspects of any interreligious hermeneutics are interdependent and have to be done simultaneously. *Perspektivenvermittelung* especially seems to be most important for Grünschloß, emphasising the self-critical[33] reconstruction of one's own understanding of faith and tradition in the light of the history of religions.[34] Seen together, these concepts, especially the latter, presuppose both 'self-relating' and 'self-change'.

Some attention should also be directed to the short but most thorough study of Cragg's 'Christian vocation Islam': Christopher Lamb's dissertation from 1987 (published in 1997).[35] Though this study aims to give a comprehensive account of Cragg's theology in the light of Anglican and Arab traditions, it also contains particular hermeneutical perspectives on Cragg that resemble those of this study. One of these is his introduction of Gadamer after having pointed to the accusation against Cragg of 'Christianizing' Islam (132-137). Based on Gadamer's hermeneutics, Lamb affirms that observation and evaluation 'are not necessarily two procedures at all' (133), and that the former 'distinction characteristic of

---

[31] Grünschloß 1994a, 308-312. At this point Grünschloß is dependent upon M. Welker, see Welker 1988.

[32] Grünschloß 1994a, 309.

[33] Grünschloß quotes in this respect Hock (regarding his radical criticism of 'autonomer Eigenmächtigkeit,' cf. Hock 1986, 360f) about the *vulnerability* of one's own 'perspective of meaning' *(Sinnperspektive)* as the most Christ-like way of encounter people of other faiths, ibid. The present study will demonstrate how this resonates with Cragg's Christology.

[34] Grünschloß 1994a, 311. Grünschloß quotes H. J. Margull from an article about vulnerability, who asserts that ' "Die Aussagekraft des eigenen Glaube ensteht nicht aus der Negation der Überzeugung anderer ... [aber] in der Entdeckung der Besonderheit des eigenen Glaubens ... Zu dieser Entdeckung braucht man jedoch die anderen ..."', Grünschloß 1994a, 311, note 167.

[35] Lamb 1997. Subsequent parenthetical references refer to this study.

phenomenological religious studies between understanding and evaluation begins to break down' (134). This leads him to acknowledge Cragg's attempt to 'apply' a Christian interpretation of Islam, and also the bringing of his 'Christian questions to Islamic material ... until they are shown to be inappropriate' *(ibid.)*. In this respect Lamb also admits the possibility of interpreting Islam from without the community of the particular Islamic tradition. Yet, such an interpretation should be 'hospitable to all the potential material' of Islam, and thus avoid 'a premature reconciliation, or 'fusion of horizons' (135). Lamb also draws attention to the problem of interpretation of 'another text' so as merely to 'mirror back' the thoughts and attitudes of the interpreter (136). Again, Lamb's use of Gadamer resembles the problem of the present study and is quite helpful, albeit the matter of 'self-change' is not thoroughly addressed. It remains therefore to see how 'self-relating' and 'self-change' are related to each other in Cragg.

1.4 Material Considerations

The first reason for the choice of the authorships of Kenneth Cragg and Wilfred Cantwell Smith is that both Smith and Cragg have made significant contributions to an understanding of Islam.[36] Within a major (Cragg) and considerable (Smith) part of their total literary works they seek to understand the religious tradition of Islam and the faith of Muslims. This is, however, most true of their earlier works, especially in the case of Smith. Whereas Smith writes decreasingly about Islam, though it continues to serve him as a main source of examples and illustrations, Cragg has a longer (temporal) range of Islam-studies though he increasingly relates to the plurality of religions and religiousness in general, as well as other topics.[37] It should also be mentioned they served extensively in parts of the world with a substantial or majority Muslim population.[38]

---

[36] Though some will hesitate to use the notion of *islamicists* on Cragg, due *inter alia* to what generally can be termed a criticism of his approach as 'Christianizing', which will be addressed in Chapter 5. Cf. also the fact that the Muslim reception of Cragg's studies has been very ambivalent. This includes certainly many who have been satisfied with his approach, to put it very modestly. Smith, on the other hand, established undoubtedly his position as an islamicist by his earliest (socio-historical) works, i.e., *MI* and particularly *IH,* not to mention minor studies presented in *UI.* However, this picture is not unequivocal. For a stark criticism of Smith's approach, see the Pakistan journal *Al-Islam* (April, 1958) where Smith is branded 'the great enemy of Islam,' Tibawi 1963, 299, n45.

[37] More about this in Chapter 4.1.

[38] Cragg served especially in Beirut, Cairo and Jerusalem, Smith in Lahore (previously India, now Pakistan). For a survey of their manifold education, offices and posts, cf. the brief Biography and References below.

Secondly, both have also aimed to interpret Islam in *theological categories* and thus aimed at connecting their interpretations of Islam (or as Smith would like to differentiate it, the Islamic tradition and faith among Muslim persons) with larger and superior frameworks. Yet, these theologies of Islam are very different in shape and content. Whereas Cragg conveys a considerable amount of substantial, Christian dogmatic issues into the dialogue with Islam, partly clothed by an inventive and elastic use of language, the features of Smith's approach are that of an untiring historian with strong personalist and (religious) humanist strains, one might well say, that of an academician. Yet, one common feature is that both lack a degree of a systematic-philosophical stringency. Their style is more shaped by their different interests in poetry and imagination (Cragg) and comparative religion and the history of religion (Smith). But there are also obvious correlations, for example with regard to semantic innovation and reformulation. These differences and similarities both complicate and make possible the endeavour to compare and treat them in relation to a common issue: 'self-relating' and 'self-change'. It is my contention that 'self-relating' and 'self-change', and their mutual relation, can be identified and characterized in Smith and Cragg.

For the main exploration and analysis of Smith and Cragg's writings, I will concentrate on materials which expose Smith and Cragg's distinctive theologies of Islam. In this, an important fact must be considered: A vast (Smith) and considerable (Cragg) part of their works are general contexts for any interpretation of what they specifically contribute in respect of the problem of the present study. As this general context also comprehends important normative-theological and hermeneutical issues related to the questions dealt with in this study, this 'larger context' will have to be considered extensively.

The primary concern in Smith's works is to rethink the way students of religion depict and conceptualize the religiousness of humankind worldwide. His replacement of 'religion' and 'religions', as well as all the '-isms,' by 'personal faith' and 'cumulative tradition' in *The Meaning and End of Religion* (*ME,* 1963) is the prominent example of this. Yet, by executing these replacements he also develops a distinctive relation between his Christian 'faith' and the 'faith' of other religious persons. For Smith the human quality of faith is seen as a human universal, yet not identical from tradition to tradition, or from person to person. By his emphasis on faith, the differences of 'externals' and 'beliefs' are confined to serve the evolution of faith, albeit they are never confused with it. In short, and in relational language, faith converge (!),[39] beliefs diverge. In his studies of Islam the same picture of faith and belief/believing can be

---

[39] Because of its function as a universal human quality, Smith avoids use of the plural of 'faith'.

13

seen, or even, Smith's general view of faith and belief seems to depend upon his studies of Islam. In that respect, self-relating, that is his attempt to grasp the meaning of Islam, has changed his self-understanding. In all this, Smith sees himself as a reformer. Yet, on the other hand, Smith admits that his particular perspective on faith and belief is a contribution of his as a Christian theologian. Consequently, the faith that he has inherited from his Calvinist background, as he understands it, and has developed in it, is regarded by him as of the same quality as that of a Muslim (for example). In short, a Muslim and Christian faith can well be combined and is ultimately enabled by his understanding of and emphasis on God as 'transcendent'. To this corresponds a near absence of a material Christology in his writings.

Cragg's approach is in many respects almost opposite, based on a Christology that emphasizes the Incarnation, suffering and inclusiveness of Christ, in many ways a *kenotic* Christology, Cragg aims to make Christ relevant within an Islamic environment. For this purpose his Christology becomes the overall important pattern. Based on this pattern, he makes a twofold approach: On the one hand he searches in the Muslim context for what may eventually resonate with the Christic pattern and thus move Muslims 'Christwards'. In this the Christ-event works as a heuristical tool. This implies a serious concern to engage with modern Muslim intellectuals and poets but also a sense for the conditions of human life in general, which Muslims live under, and which they share with Christians. On the other hand, the Christic pattern of suffering and renunciation of power and prestige becomes a critical tool for his interpretation of Islam. This is particularly the case in his criticism of the Prophet after the Hijrah, in Medina, as well as the Islamic understanding of God's transcendence. Nevertheless, with regards to both the heuristic and critical aspects of the Christ-event, Cragg sees the possibilities of making Christ relevant for Muslims, as well as recruiting that in Islam which can be held together with a faith in Christ. For this 'making Christ relevant', his inventions of concepts, often based on poems or the Qur'an, and often rather abstract and idiosyncratic, play a significant role. Yet, this encounter with Islam has also had an impact on Cragg's self-understanding. With Cragg's own words, his Christian faith has been refined and purified, although not rethought, which for him would have implied an undue agnosticism.

1.5 *The Larger Context of the Study*

Firstly, the study addresses the debate on how non-Christian religions present a challenge to Christian systematic theology,[40] in my case a Lutheran theology, and whether and how their existence and expressions can be affirmed from within, for example, a Trinitarian theology. The particular approach of the study is to comprehend the interreligious hermeneutics included in the effort to construct relations between one's Christian self-understanding and another religion. I have therefore chosen materials that primarily seek to develop relations to only one other religion: Islam.[41] I have already denoted the ways in which Smith and Cragg develop comprehensive relations to Islam as 'comparative theologies' (Chapter 1.4). This presupposes a theological interest in Smith and Cragg. If on the other hand one chooses to emphasize the hermeneutical aspect of their approaches, and consequently in the present study, 'cross-cultural philosophy of religion'[42] should also be mentioned as a field to which the

---

[40] In this respect, this study is a follow-up of an article (Mæland 1997a) concerning the religions as representing a challenge to be taken up by systematic theology and not merely by history of religion, comparative religion, etc. See also Leuze 1994, 18f, n48, for a short introduction to various systematic-theological challenges the religions may present to Christian theology: a) with regards to explication of one's own faith, b) a systematic elaboration of issues related to dialogue, and c) the very foundation of Christian theology, that is: not only to be classified terminologically within systematic theology, but treated as a matter of *Fundamentaltheologie*.

[41] Hence I delimit my material to those parts of Smith and Cragg's works that make the relation to Islam a theme. Other religions are treated in their writings, although they play a minor role compared to the concentration on Islam, yet this being more true of Cragg than of Smith.

[42] This term is a designation of a working group sponsored by the American Academy of Religion from the late 1970s into the 1980s, Dean 1995, ix. The group was joined by such scholars as Thomas Dean, Ninian Smart, Raimundo Panikkar, Harold Coward, William J. Wainwright, Mary Ann Stenger, William A. Christian, Sr., Joseph A. Di Noia, Norbert M. Samuelson, Conrad Hyers, John Y. Fenton, Fredrick J. Streng and Ashok K. Gangadean. Dean poses four criteria that should be satisfied before a study may be called cross-cultural philosophy of religion: 1. It has to be philosophically sophisticated (analytical, pragmatist as well as hermeneutic), 2. It must subscribe to the rule that no philosophy of religion shall be done without constant reference to the history of religions (N. Smart), 3. The requirement of scholarly expertise in one or more religious traditions, and, finally, 4. One must be dissatisfied with the traditional way of doing philosophy of religion, *ibid.*, 5. Most interestingly for the present study, two works of Smith are explicitly mentioned as milestones in the story of the emergence of cross-cultural philosophy of religion: *The Meaning and End of Religion*, 1962, which served as an opener for 'a new formulation of the problem of understanding across cultures and religions,' and *Towards a World Theology*, 1981, which is seen as one of the fully developed reflections in the 80s of authors who incipiently contributed to the development of the discipline (Smith, Smart, Hick). Also works of *both* Smith and Cragg are mentioned because the important work *Truth and Dialogue in World Religions: Conflicting Truth Claims, ed.* John Hick, 1974, is mentioned from the story of the 70s. In this work Smith contributed with 'A human view of truth,' Smith 1974a,

present study belongs. The common aim of both 'comparative theology' and 'cross-cultural philosophy of religion' is, however, to work in a 'normative-constructive' way, especially related to the question of truth.[43]

Secondly, the study is also an indirect contribution to the Norwegian educational curricula of an increasing multicultural and multireligious population. This 'project' was especially related to a preparatory report leading up to a new Core Curriculum for Primary, Secondary and Adult Education in Norway, namely: *Identity and Dialogue* (Norwegian: 'Identitet og dialog'), with which certainly the present study resonates,[44] but also the curriculum itself, in use from 1997. The discussion about these, as well as a range of connected principal and practical issues, has been passionate. I see this study as a contribution to the simple but highly existential matters of how to 'understand my neighbour as myself,' as well as how to 'understand myself by understanding my neighbour,' to rephrase doubly the latter part of the Greatest Commandment. With regards to this, the most important contribution of the study will probably be my examination and interpretation of the relation between understanding Oneself and understanding the Other, *in casu* Islam. In all this, I see the study as contributing to a theological and discursive dialogue.[45]

---

and 'Conflicting truth-claims,' Smith 1974b, whereas Cragg was represented with 'Islam and Incarnation,' Cragg 1974. Hence, our material belongs to the field which Dean names cross-cultural philosophy of religion.

[43] Dean 1995, 3.

[44] Which is, in content and approach, anticipated in an article from 1997: Mæland 1997b.

[45] Based on Eric Sharpe's reasonable, though typological, discernment between a *discursive* dialogue (or dialectic or debate), a *human* dialogue, and an *interior* dialogue, in 'Dialogue and Faith,' Sharpe 1973, 93f, I see my study as justified as a contribution to 'dialogue', that is, as a *discursive dialogue*. Whereas the discursive kind of dialogue, according to Sharpe, is normally based upon the assumption that 'the human reason is competent to lead to a closer approximation to the truth than that which is originally known,' the human dialogue ("Buberian dialogue") assumes the 'common humanity' where 'appreciation' and 'complete acceptance of the other person,' but not reciprocity, is strictly necessary. The third has its locus in 'the mystical, contemplative tradition' and assumes that 'all intellectualization, doctrinal or otherwise, is of limited relevance.'
I do not regard it sensible to maintain an undifferentiated concept of dialogue as found e.g. in the *Guidelines for Dialogue between Christians and Muslims* of the Pontifical Council for Interreligious Dialogue, 1981/1990: 'Dialogue only takes place between people and communities, not between systems of thought or religions,' 1. Nor do I think discursive interreligious dialogue should be confined to only 'the logical relationship between the various religions' as an 'objective, impartial or neutral,' opposed to a 'theologically normative way,' see da Silva 1986.
Moreover, Sharpe maintains that the discursive dialogue includes an understanding

1.6 Approach

I have already outlined what kind of systematic relations Smith and Cragg conceive between their interpretations of Islam and their Christian self-understandings. I will now describe how these findings can be reached by a process of 'reconstruction' and an 'increasing degree of determination'.[46]

In Chapters 2-5, the study aims to *explore* and *identify,* based on selected studies of Smith and Cragg, what kind of systematic relations they develop between the interpretations of Islam and their Christian self-understandings. This will form the predominant part of the study (Chapters 2/3). As far as this exploration is strictly dependent upon the examination of a particular issue (extensification/self-relating *vs.* intensification/self-change), and is thus directed by this as it proceeds, it employs a theoretical rather than a merely historical method. Despite using historical material on which I occasionally make some diachronic remarks (that is, noting changes and developments in Smith and Cragg's arguments across the span of time of their respective studies), the overall concern of this part of the study is not a reconstruction of the works of Smith and Cragg *per se,* but the reconstruction of positions that reflect the problem before us.

---

of faith as *fiducia* and faith as *assensus* as 'normally inextricably interwoven,' ibid. 98. This enables me to establish a critical point of view against Smith which I will utilize later in the study. Interestingly, Sharpe locates Smith mostly to the *human* dialogue, and his criticism of Smith is particularly concerned with the 'disintegration of person and context' which he asserts to see in the works of Smith, ibid. 102. This enables me to operate with categories like 'system of coordinates' or 'ground pattern,' where both intellectual and emotional aspects are included, cf. Küng 1986, xiv. See also Aydin 1998, where Mahmut Aydin draws attention to the term 'theological dialogue' which he defines in the Christian instance as 'how Christians may seek officially and individually to explicate the contemporary meaning of their own religious tradition in relation to the intellectual and theological challenges made by other religious traditions in the process of dialogue,' 3. This definition comes very close to the aim of my study.

[46] See Puntel 1990, 91f. Lorentz B. Puntel sees any process of determination within what he calls 'rational-systematic reconstruction' as to be situated between a 'natural-linguistical' point of departure on the one hand, and a 'full-determined' final settlement on the other. Puntel maintains that the division of this process of determination into various 'periods' (*Abschnitte*), e.g. as 'paraphrase', 'elucidation', 'clarification', 'analysis', 'explanation', etc., what he undifferentiatedly calls: explanation (*Erklärung*), which he understands as the middle phase towards 'full-determination' (i.e. definition), *will all convey significant normative aspects.*
I see my study as situated within this middle segment of the process of determination, that is: between the texts of Smith and Cragg on the one hand, and a full determination (definition) on the other, which I see as far too pretentious for what I in effect am doing. A differentiation within this middle segment is to follow.

Following my consideration of the relation between general framework and the 'special case' of Islam, I will proceed as follows: first, by reconstructing the general interreligious hermeneutics of Smith and Cragg, and then identifying the systematic relations between their Islam interpretation and their normative theological framework. This part uses an analytical language that will be developed in close connection to the primary sources. Yet, as Smith and Cragg's style and argument vary to a great extent, this requires stringency in connection to the problem of the study, as well as flexibility in order to treat them adequately with regards to differences in the content of their works. The method employed is also discursive as it aims to discuss the positions of Smith and Cragg in relation to relevant hermeneutic theory and explicit external criticism, on what I perceive as *strategic points.*

In Chapters 6/7, the study aims to characterize and develop further the results of the reconstruction of Smith and Cragg's relations to the problem of the study. Using a complex model of interreligious perception as developed by Andreas Grünschloß, I aim to refine my analysis in the first part into more detailed results (Chapter 6). The approaches of Smith and Cragg will be related to this model, also by comparison of the two. Based on the systematic apparatus of the interreligious model of Grünschloß, I will also outline some problems attached to Smith and Cragg's positions that will be discussed in the final chapter. The main method employed in Chapter 6 is still one of reconstruction but now reinforced with more precise analytical tools provided by a model which belongs to the systematic science of religion/systematic comparative religion (Ger. *systematische Religionswissenschaft*).

In Chapter 7 I will interpret theologically—critically as well as constructively—the approaches of Smith and Cragg from a hermeneutical and Trinitarian perspective. The normativity of the study can especially be found here, but not exclusively here since also the aforementioned reconstructions will be normative as they aim to raise and answer theoretical questions which have not necessarily been raised and answered in the same way by Smith and Cragg.[47] The method employed will be reconstructive in the sense of a theological interpretation and integration of theory as developed in Chapters 1-6. Hence, I see this last chapter as contributing to a doctrinal discussion and development.

---

[47] See note 46 above.

18

1.7 Note on Language and Style

The study uses the author-date system and, consequently, reference lists. Regarding abbreviations, most of the monographs of the primary sources have been abbreviated (see Biography and References). Other abbreviations of periodicals, lexica, etc., follow *IAGT²* when suggestions are given there. When confusion is likely to occur the abbreviation of works of Smith and Cragg seeks to avoid identical abbreviations listed in *IAGT²*.

Moreover, I use a simplified form of transliteration from Arabic where confusion is unlikely to happen, that is, without diacritical marks except by the letters *hamzah (')* and *'ayn (')*. Beside the matter of readability, the major reason for this is my own unfamiliarity with Arabic. Transliterations in quotations and titles, however, are unchanged. Finally, the *hamzah* and *'ayn* are disregarded in the alphabetical ordering of the bibliography.

If not stated, the citations from the Bible and the Qur'an follow the sources of Smith and Cragg respectively. Otherwise I use the New International Version of the Bible and Arthur J. Arberry's translation/ interpretation of the Qur'an (*The Koran Interpreted*).

2
WILFRED CANTWELL SMITH'S INTERRELIGIOUS HERMENEUTICS

2.1 Introduction

The works of Wilfred Cantwell Smith represent a quite distinctive contribution to how Christian theology and an interpretation of Islam can be held together. The examination of Smith's writings will start with addressing the general hermeneutic framework for interreligious matters (Chapter 2). This will predominantly consist of treatment of methodological issues as well as his understanding of religion. Through this characteristic features of his position will appear. In fact, both the ways Smith solves the methodological issues, and the way in which 'religion' is understood, determine the systematic relations between his interpretation of Islam and Christian self-understanding. This does not imply that rather material questions, such as the understanding of Christ, the Qur'an, the Prophecy, and so on, are out of Smith's interest, only that these issues have to be interpreted in light of the more general and conceptual issues. Yet, it will also be argued that his generalizations are dependent on his particular Islamic studies (Chapter 3). This progress could therefore have been ordered the opposite way: from the specific to the general, using the general theory as an integration of the particular findings from the case-studies on Islam. Sometimes Smith gives explicit statements about this.[1]

However, the relation between the general framework and the particular can be elaborated further. Firstly, the works of Smith that are of particular interest have been written after the beginning of his comparative phase.[2] At that time, his major concepts and theories had already gained their basic shape. Secondly, the studies of Islam seem to follow and comprehend his major works in comparative religion. Either they are (exemplary) parts in a work on a specific topic, or very often, and some years in advance, appeared as separate case-studies on Islam, on topics or concepts which later appear as titles of books, in many ways collecting and integrating views of many religious traditions. In the first case the Islam-studies serve as illustrations of a general theory based on prior

---

[1] Cf. e.g. Chapter 3.2 where *The Meaning and End of Religion (ME)* is seen as a resolution of problems raised in a study on the historical development of the understanding of the notion 'Islam' in Islam (!).

[2] Cf. immediately below for an outline of different phases of his production.

assumptions.[3] In the latter they serve as preliminary studies on the way towards a general theory. There is no reason to exclude any of the views as presented here, though we choose to start with Smith's general concerns, theories and concepts.

It is also important to place rightly the diverse studies from Smith's hand. A contextual understanding of these must recognize different kinds of emphases in these works. As Andreas Grünschloß discovers in his dissertation,[4] partly in a schematic outline, at least three (four) major strands can be discerned. They are as follows: a. Islamics ('Islamwissenschaft'), b. Science of Religion ('Religionswissenschaft'), c. Christian theology, (d. and others). These labels are certainly too general and unspecified. Yet, they serve the purpose, as major thematic discernments. Moreover, they represent the major subjects Smith's various works are directed toward. Most important, however, the ambivalence of these labels should be emphasized. This is especially true of the notion 'Christian theology', which is quite distinctively understood within his 'world' (global) theological approach, to which it is also subordinated.

Even more intriguing is tracing an epistemological development throughout Smith's works. In his very instructive 'Werkgeschichte', Grünschloß maintains that Smith's authorship consists not only of different emphases, but also of correlated epistemological shifts. This has bearing not only for his approach to Islam in particular, but also for religious traditions in general.[5] These shifts are:

(a) Until and during the World War II Smith's works are employed with a socio-historical method. During this period he is a committed socialist, he lives in the Muslim part of Lahore[6] and his major work is *Modern Islam in India (MI)*, published already in 1943 at the age of 26 or 27.[7]

---

[3] It is a major suggestion of the dissertation of Klaus Hock (Hock 1986) that the Christian theologians who interpret Islam, whom his work surveys, are doing this in a way that can be described as *reflections of their prior theological as well as extra-theological presuppositions and premises* (Ger. *Interpretation als Reflex*). In light of this general suggestion, the criteria Smith utilizes in his assessment of Islam are seen as deducted from his general theory of theology of religion (Ger. *allgemeinen religionstheologischen Theorie*), *ibid.* 337. Even though his approach avoids perceiving Islam as deficient, the structure of his theological assessment of Islam reflects his theological premises, *ibid.*, 338f (the general conclusion of Hock's thesis which is likely to apply to Smith).

[4] Grünschloß 1994a.

[5] Grünschloß 1994a, 64-66.

[6] See the Biography and References at the very end of this study.

[7] See e.g. the preface to *MI*, viii, where he very explicitly admits that he is a 'socialist with pronounced ethical convictions' and with a belief in 'scientific method'. His describes his study as a contribution to sociology of religion as well as to the

(b) In 1946-47 Grünschloß suggests that an epistemological shift takes place.[8] From now on and until the late 50s Smith uses a method of 'verstehende Religionswissenschaft.' Popularly speaking, Muslim religiousness tends to play a more significant role in his writing. Most notably, he is still in Muslim-dominated India. His inaugural lecture at McGill (Smith 1950) takes place in this period, as do also his M.A. and Ph.D. at Princeton (1947-48). Major works from Smith's hand are *Pakistan as an Islamic State* (1954), and especially *Islam in Modern History* (1957).[9]

(c) After his programmatic article 'Comparative Religion: Whither and Why?' (Smith 1959/1966) he increasingly follows a comparative and personalist approach in the study of the religious life of humankind, although the previous *verstehende* approach more or less is integrated in the comparative method.[10] His first comparative work appears the same year: 'Some Similarities and Some Differences Between Christianity and Islam' (Smith 1959/ 1981m). Major works from this period are *The Meaning and End of Religion* (1963), *Belief and History* (1977) and *Faith and Belief* (1979). His notions of '(personal) faith', 'belief' and 'cumulative tradition' are also introduced and developed during this period.

(d) His interest in theological issues can be discovered already at early stages of his writings. Many articles on various aspects of comparative religion contain the theological view as a partial aspect. These studies culminate, however, in *Towards a World Theology* in 1981. From then on he produces more on theological issues than before. My contention is that this theological concern should be understood as an attempt at integration of his understanding of the history of 'the so-called religions,' as he prefers to state it.

'political and social understanding of one important segment of this modern world.' Both the terminology (see e.g. 377-381) and thematic structure ('ideological issues' and 'politics,' see viii) of this study reveals a strong socialist orientation. Kenneth Cragg claims that *MI* was rejected by Cambridge (presumably as an MA thesis) because the approach it embodies was regarded as unacceptable. See Cragg 2000c.

[8] See also, most interestingly, how Kenneth Cragg describes the difference between Smith's earliest works and the later emphasis on the 'religious factor' as a *conversion, TT,* 243. Cragg, however, does not, like Grünschloß, depict the date for this shift, although he shows an intimate knowledge at this point about development and distinctive emphases in Smith's thinking.

[9] The former (*Pakistan as an Islamic State*) is however integrated in *IH* in a revised form: as ch. 5. In *IH* Smith's social historian background is still evident, see e.g. p. vi ('politico-economic-social study'), albeit his concern for the study of religion as 'comparative and contemporary' ('in another sense, not contradicting' the 'politico-economic-social' approach) seems to be the fundamental concern, *ibid.*

[10] E.g. his inaugural lecture at McGill from 1950, Smith 1950. But also *IH*, see e.g. its ch. 1 and 8.

For the present work the latter two periods are of particular interest. Not only as marking two divergent emphases—the comparative and the theological—but the very combination and intersection of the two. As mentioned above, this is also the case and intention of Smith, especially in his *Towards a World Theology,* but also in proceeding works (e.g. *Faith and Belief*). This corresponds also with the approach of this chapter: an elaboration of his general approach to the religious traditions as a backdrop for the second part: the interpretation of Islam and its relation to Smith's normative theological self-understanding.

2.2   The Delineation of a Programme for the Comparative Study of Religion

A milestone in the comparative thought of Smith is presented in an article from 1959: 'Comparative Religion: Whither—and Why?'[11] This study develops a programme and its features can be observed in subsequent works from his hand.

Smith sees his programmatic article as an advancement from a first stage of scholarship (in general) characterized by 'the accumulation, organization, and analysis of facts' (31), with its culmination in the *Encyclopaedia of Religion and Ethics* (1908-21), to a 'second phase' where 'a large-scale face-to-face meeting between persons of diverse faiths' (32) has taken place, where 'all mankind for the first time became one community' (33).[12] Visionary, indeed, but according to Smith, with great academic impact for the comparative study of religion, especially due to the modification which can be represented by the keyword personalization.

An approach directed by this term, he suggests, may give the studies a 'more realistic, truer' direction (33). To conceptualize 'personalization' adequately means to explore what Smith denotes 'the essentially human quality of the subject matter' (33). The culmination of such a 'progress' will occur 'when 'we all' are talking *with* each other about 'us'" (34, emphasis Smith's). We will soon realize how central this aim is to all his subsequent works. Before that, let us first see how Smith comprehends this programme.

---

[11] *CR* (Smith 1959/66). Subsequent parenthetical references refer to this work. Although Smith in a major part of this article sets forth to 'analyse trends,' he also aims to 'urge desiderata,' 34.

[12] Smith gives several examples from other scholars whose works on 'people's religious life,' both of 'major living religions' and traditions that have ceased to exist, support his impression, *ibid.* 36f.

The first, and altogether fundamental step, he contends, is the recognition that 'the study of religion is the study of persons' (34). Religions are 'human involvements' (36). And at the heart of this religious personalism lies the notion of faith. That is, faith as 'a quality of men's lives' (34). One may however ask his intention in stating the affairs thus? Smith's answer to that relates to the distinction between 'externals' and 'internals':

> What I am contending is that the study of religious faith, and especially the faith of persons belonging to a tradition other than one's own, must be a study not only of tangible externals but of human hopes and aspirations and interpretations of those externals (34).

How, then, are these 'qualities' observable? Smith admits that he is not talking of something directly observable. Yet, 'their role in human history is not less consequential, nor their study less significant or valid' (35). Hence, functions and consequences become important in the comparative study of religion. Yet, Smith sees it as a 'fundamental lapse' to think of the observable manifestations of a concern as the very nature of that concern. The all-important task is therefore to discern what the externals, the religious systems or traditions, mean to those involved: the religious persons (35).[13]

Yet, this does not reveal a disinterest in 'the realm of tangible data', though the study of externals should only be recognized as preliminary to the study of internals. On the other hand, however, 'the latter /must/ continually be revised as the former become more exactly known' (35). This point, the interdependency of internals and externals, should however be kept in mind, especially since Smith in all his subsequent studies gives a preference to the internals, to the 'religions *themselves*' (36, my emphasis). If this is not noticed, one may easily forget the role of externals in his approach.

According to Smith, this fundamental clarification is not only a matter of conceptions but also of methods and epistemology (38). He sees the possibility that the knowledge of the 'externals' of a religion (institutions, formulations, overt history) may function as clues to the personal quality of men's lives, especially by 'having adherents of that faith as informants and perhaps as friends' (38f). At this point, Smith combines epistemology with altruistic ethics.[14]

---

[13] Interestingly, Smith considers at this point the possibility of *gradations of reality*, *ibid.* 35, note 8.

[14] 'I cannot know my neighbour more than superficially unless I love him,' *ibid.* 39, note 18. See also 41f, where the moral concern is 'mutual understanding and good relations between religious communities.'

Moreover, as a comparative religionist, Smith sees his audience to be a 'world audience'. The significance of this is that those studied are simultaneously those who are concerned with what has been written about themselves (40f). According to Smith, the implication of this is moral: One must write not only more courteously but also more responsibly (42). To this moral matter belongs also his famous principle of validity:

No statement about a religion is valid unless it can be acknowledged by that religion's believers (42, 52).

The reason for this principle is that one cannot 'go beyond the believer', and: 'the piety *is* the faith.' Smith sees this rule as 'revolutionary ... but ... profoundly true and important,' and it accompanies his later works in different versions. Smith recognizes this as a 'creative principle' (43) and does not see himself as a slave under the statements of faith made by the believers of a certain tradition. Interestingly, Smith seeks also to reverse his principle: that every statement about a religion that is acceptable to its believers is true. The reasons for this constructive, external position seem to be:

1. The fact that 'a religion develops' (42f),
2. His contention that 'it is possible both in theory and practice for an outside scholar to break new ground in stating the meaning of a faith in, say, modern terms more successfully than a believer' (43),[15] and
3. His responsibility to the Western academic tradition (44).

With his notion of historical change, which in this shape could almost be described as invention, Smith equips the academic scholar with a certain freedom to work independently of the believers of a positive tradition. Nevertheless, the dependency between the scholar and the observed tradition should be recognized as normative for any scholar of comparative religion, that is, the obligation to 'do justice to the faith of men's hearts' (44). However, the borders between religious traditions, on the one hand, and the scholar of religion on the other, are seen as permeable.

---

[15] With interest for this particular study, Smith refers to the Muslim reception of part I of Cragg's *The Call of the Minaret (CM)* [it must have been part II that was intended since part I is only a brief introduction to the situation of the post-war Muslim world] as an example of how a Western scholar has been more successful than Muslims in exposing Islam to Christians, *ibid.* 44, note 26. See also his review of *CM*, Smith 1957b. Likewise, he sees his own *Islam in Modern History (IH)* in the same vein, *ibid.*, note 27.

Consequently, this personalist programme for the comparative study of religions is also seen as relevant for the investigator and the relationship between the investigator and what is being studied. Smith asserts on historical grounds within the twentieth century that it is not possible to maintain the ideal of the scholar as 'the detached academic intellect, surveying its material impersonally ... reporting on it objectively' (44). The present situation, Smith asserts, is an encounter (47). The time of descriptions, therefore, has turned toward dialogues: the time has come for learning and enrichment (48). With this statement, Smith has made the relation between extensification and intensification a theme. The hermeneutical development of this position is undertaken in the next section (Chapter 3.3).

Most interestingly, Smith's argument turns to the perspective of the Church and sees this approach as a legitimate evangelical means for the Church's mission. The benefit of a dialogue may thus be described as:

> A Christian learning at last to *apprehend one's own faith*
> and loyally (and perhaps more truly?) and simultaneously
> to *appreciate the quality and* even the *ultimate validity*
> (in the eyes of God) of others' (49, emphasis mine).

The theological implications of the latter point are explicated further at the same place:

> One has not fully understood the faith of a community
> other than one's own until one has seen how that faith can
> serve (does serve, has served) as the channel between God
> and those persons.

Consequently, Smith does not see the Christian tradition of what he calls 'exclusivism' and 'proselytism' as 'obligatory elements of the Christian faith' (49).[16] As theological statements, these contribute to developing a distinctive position regarding the approach of the present study by the way in which the impact of dialogue is perceived. His rather bold statement of what the outcome should be regarding the affirmative assessment of the faith of the other will be inquired into later (Chapter 6 and 7) as I do not recognize it as a cogent statement but a suggestion open to counter-arguments. The same applies to his reference to 'in the eyes of God'.

---

[16] As would be expected at that time, Smith disqualifies the approach and especially the *attitude* of Hendrik Kraemer, *inter alia* because of his lack of 'humility and love,' *ibid.* 49f, note 39. Interestingly, Kraemer is also criticized by Cragg, see Chapter 4.4.3.

Moreover, Smith sees the role of comparative religion in the dialogues as directly connected to a variation of the principle of validity (cf. above), that is, 'to construct statements about religion that are intelligible within at least two traditions' (52). [17] This constructive work, however, is to be understood as invention. Despite Smith's contention that any such work should be done in continuity with the tradition of the religion, he nevertheless emphasizes the 'construction of *new forms* that will subsume but *transcend the present* pattern.'[18] What seems to accompany such statements is a downplaying of the existing forms of religions.[19] At this point Smith remains a reforming scholar of comparative religion. Simultaneously, he considers the effort of comparative religion to be necessary 'in order to provide the intellectual basis for the meetings between communities' (54). Thus, the theoretical function of comparative religion is obvious, as much as it also cannot detach itself from the real meeting of people across particular traditions.

According to Smith, the implications of dialogue are far-reaching. One is that it enables an enlarged sense of community (54).[20] Another is that it will be recognized that 'in comparative religion man is studying

---

[17] The reason for the 'at least' may be Smith's opinion that where a Western scholar enters into a dialogue between for example Christianity and Islam, the scholar's work has to be cogent to the academic, the Christian and the Muslim traditions, *ibid.* 53. Smith sees himself and W.M. Watt as two examples of this combination, *ibid.* 53, note 42. See also Smith 1957b, cf. my n15, p. 24 above.

[18] My emphasis. In fact, Smith quotes here the regulations of the degree of PhD in Islamic Studies at McGill University, *ibid.* 52, note 41. However, no doubt this statement coincides with his position. He was also the Director of Institute of Islamic Studies at McGill at the time when this article was published (and probably written), cf. the brief Biography and References at the end of this study.

[19] This is clearly enough formulated by himself, *ibid.* 50, note 39, when, based on the 'fact' that 'every religion has to do with transcendent reality,' he maintains that 'it is part of the truth of that religion to be dissatisfied with its extant forms.'

[20] For the key role of the concept 'world community' in the writings of Smith, see Pruett 1990. For Smith, 'world community' is a moral challenge that relates intimately to religious diversity which may disrupt community and thus entails a moral problem. Smith sees in this respect one of the most threatening ideas within the Christian Church as that which traditionally has divided the human race between those who are saved and those who are not, see especially *FOM*, 117ff. Smith sees this as an *incoherent* position because it divides between 'the moral and intellectual facets of our relations with our fellow men,' *ibid.* 117. Throughout his writings, Smith only wants to maintain the former part of this position (that God saves) and the moral imperatives of Christ's death on the cross, that is, reconciliation, unity, harmony, and brotherhood. The latter does also answer the question 'to what?' one is saved. One might call Smith's position at this point *soterio-monism*.
See also *ME*, 8f, where Smith asserts that the two most fundamental questions confronting 'twentieth century man' are: a) that of a 'world community' on the social level; and b) that of 'meaning in modern life' on the personal level. These

himself' (55).[21] Hence, 'comparative religion may become the disciplined self-consciousness[22] of man's variegated and developing religious life' (55), and: 'in the eyes of God [or 'of reason', cf. his note 48, *ibid.*] the human community is the only real community there is' (58). Here, the focus is upon commonalities, which Smith finds located in 'man's religiousness' despite the disparity of religions. He seems, therefore, to be conscious of a situation where the great religions cease to be as separate as they used to, and perhaps also not 'quite so surely entities' (56).

This latter statement introduces his major work, *The Meaning and End of Religion* (*ME*, 1963). This work aims at both a deconstruction of the notion of 'religion' and a constructive proposal for clarifying the ambiguity between 'personal faith'/religiousness, on the one hand, and 'cumulative tradition' on the other. This pair of concepts is important for the further develoment of his interreligious hermeneutics. Yet, before we turn to that work some attention should be given to another work, *The Faith of Other Men*, where his notion of 'appreciation', which we encountered in one of the passing quotations above, appears to be of profound relevance for the approach of the present study.

2.3 The Hermeneutics of 'Appreciation'

In his popular comparative study, *The Faith of Other Men* (Smith 1962/ 1965), first given as radio talks for the Canadian Broadcasting Corporation in 1961, Smith makes some further remarks on the task of comparative religion.

He starts by saying that comparative religion should be done on three levels, including[23]

---

questions require, according to Smith, a new understanding of religion. See also Smith 1987a, 59, where he quotes his reconceptualization and replacement of 'religion' and 'religions' by 'personal faith' and 'cumulative tradition'. Most interestingly, he suggests in Smith 1987a that these two should have added a third namely, c) *participating in a community.* The notion of community is not to be interpreted as a naive conception of harmony since the alternative is clearly stated as 'conflict,' see e.g. *FB*, ix.

[21] At this point Smith seems to identify dialogue and comparative religion. This is not incoherent with his previous argument as far as the *role of the academician* in the dialogue is concerned.

[22] Cf. also Smith 1964, 17. The notion of 'consciousness' is important, though not developed at this stage. This development takes place successively towards his concept of 'corporate critical consciousness' in *WT,* cf. in particular Chapter 2.6.2 below.

[23] *FOM,*14ff. The subsequent parenthetical remarks refer to this work. For a comparable threefold listing, see his Inaugural Lecture at Harvard 1964, Smith 1964.

1. Discovery of the outward facts of the religious life in the
religious communities
2. Interpretation of religious meanings; the appreciation
of faith
3. Drawing generalizations

As should be recognized, none of these are unimportant to Smith.
The relation to the preceding chapter is that the first refers to the
'externals', whereas the second to the 'internals' or 'religious life' of
believers. Yet, both represent an 'ascertaining of data' (15). The difference,
however, between person/meaning and system/customs/beliefs/outward
facts, is a major concern for Smith. The third level (generalizations) will be
considered in the next chapter.

An implicit interpretation of level two, the appreciation of others'
faith, is to be found at the end of his popular work where the aims of comparative
religion are presented with direct relevance for the present study:

> The problems of comparative religion involve not only an
> appreciation of others' faith, but also a widening and
> deepening of one's own (99).

Smith also warns about loosing one's original allegiance in appreciating
'other men's values' (13).[24] Moreover, these statements should also be
interpreted as a suggestion about the challenge that comparative religion
makes for the Church and any Christian theology. He therefore argues
that: 'Philosophy and science have impinged so far on theological thought
more effectively than has comparative religion, but this will not last' (113).
At the beginning of the third millennium it can easily be demonstrated
that and how a (partial) change according to his prognosis has come true.

In these understandings of 'appreciation' Smith reiterates his
personalist concern for mutuality. He seems also to resonate with the
philosophical hermeneutics of Gadamer, although this is not explicitly
stated.[25] Both the possibility of change and deepening of one's own faith

---

[24] On the other hand, the importance of one's own value shall not be understood as
superseding other's values, since the 'primary fact [is] that we do worship God,' *ibid.*
13, but only as one particular possibility among many other particular possibilities.

[25] Cf. Stenger 1995, 152f, who in her discussion of the use of Gadamer for a cross-
cultural philosophy of religion addresses 'change' and 'continuous testing' of one's
own horizon related to 'the phenomena to be interpreted.' It is not easy to see that
Gadamer has played any significant role in the development of Smith's interreligious
hermeneutics. I have only found one positive reference to Gadamer's treatment of
Spiel after having made some reservations about Wittgenstein's concept of 'games',
WS, 366, n 55.

are involved, as is also the importance of retaining a particular point of view. It would be false to maintain that 'appreciation' is developed into a precise hermeneutical term here. Yet, on the other hand, Smith makes illuminating connections to this term, which also disclose obvious relations to the approach of the present study (self-relating and self-change).[26]

One of these connections concerns the way in which Smith makes a preference for people of religious faith in his studies in comparative religion. Of even more interest is the way in which this concerns himself in person: in a chapter on Christian and Jews (Ch. 6) Smith contends that his 'being Christian,' has been much involved in his awareness of other men's faith, but also *vice versa*. This has happened, he continues, at least in the matter of: a. personal experience, b. theological doctrine, and c. moral imperative (77).

[a] Regarding the first, personal experience, Smith relates the matter of learning related to previous understanding, and 'its extension' (77), through the example of understanding various parts of Muslim's beliefs (Creation, Day of Judgement, etc.): the 'capacity to grasp what they are talking about is obviously related to my own prior notion of what these terms mean.' A valid interpretation of this statement must be that his capacity for interpretation of Islam is a Christian one. Or simply, extensification presupposes a self-reference. Evidence for this is given a page later (78):

> I am simply asserting the basic point that my capacity to apprehend significantly and truly the religious stand of other men turns *in part* on the understanding that *I bring to it*—the religious understanding ... my own Christian faith (emphasis mine).

That it only does so 'in part', indicates that there is more to his perception of the interreligious hermeneutic process, and that there are 'subtleties' that are not easily understood.[27] Yet, his Christian faith enables him to see things in different religious traditions 'more truly, more richly, than I otherwise would' (81). But also the other way around: 'By my seeing them, my Christian faith becomes more true, more rich, than it would otherwise be' (81f).

These rather formula-like expressions are exemplified by his studies of the Muslim mystics. Being introduced to the Persian poets he

---

[26] See also *ME*, p. 7, where the term 'appreciative understanding' is used together with 'imaginative sympathy' and ('even')'experiential participation'.

[27] Smith mentions, 1. how differences between religious traditions are to be interpreted, and 2. his Christian knowledge that God is greater than his idea of him, *ibid.* 79.

learned more of 'the world, about God, and about myself' (82). He became also for the first time aware of the mystical strands in Christianity. Interestingly, the other way around (and back again!), his Calvinist background

> has certainly helped me to understand and appreciate the more rigid Islamic theologians; but in turn, my study of these has illuminated for me, and helped me greatly to understand, the conservative Christian thinker Karl Barth, the power of whose position I have only lately come to appreciate (82).

Thus, the personal hermeneutical experiences of Smith are very complex. They include an explicit mutuality, in which his Christian faith both determines and helps the understanding of other religious strands, and, subsequently, is also enriched and formed by the same studies. In Smith extensification and intensification thus seem to relate intimately.

[b] Concerning the theological realm where Smith sees his faith as relevant for the interreligious study, he deliberately speaks of Christian theology (83). He holds, in contrast to traditional views, that 'the Church has as yet not produced an adequate theology in the fields of relations with other men' (84). Smith asks for a 'theology that will be truer, because more truly Christian.'

The very logic behind this statement seems to be a division between (Christian) theology and (Christian) faith, where the latter has priority.[28] Smith maintains that if the former disqualifies the faith of other men as false, the premise, that is, theology, is false, since 'the conclusion conflicts with the faith itself' (85). Smith projects his hope for a resolution into the future:

> ... when men will see rather that if the Christian revelation is valid, then it follows from this very fact that other men's faith is genuine, is the form through which God encounters those other men, and saves them (85).

This is the meaning of Smith's requirement that theology become more truly Christian. Yet, he does not develop the argument further, only stating its importance and, of course, making certain consequences of Christian theology the governing principles for the truth of it. This *dictum* may at

---

[28] Cf. *FOM,* 84, where Smith says that theology 'is the attempt on the part of the theologian, who is quite human, to give an intellectual statement for his faith.'

first glance seem awkward, but becomes clearer, if not (dis)solved, as it is related to the next point.

[c] The third interrelation, the *moral* one, becomes an important part of the approach of Smith. This relates profoundly to the fact that the recognition of the starting point of Christian faith as 'God in Christ' has 'two orders of inference' (86): one intellectual (ideas, concepts), and one moral (personal relations and actions). Whereas he sees the former to have been active in dividing people from each other, the latter may 'bridge gulfs.' Also, if forced to, he would have chosen the latter over the former. Regarding moral implications in relation to other religious persons, Smith sees a) the demand to appreciate their faith, and b) 'to construct a world of reconciliation and peace, of mutual understanding and global community, of universal human dignity' (87).

These moral imperatives are central to Smith's interreligious hermeneutics. Terms like 'appreciate', 'global/world community' and 'human', are frequent in the writings of Smith, and all seem to be inspired by his understanding of the revelation of God in Christ. Because these function as moral-hermeneutical terms for interreligious relations, the theologian and the historian, or comparativist of religion, should be guided by them. This leads us, however, to his seminal encounter with one of the most prominent signs of the process of division between religious traditions: The concept of 'religion' itself.

2.4 The Reconceptualization of 'Religion' and 'Religions' as 'Personal Faith' and 'Cumulative Tradition'

2.4.1 INTRODUCTION

The last section (Chapter 2.3) began with a listing of three suggested elements of comparative religion of which appreciation was the second. The others were the level of facts, and of generalizations to be drawn from 'facts' as well as from 'appreciation'.

It is the latter that will concern us now—the drawing of generalizations, which, according to Smith, is comparative religion proper, that is:

> To induce some general truths ... [of] man's religiousness itself ... of faith itself ... as a universal human phenomenon, immensely diversified in particular, remarkably persistent in general.[29]

---

[29] *FOM*, 18f.

Moreover, the aim of this general theory is

> to formulate ideas that attempt to do justice to both the
> profundity and the diversity—in the hopes of constructing
> theories that would prove acceptable both to Jews and to
> Buddhists, both to Muslims and to Christians, as well as
> being cogent with the academic tradition.[30]

In these statements a key to his subsequent conceptual, major works is
given, especially *The Meaning and End of Religion* (*ME,* 1963), *Belief
and History* (*BH,* 1977) and *Faith and Belief* (*FB,* 1979). For further
analysis, both the differentiation of levels within comparative religion,
the general hermeneutical perspective, and the emphasis of its major task
(generalizations) should be kept in mind in the reconstruction of the relation
between his works and the approach of the present study.

In *The Faith of Other Men* Smith decided to make the most
common general term within religious studies proper, 'religion', and its
subsections of 'Buddhism', 'Hinduism', and so forth, a theme. Yet, in this
work he deliberately dropped the idea to unfold how he was to challenge
it. This occurred in the launch of *The Meaning and End of Religion.*[31]
Nevertheless, a clue to a theory was already given in *The Faith of Other
Men,* namely that

> It is possible to know a good deal about what are called the
> various religious systems, and still not to understand the
> people whose life they involve.[32]

This takes us to the core of his classic *The Meaning and End of Religion.*
While Smith uses 'religion' in rather unruffled fashion in 'Comparative
religion: Whither—and why?' (cf. Chapter 2.2), the term is deliberatively
avoided in *The Faith of Other Men.* The use of it becomes, however,
urgent and a central theme in *The Meaning and End of Religion.* In this

---

[30] *Ibid.*, p. 89.

[31] *FOM,* 16. The link to *ME* is to be seen implicitly in the statement, that 'it would
take a sizeable book to set forth my argument that this [i.e. the challenge of 'the
religions of the world' approach] is the best way to understand what is going on,'
ibid. The dissatisfaction with the term is however also present in *MI.* Though
Smith contends that he has no final solution to the problem of defining 'religion',
he attempts to give a 'clear definition' of it, that is, 'That aspect of a person's life,
or of his society's life, which that person regards as religion,' 375. Along this line
'Islam' is defined as 'the religion of the Muslims,' and a 'Muslim' as 'any person
who calls himself a Muslim,' *ibid.*

[32] *FOM,* 16.

study a set of reconceptualizations are made available as substitutes for 'religion'.[33]

The approach of Smith is twofold. Firstly, he traces the use of 'religion', both in the West and the non-Western parts of the world. Secondly, he uses this historical and conceptual analysis to propose new concepts, most importantly the notions of 'personal faith' and 'cumulative tradition'. Whereas the former conveys a deconstruction of 'religion', the latter ends up as the primary, and legitimate, concept of religiousness, that is, religiousness as a quality of human beings. Smith maintains that his contribution is not an attempt to give superseding definitions and generalizations, but rather to explore

> the possibility of clearing the ground for a *quite new attack* on the problems by *revising the framework* within which the questions are asked (12, my emphasis).

To this purpose belong two suggestions:

> (a) That the problem 'What is the nature of religion' be set aside as inapt, and
> (b) That any understanding of 'faith' within particular traditions should not concentrate on the essence of that particular tradition.

To these, again, Smith suggests:
> There are neither entities like religion in general, nor in particular.

The constructive work of Smith, however, lies in his suggestion that a 'radical reappraisal of our conceptualizations may prove rewarding.' Hence he aims to ask 'smaller questions but at the same time also larger ones' (13). At this place, 'smaller questions' means smaller than 'What is the nature of religion'? On the other hand, 'larger ones' means for example the question of the personal quality of humankind's religiousness, that is, 'faith'.

There is a certain, presumably deliberate, ambiguity in Smith's approach. On the one hand, he wants to serve the Christian, Muslim, or the 'outside student' (scholar) in their questioning about the 'true nature' of Christianity, Islam, and so on (14). Yet, on the other hand, he sees these questions as 'apparent'. His demand is therefore programmatically

---

[33] Subsequent parenthetical references in the text refer to *ME*.

described as a willingness to revise, but not to abandon a Christian (and other religious) understanding (14). This ambiguity of continuity and revision, which possibly can be contained in 'reformation',[34] is in many ways the framework of his first major conceptual study (*ME*).

Stated thus, this resonates with the issue of intensification and self-change in this study. Put briefly, Smith claims on the one hand his self-understanding to be continuous with the 'true nature of Christianity,' on the other hand the encounter with people of other traditions requires a revision of previously held concepts in the Christian view of the Other based on a criticism of the use of 'religion'. Whether this makes Smith's position reformatory can only be demonstrated in examining further parts of his writings.

Let us first look at what his historical findings are, and how he argues for his reconceptualizations.

2.4.2 TRACING THE USE OF 'RELIGION' IN THE WEST

In his discussion of the West Smith identifies a reification process in the very use 'religion'. A brief survey of his findings may illustrate this. This survey includes *inter alia* the following milestones.

[a] In Classical times the Latin term, *religio,* was originally used in a variety of senses: of taboo, external power with obligations upon man, or the feeling of man towards this power, but the adjectival sense (a quality of men's lives) persisted better that the substantive use (some independent substance or entity) (19f). The ritual and cultic use was also most prominent. In Lucretius and Cicero (21-23) this changes to the possibility of the perception of religion and 'gods' by a reflective and critical intellect, standing aside from religious practice. Whereas Lucretius conceives religion as a Great Something, as an entity, Cicero, on the other hand, develops religion as a generic, inner quality of human life, that is, as an appropriate attitude towards the gods. Hence, the situation of Classical times is compound.

[b] A major shift emerges with the *Christian community* (23-26). Smith sees this as a 'new kind of religion' because of the 'large-scale order of systematized and coherent religious life'. Moreover, until the fourth century, the Christians use *religio* frequently as well as a range of other inherited words. A new word occurs also: 'faith'. The frequent use of 'religion' in this period is most importantly seen as a correlate to a situation of religious plurality and competition, which of course relates to the very situation of that time. At this time the awareness of *nostra religio*

---

[34] Cf. *ME*, 17: 'What appears for the moment as a revolutionary reversal will be seen as rather a return to the long-range lines of classical advance.'

('our religion') versus *vestra religio/vestrae religiones* ('your religion(s)')
is apparent.

In Lactantius (27f), introducing the notions of *vera vs. falsa
religio*, the involvement with philosophy *(sapientia)* becomes evident.
Smith sees it already at work, however incipiently, in the writings of
Lucretius and Cicero. Yet, the concept of religion was most promisingly
developed by St. Augustine (28-31), whom he sees as the last writer with
a significant interest in the notion.[35] His *De vera religione* is 'a vivid and
personal confrontation with the splendour and the love of God' and bears
no sign of using the term in the sense of 'system of observances or
beliefs, nor an historical tradition, institutionalized of outside observation'
(29).

Smith affirms St. Augustine's Platonic notion of a 'true religion'
that refers to an ideal, perfect, and essentially personal relationship between
God and humankind, enabled through Christ. The new idea of a true
religion, though personal, is, however, still universal and so 'transferable'
to the later conceptions of religion as institution or entity. Smith, therefore,
sees both a sign of hope (personal faith) in the Augustinian invention of
'true religion' as well as seeds for a misleading use of it, that is, reification
and institutionalization.

[c] Whereas 'religion' does not play any significant role in
medieval times (though 'faith' does), it does so in the modern period, from
the Renaissance onwards. Smith pays particular attention to the
Renaissance writer Ficino (32-34). Ficino conceived *religio* as that which
is universal to man, namely a divinely provided instinct by which humans
perceive and worship God. Smith chooses to translate this as
'religiousness', understood as 'a quality of human nature derived from
God'. As such it is senseless to talk of different kinds of this quality,
rather, following the Platonic pattern, we speak of 'differing degrees of
genuineness'. Again, an *adjectival* understanding of religion lies close at
hand. This is also the basis of the use of '*Christiana*' in his title *De
Christiana Religione*, which Smith translates 'On the Christ-Oriented
Nature of Universal Human Religiousness, in its ideal form.' Interpreted
thus, Ficino becomes almost the prototype of Smith's own position. Smith
also recognizes Zwingli and Calvin (35-37) as approximating his own
emphasis on personal faith.[36] Calvin especially is praised for his 'sense of
piety that prompts a man to worship ... innate in everyman ... an inner

---

[35] Cf. Grünschloß 1994a, 157: 'Augustin spielt für Smith eine nahezu paradigmatische
Rolle, da er in ihm ein Religionsverständnis zu entdecken glaubt, das eine
'Platonische Form' darstellt.'
[36] Smith does not spend much time on Luther since 'he seems not to have concerned
himself with a concept of religion,' *ME*, 35.

personal attitude' (36).

[d] Yet, the great decline from this notion of an inner personal attitude towards the divine appears in the seventeenth and eighteenth centuries (37ff). With the interest in intellectual constructs, 'a long-range development, accumulating until today, of diversion of interest from man's personal sense of the holy to ... the observable product or historical deposit of its outworking' began (38). The meaning of this citation is that a development took place, from: 1) the dynamic of the heart to impersonal system, 2) from religion in singular to plural, and 3) from a Platonic view of truth to a propositional[37] one (39). Significant (Protestant!) authors associated with this change of approach, are Hugo Grotius, Herbert of Cherbury and Bishop Butler. Most interestingly, Smith compares this time of controversies and conflicts with the time of the Fathers. He also sees a connection between works on religion as a 'systematic entity' and the use of concepts of polemics and apologetics (42f).[38] In this situation characterized by conflict and 'observation from the outside', the notion of religions in plural is developed:

> The plural arises ... when one contemplates from the outside, and abstracts, depersonalizes, and reifies, the various systems of other people of which one does not oneself see the meaning or appreciate the point, let alone accept the validity (43).

But also the notion of religion *in general*, that is, generic religion, appears, which means

> to designate as an external entity the total system or sum of all systems of beliefs, or simply the generalization that they are there (43).

These developments seem to have been caused by 'new information from beyond the seas' (religion 'in plural') and by a 'triumphant intellectualism' (religion 'in general') (44). Nevertheless, the keywords remain externalization and reification.

[e] During the nineteenth century Smith pays particular attention

---

[37] Smith does not define the meaning of the latter ('propositional') more precisely.

[38] This is to be seen as contrasts to his vision of a world community, where the lack of 'religion(s)' is one of its components. Moreover, his experience with Muslim-Hindu conflicts in the area of (nowadays) Pakistan may certainly also have contributed to the emphasis on conflicts and aggression on the one hand, and community and fellowship on the other.

to Schleiermacher (45f). Yet, his view of him is somewhat ambiguous. On the one hand, he sees in him a pertinent reaction against the rationalization which he addresses (cf. the subtitle of Schleiermacher's *On Religion*[39]), in particular his emphasis on inner piety and feelings. On the other hand, however, Schleiermacher and the romantic movement do not represent a shift in the meaning of religion in direction of the inward and non-intellectual, although he might be recognized as 'expand[ing] the concept 'religion.''

Furthermore, Smith applauds Hegel's 'conceptualizing religion in flux' (47), which is a theme I will return to later (Chapter 2.4.4). Yet, Smith observes that in Hegel the notion of religion in singular, as a self-subsisting transcendent *Begriff*, which precedes all historical manifestations, is most clearly stated. This development, he asserts, reaches its 'logical extreme' in the notion of 'the essence of religion' in Ludwig Feuerbach (48).

Based on this 'reification process,' Smith highlights four meanings, or better, four types, of 'religion':

(1) Religion as personal piety,
(2) Religion as system, either as i) an ideal system, or ii) as an empirical phenomenon
(3) Religion in general

No doubt, Smith prefers the first option. Connected to this is also his rejection to offer any definition of religion. Consequently, he suggests that 'religion' as a term is confusing, unnecessary and distorting, and hence should be dropped. His constructive attempts to substitute alternatives to 'religion' will be addressed below. Before that, it remains to see how Smith interprets the relation between the historical and present namings of religion in plural and the realities they designate. The particular case of Islam belongs, however, to another chapter (Chapter 3.3).

2.4.3 THE DESCRIPTIONS OF EXTRA-WESTERN RELIGIOUS SYSTEMS

In short, Smith sees a similar and comparable reification process in the 'series' of 'religion', that is, not only in 'religion in general,' but in 'the religions of the world.' This process, he contends, can be traced as follows:

[a] Originally there were no entities like 'Sikhism', 'Buddhism', 'Hinduism', 'Christianity', 'Judaism', and so on. Any concept of a

---

[39] *Über die Religion: Reden an die Gebildeten unter ihren Verächtern*, Berlin, 1799.

systematic or historic entity seems to have been missing in all cases considered but Islam (which is handled in a separate chapter by Smith, and in Chapter 3 below). Until modern times, Smith's asserts, it was very well possible 'to be religious without reifying' (57). Hence, religiousness should be recognized as an adjectival activity, not as a substantive generalization of the adjective (52f). That does however not rule out that there *are* religious phenomena. Yet, the 'umbrella,' under which they are subsumed, needs to be replaced (66).[40]

[b] Where the reifying processes did take place, in various regions, they were linked together, and also related to the Western development (cf. the last chapter).

[c] Furthermore, when the specific names and labels were given, they seem to have been given by outsiders: Either by outsiders who were in conflict with the group of people that was named (e.g. Hindus by Muslims, 64f), or by scholars of the Western process of naming in the nineteenth century (following the process of reifying 'religion' itself), or where the religious tradition of one community developed in order to transcend the boundaries of the original people among whom it first emerged (62), or lastly, where insiders wanted to identify the (intellectual) ideal of the particular tradition or community of which they were a part (67).

This coincides therefore with what he sees worldwide: a process of reification, from a personal orientation, to an ideal or to an abstraction, and finally to an institution (76). Most significantly, this process of naming did not take place where 'people's religious life remained integrated and coterminous with their social existence' (e.g. the Incas, the Samoans and the Babylonians, 61f).[41] Moreover, Smith finds that there has been a kind of evolution by observers of realizing that the data do not fit the names of religions given in the last centuries (51, 62f, 132f). This has been particularly evident in regions (Egypt, India, China and Japan) where scholars of religion always have had severe problems in identifying specific religions,[42] but is also reflected in new ways of specifying particular parts of Christianity and its history (133). On the other hand, however, one has

---

[40] See also *ME*, 122, where he makes the point that the namings of 'religions' 'represent *something real* ... but ... what was happening in these cases needs to be understood more carefully and adequately than the single noun formulation makes possible' (my emphasis).

[41] Cf. his opposite argument *for* an understanding of the reasons in the West for the adoption of the concept of 'religion' based on the 'great process of differentiation,' identified as 'secularism ... in which an earlier cohesiveness or integrity of man's social and personal life ... has been fragmented,' *ME*, 124.

[42] E.g. the scholarly debate whether 'Buddhism' was a religion or not, but also the way Chinese people used to let more than one tradition serve their religiousness.

attempted to adjust the data to fit into existing concepts (51), or at least accepted the concepts constructed 'by other observers for other situations' without altering the original concepts (133). Smith's suggestion is that both approaches are in need of conceptual evolvement (52), and that the co-ordination of these observations and the discernment of the general significance of them await somebody's effort (53). It is to this task that Smith attempts to contribute.

2.4.4 THEORETICAL REVISION ON THE GROUNDS OF 'TRANSCENDENCE' AND 'HISTORICAL FLUX'

Smith's suggestion about general significance is related to his theoretical considerations about a) 'transcendence', or 'God' (133ff), and b) history and its nature of change and flux (141ff). It is a renewed understanding of these core concepts of theology and history that should lead to an eventual *change of concepts* (120f, 154ff).

[a] Regarding 'transcendence, Smith adduces most remarkably support for his critical analysis from Christian theologians (Christian 'participants of religious life') like Karl Barth, Emil Brunner, Paul Tillich, C. S. Lewis and D. Bonhoeffer. In this respect, it is their criticism of 'religion' he draws on (125). Although he does not acknowledge their criticism on one level, for example in the form of Brunner's expression 'The God of the "other religions" is always an idol,'[43] on another level he accepts it as a perspective remark, which should be formulated even more generally than Brunner himself did. If formulated as the 'task of a modern reformer', his attempt is, indirectly, to 'help men not let their religion stand between them and God' (127). Having reached a self-description as reformer, the meaning of it is qualified: as reformer, one does not reform a religion, but 'men's awareness of their total environment, and men's lives' (128), including an important statement about idols: 'No one in the whole history has ever worshipped an idol' (141).[44] To all this belongs that which is beyond the religious movement itself; that which the believer sees the

---

[43] Which, according to Smith, certainly reveals Brunner as 'Christian narrow-minded,' *ME,* 140. The quotation is from Brunner's *Revelation and Reason: The Christian Doctrine of Faith and Knowledge (Offenbarung und Vernunft) 1946,* 264.

[44] This apparently bold interpretion of idols does not anymore represent a curious understanding of the function of idols. E.g. see Pannenberg 1988 where he maintains that 'die Religionen im allgemeinen sehr wohl zwischen den Beständen der Weltwirklichkeit, in denen die göttliche Macht sich bekundet, und der Gottheit selbst unterschieden haben,' 197. Moreover, Pannenberg quotes in passing G. van der Leeuw (*Phänomenologie der Religion*), that it is 'weder die Natur noch die Naturobjekte, welche der Mensch verehrt, sondern die sich in ihnen offenbarende

religious tradition to signify (129). However, this is neither in practice nor in principle observable to the observer who is concerned with 'religion'. The reasons for this relate firstly to the outsider-insider problem:

> A religious tradition has no meaning unless it enables those within it to see something that those without do not see (130)

and secondly, to the nature of transcendence, namely that

> the whole pith and substance of religious life lies in its relation to what cannot be observed (136).

Yet, Smith does not draw the conclusion that it is impossible to understand the faith of people of another religious tradition. His point is rather that an adequate understanding has to attempt to comprehend the 'religious life of him whom one observes' (135). Thus, there is a principal difference between 'knowing a doctrine of salvation, and being saved' (136). It is thus interesting to read his consequential description of what 'a Christian's life' should mean:

> Not what the Christian does, but that he does it as a child of God; not that what he believes, but that God has granted him the gift of believing; not that he is in the Church, but that in the Church he is living in communion with Christ as a personal friend and with fellow members in a fellowship

---

Macht,' *ibid.* The point made by Smith here, however, illustrated by seing these two quotations together, is the function of religion as something similar to the role of 'sin' or of 'idolatry' in a traditional Christian understanding of the relation between humankind and God. The interesting question, then, is to ask whether Smith's deconstruction of religion can be perceived as a redemptive activity, that is, an activity in order to reestablish the relation between God and human beings. This is probably a too far-reaching conclusion. See also Smith's article 'Idolatry: In comparative perspective,' Smith 1987a, where a main suggestion is that: 'What is substantial ... is that it is a mistake to identify one's own 'religion' or tradition with God, or with absolute truth; to regard it as divine, rather than as an avenue to, or from, the divine ... For Christians to think that Christianity is true, or final, or salvific, is a form of idolatry,' 59. Along this line runs Smith's frequent argument against the notion of *finitum capax infiniti*. This relates directly to his Calvinist emphasis on God's transcendence and the notion of *finitum non capax infiniti*, Smith 1991a, 22. See also note 103 below. Thus, there appears a certain ambiguousness in the understanding of religion and religious tradition, cf. *ME,* 129: 'For these things [i.e. the relationship to one's fellow men, to oneself, and to the Creator or ground or totality of universe] the formalities of one's religious tradition are at best a channel, and at worst a substitute.'

> not merely human, not merely social; not that he loves, but
> that he loves because of Christ; not that he sins, but that
> he sins to Christ's hurt, and yet forgivably (*ibid.*).

Such descriptions, which use distinctive Christian (if not Protestant, at least by intention) language, are, however, not confined to apply to Christians only. In a similar way, the life of a Muslim is not understandable without due recognition of his relation to transcendence, through faith (137).[45] With more general implications: those of us who would interpret the Muslim and her and his faith, must understand not his religion but his religiousness. Hence, resonating with the relation between self-understanding and understanding of the Other, Smith's attempt to rethink the use of 'religion' is an attempt to help the understanding of another humans' faith. Hence, extensification can only occur after major obstacles to such understanding have been displaced. One may however ask: what then about his own religious perception, his Christian self-understanding? Given the assumption that one has to learn to see other's faith more

> through their eyes ... to see through and beyond their [i.e.
> the Hindus'] foreground to a Reality that, if not yet
> altogether attributeless, is certainly quite without the
> attribute of being in any sense *Hindu* (138)

the inevitable question is how this approach can integrate the fact that the eyes doing the seeing are those of the interpreter, and, in the case of Smith, Christian ones. The way in which Smith answers this question will give rise to one of this study's main objections to Smith's interreligious hermeneutics. This discussion will be addressed later. Another critical track to pursue is whether Smith's own emphasis on faith and transcendence may imply subsequent reifications.

[b] This leads us to the historical argument, which is an epistemological argument against what he calls 'essentialism'. The point of departure is, however, the recognition of history as flux (141). This has bearing not only for the humanities; also in the sciences the concept of essence has been abandoned because 'the objective world itself resists against its (the essentialist's) pigeonholing dominance' (143). What is viable in our modern age when trying to define empirical objects is only

> humble approximations of an awareness of what always
> transcends our exact apprehension—and, in any case, is
> changing even when we try to apprehend it.

---

[45] At this place, Smith seems to link 'religious life' and 'faith' very closely.

Smith seems to be confident with this epistemological approach, partly against Aristotle,[46] since 'essences do not have a history. Essences do not change' (143). In that respect he also supports the results of history of religion which 'has made those essences not more but less ascertainable' (*ibid.*). Because that which 'exists cannot be defined' (144), the dichotomy between 'existence' and 'essence' becomes total. Thus, on historical grounds, it is highly problematical to speak of religions, provided that they have been characterized by a notion of essence. One of the results of this perception is that not only the existence of things is open to change: also the future gains its freedom by this perspective, as it is 'inherently unknowable' (145).

The consequences for the 'religions' are obvious. Firstly, Smith contends that the notions of religion and religions were formed before this recognition of 'change' in history (142). Therefore, there is nothing empirical such as 'Hinduism' or 'Christianity'.[47] What, then, about the possibility of an idea of ideal 'Christianity' or 'Hinduism'? This does not seem to have gained an unequivocal conclusion by Smith. On the one hand, he says, 'the definable is the pure; and purity is to be found only in theory and in God' (146). On the other hand, he maintains that

> We are in no wise concerned—neither as worshippers or as serving historians—with an ideal realm of essences *unless, and except insofar as, it is somehow, somewhere, involved in the life of man* (*ibid.*, emphasis mine).

Held together, this seems to imply recognition of an ideal realm, though inextricably interwoven with human history. Hence, Smith has some sympathy for this 'idealistic interpretation'—that historical actualities are mundane, imperfect, compromised successions of a transcendent ideal (150). This is, however, more so in the Christian and Islamic instances where the traditions start with a 'bang', than in the Jewish or Hindu instances where traditions develop more like a *crescendo*. Yet, the problem, according to Smith, is that an idealistic interpretation 'can at best serve only as self-interpretation,' which precludes one from understanding anyone else's religious tradition.

---

[46] E.g. *ME*, 142, where he uses a passage from Aristotle's *Posterior Analytics* to illustrate the idea 'that reality is definable,' and *ibid.* 148, where he runs counter the notion of a religion as that which is common to all instances, thus reflecting 'the traditional Aristotelian notion of the essence of many particulars that belong to a single species, *but shorn of Aristotle's subtleties and qualifications*' (emphasis mine).

[47] Cf. also Smith 1961a where the *fragmentation* and *unstability* of religions is argued for as historically evident.

These statements are certainly very important seen in the light of the approach adopted in the present study. Here, the very relation between self-understanding and understanding of another religious tradition is made an acute problem: How to retain one's self-understanding, allegiance and loyalty, and still be able to understand the other? Are the alternatives finally compromise and idealization/perspectivism? It remains to see how he solves this problem of understanding oneself and the other?

A clue to this can be found in what he calls the possibility of an ideal relationship (150). Smith illustrates this with how a 'perceptive Muslim' relates to the idea of 'the mind of God.' This idea, Smith asserts, is 'not some transcendent Islam' but an idea

> by which man—the only man there is: actual, imperfect, conditioned, embroiled in the historical—is related within time to eternity. The relationship may be ideal, but one term in it is, even in theory, human (*ibid.*).

Likewise for any Christian, where

> his ideal is not Christianity but Christ; and second, even that Christ is not a purely supernal, transcendent person but one whose nature it was to come into the turmoil of history in the most *engagé* and compromised of fashions, and whose significance now is his presence with the Christians not in heaven but on earth (150f).

How this emphasis on the human part of the relationship with the divine enables one to understand other humankind's faith will be followed up later.

Nevertheless, in this rather incarnational, kenotic[48] language Smith illustrates clearly what he asserts should be the meaning of what used to be called 'religions' (cf. the title of *The Meaning and End of Religion*), namely: to be involved in history on the one hand, and involved in the transcendent on the other (151). This leads to his invention of the terms 'personal faith' and 'cumulative tradition'.

---

[48] For the kenotic aspects of Smith's Christology, see Buckalew 1987 *passim*. This is however not to be regarded a fundamental perspective. The normative sources for a substantiation of Smith's approach are rather humanism, rationalism, idealism and Islamic mystics, cf. Grünschloß 1994, 278, n64.

2.4.5 INVENTION OF 'CUMULATIVE TRADITION'
AND 'PERSONAL FAITH'

Smith suggests that involvement in history and involvement in transcendence should be treated separately. Moreover, in doing this he aims at giving room for multiplicity (155), which means that he allows for diverse and even contradictory versions of the relation between history and transcendence.

Significantly, Smith sees the very intersection between transcendence and history in humankind (156).[49] Based on this, he denotes humans' involvement with history as 'cumulative tradition', and the involvement with transcendence as 'faith', or 'personal faith' (156). Whereas the former represents 'the entire mass of overt objective data that constitute the historical deposit,' and which the historian may observe and find intelligible (168), the latter refers to

> an inner religious experience or involvement of a particular person; the impingement on him of the transcendent, putative or real (*ibid.*).

Using these concepts, which Smith at this point regards rather a method of investigation than a prejudged solution, he suggests that

> it is possible to conceptualize and describe anything that has ever happened in the religious life of mankind, whether within one's own religious community ... or in other's (157).

At this point it may be rewarding to examine more thoroughly how Smith comprehends each of these concepts.

[a] His argument for the notion of cumulative tradition is simply to draw attention to the complex history of the religious community and persons throughout the world. By 'cumulative' he attempts to describe the fact that traditions, as the environments in which religious people live and die, have always been subordinated to the necessity of change (164). From another point of view, change has always been a deliberate aspect of the same history, namely that both 'great creative leaders' and 'the obscure, average' religious person have formed, transformed and modified the inherited and transmitted tradition and thus changed the historical

---

[49] Cf. also Smith's notion of revelation as bound to history, see Smith 1987d. There is, according to Smith, no revelation of transcendence without expression in history. Hence the study of history is an adequate way of approaching transcendence.

deposit for following generations (159f). Thus, history is (trans)formed by both necessity and persons.

This process of change and formation in traditions of 'receptive followers' persists, Smith contends, because it serves 'the ground of a transcendent faith' (160). Thus, there is a certain relation between cumulative tradition and faith that is not confined to what lies within history alone, or what is open for observation (161). Hence it belongs to the agent within history not only to be related to the mundane but also to transcendence. History is therefore not a closed system, and faith cannot be separated from religious history.

Smith maintains that the case of cumulative tradition is trickier in the Islamic and Christian cases (161ff) than in the Hindu (157ff), because here transcendence is directly related to contingency and the particular; God has acted in history, either 'in the pages of Qur'an' or in the historical figure of Jesus (162).

Smith, however, evades the theological issues here, which certainly would include Prophecy and Incarnation, and argues that cumulation and modification of the Islamic (163f) and Christian tradition (166f) obviously took place, observable for both believers and non-believers. In the Islamic case this means that: 'The Islamic tradition that modern Muslims inherit, and that observers see, has been the handiwork of Muslim' (164).[50] This does not, however, rule out the impact and work of God in Muslim history: 'Any divine pattern in it that Muslim faith may discern, God has put in it by working through the intermediacy of persons' (*ibid.*).

Given Smith's rejection of the notion of essence one may ask: what is the *continuum* in Smith's concept of tradition? An implicit answer can be given thus (167):

> 1. Firstly the continuity lies in the realm of faith (which is only partly observable) where believers assume a common element of transcendence across the diversity of cumulation of traditions. This may also be called a 'genetic bond of continuity,' which the observer should concentrate on.
> 2. Secondly, Smith speaks of existential association instead of essential identity without further explanation.

The meaning of the latter will probably be a looser unitary feature than that of essence, probably the unity established by the religious

---

[50] Or, more generally: 'A religious tradition then, is the historical construct, in continuous construction, of those who participate in it,' *ME*, 165.

human beings in their inner faith. Given his personalist approach, this phrasing does not surprise us. Yet, it remains that the cumulative tradition itself is not a unit but may be intellectually abstracted, and legitimately so, on lower levels of abstraction (168). The unit, ultimately, consists of the 'individual persons' and how they engage in the existing 'segments of the total cumulative tradition available' (*ibid.*).

[b] When Smith speaks of faith he does so as participant of a particular tradition. On the other hand, and more generally, without faith the cumulative traditions would simply not be there (169). Hence, there is a dialectic connected to these most central notions in Smith's proposal for a double replacement of religion and religions.

What, then, is faith, according to Smith? The answer is simply he never defines it. He only says what it is not, where its locus is to be found, and finally, how one may get an impression of what it is like. This is of course confusing, but seems to be wholly on a par with his strategy of avoiding essences, entities and forms in view of the 'religiousness' of human beings. S. Mark Heim is probably right when he says about Smith: 'To give it [i.e. faith] any content would be to make it particular.'[51] At the same time, although it is unfathomable for the observer, even as it inevitably exists (170), he predicts a time to come when one may have gained—gradually and partially—a more adequate and accurate answer as to what faith is (189). In our time, therefore, Smith argues for the use of this concept, like the concept of cumulative tradition, as a matter of method (179, 188f) and not of definition of essence. The substantiation of all this follows this pattern (171):

(1) There is some personal and inner quality in the life of some human beings that is involved with something greater than the expressions of this involvement.
(2) This quality is given the name 'faith'
(3) We do not know what it is.
(4) But for those human beings it affects it makes certain overt observables religiously significant.

The latter point is crucial to his approach. This link between faith and its implications makes it in principle possible to approximate faith by inference (188).[52] Through the expressions of faith, it is possible to get some idea of what we mean by it. The expressions themselves,

---

[51] Heim 1995, 70. Interestingly, Heim sees unbelief as ruled out by Smith's approach in this respect: 'The last thing that either an undefinable faith or an empty ultimate [cf. J. Hick's 'the Real'] has to fear is unbelief,' *ibid.* In a later chapter (Chapter 7) I will pursue the kind of criticism of Smith which this statement entails.

[52] See also *CR,* 35.

however, belong to the mundane, historical, yet religious, cumulation. Smith uses deliberately the vague term 'apprehension' to denote this 'empirical procedure' instead of the more ambitious 'comprehension' (188f). By this approach, accompanied by 'imaginative sympathy', 'intellectual rigour', 'elaborate procedures' and 'vigorous criticism', it is not impossible, Smith asserts, to infer what goes on in another's mind and heart (188). This approach could likewise be used for the understanding of art,[53] community,[54] and character,[55] and leads Smith to contend that

> to assess a religious tradition by the kind of character that its faith produces would seem more legitimate than to do so on grounds of reason, or revelation, or any impersonal standard, were it not that none of us is in a position to judge (178).

The common ground of his elaboration on faith in these instances is that it refers to a living quality of persons, rather than to its expressions, or to any tradition to which these persons belong (179). These persons are also the loci of meaning and truth: there is no truth *per se,* only meaning for persons. This kind of assertion has certainly obvious consequences for the activity of theology. Provided that 'religious statements express the faith of persons, who as persons are involved in transcendence' (183), theological statements, therefore, can at their best only serve as indirect expressions of transcendent reality, through faith (184).[56] Smith does not think that this is a radical statement, at least not so in the Christian case where 'Truth' is a 'Person' and not a theological system. Consequently, Smith sums up the relation between theology, faith and truth thus:

—*Theology* is part of the cumulative traditions,
—*Faith* lies beyond theology, in the hearts of men and
—*Truth* lies beyond faith, in the heart of God (185).

The locus of faith is thus placed between the mundane, here represented by theology, and transcendence, here represented by truth.

---

[53] Which points beyond itself to the spirit of the artist, 173, and its 'incarnate truth', e.g. in the statues of Buddha.

[54] Which would cease to exist without the faith of its members, 175.

[55] Where faith makes a significant difference between people with otherwise identical *expressions* of faith.

[56] Interestingly, at this point Smith uses an interpretation of how 'den kristna trons (innebörd)' in G. Aulén's *Den allmänneliga kristna troen* (transl. Eric H. Wahlstrom and G. Everett Arden, *The Faith of the Christian Church)* should be translated, in order to support his own view: either as 'Christian faith', which Smith argues for, or 'the Christian faith', which he argues against, *ME*, 185, and 321f, note 13.

Yet, this faith cannot be described as '*the* faith', or '*the* Christian faith' (191). Faith is personal, not a 'generic entity.' It varies from person to person, and in every person, even from day to day (189-191). The reason, then, to use the term 'faith' is to describe a living quality of human beings which reflects a continuity across different persons, a continuity that causes humans to be involved in 'God Himself', and in 'my neighbour himself' (192). These two are, alluding to the title of Smith's classic *(ME)* once more, the ends of religion.

To conclude, cumulative tradition and personal faith are related to historical flux and transcendence in the following way: traditions evolve, faith varies, and God endures (192). To phrase it thus is Smith's distinctive contribution to a revision of the term and idea of 'religion' and 'religions'. What is important for the approach of the present study, is that by this revision also the relation between Oneself and the religious Other gains a distinctive shape. In order to grasp this better, we should proceed to Smith's major work on faith: *Faith and Belief.*

2.5   *Faith and Belief: the History and Construction of their Difference and Dependence*

2.5.1   INTRODUCTION

Smith's most comprehensive exposition of 'faith' is found in *Faith and Belief (FB,* 1979).[57] This is a work which attempts to be historical, comparative, theological, and 'in various senses philosophic'.[58] The

---

[57] Subsequent parenthetical references refer to *FB*. Because I see all the results of *Belief and History (BH)* included in *FB* I choose to leave out a separate analysis of *BH* here. I only mention the following: The primary concern of *Belief and History* is the *history* of 'belief', the meaning of which Smith, *inter alia,* contends lacks of support from the scriptural witnesses of the Bible. Moreover, Smith calls *BH* the 'supplement' of *FB*. The former appeared a couple of years in advance of the latter, but within the same process, a process of 12 years, which almost fills the gap to *ME, see FB,* x. Smith himself sees *BH* as posing a thesis on behalf of the term 'belief' and its usage, a thesis of which *implications* are developed in *FB*, see *BH*, vi. In relation to *ME,* I suggest that *BH and FB* should rather be seen as a comprehension of the conclusions of *ME* than real reorientations or advancements of its arguments. Hence, *ME* should be recognized as a central work within Smith's writings. See otherwise Chapter 4.6 and 4.7 which are implicit but comprehensive abstracts of most of the arguments in *BH*.

[58] *Ibid.* vii. Implied in this way of phrasing, it is Smith's awareness that since his study is mainly historical and comparative he does not expect it to be admitted by 'present-day philosophy.' The task of clarifying concepts is however more on a par with philosophical conventions.

foundation is, however, primarily historical as it seeks to clarify the concept of 'faith'.

　　　　The introductory questions of the work read: 'What has faith to do with believing this or that? What has faith to do with being human?' These, in Smith's terminological environment, most significant questions are intended to be both conceptual and historical, and Smith boldly asserts that both theology and philosophy should deal with them (viii). In the very beginning of this study, therefore, he implies that theological issues are introduced only as far as they relate to the understanding of humankind and of faith. Furthermore, to these two questions Smiths correlates some suggestions, which can be outlined as follows (3):

> (a) 'Faith' in the modern awareness is not what it used to be because 'belief' in its modern, and distorted, fashion has become the dominant concept.
> (b) Hence, Smith asserts the importance of forging a new understanding of 'faith',
> (c) which should be accompanied by an historical and comparative perspective.

　　　　Yet, what does this mean more precisely? We may start by noticing that whereas the first and latter represent the matters of description and method, the middle suggestion is connected with certain values and normative preferences. Smith is obviously not happy with what he perceives as the present situation and hopes for a return to previous times, or better, a renaissance (or reformulation) in continuity with them:

> And yet, strikingly, the bold new positions propounded, in their novel generic pluralism, although at odds with certain recent particularist thought, turn out to be strangely closer to several classical positions than those recent particulars are (viiif) .

And,

> it will become apparent as we proceed, however, that there is in fact continuity of the new conceptions that emerge, however seemingly novel, with classical positions, both Christian and other (6).

The umbrella notion for 'classical' and 'new', or 'innovation'/'innovative', 'reformulation', 'enrichment', and so on, is thus continuity.[59]

---

[59] See also *WT,* 121. 'New' is otherwise used in a variety of senses in Smith's writings, mostly relating to the fact and emergence of religious diversity.

Nevertheless, his main purpose is to understand faith as 'a characteristic quality or potentiality' of human life (3). But, as in *The Meaning and End of Religion,* he does not identify what such a faith is, except that:

> (a) Faith goes beyond the variety of 'religious forms,' and is related to the impulse behind the diverse religious systems (3,5), by which at the same time it is 'elicited, nurtured, and shaped' (6).
> (b) Faith is characterized by involvement and engagement (5f), both in relation to particular traditions, fellow human beings, and especially towards transcendence.

Faith *per se*, however, is again left 'unspecified' (6). One might only come to know where to look for it, its *locus,* represented by 'the human side of these involvements' (8). Consequently, this opens the way for historical investigations where 'faith' may be constructed, yet only tentatively (9). Also *Faith and Belief* has to be understood within these limits. Accordingly, Smith presents the following goals for his study:

> 1. To plead the significance of the problem.
> 2. To take an interim step towards elucidating the nature of man's faith by exploring the relation between faith and belief.

This latter relation between faith and belief can, however, be seen as a further step on the track which was incipiently constructed in *The Meaning and End of Religion,* especially where the relation between 'personal faith' and 'cumulative tradition' (and 'religion') was considered (cf. Chapter 3.4.5).

It is noteworthy that Smith sees his approach as *fides quarens intellectum* (6, cf. Anselm), which he translates, with some relation to the approach of the present study, as faith in pursuit of self-understanding. Yet, faith requires, both as a fundamental religious and human category (7), a generic understanding. This is not to say that faith is identical for everyone everywhere. Rather the contrary, because we talk about the faith of *persons*, faith may vary between persons, between traditions, as well as within the same tradition (11).

To sum up so far, Smith seems to direct his study in a twofold way:

> 1. To point out a *via negativa*, that is, what faith has not been, that is, belief (9f)
> 2. And positively to contribute to 'a new planetary self-consciousness about faith' (10).

Doing this, Smith suggests an important methodological criterion, namely that

> no interpretation of faith in general is liable to be persuasive that is not solidly grounded in a wrestling with faith in particular (8).

This statement is of particular interest for our study. Despite all his attempts at generalizations, Smith is highly concerned with the role of the particulars. In short, no theory of interreligious relations is viable without considering the role of particulars in such relations. The criterion above is particularly due to his self-understanding as an historian as he sees his contribution as inducing theory based on historical investigations. This is at least his explicitly stated approach. Whether this applies to the nature of his theory in all respects, that is, regarding all particulars, will be addressed in later chapters (Chapter 6 and 7).

For Smith, 'particular' is not to be equated with 'isolated'. He sees it as inescapable that the particulars receive their place within a common framework, a 'wider context,' namely of all traditions that nurture faith across the world. Thus, for example, 'even Christian conceptualizations of faith for the Christian case, and the Muslim for the Islamic, will halt a little until they are illuminated by being set now within the wider context' (8). Consequently, within this 'wider context', the 'conceptualisations of faith' (not faith itself!) will become illuminated. In many ways, this seems to be Smith's way of expressing the hermeneutical approach which is pursued in the present study: One's self-understanding is intimately connected with the understanding of the Other. It should furthermore be noticed that the very correlation between history and hermeneutics is of importance here because the common history of mutuality guarantees the understanding of each other across the borders of diverse traditions.

Thus, Smith sees his elaborations on the relation between faith and belief in the Buddhist, Islamic, Hindu and the Roman Catholic Church, as re-interpretations 'made possible by seeing each in the context of a comparative vision' (10). Hence, re-interpretation, or an enriched or revised self-understanding, are related to a vision or a superior framework which span various traditions. A substantial part of this vision is faith, which may take the form of

> serenity and courage and loyalty and service: a quiet confidence and joy which enable one to feel at home in the universe, and to find meaning in the world and in one's own life, a meaning that is profound and ultimate, and is

stable no matter what may happen to oneself at the level of immediate event. Men and women of this kind of faith face catastrophe and confusion, affluence and sorrow, unperturped; face opportunity with conviction and drive; and face others with a cheerful charity (12).

As such, a Christian historian will observe that faith in this 'warmly humane, open' (13) sense of the word

> has been found also in the Jewish and Islamic and Hindu and Buddhist and other communities (and among humanists), throughout the centuries and throughout the world (12).

Faith is thus a quality of *human* living (12). It is not a Christian or Buddhist way of living a morally desirable life, but a human, personal way. Consequently, for example for a Christian, the opposite of faith cannot be found in something non-Christian, that is, in another religious tradition. The opposite of faith is nihilism[60] and 'blind and fanatical particularism,' (13).

What remains of the role of 'belief', then? How is this term and subject to be understood in relation to faith? It should certainly not be understood as the opposite of faith since Smith has stated the interdependence of the two. At the same time the differences are obvious. Whereas beliefs 'strike' the historian as differing radically globally, faith has been 'more approximative to constancy' (11). Thus, faith varies, but not so much as beliefs. Interestingly, Smith asserts this to be reasonable for theologians, given an assumed definition of faith as

> a direct encounter with God—mediated, no doubt, by the sacraments or the doctrines, or the moral obligations involved, but significant precisely because it transcends these, and enables the person to transcend them (*ibid.*)

Against an undue emphasis on commonality, Smith maintains that the world's religious systems 'are not all variations on a theme ... they do not

---

[60] Smith draws attention in his investigations of the Buddhist tradition to a remark originally made with a reference to 'the only true atheist,' that is, 'He who loves no one and whom no one loves; who does not care for truth, sees no beauty, strives for no justice; who knows no courage and no joy, finds no meaning, and has lost all hope' (20). Smith therefore concludes: If this is to be a description of faith, 'perhaps no human being' has been totally without it.

operate in a common mode' (13). An example of this is that belief, as one of
many expressions of faith (17), plays different roles in diverse traditions
(15). For instance, doctrine as well as theology has been central in the
Christian case, whereas it was well developed in the Islamic tradition but
after all regarded as suspect (14). Yet, the various expressions of faith, i.e.,
theology, rituals, beliefs, and so on, serve as *loci* for faith, and a description
of faith may thus be induced from these forms of a tradition.

One implication of this is that the significance of belief is
transcendent as far as it induces faith in the believer, reaching beyond
itself and its expression (19). The appearance that this is a hermeneutics
of signification, is supported by Smith's subsequent relating of belief to
two different kinds of 'truth-pressures', one 'symbolical'[61] and one
'straightforward': on the one hand, beliefs should be symbolically true as

> life lived in terms of them [i.e. the beliefs] should be true: true
> in relation to the mundane environment in which it is lived,
> and truly human, in the highest, final, cosmic sense (19).

How this cosmic sense may be described, may vary from person to person,
according to the preferences one is inclined to. On the other hand, beliefs
are subject also to the pressure of *straightforward* truth, in the form of
true statements. Smith does not exclude any of these pressures, though
the former seems to relate more immediately to his concept of faith.
Variations of this pair of truth-concepts will be identified in due course.

2.5.2 FAITH AS THE GENERIC HUMAN CAPACITY OF INVOLVEMENT WITH TRANSCENDENCE

Faith and Belief aims, as we have seen, to outline the relation between
faith and belief.[62] After an historical investigation of how these concepts
relate to each other in the Buddhist, Islamic, Hindu, and Roman Catholic
tradition, Smith draws important conclusions in a final chapter (Chapter
7). These conclusions relate to 1) faith as generically human, 2) how belief
and 'belief-systems' should be interpreted, and 3) the interrelation between
the two. I will pursue these issues in separate subsections.

Regarding the former, Smith holds that faith is 'constitutive of
man as human,' and even, faith is '*the* essential human quality' (129,
Smith's emphasis). He may also say, that 'standard man is man of faith'

---

[61] For a comprehensive understanding of 'symbol' in Smith, see Tadsen 1985, ch.
III.5.

[62] *FB*, 128. Subsequent parenthetical remarks in the text refer still to *FB*.

(135). Smith relates this to the traditional notion of *homo religiosus*, to the openness and the spirit of human beings (129). Thus, any secular view that rules out faith is to be viewed as an *addendum* (136).[63]

This does not mean that it is impossible to have an experience of 'un-faith' (142). According to Smith, faith is not to be taken for granted simply because faith is neither rare nor automatic. Faith is the 'human potentiality for being human' (*ibid.*). In his teleological description of faith Smith is able to maintain faith as both 'the prodigious hallmark of being human' as well as rejecting a deterministic or naturalistic view of the relation between faith and individuals. Faith is normal, Smith asserts, but not natural (141). The latter relates most interestingly to his notion of The Fall, in Christian terms, and the distinction between actual truth and ideal truth in Western philosophic tradition. With what is for him remarkably Christian (Anselmian!) language, he maintains that faith is the bridging of the gap between humanity in its genuine or pristine condition and its actual life, a bridging 'at a cost that only God could pay—but did pay, by Himself turning human and suffering and dying on a cross' (*ibid.*)

Previously we have noticed that Smith not only hesitates to give a definition of faith, but in principle rejects more than a delineating of the locus and fact of faith. This seems to coincide with his teleological and potential understanding of faith. Because faith always implies the possibility of growth in relation to its ideals, it simultaneously escapes any definition and is beyond apprehension (141f). To such an understanding, the notion of faith as 'capacity' is not untoward (140).[64]

What then of his theological understanding of faith?[65] How does it exceed the secularist anthropologies that Smith from time to time criticizes? An answer to this can be deduced from his concept of transcendence. 'Man' is not only an empirical concept, but also a transcendent one (139). In this respect 'man' has at least a double meaning as far as it both denotes, theologically speaking, 'man's quest for God' and 'God's initiative' (140). This double meaning is contained in the notion of humankind's participation by faith in God's on-going and multifaceted

---

[63] Smith's criticism may also take the form of *social criticism* when he blames the modern society for being 'obtuse as to the true nature of faith' based on the assumption that 'society can be organised on the assumption that faith does not really matter' (139). The consequence is 'a pitiably dehumanized society' that will have to 'pay the price' some time. Consequently, Smith labels his approach as 'modified classical humanism,' or metaphysical classical humanism (138f).

[64] For a similar notion of faith, see Panikkar 1978, ch. IV.3, 69ff.

[65] Though Smith gives some clues to his theological approach, he explicitly leaves this for 'another book (forthcoming),' which at this place must refer to *WT*. Hence, *FB* should be seen as a bridge between his conceptual studies and his major theological work.

Heilsgeschichte (*ibid.*).[66] Thus, Smith connects the history of humankind as the history of religion (!), with the history of religion as the history of salvation by faith.

The latter notion (the history of salvation by faith) requires a clarification. Since faith varies, as we have noticed, does this imply that *any* faith is included in the *Heilsgeschichte*?[67] The answer seems to depend on what one designates by 'included'. On the one hand, Smith is eager to draw attention to the faith of *homo religiosus perversus* (131), that is, the notion of man as a sinner. Although he admits that this term represents a particular, unique view, the reality it designates is, however, global. Furthermore, faith is not everywhere admirable, and hence approximates truth historically either closely or remotely (130). On the other hand, nobody should be excluded from participating in the *Heilsgeschichte*. It is rather a matter of degree, related to truth, which he implicitly defines in relation to a range of qualities and human virtues:[68] large, rich, strong, serene, generous, courageous, compassionate, patient, noble, creative (131).[69]

In the end, what matters is to become 'human properly,' or even divinized,[70] and to become this as 'one or other of them [i.e. as Jew, Muslim, etc.]' (138). This is, Smith contends, the goal of the death of Christ, and this is also the aim for traditions other than the Christian tradition. This is also the way we *differ* 'in the depth and richness and vitality, as well as in the contours, of faith,' at the same time as we *share* in common the capacity and potentiality of it (141).[71]

---

[66] Cf. Smith 1969a, 13, where Smith maintains it to be a Christian missionary task to recognize the salvation history of all human history. Not surprisingly, the notion of *Heilsgeschichte* precedes the term 'God's mission' (*missio Dei!*) at this place (in relation to the Buddhist movement).

[67] See Chapter 3.6.3 for a further elaboration of *Heilsgeschichte*.

[68] Cf. Edward J. Hughes who sees Smith's notion of faith as virtue and *habitus,* cf. immediately below, as 'more 'Catholic,'' Hughes 1985, 72. Hughes may also be right that 'Smith wishes to discuss faith in its full range of manifestation, including its inauthentic forms.' The latter makes Smith's approach different to that of Bultmann who utilizes a norm of 'authenticity' to discern between authentic and inauthentic forms of faith, *ibid.* 71. For Smith, inauthentic faith is not unfaith, *ibid.* 72.

[69] See also Smith 1987c, 'Taking goodness seriously,' which illustrates this concern.

[70] Cf. his reference to Athanasius' dictum in *De Incarnatione*: αυτος γαρ ενηνθρωπησεν ινα ημεις θεοποιηθωμεν, *FB,* 330, note 4.

[71] Cf. *FB,* 330, note 3, where he acknowledges 'the comparable thesis' of Clifford Geertz ('The Impact of the Concept of Culture on the Concept of Man,' in J.R. Platt, ed., *New Views of the Nature of Man,* Chicago & London 1965, 93-118), which he paraphrases as 'contending that human nature is not a given to which various cultures of the world have been added on, or even out of which they have been educed, but rather that a basic ingredient of human nature is the capacity, and indeed the necessity, to live in terms of one or another such culture.'

Smith seems to be making a circle of arguments here. Firstly, faith is established as a human quality. Secondly, faith varies and is more or less true. Thirdly, when truth then is related to a virtue-perspective as a kind of realization of humanity, the whole project appears to become closed to external references. Smith's argument against this conclusion is that truth ultimately lies in the heart of God.[72] Nevertheless, this matter leads us to Smith's next concern, which opens up a more extensive version of his epistemology.

2.5.3 FROM INADEQUATE BELIEVING TO CORPORATE AND COHERENT UNDERSTANDING

When Smith aims to comprehend his notion of 'belief' and 'believing' 'as such' (143) on a theoretical level (147), he actually outlines an epistemology. This is obviously relevant for the present study because it includes considerations about how religious self-understanding should be ventured in a global perspective, that is, in the perspective of diverse 'others'.

Smith starts boldly by stating that: 'Faith is a virtue. Belief is not' (142). Regarding the latter, one may immediately ask: what is it then? Smith suggests that the notion of belief should be interpreted in the light of the 'human fact' (143) that word and concepts are culture-specific. Every meaning is a function of a world-view. In the case of belief and believing, Smith contends that these have been part of a certain *Weltanschauung*, and not only that: they became also integral aspects of what he calls 'the new detranscendentalized ideology,' a secularized view of the human, which denatured the religious life and came to dominate intellectually (144). The role of this view (ideology) was to drain the transcendence out of peoples' and ages' perceptions. Accompanied by scepticism, and to a large extent by the Church, especially in the cases of others' belief, belief came to reduce 'other's faith to manageability' by translating faith into pure mundane terms (*ibid.*).

Smith regards this as the state of historical self-consciousness of the Westerner. Against this, Smith sees just one possibility to pull ourselves out of the backwater: By a reinterpretation of knowledge (143). Whereas 'truth' and 'reality' has ceased to function as objective 'values,' 'knowledge' has survived the pressure to move in the direction of mere subjectivity and non-historicity. By knowledge one still thinks of a human relation to something valid, that is, to truth or reality. Since this concept allows not only scientific knowledge, but knowledge through history, it seems to suit Smith's purposes well.

---

[72] Cf. p. 48 above.

On the other hand, since this term is so connected with knowledge 'through and of objective science', Smith decides to use other concepts, pre-eminently 'understanding' (146). A clue to this is already given in the relation between 'believing' and 'knowing' (one does not believe a proposition, but its meaning), when Smith maintains the symbolic function of 'belief'. The emphasis is thus put on meaning and especially the meaning something has for others and their world-views. By this distinction between meaning and its understanding on the one hand, and belief, on the other, Smith is able to affirm both traditional and alien doctrines, albeit people nowadays do not 'believe' them (147).

Other concepts that have not yet been depersonalized are: 'insight', 'seeing the point', 'awareness' and 'recognizing' (147). According to Smith, through these terms one may describe the way humans approach truth and knowledge. Yet, the personal dimension of these does not exhaust truth and knowledge. It only enables one to think in 'humane' categories and thus relates not only to 'objective' knowing but also to our 'critical corporate self-consciousness' (hereafter CCSC) (148).[73] Therefore, these terms demonstrate the greatness of persons, as well as the inadequacy of any statement about persons (149).

Smith's replacement of knowledge by several other concepts aims at *knowing together with* 'one's neighbour'. This is the meaningful content of 'corporate' above. Smith asserts that the perception accompanied by the 'historical ideology' of depersonalization, detranscendentalization, and denaturing (150), is not calibrated to recognize certain realities, especially not those of human faith which includes 'most human beings, and all human beings potentially' (151). The possible solution for philosophy and theology is therefore to integrate the comparative issue, namely the 'vision of diversity, and the ability to see oneself, not only others, in global perspective' (*ibid.*).

These statements about the philosophical and theological task of self-understanding in a global perspective are exacting. They are also visionary. Let me mention but one issue: Smith sees the task of constructing coherence in the present day world, what he calls 'planetary intellectual cohesion,' as an 'only once' task. By this he means that once one has changed one's conceptual system as a whole and formed a 'pluralistic unity', the coherence is established. It is to this project Smith sees his own re-thinking of 'faith' as a contribution. Most interestingly, the global context is highlighted by his suggestion that more than many other

---

[73] For the construction of 'humane' and 'critical corporate self-consciousness', see Smith 1976b, 'Objectivity and the Humane Sciences.' Both terms are elaborated further in *WT,* see Chapter 3.6.2 below.

traditions the Sufi-tradition may have the level of sophistication to facilitate this kind of construction (153).

There are also other non-Christian resources that may help his world community to come through. In his elaboration of truth which he develops against the 'either truth-or false'-view of truth, of which the notion of belief is a part as well as the opinion of 'saved-damned' represented by 'the earlier dominant ideology' of the Church (153), he makes use of an alternative to a 'propositional' view of truth, based on Indian traditions (154). In short, this abandons the principle of contradiction and offers a complementary 'principle': if two statements contradict each other, they are both partially true, and partially false. Contradictions may therefore occur on one level but not on another. Smith seems to use his new concept of knowledge to discern between 'insights' on the one hand, and statements on the other. In the case of Copernicus he asks whether it may be said that his insights were true whereas his statements were not (154).

Against the alternatives true-false, Smith suggests that we should still talk about other people's ideas (third person) and one's own (first person). Yet, the difference between these two shall be perceived as moral: One's own affirmations must be true, whereas other people's must be understood. Smith does, however, not see this as a final solution, but a first step towards coherence in the shape of 'integration in a community (in principle, world-wide)' (155). The way Smith thus locates the matter of truth to one's own self-understanding, and the matter of understanding to that of the Other, does however not dissolve the relation between Oneself and the Other. Evidence for this is present at the same place when he poses what he calls the intellectual problem of the modern world, as 'how to be relativist without being nihilist,' and

> how to be pluralist without losing an intelligent, steadfast
> loyalty to one's own vision (155).

In other words, one's self-understanding should be regarded as part of a pluralist understanding. A part of this is that 'to understand the position of others is a function of one's own position.' This may be narrowly interpreted as if one's own position colours the understanding of other people in a distorting and inadequate way. However, I think this is more reasonably interpreted as if Smith is saying, that it is impossible to approximate to an adequate—true—understanding of others unless one's own view opens up for it. Thus, relativism and pluralism are only possible, at least at this stage of history, if they are based on one's own particular world-view. Further evidence for this may be cited:

We therein constitute (potentially) a corporate global community of a now self-conscious intellectual pluralism or relativism pledged, through our several disparate loyalties to truth and our mutual respect for each other, to move severally and jointly closer to that truth, and hence away from the grosser cacophonies of that relativism (156).

Consequently, he 'speculate[s]' whether

for a comparativist, the truth may be conceptualized as something that both is immanent within, and transcends, any given formulation of it in any given system (*ibid.*).

This immanent-transcendent way of stating it parallels the 'partial-fully' feature of the Indian perception of truth. Most interestingly with regard to our study, Smith proceeds further, and suggests in a definitory style that:

Each world-view may be less or more adequate to comprehending reality in general; and besides, may be less or more adequate for comprehending and expressing the particular apprehension of a specific point (157).

In this, Smith proffers a perspective of totality, or in his own words: a perspective of transcendence. This enables certainly a wider framework for the particular self-understandings of Oneself and of Others. Additionally, the whole issue of coherence gains a distinctive meaning by this assertion. Coherence is thus related to reality in its totality, and this kind of coherence is to be established both in relation to and independence from particular views of truth.[74] This truth of reality as totality, which only can be approximated, is what Smith calls transcendent truth or 'Truth itself' (158). The approximation of this truth, however, is 'a *derivative* from their personal quality of being able to reach out towards (to be touched by) Truth itself' (*ibid.*, emphasis mine), that is, a derivative of *faith*. From this, there logically follows a demand to comprehend the relation between 'understanding' and 'faith'.

---

[74] Cf. *FB*, 157: 'Since the truth transcends not only what each of us has apprehended, let alone formulated, but also *what all of us together have*, or can, therefore every observer may in principle learn something of truth from every person—and ... from every group ... past and present,' emphasis mine. This statement is certainly necessary due to his view of transcendence.

2.5.4 FAITH AND UNDERSTANDING

Smith contends that since faith like personhood embraces the whole person (cf. 'the locus of faith is persons'), the intellectual aspect is only one of many dimensions of faith (158). Because Smith already has reconsidered the religious epistemology in contrast to 'belief', it becomes important to see how he then establishes the relation between this new 'understanding' and the quintessence of religiousness: faith.

Smith chooses to use five intellectuals from five different religious traditions, almost contemporaneous, to illustrate his own view. These are Hugh of St. Victor (Christian), Judah ha-Levi (Jew), Ghazzali (Muslim), Ramanuja (Hindu) and Chu Hsi (Buddhist neo-Confucian). Of these, Smith asserts, none held belief to be faith (159). Further, intellectuality included 'two salient components': insight and response.[75] Let us see how he uses these concepts for his purpose.

[1] Smith identifies faith with insight: 'One may aver the history of faith to be a history of insight.' Furthermore, regarding the difference between knowing that something is true, and knowing its truth, faith and insight seem to align with the latter. Therefore, faith, intellectually, is insight (160). Smith relates this insight especially to two affirmations (160f): a) The recognition of transcendence ('a reality that transcends the immediate mundane', including the transcendence of our affirmation of the transcendent reality), and b) that the transcendent truth is not totally transcendent because it is intelligible and may imply insight. Hence, one may talk about transcendent and immanent aspects of transcendent truth, and ultimately, about transcendent and immanent aspects of transcendence itself.

[2] The more emphatic intellectual dimension of faith is *response*. What is meant by response here, is 'faith as saying "Yes!" to truth' (163). Moreover, Smith relates the notion to the difference between 'truth as seen' and 'truth transcendent, truth as such'. Since truth according to Smith is multi-faceted, it follows that various groups have apprehended it in diverse forms:

> Christian forms of faith were a saying 'Yes!' to the truth
> that they saw in and through Christ (although the almost
> unitarian Christocentrism of our day is historically recent[76]).

---

[75] Cf. the differentiation of 'understanding' by 'insight', 'seeing the point', 'recognizing', and so on, in the last chapter (Chapter 3.5.3).

[76] Cf. Smith 1991a: 'There emerged in the 19th century in Christendom a novel practice of thinking and speaking of 'Christian theology', rather than of 'theology' simpliciter. Even worse, since that time many Christians have come to assume that the two ideas are synonymous,' 15.

Muslim forms were a saying 'Yes!' to the truth that they found through the Qur'an (and through other Islamic symbols and patterns) (163).

On the other hand, the truth itself is 'greater than that'.[77] Thus, the truth as apprehended, represents many ways of responding to it, whereas the truth itself transcends every way of perceiving it. Nevertheless, any way of responding to 'truth transcendent' implies a 'particular fashion' of 'words and concepts.' In the case of the five intellectuals mentioned above, however, and this is the point of Smith, 'for no one of them was faith confused with accepting that mediating complex; yet neither was it understood without it' (164).

What is not entirely clear about this, is whether 'response' is to be thought as out of the bounds of 'truth as seen', or whether it is only different from the specific 'words and concepts' of a 'particular fashion' (*ibid.*). An answer to this question may be derived from the aphoristic distinction between faith as given by God, and belief given by 'one's century or one's group' (166). Related to this distinction, Smith says that 'faith being an awareness of transcendence and *a response* to it, its intellectual dimension has included such reaching out *beyond the given* as one's mind can manage' (*ibid.*, emphasis mine). Thus, involvement with the transcendent as involvement with that which is beyond the given, is *inter alia* facilitated by response, one of the intellectual dimensions of faith, and divergent from belief, though not entirely separated from it.

Hence, faith is not 'belief in' truth, but 'assent' to truth. Smith interprets, however, the aspects of *assensus* of faith in virtue-language. Faith is an attitude (168), a virtue (142), and it requires integrity (168). Most interestingly, Smith gives an example of what this means in the realm of conceptualization, which is 'the 'belief' that goes with [faith]' (169), and which must be seen as Smith's contribution *par excellence* (172):

> Yet insofar as conceptualizing be involved at all, it must, we may affirm, if it is to be *faithful,* be *the closest approximation to the truth of which one's mind is capable* (168, emphasis original).

So, what is the difference between faith in its intellectual dimension, and conceptualization as a matter of 'belief'? How Smith precisely orders this

---

[77] In fact, Smith suggests that one should avoid 'truth' and instead speak of *goodness*, because 'truth' implies a 'truth of something', which fails to underline what may be called the *last reference* of faith, *FB,* 163.

relation cannot be easily perceived. Yet, one gets some clues to what faith is in its intellectual mode, in which it differs from belief. This consists at least of: 1) The ability to recognize transcendence, and 2) the will that is involved in this. Consequently, there are additional aspects both on the side of *what* is known: the transcendent truth, and on the side of the *knower:* to know more than what is given by the beliefs, symbols, and so on (170).

To sum up this chapter: Smith's comprehension of faith is in the end an attempt to deal with the *de facto* religious plurality. What he offers is a pluralistic relativism, where truth is that

> to which all accounts of it approximate—so that the acceptance of diversity enriches rather than undermines one's own apprehension of faith (170).

On this view, differences will persist but humankind may *converge* in the intellectual realm because reason is universal and truth is one. Or, as Smith states it in a rather condensed way: 'Our unity is real transcendently' (171). As one sees, all this relates closely to the approach of the present study and presents his general answer to the issue of the relation between One's self-understanding and the understanding of the Other. Interestingly, on his vision of faith, one's self-understanding may be enriched (self-change) rather than dissolved by diversity. How this relates to Islam in particular will be examined in another chapter (Chapter 3), after having examined his theological integration and explication of his conceptual and comparative studies.

2.6   Towards a World Theology of Comparative Religion

It is not always transparent whether Smith speaks as an historian, as a comparative religionist, as a theologian, or, to some extent, as a philosopher.[78] This is partly due to the distinctive programme which directs

---

[78] His works are characterized most differently. Jacques Waardenburg writes in a preface to *UI* that 'Professor Smith reveals himself to be at the same time an Islamicist and a scholar of religious studies and also a thinker on religion,' Waardenburg 1981, vii. David Burrell calls it (*BH, FB* and *WT*) a 'religious epistemology,' Burrell 1983, 66. That might be a suitable and loose enough label to subsume the various aspects of his approach at this place. Smith himself hesitates until late in his authorship to call himself a theologian. Even then, he calls himself 'not an erudite theologian,' *WT,* 179. One of the most outspoken self-characteristics appears in *WT* where he calls himself 'an historian of the Orient, not a philosopher of the West,' *ibid.*

his studies, but also due to his emphasis on the transcendent aspect of religious history, as well as the demand on the investigator to recognize and get involved with what believers presuppose.

At the same time, there is a certain development within Smith's authorship towards a theological view of the history of religion, and especially of comparative religion. This move is anticipated by certain studies,[79] but reaches its summation with the launch of *Towards a World Theology: Faith and the Comparative History of Religion (WT)*, in 1981. From then on, a small cluster of theological studies arises.[80]

In the publishing of his lecture series, *Questions of Religious Truth* in 1967,[81] Smith asserts in the preface: 'It is the task of the theologian to articulate in words the vision to which men of faith legitimately aspire' (5f). The particular study of our concern (*WT*) is at the same time a response to a request from John Hick to flesh out the theological consequences of his comparative and conceptual approach. This resulted first in the Cadbury Lectures of 1972 (at University of Birmingham, the home university of Hick!), and later as a revised version in *Towards a World Theology*.

2.6.1 THE EMPIRICAL CONTRIBUTION: 'CONTEXTS' AND 'PARTICIPATION' IN THE SINGULAR RELIGIOUS HISTORY

The empirical and theological understanding of the religious history of humankind, or better, the empirical and theological understanding of the unity and coherence of that history (3), is made a main theme in *Towards a World Theology*.[82] Because this study repeats much of what several of his previous studies have comprehended, the main aim of the following examination is to identify and pay due attention to the nuances and particular emphases which *Towards a World Theology* exhibits.

As an historian, Smith conceives his task to 'hold all the evolving diversities of any one religious community's developments in interrelated intelligibility; and *a fortiori*, all the evolving diversities of all religious

---

[79] E.g. in studies in mission and the rethinking of the Christian existence in a religiously plural world, e.g. 1961b, 1967a, 1969a, and 1973b; further in some of his studies on truth, e.g. *QT* (1967b); and to a certain degree in the conceptual studies, especially in the last chapter (ch. 7) of *FB*. See also *FB*, 169, where the comprehension of 'revelation' is reserved for 'another volume, on theology.'

[80] E.g. Smith 1987b, 1987d, 1988a, 1991a.

[81] Smith 1967b. This is the Taylor Lectures of 1963 held at Yale Divinity School. Smith describes this as 'my first public appearance as a theologian,' *ibid.* 7, and sees the series as 'specifically and explicitly theological.'

[82] Subsequent parenthetical references in the text refer to *WT*.

communities' (4). Along with his reconceptualization of religion by 'personal faith' and 'cumulative tradition' in *ME,* this intelligibility shall not be understood as a 'unity among the 'religions of the world' but a unity 'of religious history.' This unity, Smith contends, must both preserve history as the domain of the specific, multifarious and human, and, on the other hand, affirm the interconnections, continuities and interactions of elements within history (5). At this point, Smith maintains that one can only understand oneself in terms of 'a context of which the other forms a part.' This implies both 'growing out of' oneself and being 'influenced by' the other. Consequently, the awareness of other traditions and influences may enlarge and restore the Christian and human (!) capacity 'to feel at home in the world—the whole world' (21).

This complex and interconnected religious history is illustrated by the traditions of the rosary, greetings cards, the matter of scripture, and the idea of God (11-17). The most intriguing representation of this point is facilitated by a retracing of the *Wirkungsgeschichte* of the story about Barlaam and Josaphat (6-11). As Smith discovers, its various steps go backwards from Tolstoi through Christian hagiography, through the scenes of India and Sinai, through an Islamic original of these, and, lastly, to a Buddhist legend of Buddha. Moreover, this last version might even have a Hindu or Jain source, possibly with an Aryan origin. On the other hand, its implications also proceed forwards including both Jewish versions, the significance it had for Gandhi, and consequently for Martin Luther King Jr. Based on these findings, Smith contends that for a thousand years Buddha was a Christian saint (20).

What is the outcome of such indications of interconnectedness between communities and of historical ages? Smith sees this *Wirkungsgeschichte* as pointing towards the religious history of humankind as a global continuum (18). Moreover, and of particular importance for our study, against the alternatives of dichotomy and anachronism in respect of relating theology to other knowledge, Smith suggest a view of historical coherence (19). His vision is, therefore, integration within the global history of humankind. According to Smith, this will enable 'a more adequate theology' (33).

In *Towards a World Theology* the elaboration of the notion of a global continuum follows two tracks. These are:

(a) The fact of processes of *historical change* of religious traditions and communities (21); there is nothing like stable 'religions'.
(b) The problem of developing *concepts and theories* which may grasp this fact *adequately* (21). Without these, one

will never be able to attain a 'a theology of' comparative religion (27).

Which are these concepts and theories, then? Like in *The Meaning and End of Religion,* Smith emphasizes the interaction between four elements of 'living life religiously' (26):

—the accumulating religious *tradition,*
—the particular *personality,*
—the particular *environment* and
—the *transcendent reality,* without which the rest cannot
be interpreted intelligently

This complex picture, Smith asserts, fits both in the Buddhist (23-28) and Islamic (28-33) instances, in many ways the radical opposites of the religious spectrum. Hence, he suggests generally 'the conceptualisation of historical process as the *context* of religious life, and participation as the *mode* of religious life' (33, emphasis mine). In the Islamic instance this gains the form: 'To be a Muslim means to participate in the Islamic process, as the context of one's religious life' (31). Stated thus, Smith maintains that its form will please both the Muslims and the outsiders.

The new concepts of mode/participation and context seem to follow the structure of argument pursued in his conceptual studies (*ME, BH* and *FB*), where 'context' to a certain extent comes to replace 'cumulative tradition', and 'mode' and 'participation' are used for 'faith'. Yet, how well do these notions fit particular self-understandings? Doubtlessly, Smith's point here is that of historical change and process, not of excluding transcendence, which can be seen as included in the insiders' participation (mode) with for example the Qur'an and its meaning for Muslims (context). Thus, the historical approach does not rule out the theological answer to what participation in a 'community in motion' means (35).

With interest for the present study, Smith also sets out to test his suggestion about others, as a hypothesis about a Christian self-understanding (33). Firstly, 'to be a Christian' means for Smith:

To participate in the Christian Church: to take on its past ...
to take on its present ... with a devastating sense of one's
own inadequacy and yet leaving the outcome to God (34).

Secondly, the reason for choosing the Christian Church is that 'through it

2 *Wilfred Cantwell Smith's Interreligious Hermeneutics*

we find God ... because through it God finds us.' Hence, the Christian process, like all other processes, is, and has been, 'a divine-human complex.' The human part of this interaction is denoted by 'context'. This context is described as

> the *religious data* of specific situations in history that altogether provide a *sacramental environment* in interaction with which person's *faith occurs*—and takes a particular form (36, emphasis mine).

Smith may say that this is so in regard to 'the role of the Bible in my parent's faith'. Yet, this is also so, as a part of this changing Christian context, that Buddha may very well have been a Christian saint in medieval times as far as he contributed to the 'sacramental environment' in which 'faith occurs.' The topical relevance is that these processes are becoming self-conscious, and that we all play a significant role in others' contexts also (37f). In our days, he says,

> each person, certainly each group, participates in religious history of humankind—as self-consciously the context for faith (44).

For this situation, Smith deliberately speaks of inter-dependence and inter-involvement, not of 'influence' (38).[83] Thus, participation gains a double meaning: In the historical changes in one's own context, and in changing the contexts of others (42f). Seen together, these meanings require the recognition of 'the unitary religious history of humankind' (44), or as Smith usually ends up when his vision penetrates his intellectualist comprehensions: there is only one community world-wide and 'history-long': the community of humankind.

2.6.2 THE EPISTEMOLOGICAL CONTRIBUTION: CORPORATE CRITICAL SELF-CONSCIOUSNESS AS THE MODE OF HUMANE KNOWLEDGE

Smith's epistemological investigations seem mainly to follow two tracks in *Towards a World Theology*:

---

[83] He makes this point in relation to the way Buber, Marx, Darwin and Freud have contributed to modern Christian theology, and Aristotle and Plotinus to the Medieval and later periods, *ibid.*, 40f. Also the impact of Theodor Herzl on Islamic history is mentioned.

(a) A follow-up of the personalist and methodological concerns of his previous conceptual works, that is, (i) that the locus of faith is persons (both individually and socially, 47) and that faith helps human beings to live 'in transcendence' in the world in an integral (human) way (52), and, consequently, (ii) that the study of religion is the study of persons (at their most intimate, profound, primary and transcendent), and further, that history of religion is the humane history of man, and that comparative religion is the profound self-awareness of man in his and her unintegrated wholeness (48f)

(b) A further development of the notion of self-consciousness.

The first track has already been explored at some length. The latter track, however, has not been examined so far, and is worth pursuing because it explicitly concerns the relation between self-understanding and understanding of others. It also gathers previous attempts to comprehend this notion by the way in which it is shaped in *Towards a World Theology*.[84] We will therefore address this track in more detail.

[1] Smith's first intention is to free his concept of (critical) self-consciousness from the notion of 'objectivity' (55).[85] Since objectivity has been a key to the Western understanding of truth and a norm for intellectual inquiry, his comprehension of this is most important.

Smith starts by making 'self-consciousness' a *terminus technicus* for 'humane knowledge' (56f). Self-consciousness is thus to be understood as 'the knowledge of man by man' (as distinct from 'human knowledge', which can also be knowledge about other things than merely man). Ideally, he says, all humane knowledge is self-consciousness. Thus, self-consciousness seems to be an ideal towards which one ought to

---

[84] One of the most significant contributions is to be found in Smith's Inaugural Lecture at Harvard in 1964, see Smith 1964 ('Mankind's Religiously Divided History Approaches Self-Consciousness').

[85] His elaboration on self-consciousness in *WT* is divided into two chapters: ch. 4: 'General: Objectivity and the Humane Sciences,' 56-80, and ch. 5: 'The Field of Religion,' 81-103. There is, however, a certain amount of overlap between the two chapters.

His criticism of objectivism is mainly that it disrupts community and that it fails to do justice to both the knower and that which is known, *ibid.* 77ff. Further, he finds it to be immoral because it uses people as means for ends which are entirely independent of themselves, and in which they do not participate (73f). Moreover, objectivism does not properly acknowledge the personal level of what is investigated (74). Lastly, it is idiosyncratic in that it is developed for a particular group other than those studied (74f). As this is not only one homogenous group, but a multitude of disparate idiosyncrasies, Smith asserts that the 'objectivist ideology' is 'fissiparous within, as well as polarised against the outside' (75).

approximate. Yet, given the assumption that all humankind is one, Smith asserts that humane knowledge is *ipso facto* self-consciousness (57).

This, however, does not mean that all self-consciousness is of identical value. Smith discriminates diverse humane knowing in connection with his notion of truth. The major term in this respect is corporate critical self-consciousness (CCSC), which he introduces as an alternative to the subject-object polarity. The interconnection between self-consciousness and CCSC moves along the following path (58f):

(a) In the shift from consciousness to self-consciousness, man emerged.

(b) In the shift from self-consciousness to critical self-consciousness, man may become truly scientific and rational, and

(c) In the shift from critical self-consciousness to corporate critical self-consciousness, this rationality may embrace all human beings in their diversity, and in a personal manner. Smith's definition of this latter consequently integrates the former two:

> By 'corporate critical self-consciousness' I mean that critical, rational, inductive self-consciousness by which a community of persons—constituted at a minimum of two persons, the one being studied and the studying, but ideally by the whole human race—is aware of any given particular human condition or action as a condition or action of itself as a community, yet one part but not of the whole of itself; and is aware of it as it is experienced and understood simultaneously both subjectively (personally, existentially) and objectively (externally, critically, analytically; as one used to say, scientifically) (60).

In this definition Smith sees included what he calls a 'decisive' new principle of verification. Based on this, he also develops his verification principle from *CR*, cf. Chapter 2.2 above:

> No statement involving persons is valid ... unless theoretically its validity can be verified both by the persons involved and by critical observers not involved (*ibid.*)

Smith uses these definitions in order to do justice to the facts that 'man is patently different, in ways highly significant, from material objects' and that 'the knowing mind is human' (60f). Altogether, his approach aims to offer an alternative to the epistemology of natural science and the notion of knowledge embedded therein. This alternative seeks to proffer a knowledge 'that participates in the consciousness of those involved' (63). Hence, such knowledge will no longer be entirely external, but to some extent internal.[86] Smith maintains that only this kind of knowledge can be on a par with its material: human beings.

In CCSC Smith sees a possibility to integrate the view of the observer and those observed into one, synthesized and converging apprehension (66). CCSC is therefore an apprehension accompanied by 'interpretation, imagination, insight, perceptivity, human sympathy, humility', and so forth, standing 'imaginatively in the shoes of others' (*ibid.*), a process of understanding that requires the student to be a human person 'as fully human as may be' (68). This is the alternative to objectivism and subjectivism, a rational personalism driven by the moral objective of solidarity and self-transcendence, which precedes particularity, and where

> the truth of all of us is part of the truth of each of us (79, 103).

Because, ideally, there is nothing like *us* and *them*[87] within the concept of CCSC this is also the most adequate way of studying oneself. Smith expresses this most pithily: Differences are ultimately a matter of '[we who] self-consciously differ' (103). From this it follows that any inter-religious understanding is ultimately intra-religious, or simply religious (81).[88] One may say that the perspective has become so vast that it is almost impossible to place somebody and something outside it. Yet, on the other hand Smith sees this fact as generative of mutual understanding. At this point we may notice that Smith seems to combine a confinement (or paradoxically: expansion!) of 'inter-religious' to 'intra-religious' with 'mutuality'. From this combination it seems to follow that relations do not

---

[86] Cf. *ibid.* 57 where he maintains that although self-consciousness has been a humane knowledge, of man by man, it has, at least in the past, been perceived as *external* to what it has aimed to understand. This is not sufficient, according to Smith, because 'what man does is misunderstood if conceived wholly from the outside,' *ibid.* 69. CCSC, on the other hand, aims to integrate both the outsider's and insider's perspective, cf. the principles of verification. The vehicle for this move beyond objectivity and subjectivity seems to be *participation*.

[87] Cf. the title of *FOM (The Faith of Other Men)* from which Smith at the time when *WT* was written would have deducted 'other,' *ibid.* 103, since there has to be taken 'a next step' after recognizing the faith of other men.

[88] Cf. Smith 1960/1981e, where, in the introduction to a reprinting of a study of *shari'ah* and *shar'*, he says that his study is now (1981, the same year as the launch of *WT*) 'pushing me towards forging a synthesis between comparative history of religion and Christian (*or Islamic, or global*) theology,' 87, my emphasis.

convey a sense of difference between oneself and the other. The theological implications of this understanding of CCSC are however more thoroughly developed in the next subchapter (Chapter 3.6.3). In Chapter 6 and 7 the concept will be criticized as well.

[2] Within his treatment of the conceptualization of one's understanding of others, and of oneself, that is, precisely the approach pursued in the present study, Smith also draws attention to the matters of conceptual framework and symbols.

Smith's point regarding frameworks, or world-views, is that they confer meaning. As such they may be seen as presupposed patterns into which diverse parts of for example Islam cohere (82f). If for example a Muslim loses his faith, the various things in the world do not cease to exist, they only do not form a coherent pattern any more. On the contrary, as coherent patterns they nurture faith and work as its expressions. Smith sees this notion of framework as a fruitful point of departure for understanding others.

The notion of symbol has likewise, Smith asserts, proven helpful in interpreting others' religious life, but also as a resource for one's own self-interpretation (85). Although a symbolic understanding of, for example, Christ might neither be recognized as an adequate way of interpreting what Christ has meant to Christians, nor as a representation of the traditional Christian position, it may in several instances nevertheless serve as a helpful tool because of its humane implications (85) and because it enables participation in transcendence (87). It, then, enables us 'to think rationally about the world without automatically having depersonalized our intellectualisations' (*ibid.*).

One reason for this seems to be that a symbol is only a symbol in relation *to* somebody. And, as it is characteristic of man that things become symbolic *for* him and her, it is also characteristic of things that they become symbolic for man (86f). According to Smith, it is noteworthy how this only occurs to certain persons.[89] Symbols, therefore, are a matter of particularity. That does however not rule out mutuality, because

> once one has understood what a symbol signifies to another person, or community, then to some degree it now signifies that to oneself... . You may become a changed person in consequence (89).

---

[89] At this place Smith delimits his own approach in relation to 'Phenomenology of Religion', which he regards as a loose notion, *ibid.* 86. Whereas he assumes that this discipline partially represents a recognition that symbols carry their meaning in themselves, Smith, as an historian, suggests that things are not objectively symbols; only in relation to certain persons and not others. Cf. also *FB*, 7.

Further:

> Accordingly, it can happen that in coming to understand
> the meaning that an alien symbol has had for an alien
> community, you may discover therein a meaning—of life,
> of the universe, of man's destiny, or whatever—that was in
> your own heritage all along but that previously you
> personally had not seen (90).

This includes certainly a kind of relation between the others and oneself, 'the effect on oneself of new humane knowing' (88). Smith suggests that this relation takes place at two different levels (90): 1) The accepting and sharing of others' symbols, which constitutes human community, and 2) The understanding of others' symbols, which is humane but does not imply a sharing of community and accepting of the meaning of the symbols. Hence, the questions of truth and diversity become parts of his agenda. Or, as Smith puts it:

> How to enlarge one's vision of truth without losing loyalty
> to one's own, however finite, hold upon it (by it)? (89).

The treatment at these two levels of the relation between 'self-consciousness' on the one hand, and world-views and symbols on the other, as well as his discernment between faith and belief, is Smith's contribution to solving the tension between 'enlarge' and '[keeping] loyalty'.

Smith sees, moreover, the process towards self-consciousness of oneself and of other as opposite to the reifications which took place in Western studies of other 'religions' (cf. Chapter 2.4). According to Smith, this process can only be a corporate one (93f), which is his proposal to remedy the subject-object polarization which has often ended in a state where every religion has become equally true to the believer and equally false to the philosopher. Instead of simplistic logic, the religious orientations must be seen as

> less or more true in the sense of *enabling those who looked*
> at life and the universe through their patterns *to perceive*
> *smaller or larger,* less important or more important, *areas*
> *of reality,* to formulate and to ponder less or more significant
> issues, to act less or more truly, less or more truly to be (94,
> emphasis mine).

This is the consequence of religious patterns which have previously been general presuppositions (patterns) of reality and truth as such. Given the fact that this form of consciousness, which once was existential, has now moved towards a presupposed recognition of the objects of consciousness,[90] 'a quite new mode of thinking becomes imperative.' It is his corporate critical self-consciousness that is supposed to inherit this role. The ultimate reason for this seems in Smith to be a coincidence between the presupposed patterns once in the past on the one hand, that is, patterns that conveyed universal validity, and the aim of 'corporate' within the concept of CCSC in order to approximate the (general) truth on the other. This may be called a coincidence about generality, that is, as the citation immediately above showed, an emphasis on totality, coherence and integration.[91] How this 'coincidence of generality' is most adequately interpreted, will be a major issue to discuss in the last chapter (Chapter 7.3).

---

[90] Cf. his historical investigations of 'belief' in *BH*, see note 57.

[91] Cf. also 1987d, 10: 'As intellectuals ... we face the further—or preliminary—task of ensuring that our answers to these questions be coherent with everything else that we know about the universe.' This must therefore take place as an attempt at *integration*, in particular related to 'new knowledge,' which in Smith's case is especially connected to the fact of *religious diversity*, 12f. Stated thus Smith comes close to the *criteria* which Wolfhart Pannenberg applies to theology related to philosophy of science, see e.g. Pannenberg 1976, 344f (= *Wissenschaftstheorie und Theologie*, 1973, 348). According to Pannenberg, theological hypotheses are not be judged as substantiated 'if and only if' (2) 'they have no connection with reality as a whole ... ,' and (3) 'they are incapable of being integrated with the appropriate area of experience or no attempt is made to integrated them ...' The other criteria, are (1) if 'they are intended as hypotheses about the implications of the Israelite-Christian faith but cannot be shown to express implications of biblical traditions (even when changes in experience are allowed for),' and that (4) 'their explanatory force is inadequate to the stage reached in theological discussion ... and does not overcome limitations of these which emerge in discussion.' Whereas Smith's statements obviously coincide with Pannenberg's middle criteria (2 and 3), I regard it pertinent to pursue in another chapter (Chapter 7.3.2) how Smith relates to *the first criteria* (relatedness to the Jewish-Christian tradition). Despite coincidences, the language of Smith and Pannenberg in respect of 'faith' and 'tradition' divide significantly. This becomes obvious when Pannenberg's writings about theology of religions are considered, which also makes my critical point of concern overt, see e.g. Pannenberg 1990/ 1995, 104, n. 7, which we will return to later (Chapter 7.3.1). One will see that Pannenberg's position in this respect comes close to, if not being identical with, that of Cragg (Chapter 4).

Cf. also how the rest of 1987d coincides with Pannenberg in respect of the possibility and necessity of studying theology and religious history at the university, as well as his understanding of revelation as an historical and therefore academic question (cf. Pannenberg's theology of history, in particular his contribution to the German 'Offenbarung als Geschichte' project in the 60s).

Yet, this path is not left without problems. Regarding the notion of symbol, Smith maintains that to understand the Qur'an as symbol and how it has served symbolically for Muslims (first level) can be understood by Western students, but only on the second level of understanding. The case is comparably illustrated by the problems of speaking of Christ as a symbol ('the Divine Himself'), that is, what outsiders see as a symbol is not recognized as a symbol at all but as something at a 'zero level', that is, higher than the first level, where it is presupposed (95). The observer has to take notice of this situation. Obviously, Smith sees what kind of problems arise here. Yet, he also sees a possible solution to the problem in developments of the notions of 'symbol', 'revelation', and of 'faith' and 'involvement' (96), the crucial point being whether one takes the person or the religious object as one's focal point.

Nevertheless, CCSC is the mode of humane knowledge that emerges as an imperative on 'all intelligent men and women' (102). At its pragmatic level it is, Smith maintains, rewarding in its conception of truth and validity, which includes both the observer, the participant and the community between the two ('no observer's statement about a group of persons is valid that cannot be appropriated[92] by those persons,' 97), where ultimately 'the truth of all of us is part of the truth of each of us' (103, cf. above).

On a theological level, this may have great implications for, for example, the Christian approach towards the Muslim tradition if it is to be regarded as a theology 'from within all'. How this can be justified theologically belongs to the next chapter.

2.6.3 THE THEOLOGICAL INTEGRATION: A THEOLOGY 'FROM WITHIN ALL'

It seems inevitable for Smith to make explicit the theological reasons for his assumption that the history of religion 'is intrinsically the locus of

---

[92] This is certainly a loose term. It does not seem to require more than the saying 'Yes! That is what we hold' on the side of the 'other', and a satisfaction of 'all the most exacting requirements of rational enquiry and academic rigour' on the side of the observer, *WT,* 97. To the question of representativeness of those observed, Smith does not delimit himself. This seems to resonate with both his anti-reificationist and personalist attitude, *ibid.,* 97f. Yet, in practice it is the intellectual representatives who occupy his interest, 98ff. It also seems that he thinks intellectuals may avoid the isolationist stance in a better way. The other group which gains most positive attention in Smith's works, is the mystics, especially the Sufis, see e.g. *ibid.,* 135.

both the mundane and the transcendent, unbifurcated' and that this history 'since it is human, therein has transcendent ... overtones' (3). Or stated oppositely:

> Those who believe in the unity of humankind, and those who believe in the unity of God, should be prepared therefore to discover a unity of humankind's religious history (4).

At this point of departure, Smith thus assumes a close relation between the unity of God and the unity of humankind's religious history.

His first objective in his explicit theological chapters is, however, to ponder the notion of a 'theology of religions'. The fact that he sees this term as highly problematic should not surprise anyone familiar with his reconceptualization of 'religion'. Yet, his theological elaboration on this here is more intriguing than elsewhere in his writings.

Smith asserts first that both the subject (theology) and object (religions) are problematic (107). The former, as it is mostly understood as 'Christian theology of', involves two problems once one sees it as one in a series: Either it becomes relativistic, as one option among many. Or it becomes dogmatic, that is, as apologetics against other positions (109). Smith finds neither persuasive and contends that the starting point itself is wrong. The latter, for instance, may serve the apologist but not the enquirer. This is also the case with an 'Islamic theology of religion', which may be a legitimate Islamic position grounded on Islamic reasons, but not a position that can be held in relation to Christian faith (109f).

Thus, 'theologies of religion' do not develop relations to faiths other than one's own. Hence, a 'Christian theology of religions' is an inadequate concept (110). Yet, Smith modifies this immediately by saying that this is at least so 'in so far as a Christian (or Islamic, or Hindu) theology of religions involves an objective genitive ... a theology that has the religions as its object' (110). Smith, thus, welcomes a subjective understanding of the genitive of these terms, a theology induced and represented by the religions, that is, a theology embedded in the religions themselves.[93] On the question: 'Of what, exactly, is to proffer an interpretation?,' Smith therefore asserts:

> There cannot be a Christian theology of the other religions, because religion embraces more than an outsider perceives.

---

[93] For a comprehension of the genitives of subject and of object respectively in 'theology of religions', see Leuze 1978.

> Theology theologises about things, garnering them into
> coherence, *because faith, which it verbalises, is central,*
> *total, supreme;* but for this very reason faith cannot be
> theologised about by an outsider. It is *itself an organising*
> *principle...* . Faith can only be theologised from the inside
> (110f, emphasis mine).

In other words, theology is an interpretation of faith, and since faith is the
ultimate expression of coherence and integration of a given community's
faith, this level of integration cannot be reached by any outsiders. The
coherence belongs to the community and its faith, and not to the perception
and investigation of an outsider, be it theological or whatsoever. Theology,
which in its nature aims at integration, is, therefore, only possible as 'self-
theology,' from the inside (111). One may, however, ask: Has Smith by this
statement *de facto* moved to a particularist stance?

    Firstly, one has to bear in mind that Smith has never rendered
such 'self-theologies' totally inadequate. His point is rather synthetic,
based on the dynamics of history, namely, that in the light of a 'new
context and a new consciousness' we should proceed to a larger, older (!),
and universal 'truth,' which is

> not less than Christian, or Islamic or whatever, and no longer
> even only Christian or Islamic or whatever, but a truth in
> some sense *more than* Christian, or at least more than what
> recently has been called that; more than Islamic, in the
> particularised sense of the term; transcending the adjectival
> truth of any partial group (112, my emphasis).

This understanding of truth is well illustrated by the particular
understanding of faith, as for example 'Christian faith'. As he has argued
in *Belief and History*, faith is central to the New Testament, but it never
denotes the 'Christian faith', about which nobody writes until
Schleiermacher onwards. On the contrary,

> faith is an orientation of the personality, to oneself, one's
> neighbour, to the universe; a total response; a way of seeing
> the world and of handling it; a capacity to live at a more
> than mundane level; to see, to feel, to act in terms of, a
> transcendent dimension... . today we should add, to find
> life meaningful, to overcome alienation, to be bound in
> community with one's neighbour, and in integrity with
> oneself (113f).

Smith affirms this understanding of faith.[94] Hence, the relation between particularism and universalism can be stated thus: every particular view of faith and of God will be a view of faith generically and of God absolutely. The beliefs, on the other hand, should be reflected upon comparatively. This is his anti-fragmentary vision, a vision which seeks to restore the 'integrity of our older visions' of pluralism (113). His arguments for this gain evidence from his previous conceptual studies.

As we noted above, Smith rendered it impossible for a theology to attain a total understanding of another community's faith, because of the role of faith as a particular organizing principle. When he at this point, however, draws attention to his understanding of coherence in relation to the universalist vision which breaks out of the particularist bounds, this can be understood as the proffering of another level for universalism and relations. The level of mutual relations between people is not that of theology and beliefs, but of generic faith. Consequently, this has certain impacts on the possibility of doing comparative theology, or 'theology of comparative religion' as Smith prefers to state it, or simply, 'a theology of the religious history of humankind' (117, 125).

Smith aims certainly at a subjective understanding of 'theology of religions', understood as the induced expressions of the generic religious quality embedded in the history of human religiousness (faith), that is, 'a theology that emerges out of 'all the religions of the world'' (124).[95] Consequently, theology becomes in the end an object, subordinated faith. Or as he states in respect of Muslim *kalam*: 'Muslim theology (*kalam*) is a statement within, not about, their total position' (119f). Theology of comparative religion is thus a theology of faith in its many forms (124), or a statement of God and His diverse involvements with humankind (126).

On the other hand, however, he seems to establish a constructive development of a theology of comparative religion which is based upon the fact of faith *and* the corporate critical self-consciousness. But how can these be combined, a theology that on the one hand can only be self-theology, and the CCSC on the other? The (emerging[96]) solution is a

---

[94] And sees it also as reflected in Luther's 'by [faith], and by it alone man is saved' (114). It is of course quite doubtful whether faith as the contrast to nihilism and despair can be identified with Luther that easily.

[95] Yet, he does not set out to anything further than a delineation of what such a theology will be in the future (123).

[96] Smith does not see this solution as already realized but as a possible attainment of the future. Most significantly, Smith sees (again) the *mystics* as prototypes of what this programme can become. These are the only ones in the past that, if only approximately, deserve to be called theologians of religion, *WT,* 126. No wonder that, according to Smith, the theology of comparative religion understood as 'interpreting, intellectualising, our multiform faith' has never been written.

theology that is a product of thinkers who recognize and know persons of all religious traditions and ages, and who themselves participate in one of the communities (125). Thus, the theological data must be the data of the history of religion which is defined as 'the history of man's (Christian and other) continuing involvement, within history, in transcendence' (126). The ultimate goal is, therefore, to subsume the sectional parts into a world theology (130).

Along the way towards this, Smith offers a 'Christian contribution to it ... inadequately Christian, certainly: yet, inescapably so' (129).[97] This is his way of participating 'Christianly' in the total life (intellectual, religious, political, economic) of humankind, ultimately towards the building of a world community on earth. Yet, 'Christian, plus' (125).[98]

What then about other communities? As mentioned above, Smith aims to subsume Christian, Islamic, Hindu, etc., contributions into a world theology. Further, and most interesting *vis-à-vis* Cragg's approach (see Chapter 4), this activity is seen as an ability that theology of comparative religion should fulfil (130). This underscores Smith's aim of convergence in difference to a view of uniformity or common core.[99] Yet, as Smith himself has been aware of so far, 'fulfil' has been a Christian concept. If it is going to gain universal validity, one has to ask how this turns out for other traditions. A most interesting remark on this by Smith, based on several objections from 'pseudo-representatives' from other religious traditions, is that his

> aspiration ... to transcend 'Christian theology', to get back to an earlier and more innocent 'theology' *simpliciter* or to move forwards towards it, may be seen more clearly as unduly pretentious (or anachronistic) (150).

One may therefore ask: How Christian and how generic may his approach be recognized then? On the one hand, he admits that his concern for truth has its theological origin in the Church's development and its intellectual origin in the Western university (150f). This emphasis relates to his concept of historical apprehension of truth (151). On the other hand, he maintains

---

[97] Smith sees the 'Christian' particularly represented in both the notion of *theology* which came from Greek thought but became a salient Christian activity, and in *faith* which is the very core of Christian religiousness, *ibid.* 128.

[98] In this phrasing Smith seeks to take advantage of the analogy from the 'ecumenical Church,' i.e. the difference between and interdependence of an ecumenical (Christian) theology and a Presbyterian theology of ecumenicism, *ibid.* 125. His point is that to be theological enough one has to expand the particularist perspective, although the 'greater vision' is not accessible without it.

[99] Cf. Burrel 1983.

that this degree of truth is continuous with other communities' developments in their approximations of (ultimate) truth. Thirdly, Smith finds it pertinent to use the concept 'theology' in this respect, although he suggests using it in an informal sense, and not within a systematic theology. The informal sense is understood thus:

> Talk about God; or more generically, about the transcendent dimension of human life and of the universe to which the history of religion (the history of man's spirit) bears witness and which it elucidates, and to which Christians have historically given the name 'God' (*ibid.*).

This interim step leads us into Smith's concluding and integrative elaboration about theology and comparative religion.

On the way towards a theory that 'aspires to be part of the movement towards the truth' (that is, CCSC), Smith requires that it should be justified in the light of both the data of history of religion and of the group from which the theory emerges (152f). This means in Smith's case that one has to ask whether his theory of comparative religion fits into a Christian self-understanding, or not. For the critical appraisal of his position in Chapter 7, this criterion will play a most important role. Smith's own standard of norms seems, however, to determine the result. For him, his theory must fit both 'more traditional modes' and 'the newer awareness that is emerging' (154). Shortly, it must be 'classically new'. Yet, what does this exactly mean?

Firstly, it does not mean that the history of religion should be studied 'backwards' in the light of a kind of Big-Bang theory, an attitude he in the Christian case locates to the Protestant Reformation ('back to the original, to the pristine') (154f). Time's arrow, Smith reminds us, is pointing the other way, a kind of *creatio continua*. Hence, every historical study is the study of movement and process. On the other hand, regarding truth, both origins and consequences belong to truth (156). Studying persons, therefore, means keeping an eye on how persons are interconnected with both the things that formed their past and which forms their future (157). Yet, one may still ask: What is the theological relevance of this? Smith answers with something like a job-description for the theologian:

> To interpret not a system at all—no more than it is the task of the historian; nor even a movement, if that distract from *the locus of religious reality that cosmically counts*, the lives of the persons who made up the movement and who have interacted with whatever successive patterns there

> may have been, and with each other, and with God (160, my emphasis).

Consequently, the ultimate theological objective is to understand the relations a person participates in, particularly the relation with God as given in faith. These relations, and especially the one with God, shape the very meaning any tradition might have for the persons who participate in it. Hence, in the case of the Islamic tradition, Smith suggests:

> The faith of a particular Muslim ... had a specific form
> constituted by his participation in the Islamic context of his
> life that was that particular moment of the total process of
> the Islamic strand in the world religious history; and that in
> that faith in that particular form he was in touch with God,
> and God with him (164).

Smith follows up the Protestant feature of the preceding suggestion with a distinctive statement:

> By that faith, I believe and suggest, he was saved. A sinner,
> yes; but *simul justus et peccator* (165).

This salvation is then connected with the hearing of God, which may be more or less clear, and to the listening of the particular Muslim, which also may be limited.

Smith asserts that this is an interpretation that he can defend warmly as an historian, and even demonstrate (165, 167). The demonstration on the historical and empirical level ('the mundane level') takes the following pattern: It was a faith that saved him

> from nihilism, from aleniation, anomie, despair; from the
> bleak despondency of meaninglessness. Saved from
> unfreedom; from being the victim of one's own whims within,
> or of pressures without; saved from being merely an
> organism reacting to its environment (168).

Yet, in this meaning, no man on earth is fully saved, but 'in so far as he *is* saved, he is saved by faith,' be it a Muslim or whatever (167f). Smith's contention is 'that faith differs in form, but not in kind' (168).[100] What then about the theological meaning of 'saved'?

---

[100] This distinction is quite important and makes visible a discernment within 'faith'. See also Andreas Grünschloß' ontological scheme about faith in Smith's writings

Although Smith includes the mundane part of salvation in his notion of 'saved', he argues independently for his submission to this view by theological arguments. His first thesis is that as the Church forms 'a divine-human complex in motion', so do also other religious communities (169f). Hence the divine-human relationship of faith is nurtured and created 'primarily by a participation in the on-going historical movement of one or another of the world's religious communities' (170). Consequently, his general thesis is that

> God has participated more richly in human affairs, man has participated more diversely in God, than we once knew (172).

This is the complex way of recognizing that 'God has found effective [forms and doctrines and structures that many Christians find odd]' and that

> all human history is *Heilsgeschichte* (*ibid.*).

Yet, when he is going to justify this view ('how I know that'), he says that he knows the historical dimension from his historical studies and his friendships (induction), and that he knows the theological dimension (deduction), which is primarily related to the cosmic (eternal) dimension of salvation, and which he affirms for all persons whatever tradition they belonged to,

> because of what I know of God; by what I find revealed to me of Him in Christ (170f).

Though he might not be totally sure how to relate the mundane to the cosmic, he is convinced that 'it contradicts the central revelation of Christ to say anything else' (171). That God saved through other *forms* of faith, therefore, corroborates 'our Christian vision of God as active in history, redemptive, reaching out to all men to love and to embrace them' (*ibid.*). This, he suggests, is 'continuous both with the central (major) emphases of Christian theology over most of its course, and with modern historical

---

where he discerns between 'existence' (contextual 'limited' faith/'specific historical form') and 'essence' (ideal faith/'timeless substance') within Smith's concept of faith, Grünschloß 1994a, 197. It is central to Grünschloß' scheme that the latter manifests itself in the former but that Smith hesitates to identify 'that which manifests itself' for various reasons/reservations (based on arguments of intersubjectivity, nominalism, idealism, transcendence).

knowledge of the human condition.' Thus, it should be recognized as justified on Christian grounds.

Most interestingly, at this place Smith uses the terms 'central revelation' and 'central emphases'. These do also fit well with how he depicts their contents. Yet, this is interesting because he, in the near context after these statements, criticizes the distinction between general and special revelation. His own understanding of revelation is one of 'continuing contemporaneity' (173), which includes:

> (a) That revelation is understood as *humane*, as revelation
> *to* somebody, and not as an objective concept.[101]
> (b) That what God reveals is *Himself.*

The latter point is the explicit theological one, though a rather complex one. This is, Smith maintains, a point partly based on his Christian conviction, partly on his comparative studies, partly on his awareness of historical dynamics, and lastly, on resolute rationalism (173).

For purposes of illumination Smith draws our attention to the instances of the Qur'an and of Christ. Regarding the former, instead of saying that the Qur'an was or was not God's revelation, he suggests we ask whether it was or was not a channel for God's self-revealing to somebody, for example al-Ghazzali. Likewise, 'God was not revealed in Jesus Christ,' but in Him God was revealed to Smith and other Christians. Yet, God was not fully revealed in Jesus Christ (174f), because

> all revelation is potentially fuller than it is actually (175).

By the usage of 'channel' and 'through' he underscores this point further.[102] Revelation is actual potentiality, of which the Qur'an, Christ, and so on, can only approximate. The two ultimate points that he aims to emphasize here (again), are transcendence and history as movement forward (*ibid.*). This is implicitly also the reason why he opposes any attempts to develop concepts that differentiate between various degrees of fullness of revelation.

Within this framework of 'humane revelation of God Himself,' the Incarnation also (and Resurrection) gains a distinctive interpretation, namely that

---

[101] He sees this point as resonating with his notion of symbols (which do not carry their meaning themselves) and of transcendence (immanent and transcendent transcendence). This is illuminating for how complexly Smith interprets 'theology', *ibid.*

[102] For the use of channel and revelation about Christ, see Smith 1987a.

God in the shape of Christ did indeed enter the world of man, in the lives of Christians in the course of many centuries, until now (176).

This represents Smith's overall concern: the 'presence of God from day to day in the life of the community. To this all is ancillary' (177). Included in 'to this all is ancillary,' is any kind of christocentrism. Smith characterizes his position as theocentrism, and asserts that 'if Christians insist that Christ is the centre of their lives, it is time that we rediscovered that God is the centre of the universe' (*ibid.*).[103] Resulting from this statement is a somewhat rare assertion, namely that his position of being Christian is 'by way of faithful participation in the Christian process' (178). What is involved in this statement, is his investigation of how Christian thinkers in the past understood faith in contradiction to a modern and christocentric understanding of it.

Furthermore, he maintains that his position is continuous with the following doctrines (178):

—'salvation by faith,'
—that 'God is as Christ reveals Him to be,'
—the 'deep Christian commission of concern for and outreach toward the neighbour, and of reconciliation and

---

[103] Smith's aim is not to dissolve a Trinitarian theology, rather the opposite: to maintain not only a concentration on Christ, but also on God the Creator, known (partially) in creation, and the Holy Spirit as active in world history. See for example Smith 1961b, 125. Most interestingly Smith applies the limited knowledge of God outside Christianity to Christians as well ('Christians know God only in part,' 126). This relates intimately to his acknowledgment of *finitum non capax infiniti* ('the finite cannot comprehend the infinite,' 125). Cf. also note 44 above. Cf. also 1991a, 22, where Smith in an identical context reiterates his distinction between 'comprehension' and 'apprehension' in this respect, of which the latter is recommended. Cf. also 1987d, 13: Theologians may seek to 'express in specific, finite terms as much of infinity as we are enabled to envision.' Lastly, this relates directly to his core notion of 'transcendence', which resembles Kantian features, cf. Hughes 1985, 164, and which contains a variety of nuances and connotations. See e.g. in his programmatic Ingersoll Lecture on 'transcendence', Smith 1988b, 10, third col.: 'Transcendence is not to be comprehended though it is to be apprehended.' This corresponds to what was mentioned above (end of Chapter 2.4.5, p. 48) about truth that lies beyond not only theology but also faith; in the heart of God. One may however ask whether Smith runs the risk of minimizing Christology unduly. See e.g. E. Hughes' dissertation, which on the one hand suggests that Smith's approach is 'coherent, cogent, and helpful for furthering an understanding of planetary religious existence,' but on the other hand objects 'to elements of Smith's rationalism and to his minimizing of Y,' Hughes 1985, 4 and 328.

the building of community,'
—the 'doctrines of sacrament,' including the doctrine of
'Real Presence,' and
—'God's mission in the world through the Church' though
understood as 'through Buddhist, Islamic, modern Jewish
and other movements.'

This is what Smith calls a 'not nearly Christian enough Christian's contribution' to a theology of comparative religion. Whether 'the innovations ... constitute too radical break with current Christians to be countenanced as Christian,' Smith leaves to others to judge. To this question, we will return in time (especially Chapter 7.3).

To clarify the relation of the approach of this study, and in relation to the last chapter of *Towards a World Theology* (ch. 9): to accept and relate to pluralism adequately, according to Smith, does not mean to give up faith as specifically given in one's own particular tradition (180). Smith's point is that in the light of history of religion, one should reconceptualize more adequately the relation of the specific to the generic by generic concepts. This is exemplary the case with 'faith', but also with 'salvation' (182) and 'theology' (182f). Regarding the latter, Smith suggests replacing it with the term 'transcendentology'. As with the concept of 'God', which Smith regards as a symbol, he aims to use it interchangeably with 'transcendence' (183-186). Thus, 'God' is 'a truth-reality that explicitly transcends but in so far as conceivable is that to which man's religious history has as its best been a response, human and in some senses adequate' (185).

The general point of this is important: The 'new vision must not only be seen but also intelligibly expressed' (183). Yet, 'intelligibly expressed' has to be interpreted in the light of 'corporate', 'historical' and 'bridging the gap between the specific and generic', or in other words, in the light of corporate critical self-consciousness (186). This then means that the question of truth is put in front of us. It is most interesting to see that Smith underscores the role of a 'great Other' in order to prevent CCSC from becoming a 'collective subjectivism' (186). Ultimately, therefore, the question of truth is the question of the reality of God and transcendence 'itself/himself/herself' (184,189). Hence, truth transcends history and persons, though it may only be approximated through history and the meaning propositions have and have had to persons (190). In this sense, the truth is finally that

It is through His [i.e. God's] participation in the religious
history of the world ... that He has chiefly entered human
lives to act in human history (194).

And further, with the same pathos:

> Right now he is calling us to let Him act through new forms,
> continuous with the old, as we human beings across the
> globe enter our strange new age (*ibid.*).

Thus, the conceptual and theological studies of Smith gain a central
epistemological and theological summation at the very end of *Towards a
World Theology*.

2.7   Conclusion

We have now traced Smith's development of his position of interreligous
hermeneutics, from his programmatic article of 1959 (*CR*), via his conceptual
studies (*ME, BH, FB*), and through the anticipation (*FOM*) and realization
of a 'world theology'. It remains to make some conclusive remarks about
how Smith develops his approach in relation to the problem(s) pursued in
our study.

In *CR* Smith primarily profiles his personalist approach to the
study of religion ('the study of religion is the study of persons'). In this,
Smith aims at an adequate conceptualization of the object of religious
studies. The major notion in this respect, faith, is understood as a human
quality whose functions and meanings ought to be studied. By using
'external' data as clues to the 'internal,' as well as the personal 'life of
men', Smith hopes to be better equipped in order to grasp what history of
religion is all about. In *CR* Smith also stresses the global audience of
religious studies. This becomes especially apparent in the introduction of
his principle of validity ('No statement about a religion is valid unless it
can be acknowledged of that religion's believers'). This does not, however,
prevent him from inventing new concepts in order to depict religious
meanings and the matter of faith more clearly, in particular by transcending
existing (external) 'patterns' of faith. Smith sees this as a justified means
of dialogue between the investigator and the people he tries to understand.
In this kind of dialogue it is Smith's contention that his own faith may be
enriched and apprehended as may he likewise get to appreciate the quality
and ultimate validity of other's faith. By this, one may increasingly see
oneself as a person within the human, global community, which is the
only real community. This last statement is intended to be Christian as
well as theological.

This mutuality between one's own faith-allegiance and the
interpretation of the meaning of others' faith is reiterated in FOM. In this

study Smith emphasizes, not least based on personal experiences, that one's own faith may be widened, deepened, and made more true and rich throughout the process of understanding other's faith. Understanding the Other may thus support the understanding of Oneself. In this, mutuality and complexity seem to coincide. The moral side of this is also made a theme when Smith introduces the acute need for a reconsideration of the moral impulses of 'God in Christ,' thus also making the requirement for an adequate theology obvious.

Smith's primary concern in *ME* is to break up the use of 'religion' as well as the perception of the world's religious traditions as entities. A part of this deconstruction is a tracing back of global processes of reification and externalization to the influence of Western scholars in modern times. Another finding is that these processes seemed to occur in times of polemics and apologetics.

Smith's project is also constructive as it replaces 'religion' with 'personal faith' and 'cumulative tradition'. It is Smith's hope that these concepts may prove helpful as continuous with the views of religious life in previous times, as well as being apt to refer properly to the 'facts of' transcendence and historical change, to which Smith submits the religiousness of living persons. However, these concepts are only employed as methodological tools, not in order to define the nature of, for example, human religiousness.

The consequences of his historical investigations are far-reaching. One is that issues of convergence and mutuality should be developed in the realm of personal faith and within the total process of human history. Because of his distinction between internal and converging faith (singular!) on the one hand, and external, dividing traditions on the other, there is nothing like '*the* Christian faith' opposed to '*the* Islamic faith.' There are only adjectival ways (e.g. Christian, Muslim) of having generic faith. This 'clearing the ground' of one's concept of religion and religiousness is ultimately an attempt to provide an adequate understanding of another person's faith from one's own perspective. It is simultaneously a rethinking of one's self-understanding in terms of continuity and revision.

An implicit attempt to clarify this matter appears in *FB* (and *BH*). The step that especially refines the argument, as found in *ME*, is the attempt to clarify the relation between faith and belief. With Anselmian language this is seen as faith in pursuit of self-understanding, that is, how faith can be conceptualized intellectually.

Smith aims to combine a *via negativa* of what faith is not, with a contribution to a new planetary self-consciousness about faith. In this, any apprehension of and approximation to faith (which eschews any definition or comprehension) needs to relate to both a particular as well as the global context. His generic understanding of faith thus seeks to be rooted in particular conceptualizations as well as to be illuminated by 'the comparative vision'.

Smith describes faith formally, as the essential human quality and potentiality and finds both faith and its relationship to belief represented in all major religious traditions. Hence, the opposite of faith is not what is non-Christian, non-Buddhist, and so on, but what is inhuman and de-human, primarily related to nihilism and what he calls 'fanatical particularism'. Faith as generic does not, however, imply that the faith of diverse persons is identical or uniform. On the one hand, obvious and severe differences between religious traditions as belief-systems may enable religious persons adhering to particular communities to live a life in faith, that is, in adequate relation to transcendence and to one's neighbour. On the other hand, this faith converges with the faith of human persons in other communities, because it represents both 'man's quest for God' and 'God's initiative', and thus forms a part of humankind's participation in God's ongoing and multifaceted *Heilsgeschichte*. At this place the theological aspects of faith becomes transparent. This is a personalist theology in which what ultimately matters is to become properly human 'as one or other'. This is interpreted as the goal of the death of Christ, but not to be seen as an exclusively Christian aim.

This position is enhanced by epistemological considerations. In order to avoid the objectivist sense of 'knowledge', Smith opts to speak of 'insight', 'awareness', and 'understanding' as intellectual derivations of faith. Using the family of these notions, Smith seeks to attain a humane epistemology, *in casu:* a critical corporate self-consciousness, which may enable a knowing together with one's neighbour in a global perspective. This epistemological option is seen as an 'only once'-task of establishing a global coherence in terms of a pluralistic unity or integration in a community. In this, Smith seems to be influenced by Sufi thoughts in respect of intellectual sophistication and refinement. He seems also to be in substantial agreement with a particular Indian complementary view of truth, which allows two apparently contradictory statements to be partially false, and partially true. The reason for this seems to be a distinction between propositional statements on the one hand, and knowledge as insight on the other. This relates to his faith-belief distinction: Whereas beliefs may differ, faiths converge.

Lastly, the notions of faith and truth both relate to transcendence, which in all its ineffability and infiniteness warrants Smith's relativizing and grading view of faith as capacity and potentiality on the one hand, and his view of truth as only approachable by approximation on the other.

This enables, however, a pluralistic relativism where 'our unity is real transcendently,' that is, where truths 'as seen' may differ and compete with each other, but where 'Truth itself' unites and enters human reality in its diverse forms. Hence these notions of transcendence and truth imply a perspective on generality and totality. Smiths contends that any particular world-view is less or more adequate in relation to reality in its totality. This perspective is developed more thoroughly in *WT.*

In *WT* Smith takes a further step towards theological integration, which indeed has been anticipated in several of his earlier writings. In this study Smith contributes by combining empirical (historical), epistemological and theological factors in an understanding of the unity and coherence of the comparative history of religion.

Smith explores first historical relations across religious boundaries in history and maintains that they constitute one intertwined religious history. Within this unitary historical context everyone participates in one's own context as well as in the contexts of others. Yet, according to Smith, the recognition of this historical coherence and global continuum requires a more adequate theology.

In *WT* Smith takes advantage of, and develops the concept of corporate critical self-consciousness (CCSC). Smith suggests that this notion of humane knowledge ('knowledge of man by man') may align rationality with an understanding of truth which is corporate and inductive in approach. It may thus span the gap between the outsider (subject) and insider of a community (object) in order to make both sides internal in one synthesized and converging apprehension. Along this corporate path one may, religiously speaking, come to understand and even accept others' symbols. The crucial point is, however, how one might keep loyal to one's original vision as this vision is enlarged in the light of other communities' symbols. As in *FB*, this is in the end a matter of perceiving smaller or larger areas of reality, that is, to relate one's faith coherently to all known areas of reality. This requires also in *WT* to make the matter of truth a theme. Truth is in this respect understood thus: 'the truth of all of us is part of the truth of each of us.' In this perspective, CCSC seems to work as Smith's proposal for demanding a return to generality and universality (classically new), which was lost by the modern development of 'belief'.

Smith's theological concern is how to relate the unity of the religious history of humankind to the unity of God, transcendence, or the like. His first offer is a subjective understanding of 'theology of religions' as a replacement of a 'Christian theology of religion', that is, the induced expressions of the generic religious quality embedded in the history of human religiousness (faith). His suggestion is that this kind of theology may represent a total coherent perspective, which would otherwise, if from only one particular perspective, dissolve. On the other hand, Smith contends that faith can only be theologized from the inside, as self-theologies. Yet, if held together, these self-theologies may contribute to a synthetic, world theology that on the one hand integrates both Christian, Buddhist, Islamic, etc., views of truth, and at the same time transcends all of these as they regard faith generically and God absolutely, as Smith puts it.

There is thus a certain ambivalence between Smith's imperative that this grand approach must be justified within each particular tradition, and his general theses that God has participated more richly in human affairs and man has participated more diversely in God than we once knew, and that, therefore, all human history is *Heilsgeschichte*. Smith aims to maintain both a particular view and a grand view induced by all particular views. It is obviously this latter suggestion that is a *novum,* despite his insistence on its continuity with views of significant theological figures of the past.

Smith asserts that he can demonstrate that all history is salvific both as historian and theologian. The historical argument, which is induced from his historical studies and friendships, pursues a concentration on how salvation by faith (alone!) in mundane terms is easily demonstrable in every strand of human history. The theological argument, which is derived from his knowledge of what he finds revealed to him (!) of God in Christ, is that the salvific nature of faith relates to any divine-human complex in motion and is not exclusively reserved for the Christian one. Because God's revelatory (and salvific) history to anybody, and of Himself, is conceived as a continuing contemporaneity present everywhere, traditions should be examined whether they serve as channels for this revelation, not whether they are to be recognized as revelation itself. This latter point relates again to his notions of the ineffable transcendence and of history in flux. It is Smith's sincere contention that this represents a 'faithful participation in the Christian process' and thus a 'not nearly Christian enough Christian's contribution' to a theology of comparative religion. Attention has been drawn to some objections to this conclusion. Further criticism belongs especially to Chapter 7.

3

'THE SPECIAL CASE OF ISLAM' RELATED TO SMITH'S GENERAL THEORY

3.1 Introduction

This part will mainly contain attempts on behalf of Smith to show how 'religion' and 'religious' have their counterparts in Islam. Central here will be how he conceives faith, belief and cumulative tradition in the Islamic tradition. As we will see, this is primarily a question that has to be answered according to how one understands 'Islam' and 'iman', and the relation between the two. Yet, also the understanding of the Qur'an is elaborated by Smith and gains in the end a theological understanding as well.

The succession of topics below will mostly follow the order in Smith's own collection of Islam-studies in *On Understanding Islam: Selected Studies (UI)*. Noteworthy, according to the original publications of the articles, this collection spans the period 1958-1977. This coincides roughly with the period we have examined in order to reconstruct his comparative concepts and theological ideas. For this reason the question of relation between the preceding chapter (Chapter 2) and what follows in this chapter, which is: the relation between Smith's general theory and his particular interpretation of selected issues within the Islamic tradition, is of particular interest though it may be difficult to discern 'what depends on what.' This problem was however highlighted at the beginning of the last chapter (Chapter 2.1).

It should also be mentioned that since the previous chapter has shown how Smith's interreligious hermeneutics, predominantly explicated by his historio-conceptual studies, is inextricably interwoven with his theological self-understanding, his 'encounter' with Islam will be of particular interest for the objective of my study: 'self-relating' and 'self-change' in the 'field' between Oneself (Smith) and the Other (Islam, the Islamic tradition).

3.2 The Historical Development of the Understanding of 'Islam' in Islam as a Request for Theory

A fruitful place to start is simply Smith's understanding of the verbal noun 'islam'. The impact his studies of this term made upon him shows how self-relating and self-change are linked within his writings, though not often made explicit. An exception is to be found in a preface to a reprinting of a study[1] of the historical development of the concept of 'islam' within (the religious tradition) Islam where Smith provides some clues to what areas of *the development of his own thought* this particular study impacted upon:

1. His understanding of Islam.

2. The general problem of the conceptualization of religious matters from within a given religious position; that is, from the outside.

3. About the divergence between 1 and 2.

4. Their—due to modern times—growing interrelatedness.

Smith contends that these issues were not solved till *ME* (1963). One might complete this by saying that the third and fourth points have been comprehended most thoroughly in *BH* (1977) and *FB* (1979). As one might see, this listing of areas that this particular study from 1958 influenced coincides to a large degree with the problem pursued in the present study.

The distinctiveness of Smith's approach is, however, primarily conceptual,[2] which also becomes quite recognizable in the results he gets to in his study of the concept of 'Islam' in Islam. Smith starts his introduction to 'the problem' by designating three different ways that human beings 'think or talk about religion in general or any one particular religion,' which certainly resembles matters of the previous main chapter (Chapter 2).[3] These 'ways' are (42f):

(a) *personal*, which considers the 'life of the spirit, the quality of faith, for a specific individual,' and which is 'immediate, concrete, and existential,'

(b) *systematic,* and (c) *institutional*. Together, these latter two represent 'the religious systems to which whole bodies of people 'belong." This may be understood as either an ideal (systematic) or historical reality (institutional), or as essence[4] (systematic) or existence (institutional).

As one may expect based on his general theory of religion, the main division is to be located between the first, on the one hand, and the second and third on the other. The two latter are of the same kind, that is, they are objectifications. Most importantly, however, Smith suggests that

---

[1] Smith 1958/1981c, 41. First presented at a conference on Muslim historiography, School of Oriental and African Studies, University of London, 1958. Subsequent parenthetical remarks refer to this study.

[2] *Ibid.*, 59: ' ... is pushing me to the conclusion that such understanding requires a fairly serious revision of many of our terms and concepts.'

[3] See for example the end of Chapter 2.4.2.

[4] Cf. again Grünschloß' identification of ontological levels in Smith's writings, Grünschloß 1994a, 197. See otherwise note 100 above, Chapter 2.

these three 'main heads' have validity in general: it fits, he says, his own 'Christian faith,' it fits 'John Doe's Christianness,' and it may also fit Islam. From these general notions, Smith proceeds by saying that the notion 'Islam' is used in three distinct ways (43):

(a) Islam as the active personal faith, the self-commitment (*taslim*) of an individual Muslim. This sense is active because of its function as a verbal noun (a *masdar*[5]).

(b) Islam as a transcendent ideal, and

(c) Islam as a historical phenomenon and empirical actuality.

Smith says that the second sense is the sense of the insider; how Islam ought to be. This is at the same time how Islam is presented to outsiders. The third sense is the conception of the outsiders. The first, personal sense is however, at least to a certain degree, opposed to both of them, though he also stresses the continuity with the ideal and actual meaning of 'Islam' (44). One may also discern Smith's own sympathy for it in his euphemistic description of it:

> It is the response of a particular person to a challenge. That
> person's whole being is involved, in a transaction, as it
> were, between his soul and the universe; and, according to
> his conviction, his eternal destiny is at stake (43).

By this 'distribution of meanings' Smith has, however, not clarified what Islam as personal faith is, or what the ideal Islam is. What he has presented are not the results of his empirical research but the launch of a heuristical set of different meanings of a single word (Islam), which in turn may help him and others, at least as a long-range ambition, to 'come closer to an understanding of what Islam (and, ultimately, religion) really is' (45). The short-range ambition is, however, to trace historically how this has been conceived by people at different times and at different places.

Smith's choice is simply to study any Arabic book-titles containing 'Islam'. These titles are divided into lists, one up to 1300 AH, one for recent titles after 1300 AH, and one based on received suggestions of works, for example from people in Cairo who added titles to the first two lists.[6] Whereas the first list is with one exception based on Brockelmann's *Geschichte der arabischen Literatur,* the second is completed by Smith from other sources as well. The results are extensively reported and all

---

[5] *Taslim* is a verbal noun of the verb *sallama,* which is the *qattala*-form of vs-l-m, see *CQur,* 1079.

[6] Cf. note 8, p. 93 below.

titles containing 'Islam' are given.[7] The most important result of this study is that Smith seems to discover some 'general trends' in his material. These are:

(a) 'In classical and medieval Muslim times religious books were numerous, yet titles on 'Islam', although they do occur, are considerably less common than today' (50). 84 titles were found in the first list.

(b) When such books occur before 1300 AH, they are either found 'actually or potentially' in combination with *iman*, or they are ambiguously designating either 'man's personal acceptance of responsibility before God' or the idealization of Islam (55f). Those ambiguous are only found after al-Ghazzali.

(c) '*Iman*' is used in only 56 titles (in the Qur'an it is used five times more often than 'Islam'), whereas in modern times the relation between '*islam*' and '*iman*' is 13:1, and a combination of the two is not found after 1300 AH (52).

(d) There is also a reasonable set of titles where Smith sees a transition from the personal meaning and the 'religion-as-ideal-or-system'-meaning, to a reference to Muslims themselves as a community or culture (56ff). This 'secularizing' transition is radical in modern times and coincides with the objectivist attitude of Western orientalists, in opposition to both the ideal of Islam, and the 'inner aspiration of [the Muslim's] heart' (59).

Smith gives at the end a short interpretation of these results: The word 'Islam' has gradually lost its relationship to God during the history, and especially in modern times (63f). This can be divided into three different shifts:

(a) From a personal piety to an ideal religious system or transcendent pattern,

(b) to an external, mundane religious system, and

(c) to the civilization that was its historical expression.

For a further interpretation of the results he refers to an as 'yet unpublished address.'[8] This address and the study of concern in this chapter form the background of *The Meaning and End of Religion*. I prefer to proceed to that work since the results and the data are mostly the same. Another reason for this is the fact that his use of particular terms anticipates the results of the study, for example when he entitles the development of Islam a reification process, which corresponds perfectly to his hypothesis in *ME*. At this stage of his writing *ME* also attains the

---

[7] Smith 1958/1981c, ch. 3.2 (data) and 3.3 (titles).

[8] *Ibid.*, 45, n 1. These are 'Is Islam the Name of a Religion?' delivered at Princeton University, January 1957, and 'Should the Great Religions Have Names?' delivered at the University of Tehran and the American University of Cairo, February 1958.

function of a developed theory of religious data in general, and of Muslim data in particular.

3.3 The Theory Found: Islam and Iman

Smith's historical examination of how 'Islam' has been used at different stages of the history of Muslims is connected with total argument for a new understanding of religion. Smith is therefore compelled to examine the Islamic case in order to return a verdict on whether Islam is a misconceived religious tradition. If so, how should this tradition be conceived? If, on the contrary, Islam cannot be recognized as misconceived, his reification-hypothesis would be significantly weakened. This examination has strong impact upon how he develops systematic relations between his normative self-understanding and Islam and is therefore worth pursuing in some detail, albeit this detour may seem unnecessary.

A way of stating his key hypothesis in the Islamic instance is to suggest that the understanding of 'Islam', not the notion itself, represents a 'reification' of an originally vivid 'ringing personal summons to men and women to have faith in God and to commit themselves wholeheartedly to [God's] commands.'[9] But the case is more complex. A prominent case is that Muslims themselves insist on using 'Islam' despite Western attempts to label it otherwise.[10] Islam is in Muslims' opinion a name given directly from God—in the Qur'an.[11] Another reason is that the notion of religion as both a personal religion and a religious system is well known through the concept of *din* (81f). The possibility of a plural of *din* (*adyan*) makes it also viable to combine an understanding of an ideal religion (one's own) with objective knowledge of other religions. According to Smith, this involves a consciousness of the existence of 'a series of phenomena of essentially the same kind' (82). Smith stresses that this runs counter to the opinion of one's own religion as a religion *sui generis*. If Islam is to be reckoned as the best religion, it is only of its kind.

This does not, however, lead Smith to underestimate the significant differences between Islam and other religions, which from a

---

[9] *ME*, 118. Subsequent parenthetical references refer to *ME*.

[10] *ME*, 80f og 83f. E.g. 'the heresy/sect of the Saracenes', 'the religion of the Tartars/Turks', 'Muhammadanism', and so on.

[11] Surah 5.3 and 3.19. The translations are Smith's own though he claims to have sufficient support for them. The translations are: 'This day I have perfected your religion for you, and completed my favour unto you; and has chosen for you as a religion *Islam*' (5.3), and: 'Verily, *the* Religion in the eyes of God is Islam' (3.19). Noteworthy, the translation of N.J. Dawood reads 'faith' instead of 'r/Religion' in these Surahs. Arberry, however, reads 'religion' at both places.

comparativist perspective must be maintained if not to unduly harmonize various traditions. He even admits that not only are they different; they also ask different questions (84). Hence they are not merely variations on a single theme. Islam, Smith continues, may in fact be the most closed, 'entity-like' or 'morphous' of the different religions (84f). On the other hand, there is Islamic evidence against this, most prominently the Sufi mystics who point in a more personalist and less formal direction. Nevertheless, the particularist aspect of Islam is well pointed out.

Moreover, Smith suggests this to be the result of a strong reification process. He therefore wants to trace the path which lead to this. One of his hypotheses is that the reification of Islam is less deep-rooted than one would expect, which would certainly strengthen Smith's interpretation of 'religion'. He therefore states:

> What makes the Muslims specifically different from other groups is the very fact that makes them generically the same as other groups; namely, that they are persons living *sub specie aeternitatis* in concrete and particular historical situations (86).

Let us now look at the processes Smith examines. In short, there are three of them which, according to Smith, have formed the reification-process of Islam.

The pre-Islamic possibilities ('the Middle Eastern tradition') of independent religious communities as an environment for the launch of the Islamic tradition and community. These possibilities can be approached both historically, linguistically and in the light of the rise of Islam.

Historically this is represented by the phenomena of the appearance of the Church in the Mediterranean world and of the Diaspora of the Jews (86-108). This development also impinged on Arabia at the time of Muhammad, which is illustrated by Smith when he, tracing the underlying process, draws the attention to Zarathustra who 'was preaching faith' and thus 'participated within the total religious history of mankind' without having any pretensions of establishing a 'religion' (88), and likewise to Mani (216-277 CE, 95f). Smith interprets this as a significant turn in the religious history of humankind, from a preoccupation with content, to one with form. After this, from the second to the sixth century, a development toward 'systematization, crystallization, and definition of what previously had been a more chaotic welter of unorganized movements' was inevitable (97).

Linguistically Smith traces the roots of the aforementioned *din* back to the Persian *daena* (99-102). The etymology is not entirely clear but Smith asserts that the word originally designated something inner and personal. As such, he sees this as representing a personal religion, and thus 'approximates more significantly to personal "faith"' (99). The first development away from this is the development of a generic *daena*. Later it also gains a plural form, which of course matters in Smith's theory of a development away from the inner personal, via the generic, to the reified and, lastly, 'pluralized.' Smith also shows how the understanding of *daena* or *den* corresponds to the meaning of *din* in the Arabic environment at the time when Islam appeared on the historical scene.[12]

The third matter is the question of how these 'reification trends' impacted on the rise of Islam (103-108). Here, as Smith comments, 'the argument becomes very delicate ... since the issue raises the questions of the relation between revelation and history,' and of the relation between religious truth and religious language (103). The delicacy is illustrated when Smith maintains on the one hand that: 'faith does not alter, and must not and need not evade, the facts of particularist history,' and on the other refers to the traditional Islamic refusal of the Qur'an being translated into 'words ... of human constructs.'[13] Nevertheless, Smith wants to acknowledge the importance of the Qur'an for Muslims and give attention to the fact that these God-given words mean something to people, either at the times when the Qur'an was presented, or later. As a part of this issue, meanings have evolved and changed during history. It is this fact Smith wants to elaborate on, in which he supposes Muslims to take an interest.

Related to this, Smith sees Muhammad as a 'founder of a religion' (Mani being the only predecessor) (106). This does not exclude God as the ideal originator of Islam, but emphasizes the systematical, sociological and political organizing in the hands of Muhammad. In this respect, Muhammad constructs Islam. Moreover, which is a particular Islamic point, Muhammad did not primarily offer a revision of the existing indigenous religious traditions, but a 'reformulation of ... the tradition of Christians and Jews.'[14] Thus, the reception of this reformulated faith by people outside

---

[12] According to Smith *din* has three meanings at that time: a. It works as an invention from the surroundings, designating systematic religion, b. As a verbal noun it can have the meaning of judging and the like, and, finally, c. also as a verbal noun with the meaning: 'to conduct oneself, to behave, to conform,' and so forth, or as an abstract noun: 'conformity, propriety, obedience.'

[13] *ME,* 103 and 291, n 74.

[14] *ME,* 107f. In this argument Smith is dependant on Arthur Jefferey: 'It comes, therefore, as no little surprise, to find how little of the religious life of this Arabian paganism is reflected in the pages of the Qur'an ... Even a cursory reading ... makes it plain that he drew his inspiration ... from the great monotheistic religions ...'

those two existing traditions marks a unique event in the history of religions. The outsiders become insiders.

As a counterpart to these external forces in the Arabian environment there is also an internal reification process of which Muslims themselves reified the notion of faith (108-115). However, Smith does not spend much time on this, it being obvious enough in, for example, Muslim theology. He therefore proceeds to consider 'what mighty forces within the Islamic community were originally at work *against* reification' (109, my emphasis). His thesis is that a reified interpretation of *islam* and *din* is not the most adequate interpretation of them. A threefold evidence for this can be given:

(a) A non-reifying interpretation emphasizing the personal and vivid 'fundamental orientation' with perception of 'transcendent overtones' complies better with the way in which the notions mentioned above were traditionally used in Arabic language. It is also in better accordance with how leaders in early Islamic times understood them (110).

(b) *Islam,* as verbal noun, is seldom used in the Qur'an (eight times) and when it is used it designates a decisive personal act, not a systematized religion (110). Moreover, its foundation verb (*aslama*) is used three times more than *islam.*

(c) Moreover, Smith gives attention to the fact that 'God' is used 2,697 times in the Qur'an, and that the 'great term [for the manward side]' is *iman* ('faith'), which is used 45 times in the Qur'an, as well as the corresponding *mu'min,* which is used in opposition to the more impersonal and less vivid 'Muslim', and five times more frequently. For Smith, the verbs and verbal nouns precede the nouns logically, structurally and are in correspondence with the Qur'anic usage. Also the verbal noun *iman* is found less than a tenth as often as its verbal counterparts. Nevertheless, Smith ties the usages of this notion mostly to 'faith', and not to 'belief', based on the following definition of the former as

> an active quality, one that commits the person and by which he is caught up into a relationship with his Maker and his fellows. It is the ability to see the transcendent, and to respond to it; to hear God's voice, and to act accordingly (111f).

From this, Smith draws the conclusion, which he claims to be a 'perfectly possible reading' though not necessarily 'the right or transcendent one,' that:

> The Qur'an is concerned, and presents God as being

concerned, with something that persons do, and with the persons who do it, rather with an abstract entity (111).

And, likewise:

> Vivid and personal: these are the qualities of the term of *islam* in the Qur'an. What was proclaimed was a challenge, not a religion (113).

Thus, the Qur'an presents 'a great drama of decision.' Hence, *islam* is to be understood as commitment or obedience, in partial contradiction to the reifying forces, especially those of the loan-words from Persia (*den/din*).[15]

The third process that Smith locates is the reaction to Western pressure since the end of the 19th century. According to Smith, there has been an almost complete shift among Muslims towards using the term Islam to name a religion (106). Smith interprets this as a result of the demand for apologetics, which is a strong reifying force, that is, fixing the internals for the use against outsiders. Smith ends his study in the history of ideas by repeating his general suggestion in the previous subsection; that 'Islam' in recent times is used in three distinct, yet generalized senses:[16]

(a) As a verbal noun; a 'submittingness' that varies from person to person.

(b) As the empirical actuality (historical and sociological), and

(c) As the Platonic ideal of a total Islamic system as an institutionalized entity.

Smith's conclusion is that whereas the first is chronologically and logically the first, the latter two are the dominant ones. Smith's conclusion from all these processes is therefore that Islam has been 'the first and most reified of all man's living religious movements;' it all started at its very birth! As a conclusion Smith takes this as a strong confirmation of his general understanding of 'religion' as reification and a very limited conceptualization of an originally vivid personal faith. As such, the Islamic instance is a very intricate, but revealing illustration (118).

---

[15] *ME,* 110 and 112. This does also correspond to original meanings of one of the traditional 'proof-texts' for Islam as a reified system, Surah 3.19 ('true religion (*not* 'the true religion') is obeisance'). Cf. *ME,* 113. Cf. also note 11, p. 94, above in the present chapter.

[16] *ME,* 117. Cf. above p. 92.

3.4 Arkan: *Pillars of Islam or Pious Acts?*

Another example of this reification tendency, which also may function as a bridge to further studies of faith, can be found in Smith's study of the concept of *arkan*.[17] In short, this term highlights the relation between faith and works on the one hand, and between faith and its fixed, credal confessions on the other. Smith's point of departure is the meaning of *arkan* in a medieval formula (cf. below). There exist two different readings of this term, namely: either the pillars of Islam, or the limbs of the human body. The consequences of either are, however, far-reaching. In a study of the various arguments Smith seeks to enhance the meaning of faith itself. Having the objective of 'systematic relations' of the present study in mind, Smith interestingly places his concern in a context similar to ours. He starts namely by stating what he finds to be common elements which Christian and Muslims agree upon, namely, faith as 'man's most decisive quality' and the Day of Judgement as a day of 'determining of who has had it and who not.'[18] To these fundamental aspects of 'various of the world's cultural traditions' the question about how to conceive faith itself becomes important.

Smith's approach makes *arkan* a theme as an ambiguous term within Muslim conceptions. Accordingly, Smith places his exploration of *arkan* within an understanding of faith as controversial both in general, and among Muslims (164).[19] Because it is the relation between faith (*iman*) and *arkan* that matters here, Smith starts by asserting generally that there are three Islamic positions for understanding *iman*. These are, *iman* as: a) an act of the heart, b) a public confession, and c) works/deeds.

These positions, or meanings of faith, correspond in addition to groups of Muslims, which make various combinations possible: (a) is represented by the most recognized theological schools. Smith sees this as 'no simple [but a] vulnerable position' (*ibid.*), whereas (b) is maintained by the majority community. This understanding has been adopted for all purposes in mundane and social life, and in law. The *mu'min* is the one who recites the *shahadah*. Lastly, (c) is represented by the *Khariji*

---

[17] See immediately below.

[18] Smith 1974/1981h, 163. Subsequent parenthetical references refer to this study. Smith's elaboration on the word *arkan* fits into a series of conceptual studies leading up to the main conceptual and comparative studies, *BH* and *FB*. One should have in mind that his emphasis in these studies lies on how words should be understood *as meaning* (164).

[19] Cf. his statement in *CR* about his relation to the Western academic tradition in respect of equipping the freedom of the academic scholar to work both independently and dependently of the believers of a positive tradition, 44. See Chapter 2.2.

movement. As an illustration about how these triple options may belong together, Smith quotes a standard, rhyming, 'major' formula, which in later centuries was held to be 'the position of generality' of scholars, namely that faith is:

> *tasdiq bi-al-janan* / *wa-iqrar bi-al-lisan* / *wa-'amal bi-al-arkan*[20]
> [knowing with the heart / confessing with the tongue / and performing the chief works]

Smith's purpose is to examine how *arkan* should be understood in this formula, and by this to throw light upon the whole understanding of faith.[21] As I mentioned, there are two options for conceiving the meaning of *arkan*: Either a) as 'the pillars' of Islam, that is, as a *terminus technicus*, or b) that it signifies the limbs of the body. Whereas the former position is widely held by Muslims and Western Arabists, Smith suggest that the latter has 'more persuasive logical, contextual, and empirical support' (165). Yet, what are his arguments for this?

(a) Firstly, the root of *arkan*, *r-k-n*, means to 'incline towards, to lean upon,' and so on (165). The plural of the noun, *arkan* (sg. *rukn*), signifies 'that upon which something rests ... is supported.' This meaning is confirmed in classical dictionaries where it means 'the strongest side of a thing ... that on which something or someone rests or relies.' It may therefore designate both a corner of a building or the pole of a tent. Interestingly, in philosophical discourse it denotes an 'essential condition.' In this sense, both the 'the pillars'-meaning and the 'limbs'meaning are possible renderings of the noun. Smith's suggestion, therefore, is that the

---

[20] The formula is taken from Taftazani (cf. note 51 below), who did not himself use the triple formula but makes a critical comment about Nasafi whom he is commenting on, *ibid.* 320, n2. Smith finds moreover an earlier version of the triple formula in the Hanbali writer Ibn Battah (died 387AH/ 997AD). Smith does not translate the formula himself but refers in another footnote to a translation of A.J. Wensick, *ibid.* 321, n3, which supports his view about the formula, in particular the meaning of *arkan*. This translation of Wensick reads: 'Faith is knowing with the heart, confessing with the tongue and performing *the chief works*' (Smith's emphasis), Wensick, *The Muslim Creed,* Cambridge: Cambridge University Press, 1932, 267.

[21] The way Smith identifies different methodological levels within his entire studies on faith is most interestingly illustrated here, Smith 1974/1981h, 165, where i) the 'religious or human' question is 'What is faith?' ii) the historical 'What have Muslims affirmed it to be?' iii) the linguistic question—as is his concern here—'What have they meant when they affirmed (in Arabic) such-and-such,' and the quasi-hermeneutical question of 'What do we mean when we say that in affirming it to be x they have meant a?'

elaboration should advance since 'careful reflection and a critical scrutiny of many instances push one inescapably in the direction of a *jawarih*,' *which* designates unequivocally 'limbs' (166).

(b) One of the more 'substantial' matters concerns the relation between faith and works (167). The question of whether faith included doing as such was a highly debated issue within the Islamic world as it was in the Christian one.[22] What Smith makes a point, is that in this general debate the terms *al-jawarih* and *al-arkan* were used almost interchangeably, without any shift in usage during the time.

(c) Still more substantially, Smith contends, 'works of faith, for a Muslim, involve a good deal more than just 'the pillars'' (168). The implicit point is that if works were to be included in the tripartite formula cited above, it there would have been a considerable limitation to reserve *al-arkan* to only the pillars. A problem in itself is that *Shahadah,* the creed (cf. the section 2.5), which is included in the second part of the formula (*iqrar bi-al-lisan*), is one of the pillars itself.

(d) Smith also discusses the issue of chronology (169). He takes as a given fact that *al-jawarih* has been used at earlier stages of the development of the formula. Why should then *arkan* take its place? In this respect, Smith argues persuasively for the reason and weight of *rhyme* instead of theology.[23]

(e) In the authorship of for example Baqillani and al-Ghazzali, Smith finds that when they are quoting the standard tripartite formula of faith they use *arkan*, whereas they are inclined to use *jawarih* in their own discussions of faith and works (170).

Based on all these arguments Smith therefore concludes that

> in classical and medieval Islamic texts the word *arkan* as part of a definition of faith [i.e. the tripartite formula] designated the limbs of the human body, and was a synonym of *jawarih*; and was so understood [as] the pillars and other pious acts (171f).

---

[22] Most interestingly, 'faith without deeds does not save' (cf. James 2.14ff), was a central point of the Islamic Khariji sect mentioned above, see *CEIsl*, 222f.

[23] In short his argumentation runs as follows: In the aftermath of an introduction of *janan* in the first phrase (substituting *qalb*), *al-arkan* has been introduced at the cost of *al-jawarih*. The result is *janan-lisan-arkan*, instead of *qalb-lisan-jawarih*, while the meaning is kept the same. A further convincing argument is that Smith has not found that *janan* or *arkan* occurred in contexts other than rhymes, and when found in rhymes, always with either or both of the two other words at the end of each phrase, Smith 1974/1981h, 169f.

Hence works is part of what faith is, as pious acts, and on the other hand, they are more than observance of the pillars.

Smith does however not stop there. He places the meaning of *arkan* within 'a history of meanings' (*ibid.*). By this he finds that *arkan* has, as an inescapable fact for scholars as well as villagers, changed its meaning from 'limbs' to 'the pillars'. As a similar fact, the *fiqh* (legal) usage came to dominate over the *kalam* (theological) one. Smith sees this development as 'not surprising' and 'plausible' (172): 'The five pillars are handy and in some ways obvious illustrations of what is meant by pious behaviour, by religious bodily actions.' Thus his thesis about the reification process as well as the meaning of faith is enhanced.

3.5   *The faith of Muslims seen through the* Shahadah

At about the same time as *ME* was published Smith was asked to give some radio talks on 'the religions of the world.'[24] Smith interprets this as a challenge, having only been an Islamicist so far, to become 'something wider than an Islamicist.' Consequently, in the radio-speech on the Muslim instance,[25] he tried to 'convey a sense of what it might be like to be a human being *living in the light of one or another of them* [i.e. the various 'systems']' (my emphasis). This corresponds also with the characteristics of the third stage in the development of Smith's ideas according to Andreas Grünschloß: the comparative and the personalist phases.[26] At this stage Smith had come to see Islam as 'a human involvement ... within the general pattern of humankind's religious and cultural life.'[27] Because Smith reckons on the one hand *ME* as 'general theory,' and *FOM* as 'popularized application,' I find it interesting to make a short survey of how Smith conceives 'Muslims,' which is the title of the chapter (and speech), in a different context than that of a 'careful scholarly documentation.'

Smith starts by giving attention to the diversity of Hindu and Muslim architecture represented by the temple and the mosque. Whereas complexity shapes both the temple as building and worship within it, the mosque undergirds simplicity both in its architecture and the devotion of

---

[24] For the following quotations, see the preface to the reprint of the section on Islam taken from *FOM* in Smith 1981b, 26f. Other parenthetical references refer to Smith 1981b.

[25] Published in *FOM*.

[26] Cf. p. 22.

[27] He relates this emphasis to his moving from McGill (and the specialization as an Islamicist) to work 'in the wider field of Comparative Religion' at Harvard, although he originally was 'Professor in Comparative Religion' at McGill, cf. the brief Biography and References at the end of this study.

3 'The Special Case of Islam' Related to Smith's General Theory

Muslims. And, contrary to the Hindu who is allowed to choose from various systems of ideas, the Muslim community 'symbolizes its belief' in the *Shahadah*,[28] referred to as 'the (two) word(s)' by Muslims (28). Smith, therefore, suggests that to understand this 'simplest, tidiest creed in all the world' perhaps is to understand a Muslim, albeit he 'cannot suggest something of the richness of what lies behind' (28f).

Smith suggests that the 'coherence and simplicity' of the Muslim faith is symbolized by the *Shahadah* (29). This does not entail that the Muslim faith is narrow or superficial. On the contrary, it only implies that details are strictly subordinated to 'an over-all pattern that is essentially simple,' or 'to the higher truth, the simpler truth, of the creed.' This corresponds perfectly to the strict Muslim notion of God's oneness (*tawhid*), which is opposed to that of *shirk* (associating God with other things). This is, according to Smith, the content of *Shahadah*.

Smith calls the *Shahadah* a symbol (31). And as a symbol, he says, it plays a role similar to that of the *cross* for Christians.[29] That a word may function as a symbol in Islam, relates to the verbal form of revelation. It seems, therefore, that both symbol and revelation play the comparative role, the *tertium comparationis,* when Smith tries to characterize the role of the *Shahadah* as a creed.

On the other hand, Smith gives attention to the fact that the 'two words' is called a witness (31f).[30] Thus, it stresses the function of Islam as a missionary movement. This proclamation of conviction is, according to Smith, more a kind of presupposition than an affirmation of belief. A Muslim does not suppose that God exists, he takes it for granted—and witnesses about it. At this place Smith uses the opportunity to also make a differentiation within the single Western notion *credo,* which confuses profoundly different aspects within it, on the one hand (intellectual) belief, and on the other (religious) faith.[31] According to Smith, 'one of the

---

[28] The Creed, that is, 'There is no God but God, and Muhammad is God's apostle.'

[29] For a more precise understanding of 'symbol' in Smith, see Tadsen 1985, ch. III.5. As we noticed in the end of one of the previous chapters (2.6.2), Smith understands symbol in relation to persons and as means of mediating to/from transcendence. As such it transcends a mere 'belief-in-proposition.' On the other hand, Smith seems to have some doubts about how rewarding the use of symbols may prove in the end. As we have seen in *WT,* he is quite balanced as to whether symbols may prove strong enough to carry the weight they are asked to and introduces therefore a 'zero-level' in distinction to symbols on a first (for adherents) and second level (for outsiders).

[30] Cf. the introduction to *Shahadah:* 'I (perceive and) bear witness that ...' 'Shahadah' comes from the verb *shahida* which has a double meaning: On the one hand: 'to observe', 'to perceive', and on the other: 'to witness', 'to testify',and so on, see *CEIsl,* 359.

[31] Smith 1981b, 32. This is elaborated further in *FB,* ch. 5.

fundamental problems arising from a recognition of religious diversity' is that, that which used to be taken for granted becomes 'scrutinized intellectualisations' and 'true-or-false-propositions.'

One might therefore argue that Smith's understanding of how the *Shahadah* functions in the life of Muslims illuminates how the modern notion of 'belief' has become something different from personal faith; it has become an intellectualization, and thus on the outside of what religiously counts: faith as 'commitment,' and 'doing something about it' (33). Noteworthy here is also the aspect of activity/commitment that faith is involved in.[32]

What about the *Shahadah* then, and its meaning of it for Muslims? Smith locates four different meanings the *Shahadah* may have for Muslims:

(a) The rejection of polytheism and its uncompromising insistence on transcendence, as it first functioned in pagan Arabia.

(b) The rejection of human tyranny because God alone is to be served and to be given human's allegiance. Smith is not blind to the fatalist notions whereby the activist line was suppressed, but he follows the principle of 'interpreting other men's faith as ... one's own' and maintains that an activist interpretation of the *Shahadah* is historically and actually available to Muslims (34).

(c) A turning aside from moral polytheism, from false values and false gods of heart. The believer must thus 'fear no other power, honour no other prize, pursue no other goal' and cannot 'look for help to purely mundane forces, ... rely upon armies or clever stratagems, to trust anything that is not intrinsically good' (35). According to Smith, this is learned from the Sufi mystics of the medieval period, who corresponds with 'the sensitive Muslim conscience.'

(d) The 'movement in faith' understanding. Smith admits attraction to another understanding given by mystics, namely an understanding of *Shahadah* which represents the process from unbelief to faith. 'There is no god' comes first, and 'but God' follows after. Or in Smith's own words:

> A person brought up in a religious tradition must have seen through that tradition ... he must have learned the bleakness of atheism, and have experienced its meaninglessness and eventually its dread. Only such a

---

[32] It is here obvious that 'faith' seen in an Islamic context gains a quite 'active' determination if compared with his more general formulations about it as examined in Chapter 2. This moment of action, commitment, and so on, can be seen in Chapter 3.7 below.

person is able to go on, perhaps only years later, to a faith
that is without superficiality and without merely cheap and
second-half glibness (35).

Most interestingly, Smith is most concerned with the second aspect of
the testimony: 'the apostle of God,' which he sees as a statement about
Muhammad's function and not about his status. Consequently, Smith
asserts, there is no reason for comparing him with Christ. If he should be
compared functionally with something in the Christian tradition, it would
be with St. Paul and St. Peter in their witness to the central event of their
tradition. Nevertheless, what Smith sees as presupposed in Muhammad
is that God has something to tell human beings: the moral law, and hence
that God is not to remain transcendent, inscrutable or passive. On the
contrary, God is by his nature active and communicating. The phrase of
the *Shahadah* referring to the Apostle implies therefore that the initiative
is God's own. From this it follows that:

> Man's business in the religious life is not a quest but a
> response (36).

Smith is of course balancing here between interpreting the *Shahadah* as a
Muslim would recognize and find appropriate on the one hand, and using
language that quite obviously pulls the phrases of the Muslim creed towards
a Christian universe of meaning (God as active, not remaining transcendent,
communicating, initiative vs. response). I think this 'sample' of his
interpretation of *Shahadah* may illustrate how he sees diverse forms of
faith as converging towards each other. In this is also included the importance
of the (external) expressions that serve as vehicles for faith.

That external expressions matter becomes even more important
when he in the end characterizes the 'apostle-part' of the formula as one
about what is right rather than what is true (36f). This, he relates to the
revelational difference between Christians and Muslims, that is, in the
Christian case, revelation *of* God, and in the Muslim case, revelation *from*
God (Muslims). This matter is, however, not discussed thoroughly but is
balanced quite irenically, yet far-reachingly, by maintaining that those
who do not call themselves Muslims should

> nonetheless *not allow this to obscure from us the cosmic*
> *things* that those inspired from this source are saying about
> morality, about man, and about God (37, my emphasis).

How 'not allow to obscure' and 'cosmic things' should be understood here, is not entirely clear. One possibility is to see them as resonating with the ambivalence in Smith's notion of truth, that is, on the one hand, mundane truth (which is demonstrable), and on the other: cosmic truth (faith, transcendence, etc.). It is, however, evident that those things which are normally reckoned as significant differences (e.g. 'revelational difference') are neutralized in Smith's approach. Or better, an attempt is done at integration into a superior perspective where differences do not matter as much as they in particular periods and places have been thought to do.

3.6 Faith and Belief in the Qur'an: Theocentrism and Anthropocentrism

In a preface to a reprinting of one of two lectures delivered as the *Iqbal Memorial Lectures* at the University of the Punjab thirty years after he taught there,[33] Smith gives attention to the fact that the results of his previous studies on the Islamic concept of faith were dramatic. 'Dramatic' because they showed him that he had been wrong in connecting too tightly, and confusingly, faith and belief. They were also dramatic in the sense that the very foundations of Christian theology, and the central question of philosophy, the meaning and form of truth were at stake.[34] Pondering these questions entailed therefore 'a confronting of the ultimate questions of both life and intellect.' Needless to say, such personal statements on behalf of Smith are entirely consonant with the present study in the following way: Smith's Islam-interpretation involves self-change with regards to central matters of his self-understanding.

The article itself concerns the relation between faith and belief in the Qur'an.[35] As such it also anticipates, and is almost identical with the first part of the Islamic chapter in his 'second substantial comparativist

---

[33] Smith 1974/1981f, 110f. Subsequent parenthetical references refer to this reprinted lecture. Besides, Smith taught at Forman Christian College, Univ. of Punjab, Lahore, then India, 1941-45. Cf. otherwise Biography and References.

[34] Smith 1974/1981f, 110.

[35] This first of these lectures was delivered under the title 'Faith and Belief,' whereas the title of the printed version is: 'Faith, in the Qur'ân: And Its Relation to Belief.' The lectures contained two presentations, one with the subtitle 'some considerations from the Islamic instance,' printed as Smith 1974/1981f, and one with 'some considerations from the Christian instance,' of which excerpts—those that 'draw theological inferences' from his 'new understanding'—are printed as Smith 1974/1981o, cf. *ibid.* 266.

volume,' that is, *Faith and Belief* (1979).[36] Smith maintains that at the time he was elaborating these issues, he was

> agog at finding that the new understanding powerfully illuminated not only Islamic matters but also both Christian thought and the comparative question as to the relation between Christian and Islamic (111).

In his lecture he also explicitly addresses the audience by saying that in the light of his engagement with faith and belief in Islamic life he was able 'to understand also my own Christian heritage' (113). How this should be interpreted is a clue to that which follows.

Before I trace how Smith systematically explores the relation between faith and belief in the Qur'an, I would like to draw the attention to a most interesting passage from Smith's lecture which reveals how he has been influenced by a particular, yet significant Muslim, Sir Muhammad Iqbal,[37] to whom this memorial lecture was dedicated. In personal language this extract indicates how Smith became influenced by an Islamic vision of what he calls a 'generic human issue,' that is, of human life and faith.

> Iqbal had died two years before I reached Lahore. I do not exactly remember when I first read his Sic Lectures; perhaps before I arrived in these parts, although it was here that I learned to take them very seriously. I do remember clearly, vividly, when I was in process of learning Urdu here, my first introduction to his poetry. I began with *Bang-i Dara*. My heart and my mind were stirred, my imagination was enriched, *my vision of the world* and certainly of Muslim culture *was deepened and enlarged,* by the encounter with Iqbal then begun. For thirty or more years that vivifying experience has developed in my thought and feeling; and

---

[36] A later version of Smith 1974/1981f constitutes the Islamic Chapter in *FB*, which also includes a section on faith in Islamic theology, *ibid*. 111. Noteworthy is Smith's own assertion: 'It has been my custom to publish things having to do with Islâm only after first submitting them, if feasible, for critique and comment to Muslim friends, so as to have their reaction,' *ibid*. 114.

[37] 1877(?)-1938. Indian philosopher, poet, politician and spiritual leader of Indian modernism. Iqbal was strongly affected by European philosophy (e.g. Bergson and Nietzsche), which he tried to combine with the Qur'an and Sufi Islam, see *CEIsl*, 190f, Lapidus 1988/1995, 737f and Nagel 1990, 53ff. Iqbal was also President of the Muslim League and one of the major spokesmen for a Muslim homeland; Pakistan. After the partition of India Iqbal became probably the most prominent national figure of Pakistan.

> *any understanding of life and faith*—not only of Muslim
> life and faith, but of human life and faith—that I may have
> since attained, *owes something indelible to him* (113, my
> emphasis).

The general context of this lecture is, as mentioned above, his work with the problem of the 'relation of religious faith to intellectual belief, to conceptual formulation, to theology.' For Smith this matter is important both in respect of recognizing what kind of level one operates on by doing theology, and, on the other hand, on what level one is 'faith-ing.'[38]

The strategy of Smith is to stress the ambiguousness of faith and belief. Hence his theses:

(a) faith and belief are quite different, and

(b) believing is not what religious people do; it is not of ultimate significance; and it is not a classical religious category

Yet, what is his positive contribution, then? What is faith, for instance? Smith evades this question first by saying that 'it is easier to say what believing is, although it is much more important to know what faith is' (115). After that he makes 'faith' equivalent to the Arabic *iman*. Consequently, *iman*, as a matter of ultimate significance, should not be translated with 'belief', at least in its modern notion. As one may remember, one of his major arguments is that the meaning of 'believe' has changed from 'to have faith' to a quite different, modern meaning, which I will investigate in Smith's study in the following.[39]

Belief, Smith says, is in the modern sense connected to knowledge. Yet, Smith's interest is not how knowledge is understood logically or philosophically, but how it is used in ordinary language (116). According to him, the language of 'the man in the street' involves two meanings for knowledge:

(a) certitude; relation to inner conviction, and

(b) correctness; positive relation to objective facts, that is, in what one knows (117).

It is in this environment that 'believing' occurs, as a 'common-sense notion,' but it seems to Smith that it differs from knowing by involving one or both of two things:

(a') a lack of certitude

(b') an openness to the correctness or otherwise of what is believed.

Despite the fact that the latter believing-view of knowledge to

---

[38] As Smith describes the act of faith by a verbal form.

[39] Smith 1974/1981f, 116. This is primarily elaborated in *BH*.

some extent also includes the former common-sense understanding of knowledge, 'believing' becomes

> the concept by which we convey the fact that a view is held, without a decision as to its validity—explicitly without that decision (117).

Believing has therefore no pretensions to validity. Smith says, this being so, and the religious domain not differing from the ordinary/secular, 'small wonder that believing has become then the characterization *par excellence* for religious positions, in the modern world' (117f). It enables people to keep their religious belief though they are not fully sure about its correctness. It also enables religious people to integrate the fact that religious beliefs vary in the contemporary world. Also particular positions can be upheld, but at the cost of certitude. Lastly, it is only used, Smith argues, as an over-simplifying notion, in clear opposition to previous times.[40] This is most obvious as it 'leave[s] theoretically unresolved the question of its objective intellectual validity' (120). Both theologians and anthropologists should therefore be in need of more refined notions on a critical level. No wonder that Smith concludes that this notion is 'altogether foreign to the Qur'an.'[41] Hence, his thesis

> that in the Qur'an, the concept 'believe' (as a religious activity) does not occur (and does not occur for very good reasons) (120).

Consequently, any use of the concept in English translations of the Qur'an should be rendered as mistranslation, which of course is a severe attack that applies to most translations, if not all. One may ask: why this bold assessment? Smith's answer is that it is probably more obvious than it is radical, and it is doubtful whether it represents a novelty. The latter is demonstrated by an examination of the relation between the notions of 'knowledge' and 'believe' within the Qur'an. The results are as follows (121ff):

(1) Words for 'knowing' are frequent and emphatic (*'arafa* and especially *'alima*)

---

[40] Smith 1974/1981f, 119. Smith's thesis is that 'believing has become an apparently appropriate category for the modern world and *therefore* is not appropriate for other times and places.' In *FB* he adds to the identical sentence, that 'its seeming modern aptness is correlated with its not having been a classical religious category,' 37.

[41] Smith 1974/1981f, 120. He also maintains that it is foreign to the Bible, cf. his second lecture of the two Iqbal memorial lectures, see note 35, p. 106 above. Cf. also ch. III of *BH*.

(2) The presumably standard word for 'believing' in later Islamic theology (*i'taqada*, and its derivations) does not occur in the Qur'an, and in its medieval usage it starts to mean 'to bind oneself,' and only centuries later it means to believe intellectually.

Smith goes also the opposite way by asking: which terms in the Qur'an are translated by 'believe'? To two of these terms, he pays special attention: *amana* (with *iman* as verbal noun), and *zanna/yazunnu* ('to think/opine', 'to hold an opinion').

(3) Smith holds that the fundamental category on the manward side is faith, *iman*, which presupposes what he calls 'the fundamental concept in the Qur'an':

> that of God, presented as Creator, Sovereign, and Judge, powerful, demanding, succouring, majestic, laying upon humankind inescapable imperatives and offering us inexhaustible rewards (122).

Related to this, faith is

> the positive recognition and acceptance of the divine summons, the committing of oneself to the demands, and thus being led to the ultimate succour (*ibid.*).

Smith maintains that faith, therefore, is always an act of faith, due also to the fact that *iman* is a *masdar*; a verbal noun. As a presupposition to this 'act of faith', Smith sees the very fact of God's own 'self-disclosure' and the 'great drama of decision' made known to humankind with a 'resonant clarity and force' (*ibid.*).

Iman should also be seen in the light of the opposite reaction to the revelation of God: rejection, *jahada/kufr*. His point is that this rejection does not mean anything like 'not to believe', but rather 'haughtiness, arrogance, stubborn wilfulness'. This is therefore 'man's dramatic negative response to this spectacular divine initiative [that is, when God speaks out of his authority and compassion]' (123).

We have seen above in this chapter that faith was formally defined as 'self-commitment,' or simply *s'engager*—engagement.[42] He

---

[42] Smith is here dependent on Najm al-Din al-Taftazani, whom he calls 'perhaps my favorite *mutakallim*,' and his interpretation of the Persian notion of *giravidan*, *ibid.* 123f. Indirectly, Smith sees here a connection between Sufis and modern existentialists. See also note 51 below. Smith describes faith otherwise in a variety of contexts, see Hughes 1985, 342-347, who in his dissertation has made an appendix of a certain number of the descriptions found in some of Smith's major works (*FOM, ME, BH*, and *FB*).

also finds in the English 'amen' and the Arabic *amin* (cf. the Hebrew root *'-m-n*) a suggestive illustration of what it means to be 'a man of faith': a *mu'min* (124). Amen is the act whereby the congregation participates in what its leader says, 'incorporating themselves into his act, saying 'yes' to it.' By faith, therefore, the *mu'min* 'identifies himself with the communal and cosmic activity.'[43] A human who incorporates the opposite attitude is, however, a *mushrik*. According to Smith this term should not be translated into English as 'polytheist' though this might be a consequence of being *mushrik*. The right translation of the root of the word (*sh-r-k*) is 'to associate'.[44] The verbal noun, *shirk,* thus means 'associating other beings with God' (sc. which are not so). Given this meaning of *shirk,* it follows that a *mushrik*

> is not that man who simply believes in many gods; but, if one is to use the term 'believe' at all, it is the man who *perversely* believes in many gods. Or, more precisely ... 'to believe in more gods than there are' (124f).

However, to say 'I am a *mushrik*' is, according to Smith, a logical self-contradiction. It does not give a self-description of a belief that believes there is more than one god.[45] On the contrary, it analyses this belief 'from the point of view of those who reject it. It is a monotheist concept of a polytheist' (125).

Like Cragg, Smith also tries to present examples of what *mushrik* and *shirk* would currently mean. By giving attention to the fundamental difference in the origins of Islam of recognizing the existence of 'sticks and stones' on the one hand, but not worshipping them or treating them as divine on the other, Smith maintains that there is no doubt of the existence of money, devotion to advancement of careers, self-gratification, and so forth, but those who worship them are mistaken.

> in that they are associating them with God in ... their scheme of values, are consecrating[46] their life in part to them rather

---

[43] Smith stresses here, and elsewhere, that the *voluntary* element should not be overemphasized since Muslim writers differ on this point. Neither should the element of intellectual recognition be excluded, cf. *ibid.* 132 where a certain intellectual component of *amana* is conceded.

[44] This is the same meaning as Kenneth Cragg uses, cf. Chapter 5.4 below.

[45] Yet, Smith admits exceptions for a) the 'penitent Muslim' 'who was repudiating his former sin and blindness' and b) the 'mystic Muslim' 'who confessed in tears imperfection in his sincerity, pleading that his intellectual recognition of God's oneness was not matched in full purity by a total singleness of heart in his devotion,' *ibid.* 125.

[46] This use of *sacramental* language will be addressed in a later Chapter (Chapter 3.9).

than consecrating it solely to the only reality that is
worthwhile, worshipful, worthy our pursuit: namely, God
(125).

Consequently, both the person-of-faith (*mu'min*), the infidel (*kafir*) and
the associator (*mushrik*) have to be understood within a monotheistic
frame, that is, from the point of *al-Haqq*, the Truth. It applies to both the
'yes' and 'no' answers that the existence of God is not 'believed', but
presupposed.[47] The difference between believe and presuppose is
therefore 'crucial' to Smith (127). It is, furthermore, what one does with the
presupposed fact that makes every difference. In that respect being faithful
is quite different from believing or recognizing (128).

   (4) Let us then turn to the second of the Qur'anic terms that
Smith examines, and which by the time has been translated 'believe':
zanna, yazunnu, zannan. According to Smith, this is an illustrative
instance for 'the whole matter' (128ff).

   Smith maintains that the set of words means: 'to think something,
to form in the imagination an idea or opinion or assessment, to adjudge, to
conceive' (129). Moreover, the validity and correctness of the conception
is left open. Besides this neutral sense concerning 'the mundane world,'
which is in a minority (15-20 of 70 occurrences), the words may also
function as religious categories (49 or 50 of 70 times). In this case the
meaning is of 'men's having an opinion about God or His doings, but one
that is woefully and manifestly awry' (129). Hence, it designates a belief,
which is a wrong one. The term is therefore used in order to show 'the
absurdity or perversity of that view.' As such, it runs contrary to both
knowledge and faith.

   At this place Smith parallels what he sees as the Qur'anic view
with John Calvin's dichotomy between God's revelation and the 'arrant
absurdities of depraved human imagination' (130). The contrast between
zanna and *amana* is therefore 'stark.' The contrast is connected to two
differing approaches to knowledge, which coincide with what was
mentioned above: a) whereas faith (*iman*) is closely correlated to
knowledge in the Qur'an in the way that the person-of-faith accepts that
which he or she knows, b) the man of *zanna* opposes the same
knowledge.[48] In both cases knowledge comes first, given by God, but is
responded to differently. Whereas *zanna* means believe wrongly, Smith

---

[47] Smith 1974/1981f, 126. Cf. Smith's commentary on *Shahadah,* Chapter 3.5, and
   the Islamic Chapter in *FOM.*

[48] Smith 1974/1981f, 130f. Here, Smith gives several examples from the Qur'an
   where sentences are *structured* in a way that knowledge and *zanna* are established
   as alternatives.

hesitatingly says that faith means 'to believe rightly,' if at all it should be translated by 'believe'. Or, better, without any hesitation: the intellectual component in *amana* should be translated as *to recognize* or 'to become aware of the situation as it in fact is' (132). If so, faith runs contrary to the modern concept of 'believe' as well.

Smith sees this difference between *amana* and *zanna* as coinciding with the scheme anthropocentrism-theocentrism, which also makes him see 'faith' and 'believe' as distinctive alternatives (132f). 'Believe' in its modern sense is thus an anthropocentric concept, whereas the world of the Qur'an is theocentric 'not only as a whole, but in all its parts.' Smith finds this 'all very natural, very much to be expected ... since God knows what is right and what is wrong' (132). It was 'in order to salvage us from [our human epistemological bewilderments] that in this scripture He mercifully came to our rescue' (133).

We see here that the qur'anic view of Muslim reverence related to the alternatives of faith and modern believing are interpreted in distinctive Christian (Pauline?) language of salvation. Thus Smith indirectly establishes a linguistic as well as a factual correlation between the work of Christ in Christian doctrine on the one hand, and God's mercy as a verdict on 'human epistemological bewilderment' through the Qur'an, on the other. This relation seems to have been developed out of his Christian language and Calvin's perspective of anthropocentrism as opposed to theocentrism.[49]

On the other hand, it seems that he has learnt a lesson from his Qur'an studies that has bearing and interpretative impact upon Christian theology. A passage from another study[50] may illuminate this, related to his emphasis on theocentrism:

> one of the handful of what some would call 'mystical experiences' that I happen to have had ... was an ocean liner one evening en route to India, with a magnificent sunset transforming the distant horizon. I chanced to be undergoing some grave personal difficulties at that time, when suddenly my spirit was quieted by a verse from the Qur'an coming to me, as it were audibly over the broad expanse of the calm waters, in Arabic: *huwa al-kāfī*—'He is sufficient,' or more exactly, 'It is He who suffices.' Now quite obviously II Corinthians 12:9 might have served

---

[49] Cf. also his (partial) sympathy for Barth, Brunner, and others, in a similar respect, referred to at the beginning of Chapter 2.4.4.
[50] Smith 1992, 57f.

precisely the same purpose ... The fact is, however, that in
my case it was this verse from the Qur'an that arrived out of
the blue, to my vast surprise ... and left me with a rather
serene assurance of divine strengthening and support ... I
have sometimes wondered whether perchance my strong
theocentrism (which contrasts at times a whit starkly with
some of my fellow Christians' Christocentrism, or
fundamentalists' bibliocentrism) *may have something to
do—in part—with my having studied the Qur'an, and
Muslim theological and moral thought based upon it*, for
some decades and with some sensitivity. There is a great
deal in our Christian heritage ... especially in its pre-modern
eras, on which such theocentrism could and often has been
grounded... . Current Christocentrism is both modern and
heretic ... although it is strong (emphasis mine).

This point is also evident when he sums up his article on faith and belief
in the Qur'an by saying that whereas faith in classical Islam presupposed
belief it presupposes scepticism in modern times. This is equally valid for
Christians, according to Smith. And, moreover, at the level of faith,
Christians and Muslims differ from each other 'conceivably less that one
might imagine' (134). At this point Smith establishes the strongest
systematic relation between Muslims and Christians. This relation on the
level of faith, enabled by a particular, definitive view of transcendence,
seems to be dependent upon both Smith's Christian self-understanding
and his Islam-interpretation.

3.7 Faith, Truth and Activist Sincerity: Iman as Tasdiq

In an encounter with Taftazani's[51] theological commentary on Nasafi's[52]
statement on faith *('Aqa'id)*, Smith found one of 'the ten books that have

---

[51] Al-Taftazani (AH 722-791?/1322-1389 CE), born in Taftazan in Khorasan,
primarily known for his breadth and quality of scholarship, spanning from rhetoric
to Qur'anic exegesis. Taftazani's major work is exactly the one that Smith refers
to; his commentary on the creed on Islam of al-Nasafi, *EncRel(E)*, Vol. 14, 244.
See also note 42 above.

[52] Abu Hafs Umar Nadim al-Din al-Maturidi al-Nasafi (d. AH 537/1142 CE), jurist
and theologian, mostly known for his abridged and catechism-like creed *(Aqa'id)*
(according to the scholastic method used at that time). The creed became well
known through the commentaries on it, *EI*, 7:968f, 'al-Nasafi' (by A.J. Wensick).

changed [my] life.'[53] Through a review of a translation of Nasafi's commentary he came to recognize Taftazani as to 'be numbered among my friends' (135). What especially came to impact him was the fact that he found something 'important, insightful and even 'true': humanly true' in the work of Taftazani, although he did not 'believe' his theology (*ibid.*). Significantly for the present study, we therefore find that the Christian, Reformed theologian Smith finds something 'true' in the humane sense of the word in a commentary of a Muslim on a Muslim statement of Muslim faith. More generally, through his entire encounter with Muslim theology, *kalam*, especially at McGill and Harvard,[54] Smith seems not merely to have found true parts, but

> a new apprehension of what theology, medieval or whenever, Islamic or Christian or whatever, at heart consists in: what theology as such, what human theologizing, has fundamentally been (and may yet become)—and indeed, human conceptualizing (136).

This 'new apprehension' has been partly reached in the aforementioned conclusion that faith, *iman,* has been translated wrongly by 'believe'. It seems that this conclusion was partly attained by a study of the translation of Taftazani's commentary from the 14th century.[55] As Smith states it: 'It [i.e. the translation by 'believe'] did *not* finally *cohere* with what Taftazani was saying about [*iman*]' (136, emphasis mine). Let us therefore look at how this general finding of incoherence influenced his understanding of theology.

Smith starts by designating three meanings of *iman* held by Muslims (137):
  (a) as doing something
  (b) as saying something
  (c) as an inner act
Whereas only some Muslims hold each of the two former opinions, the third one is held by most. Smith's concern here is however

---

[53] Smith 1971/1981g, 135. Originally a book review, this was later delivered at a conference in honour of Harry A. Wolfson, Professor Emeritus at Harvard, and printed 'probably' (*ibid.* 136f) for the first time as a part of *UI*. The study appears later in various, hardly altered, versions, e.g. 1974a and *FB*. Subsequent parenthetical remarks refer to the former study.
[54] Cf. the Biography and References for this period.
[55] Smith contends that his findings in this translation, compared with the original work of Taftazani, impacted on what later became two of his major historio-conceptual works: *BH* and *FB*.

the last one, that is, faith, *iman,* and its relation to *tasdiq.*[56] Smith sees this as a 'subtle, complex, and important' matter (137), which he aims to approach by asking what the meaning of *tasdiq* really is to be understood as.

His thesis is that in addition to the philosophical (*falsafah*) meaning of the notion (that is, making a judgement), there is one in *kalam* that has another sense. This latter theological sense has, according to Smith, important, even decisive, bearing on the 'major formula' in *kalam: al-iman huwa al-tasdiq* (138), which linguistically links *iman* and *tasdiq.* Smith sees, however, the quest for the meaning of faith and *tasdiq* as 'a delicate and problematic affair' and warns, as he often does, against attempts to define faith, either in a general or a particular sense (138f). Yet, Smith himself takes faith as 'a virtually universal human quality or characteristic' as a point of departure. By this, one may say that faith gains a heuristic and formal definition.[57] As such, faith appears at least without a defined content. In his elaboration on the meaning of *tasdiq,* which in the formula above serves as the predicate of *iman,* he hopes to gain an answer to what the meaning of *iman* 'inherently is' (141).

A part of this warning about definitions is that concepts that make an understanding of *iman* and *tasdiq* available are themselves particular, and therefore limited (139). Interestingly, Smith gives attention to the concept of 'faith'. He maintains that there are two currents that the diverse connotations of this notion derive from. These are: a) the Christian current, based on the New Testament and incorporating the tradition of ancient Israel as well as much of the Greek thought, and b) the objective-critical and academic current, especially since the Enlightenment, that 'considers faith from the outside, and more recently that observes it, generically but passively, in a wide variety of forms across the world' (139). Smith says:

> The Islamic concept of faith, classically, is and must be formally and in principle different from both these (*ibid.*).

One should at this point have in mind that Smith is operating on a conceptual level. He is speaking of the concept of faith, and concedes therefore differences between the Christian, objective-critical, and the Islamic concepts of faith. A pertinent question that may be raised in the light of the approach and thesis of our study, and which certainly resonates with what has hitherto been explored in Smith's conceptual studies, is. How far-reaching are these differences to be conceived? Let us answer

---

[56] *Tasdiq* is in *CQur* translated 'confirmation; accepting as true; belief,' 1176.

[57] Cf. how 'personal faith' and 'cumulative tradition' were introduced in *ME* for methodological and heuristical reasons.

this by reconstructing Smith's conception of *iman* and *tasdiq* in classical Islamic *kalam*.

Smith's strategy is to suggest that *iman* should be translated by 'faith', and takes this as a point of departure for his understanding of the predicate of *iman* in the formula: *tasdiq*. By putting things thus, he keeps *iman* open for a variety of interpretations, though he suggests his own definition to be based on classical Islamic writings. Smith's postulate is that 'none of us adequately understands 'faith', either in general or in the particular Islamic case' (140). This corresponds to the intimate relation between 'faith' and his conception of 'transcendence' in the range of its meanings.[58]

What then about *tasdiq*? Smith seems to answer this by drawing the attention to what kind of truth one employs by translating *tasdiq* (142ff). In translating it by 'belief' one renders it as 'holding to be true', corresponding more or less with logicians in classical Arabic, Greek thought and the modern notion of 'believing'. However, the *kalam* tradition requires more of the concept. Smith, therefore, elaborates the term first by interpreting it within the context of 'a comprehensive Islamic view of truth.' Then, he tests his understanding of *tasdiq* within a general Islamic context of truth by confronting specific passages of *kalam* writing that, according to him, illustrate and confirm his interpretation.

Smith starts his development of an interpretation within the Islamic conception of truth by recalling a cluster of three verbs 'which crystallized Muslim's concepts on this mighty question' (142). These are *haqqa*, *sadaqa*, and *sahha*.

(a) *Haqqa* is related to both 'true' and 'real' (cf. Lat. *verus*, Skt. *satyam*). To modern people, Smith asserts, these two meanings may seem to diverge.[59] Against this opinion, Smith maintains that on the contrary there used to be 'a single truth-reality,' that is, where what was true was real (143). This is explicated by his criticism of the opinion that 'things are just there,' and that it is only propositions about them that judge them as true or false. Smith, however, maintains that things can be true 'in and of themselves by dint of metaphysical or cosmic status.' Hence *haqq* is a denotation *par excellence* of God, but also of other things that are 'real, genuine, [and] authentic.' It follows from this that *haqq* is 'truth in the sense of real, with or without a capital R' (143). One might call this pre-suppositional truth.

---

[58] See Chapter 2 *passim*. See also how Smith here uses transcendence-language about 'faith' and the (impossibility of a full) apprehension of it: 'beyond our intellectual apprehension', 'towards a partial clarification of which we can hope'.

[59] Cf. *BH*.

(b) *Sadaqa* refers to 'truth of persons' (143). It may involve truth both to oneself and to others, as well as to the 'objective situation' with which one is dealing (144). The relation between this personalist sense of truth and propositional truth is that the latter is subordinated to the former (cf. immediately below). Interestingly, Smith gives attention to the fact that the English language, different from the Arabic, lacks a personalized concept of truth. It contains words for the opposite: to be a liar (cf. Arab. *kadhiba*), but not for the person who maintains or tells the truth (cf. Arab. *sidq*). This personalist notion of truth is central to Smith's entire argument.

(c) The third root for truth in Arabic, *sahha,* designates what is 'sound' and 'appropriate'. This has been a minor notion of truth in Islamic life and is hardly interesting for the development of Smith's argument. The root does not even occur in the Qur'an.

Hence, it is the former two that are at stake in the Islamic vision, that is, humankind's 'dramatic freedom and moral choice, in a world where decisions matter' (145). In this drama one has to choose between *haqq* and *batil*, the 'real' and the 'phoney', and between being a *sidq/sadiq* or a *kadhib*. The notion of truth is primarily a notion of the *true person.* Smith therefore admits that these conceptions of truth, the realist and personalist, are 'highly moralistic' and that human destiny and quality are at stake with them (145). This is 'mightily' reverberated in the Qur'an represented by both *haqqa* and *sadaqa*.

Smith continues by concentrating on different forms of the second verb for truth, *sadaqa,* first in its first form *(qatala[60]): sadaqa, yasduqu* and *sidqun.* For Muslims, he contends, this term 'formulates a cosmic category, constituting one of the basic points of reference in relation to which human life and society take on meaning in the Islamic complex' (146). If Smith is right, he is of course pursuing one of the fundamentals in the Islamic tradition, nothing but a 'cosmic category.' Let us therefore examine more closely how he determines this category.

First, Smith searches out the meaning of the term by consulting Arabic dictionaries. There, he finds that the word in almost every case is put together with *kadhiba*. Furthermore, *sadaqa* and *kadhiba* are connected to speech in a way that two things have to be in conformity with each other, that is: a) that which is in the speaker's mind, has to conform with b) what is actually the case. Thus, true speech has both an inner side (speaker's intention) and an *outer side* (correspondence to reality). Interestingly, this outer side of *sadaqa* may also, in cases where

---

[60] Qur'anic Arabic like the Hebrew Bible uses several forms of each verb (ten forms are most frequently used). The first two of these forms (*qatala, qattala,* depending upon which verbal root one bases the verb inflection) are of especial interest here.

the future is referred to, require conformity between intention and subsequent deeds. Thus:

> *Sidq* is that quality by which a person speaks or acts with
> a combination of inner integrity and objective overt
> appropriateness (147f).

In this, the person aligns to reality. This *is* truth in as much as both 'halves' become appropriate to each other, which is enabled by human behaviour (148).

> Human behaviour ... is the nexus between man's inner life
> and the surrounding world. Truth at the personalist level is
> that quality by which both halves of that relationship are
> chaste and appropriate—are true.

These observations are enhanced by his consideration of the second form of *sadaqa (saddaqa, yusaddiqu* including the *masdar tasdiqun*), which forms 'an intricate causative[61] or double transitive of wide potentiality' (148). In this material he again finds[62] that the standard implication is 'strongly one of objective truth as well of sincerity,' which makes Smith see *tasdiq* as 'a cosmic human quality' (149). Consequently the relevant Arabic terms cannot be translated by 'believe' because this may also be used in cases where falseness is presumed. Based on linguistic reasons, as well as his examination of 'ordinary language,' Smith therefore summarizes his findings in medieval Arabic dictionaries thus:

> *Tasdiq* is to recognize a truth, to appropriate it, to affirm it,
> to confirm it, to actualize it. And the truth, in each case, is
> personalist and sincere (150).

---

[61] The *taf'il/qattala* forms, that is, the second forms, are formed by doubling the middle consonant; generally intensive and causative in meaning, *CQur*, xxvii.

[62] Smith finds four meanings related to this verb form: (a) 'To regard as true' (148f). Primary object, he says, can be either a person (e.g. 'He held him to be a speaker of truth') or sentence (e.g. 'He held it to be spoken truly'). But for both cases the presupposition is that 'he' trusted the *person* involved as speaker. (b) 'He *found* him to be a speaker of truth' (150). The aspect of subsequent reason and experience is included in this form. (c) 'He *proved* him to be a speaker of truth' (150). In this form *tasdiq* has become the term for scientific experimental verification. (d) 'He who validates what he says in what he does'. This is the more *deliberate* form of *tasdiq*. Truth is a consequence of conformity between speech/conviction and deeds, as pointed out above.

Again, truth, is in the end conceived as a (personalist) moral matter, or even more precisely: a virtue-oriented moral matter.[63] In this, his notion of truth in form of 'true speech' supports his conclusion: that such true-ness has to make both the intention of the speech cohere with its correspondence to reality. Consequently, truth cannot be true if it does not correspond to things as they really are. One might say: coherence must involve correspondence. Yet, how is the 'surrounding world' to be conceived more precisely? If there is some notion of coherence embedded in his perception of human behaviour and speech as 'nexus' between intention and reality, what is this coherence more precisely? Is it for example possible to say something about this coherence that enables it to assess whether things belong within or without the coherence? Or are his statements about coherence only to be recognized as formal presuppositions that are never substantiated more thoroughly. I will return to these questions later.

What about the corresponding theological *(kalam)* statements and interpretations of this linguistic usage? Smith seems to start with the very conclusion about what 'men of religion' (that is, theologians in classical *kalam*) thought when they placed *tasdiq* as a predicate to *iman* (cf. the *kalam* 'major formula' above). That is:

Faith is doing or making or activating truth: doing personal truth, or making truth personal (151).

If *iman* and *tasdiq* are thus linked (subject-predicate) and understood, some preliminary linguistic implications may be as follows:

(a) That faith is recognition of divine truth at a personal level (151). Hence, 'what is cosmically true come true on earth—the actualization of truth.' If conceived thus, this becomes a process of inner appropriation of what 'God—or Reality—intends for man.'

(b) That faith is the discovery of (the deeper) truth of 'the Islamic injunctions.' This sense is personal but also involves a 'more mystical' process of verification, where the 'Islamic injunctions ... become true [by living them out].'

(c) That faith is the ability to trust, and to act in terms of what one knows to be true. Faith is more than knowledge; it is a response to truth.

These definitions of faith are what Smith calls 'not bad definitions of faith.' Yet, they are not definitions of *Islamic* faith. They are 'Islamic definitions of human faith.' 'Islamic' is only an adjective to the noun,

---

[63] Cf. e.g. his use of 'moral integrity', *ibid.* 149.

which, after all, counts, faith. Phrased differently: faith is generic, whereby Islam is particular and contingent. Or, as Smith poses it:

> At issue here is not the content of faith but its form, not its object but its nature; in question is not what is true, but what one does with what is true (152).

Hence, it is the form and (inner) nature of humankind's adequate response to the intentions of God or Reality that makes 'the human quality of faith.' Regarding the 'particulars' of the Islamic tradition, Smith makes a point of the 'Islamic epistemological point,' that is, that Muslims are taught about the final truth through God's disclosure in the Qur'an, has had little impact on the theological discussions of faith in classical Islamic *kalam*. He uses this therefore as a premise for the conclusion that Islamic conceptions of faith are almost interchangeable with Christian discussion on the subject, and to 'some degree' with humanist discussions (152). Smith's point is not to make faith a common monolithic thing, but to maintain that a preoccupation with the 'object' of faith will inevitably distract people from exploring either the similarities or the divergences between various conceptions of faith.

Smith draws the attention to two of these different 'conceptions of faith,' which relate to: a) the fact that the Islamic sense of clarity (outside Sufi-circles) is much more fundamental than in Christian traditions, and b) that the Islamic orientation has been much more moralist and practical, the revelation being God's will understood as an imperative, whereas revelation in the Christian case is of a person. Let us first consider his first claim about clarity (and knowledge).

(a) Faith related to the Islamic notion of clarity, *mubin*, has as a consequence that faith as response to divine initiative happens on the basis of a God who 'has acted to make quite manifest to men and women what He would have them know' (153). Christian's notions of faith imply, according to Smith, that faith 'is to believe, not yet to know' (*ibid.*).[64] According to Smith, therefore, and related to knowledge, the conception of faith differs significantly. As Smith puts it: 'For Muslims ... faith is on the other side of knowledge; not on this side of it.'[65]

---

[64] This statement about the Christian notion of knowledge is of course quite simplistic and leaves out significant traditions that make *certainty* (e.g. of faith) and *clarity* (e.g. of Scripture) important if not central.

[65] This notion of 'the other side of' implies an historical critique of the position that faith is knowledge. According to Smith, the order of faith and knowledge in *kalam* is opinion/knowledge/faith or better: opinion/God's acting/knowledge/faith, whereas the order within the Christian scholastic thought was opinion/faith/knowledge,

The fact that faith in Islamic *kalam* is more than knowledge has its evident argument in the fact that *kufr*, the negative correlative to *iman*, like *iman,* presupposes knowledge though it subsequently rejects it (154f). Discussions of faith in *kalam* presuppose both that God is acting, and that one has knowledge about it, before the dramatic question of whether human beings will accept (*iman*) or reject (*kufr*). The person who accepts God's initiative is a person of faith. He knows, but faith is even more. This 'more', Smith says, is *tasdiq*.

Smith therefore asks what the meaning of *tasdiq* might be in the *kalam* context. An answer to this is given as he repeats the elaboration of his previous understanding of truth:

> [*Tasdiq* lies] clearly ... in the realm of *activist sincerity* (156, emphasis mine).

Hence, 'the more of faith' lies in both the personal commitment to truth and the 'operationalist' confirmation and actualization of it. In this sense also God is called a *mu'min* (by al-Baghdadi). God is 'faithful' because he effectuates his promises by *tasdiq*. Therefore, *tasdiq* should not be rendered 'believe'. Whereas 'believe' allows a lack of certitude and correctness, *tasdiq* means 'to recognize a truth and to existensialize[66] it' (156).

(b) This corresponds to the second characteristic of Muslim notions of faith: the moralist or practical. Moreover, the combination of the clarity and moralist lies in the fact that the knowledge that a Muslim presupposes, and responds to, is moral truth (157f). To this moral truth it belongs a moral life, which exceeds 'knowledge about'. That which brings oneself to a commitment to this truth is the quality of *tasdiq*, which equals faith. *Tasdiq*, *amana* and *saddaqa* should hence be expressed in the same breath (159).

In a very telling and fine quotation Smith lets al-Kastali[67] have 'one of the most compelling expositions' of the matter:

---

ibid. 154. Smith also quotes Taftazani, whom he paraphrases: 'Man is required to have faith in those things that are known,' *ibid.* What is immediately clear is that Smith wants to highlight the very difference between believing something in the modern sense, where knowledge is negatively presupposed and simultaneously excluded, and the Islamic (and earlier: Christian, and others) notion of faith which takes for granted certain knowledge about what could be called 'fundamentals', a cosmic framework, and so on.

[66] 'Existensializing' is important to Smith. He combines again this term with what Taftazani does when he lacks proper notions to describe *tasdiq*, that is, He borrows a Persian term—*giravidan* (157), which means exactly the same as *s'engager* as they stem etymologically from the same words. Cf. also note 42 above.

[67] This person remains unknown to me despite several attempts to gain information about him from various reference works.

> *Al-tasdiq* does not mean knowing the truth ... no, it is rather
> a yielding to what is known and a letting oneself be led by
> it, and the soul's being quiet and at peace with it and its
> accepting it, setting aside recalcitrance and stubbornness,
> and construing one's actions in accordance with it (158).

The fundamental consequence of this for a Muslim is the very difference between recognizing something *as* divine revelation on the one hand, and recognizing divine revelation as authoritative, for oneself, personally.[68] Without this difference in mind, neither *tasdiq* nor *iman* is understandable, nor is the concern of Smith for *tasdiq*. The parenthetical comment by Smith on the quotation of al-Kastali is that it is a beautiful passage 'that Christian theology could be happy and proud to take over word for word ...' How such a statement is possible is a question Smith already has answered and which he pithily answers indirectly at the end of the article:

> Faith, then, was understood by classical Muslims not in
> terms alien to modern men, nor in terms parallel to but never
> converging with other communities' involvement, but rather
> in ways deeply discerning and universally human ... *Kalam*
> is a statement within, not about, their Weltanschauung;
> and to that statement the concept of *tasdiq* could and did
> make an impressive and significant contribution (160).

Thus, the meaning of *tasdiq* is *Islamic* only as far as it is a human matter. It is not a matter of an outsider assessing the meaning of the faith of Muslims. But, through the Islamic tradition, here represented by *kalam*, the universally human matter, faith, might be reached by particular means (for example *tasdiq)*. Hence,

> the question is not what one believes, but what one does
> with what one believes or recognizes as true. At issue, in
> the matter of faith, is what kind of person one is (161).

If we sum up, Smith can be said to maintain two kinds of truth: a) 'Objective truth,' that is, as things are as facts, b) personal morality and integrity. It is the *convergence* between these two that seems to be his major concern.[69]

---

[68] Smith 1971/1981g, 159. This is Smith's own exegesis of a statement in the commentary of al-Nasafi *(al-'Aqa'id,* see note 52 above). On p. 160 he asks himself whether he reads too much into the text (eisegesis!), but answers by bringing evidence from Taftazani's comment on the actual passage.

[69] See also Smith 1974a, 36.

In this the former seems to play a *preparatory* role for the latter, which consummates truth by making it 'truth for me': faith. We may probably say that the coherence of faith exceeds the coherence of the observable facts because it presupposes the latter as an element of the former.[70] In one sense, this is Smith's answer to my question about what kind of coherence he is using. Yet, his suggestion about a return to a (pre-modern) personal, single truth-reality conveys a tension between the two. This is quite obvious when he refrains from paying attention to differences of knowledge, truth, revelation, and so forth, which he certainly indicates between Muslim and Christian traditions, and which normally are considered important. One may also ask whether this is enabled by an undue subordination of 'objective truth' (facts) to 'truth for me' (personal appropriation), despite his insistence on the integration of the two? If so, does he at the same time run the danger of divorcing faith from history and 'reality,' which in the end must make these insignificant, and faith irrational? A more thorough examination of these and further questions belongs to a later chapter (Chapter 7) where Smith's writings will be assessed in regard to his total position, and not only single studies. However, clues to answers will be found in the next two subsections.

Lastly, let me only refer to a direct statement about the relevance of this Islamic study for Smith himself. In his Islamic chapter in *Faith and Belief*, which also draws on this article, Smith relates his investigation of faith in Islamic theology (*kalam*) to the question of self-understanding, which he sees as the 'acute ... primary question of today' (*FB*, 50). Smith contends that in the classical Islamic position (*FB*, 48f), faith is understood as

a. a personal relationship to truth and goodness,
b. an inward appropriation of objectively valid truth, and
c. self-engagement with truth.

Significantly, he claims that this understanding helped him when he was confronted with the present challenges of wrestling with 'faith in a modern form, and specifically ... the question of faith and belief' (*FB*, 50). Hence his Islamic studies have obviously served as premises for his self-understanding within a context of religious diversity. The suggested

---

[70] In Smith 1974a ('A Human View of Truth,' which starts with a reprint of Smith's study of *tasdiq* in Smith 1971/1981g) Smith makes this a reasonable conclusion. With direct invitation to 'amoral' and 'impersonal' (note the constellation of pairs!) systems of conceptualization to comprehend the world of man, Smith implicitly qualifies the relation between coherence, consistence and correspondence: 'For the conceptual systems that we adopt do themselves, in their entirety, like individual statements within them, have to be related to the world in which we live, and not merely to be internally consistent', 38f. Coherence should therefore be tested in regard to how one is able to incorporate new data.

corporate critical self-understanding is primarily that we should know the difference between the final religious category (faith, response) and the self-consciousness of forms and systems of beliefs. This difference resembles the previous subsection, that is, the difference between 'anthropogenetic' and 'divine.'[71]

3.8 The Truth of the Qur'an as its Function for Muslims

It is of course impossible to comprehend the systematic relation between Christian theology and Islam without giving sufficient attention to the delicate issue of the Qur'an. Below, I will show how certain elements within this field illuminate not only Smith's view of truth (cf. the previous subsection) but also of faith. This is especially the case when Smith raises major 'historical' questions regarding the interpretation of the Qur'an in particular, and scriptures in general. These questions are:

1. What is the 'true meaning' of the Qur'an?

2. Can the Qur'an be called 'the Word of God'? And if so, how?

The first question is handled in his 'scriptureology', that is, his investigations of various 'scripturalizing processes' in *What is Scripture?* (*WS*) from 1993.[72] The latter question is tentatively pondered in an article from 1967.[73]

Since the former study can be said to propose a general theory of scripture, whereas the latter develops one particular theological issue, I choose to start with the former and then continue with the latter, despite their opposite chronological order. This will give both a more coherent account as well as a more continuous development into the next subsection.

The very purpose of *WS* is to develop a *general* theory of 'scripture'.[74] The aims include:

—To understand 'the matter' in general,

—To 'explain other cases,' that is, to recognize and interpret

---

[71] *FB*, 52.

[72] Smith's chapter on the Qur'an, 'The True Meaning of Scripture: the Qur'an as Example' (ch. 4), is a reprint of Smith 1980a, with only minor adaptations. The main argument can also be found in Smith 1976a where Smith refers to the Qur'an as a particular example from a forthcoming general theory of scripture, though the main subject is the options for studying the Bible within the (then new) departments of religion.

[73] Smith 1967/1981p. First held as one of the Taylor Lectures at Yale Divinity School for 1963 at the time when his classic (*ME*) was launched.

[74] See especially *WS*, 214ff. Subsequent parenthetical references refer to *WS*.

how other people, that do not share one's position or tradition, be it religious or not, relate to their own scriptures, and

—To consider 'the human involvement with [the various texts/scriptures]' (ix).

Smith's general suggestion, which comprises all the points made above, is that *scripture is a human activity* (18). One will soon realize how this relates to his understanding of faith. This 'programme' also sets out to approach the *true* meaning of scripture. In fact, this is what Smith holds to be his fundamental concern (65). In this respect, the dependence of the general upon the particular is evident. Consequently, his attempt to 'apprehend as nearly as we may truth about scripture generally,' entails therefore that *parts* of this truth are 'growing out of our treatment of specific cases' (*ibid.*). One of these cases is the case of the Qur'an.

In general, the people for whom the Qur'an has been recognized as scripture may be divided into two groups: a) Muslims, and b) the observers whom at least recognize it as scripture for Muslims. Smith asks both groups for a 'reconsideration interlacing scriptural and historical,' which 'may prove helpful in illuminating our generic question' (66).

Smith suggests boldly that within the variety of interpretations of passages of Muslim scripture, both internally (Muslim schools of exegesis) and externally (the Western scholarly world), 'none of them are any longer convincing.' The time has come for 'a significantly new orientation' (67). However, as the original title of the chapter indicates ('The True Meaning of Scripture: An Empirical Historian's Nonreductionist Interpretation of the Qur'an'[75]), Smith's concern is to 'enhance, rather than to reduce.' Therefore, he maintains, 'the most promising solution is one that is *continuous with each of the careful yet partial theses* that have been advanced thus far, and *subsumes* most of them, but *moves beyond* all' (67, my emphases).

This language is carefully chosen and provides an overt clue to his methodological arrangement of particulars and generals. Keywords for this 'strategy' are: *continuity*, *integration* and *transcendence*. Whereas he on the one hand gives attention to 'previous attempts' by Muslim exegesis or Western historical-critical reading of the Qur'an, he makes it clear, on the other hand, that he aims at *integration* into a superior perspective, which *transcends* ('beyond') traditional ways of handling the Qur'an.

Smith also gives attention to what he recognizes as 'observed data' of historical nature. He maintains that these data resonate with the results of various other studies of the religious meaning within and across

---

[75] = Smith 1980a.

religious traditions, and are, among others (67-69):

(a) That the Qur'an has meant many different things to many different people at different times and places. This does not, however, rule out the possibility that the people involved with it have been 'in touch with a reality transcending history.'

(b) Also Smith's study implies a participation in the historical process of the Qur'an.

(c) The great step today beyond a mere historical consciousness, is to acquire historical self-consciousness. Smith describes this in a parenthesis as 'historical appreciation'.[76]

Regarding the Muslims, Smith makes a starting point their presupposition that the Qur'an *is* the word of God (68f). Any disagreement with them on that has to be rendered a 'naive error' because one has to recognize the Qur'an as scripture before one can understand it as this. However, how this contention may be interpreted is in the next turn instantly limited, and even neutralized, by Smith's explanation that this contention should be taken in its human meaning, not in its cosmic, which depends on a distinction between human/mundane and cosmic truth.[77] Nevertheless, Smith's point is that the Qur'an is not any book whatever; it is scripture.

This point seems to be rather pragmatic. What matters, according to Smith, is only whether a book is treated as divine, not whether it *de facto* is. His view of function, form and role seems to be a major concern throughout this chapter.[78] Interestingly, this view is connected to the work of the Spirit,[79] much as it correlates to the role of Jesus Christ in the 'Christian pattern'.[80] This pragmatic concern relates however to his general thesis: that 'scripture is a major matter in human affairs' (69). Consequently, this matter invites not only theologians to careful investigation, but also historians.

Given this acknowledgement of the Qur'an, Smith continues in identifying the content of 'the Qur'an as the word of God'. As an historian

---

[76] Regarding 'appreciation', which is a significant hermeneutical term in *FOM*, see my examination in Chapter 2.3.

[77] Regarding this distinction, cf. Chapter, 2.5.1, 2.6.3, 3.5 and 3.7 above, *passim.*

[78] *WS*, 71, 74, 81, and Smith 1992, 61. See also Smith 1976a, where 'the basic issue' is identified as 'scripture as religious form' (45).

[79] 'It has become increasingly evident to careful observation and to serious reflection that what matters in religious life is not the external visible forms through which the spiritual is mediated, so much as the *role* that these play—that these *enable the Spirit* to play—in the personalities, and living, of those affected,' *WS*, 58, my emphasis.

[80] Smith 1976a, 45, a parenthetical remark, which is elaborated in Smith 1959/1981m, cf. Chapter 2.9.

he makes the following findings (70):

—For Muslims, the Qur'an has been received as the *ipsissima verba* of God Himself

—Hence the Qur'an represents the eternal breaking into time; the unknowable disclosed; the transcendent entering history and remaining here; the divine has become apparent

—To memorize or to quote the Qur'an means to enter into some sort of communion with ultimate reality, which he later compares with the Christian Eucharist[81]

—To obey the Qur'an is to leave the purely natural and to enter upon the realm where the mundane and the transcendent meet, which he compares with 'the almost universal human awareness, formalized especially in the Semitic consciousness,' where 'the moral imperative, righteousness, mediates to us something higher, more ultimate.'

In my opinion, this is a very important section in Smith's chapter on the Qur'an. Here, Smith deliberately chooses revelational, eucharistic/ mystical, transcendent, and perhaps also incarnational language, distinctively informed by the Christian tradition. This seems therefore at first sight to stand in some tension against an historian's report about Muslims' reverence of the Qur'an and their interpretation of its meaning. At least, this makes it obvious that Smith's religious formation forms his perception of Islam, as far as the meaning and function of the Qur'an is concerned. One may conclude that his general theory of scriptures is not merely an induced product of particulars, but just as much his own interpretation of particulars other than his own, at least in the case of Islam, distinctively dependent on his Christian perspective.

Nevertheless, the impact of the Qur'an upon the Muslims is regarded as considerable:

> The whole of Islamic history might in some ways be regarded as at least ideally an elaboration and implementing of its [i.e. the Qur'anic] meaning—however limited by human failing (70).

Regarding the latter part of this sentence ('however limited by human failing'), Smith sees in the Islamic history an 'on-going interplay between human and mundane distractions, on the one hand, and on the other the corporate Muslim attempt to work out in practice the meaning of the divine word' (71). An example of the latter is the diversity and on-going production of exegetical commentaries (*tafsir*) on the Qur'an (*ibid.*). To

---

[81] Cf. Smith 1959/1981m, 244f.

Smith, this indicates a certain inadequacy of previous expositions. Or stated differently: that every Muslim in any verse of the Qur'an 'sees and feels in that verse something that is surely far from simple' (*ibid.*). However, what Smith sees Muslims as asking for, given this fact, is nothing less than the 'best possible interpretation that comes to you or that you can think up' (72), in the sense of: 'what in your judgement is the closest to what is good and true absolutely, cosmically' (73). A due recognition of this would demand of any historian an openness towards the human perception of the cosmic true and absolute.

Based on this, Smith tries to figure out a view of how different pressures that have existed and still exist within the Islamic world function in mutual relation with what they consider as ideal. These 'pressures, choices, social structures, distractions' are constructive and dynamic as long as they preserve the highest and the best of the particular people. However, a critical situation may take place if

> a symbol system begins to wane, and presently collapses, when its symbols prove no longer capable of receiving and holding and activating the highest and best that a given people can imagine (74)

Thus, Smith seems to presuppose a thesis that a symbol-system is dependent upon plausibility, that is, its symbols must prove meaningful, helpful, prosperous, and so on, for people who use and feel allegiance to them. Consequently, if thus the gap between ideals and life-reality becomes too wide or unfathomable, the symbol-system, *in casu* the meaning of the Qur'an, becomes inaccessible and loses any power of persuasion. Because Smith holds that the Qur'an has been the medium of interpretation of various pressures of life in the Islamic instance, the function of the Qur'an as establishing coherence in the life and world of Muslims becomes a major theme.[82] He even asserts this to be a matter of competition between, and modification of previous interpretations and opinions. We have seen how the issue of coherence has been a theme in Smith's writings already. It does, however, seem that Smith does not make the interreligious issue a theme in this respect. His notion of coherence here relates to the Islamic tradition and community, which of course is considerably diverse and multifaceted. A larger view of coherence may be seen below.

Yet, as he maintains this to be the Muslim view, his main opponents become those who have not recognized the Muslim scripture in this manner, namely: the Western academics. His criticism of them is

---

[82] *WS*, 75. He also maintains that the Islamic movement has been 'the most systematic, the most coherent' of all major religious movements in human history, *ibid.*

simultaneously to be seen as a theoretical support of his general suggestion of scripture as a human activity. Smith's concerns in this respect divide into three subjects: the view of history, religion and language (78).

Let us start with his criticism of Western historians' approach to the Qur'an. Smith begins with an attack on 'the Muhammad theory of the Qur'an': that Muhammad was the author of it and that the task has been to reconstruct the process of producing the Qur'an (77f). Given this view, the meaning of the Qur'an is confined to the historical meaning of it at the time in the history when it originated. Against this view, Smith asserts that (79f):[83]

1. History is a process forwards. History is something that significantly 'on-goes.'

2. Synthesis, integration and effects are more important than an analytic outlook.

3. An historian, therefore, should make intelligible this process 'by which those disparate items from here and there were at a given moment creatively put together, to constitute something new.'

4. Lastly, also the historical criticisms of the Qur'an have to be understood historically within 'a more informed awareness and a more cosmopolitan vision' (82).

Regarding the Qur'an, Smith consequently states that:

> One has hardly explained the Qur'an if one explains ... what went *into it*, but does so in a way that neglects, that leaves uninterpreted, even incomprehensible, perhaps even unnoticed, what came *out of it* and for fourteen centuries has continued to come out of it (80, emphasis mine).

An adequate understanding of the Qur'an should therefore recognize its 'formative, dominating, liberating, spectacular [role]—in the lives of millions of people' (81).[84] Thus, this scripture

> has shown itself capable of serving men as a form through which they have been able (have been enabled) to deal with the problems of their lives, to confront creatively a series of varied contexts ... . He is a feeble and sorry historian who underestimates—underperceives the power of symbols in human life, or the power of a scripture to function symbolically and as an organized battery of symbols.[85]

---

[83] See also Smith 1976a, 47f.
[84] See also Smith 1976a, 45.
[85] Smith 1976a, 47.

Secondly, the misinterpretation of the Qur'an by Western scholars depends also on a certain view of religion. This resonates certainly with his deconstruction and reconstruction of 'religion' in *ME*.[86] Smith sees a conflict between certain Islamics in the West, scholarship based on Enlightenment rationality and critique of religion, on the one hand, and the religious perception of Muslims on the other. Whereas the former, through an analytical way of thinking, used to orient itself away from human wholeness, creativity and synthesis, the opposite attitude has been the case for Muslims as for all religious people who see the religious dimension as the 'primary locus of humanity's endeavour to see things whole—and to achieve integration, wholeness, oneself' (83). This has particularly been the case in Islam, according to 'the central emphasis on *tawhid*, unifying.' As one sees, the analytical strategy is common to both the view of religion and history. What Smith offers, instead of what he calls "the 'big-bang' theory' of religion,' is a notion of 'continuous creation,' which is treated as a parallel concept to 'cumulative tradition' (85).[87] Hence, Islam is not a system or a 'neat package for export' constructed or produced by a founder at the beginning of its history, but a process (85f).[88]

Regarding the understanding of language, Smith's concern goes in the same direction as his understanding of history and religion. His general position in this respect may be briefly stated thus (86-88):

1. Language is not an object, but a human quality and activity
2. Since language can be shared, it involves community.

3. Because the meaning of a sentence implies a meaning to somebody, understanding always involves more than one meaning.

Described thus, Smith sees for example poetry as far closer to the scriptural situation than other forms of language.[89]

This is what Smith calls the community aspect of language. In addition to this aspect, one should also recognize what he calls 'the

---

[86] Cf. Chapter 2.4, 3.2 and 3.3 above.

[87] *WS*, 83f. Most interestingly, Smith suggests that the attitude of the historicist search for the pristine, originates somehow from an experience of the vision of the Protestant Reformation: 'Back to the original!' *ibid*. See also Smith 1976a, 50, and 1991b, 189, for the same argument.

[88] This negative evaluation of 'system' should not be interpreted too strictly. As one may have noticed, Smith occasionally refers to the Islamic tradition as a coherent and systematic tradition. The point here is that Islam should not be recognized as a given, fixed entity which originated in the seventh century and stayed as it was 'launched.' Within a synchronic view, however, Islam may to some degree be seen as a system.

[89] This aspect is loosely connected here to the other elements but is developed later in *WS*.

Muslim-community (*ummah*) aspect of the Qur'an as scripture.' The major element here is, as we have already seen, that: What has made the Qur'an scripture, is that for Muslims it has been received as the word of God. With this, Smith maintains that the true meaning of the Qur'an has already been outlined, that is:

> The solid historical reality of the continuum of actual
> meanings over the centuries to actual people (89).

As one may see, the key terms are: 'the reality of', 'continuum of', and 'actual'. By these terms, Smith seems to combine a cognitive view of reality, a coherential view of truth, and a personalist approach. Meaning is not, when it comes to terms, isolated personal meanings, but the totality of meanings situated in the total complex of history.[90]

    In addition to this, Smith concludes his development of the chapter with an option of falsification for the person who is certainly most involved by this theory: the devout Muslim. According to Smith, he or she 'may reasonably dispute this conclusion' (89f). Smith therefore offers arguments against his theory, namely, that 'the true meaning of the Qur'an is what God means by it,' and that 'the various meanings that history evinces in the process of their earthly development constitute an ongoing and ever-varying approximation.' The answer of Smith to that is, 'We shall strive to incorporate into our final theory its discernments (not necessarily involving the particular concept of 'God')' and further, 'We contend that the Muslim community's perception of the Qur'an as scripture through time must be recognized as basic.' This is an important remark because it stresses the point that the generic category of 'scripture' should open up for 'differences significant for a generic concept.'[91] Whether Smith succeeds in this 'incorporation' remains however doubtful.

    However, both the philosophical and theological implications of these statements are far-reaching, and pondering these should be rewarding. It is, therefore, pertinent to switch over to his theological article on this subject; 'Is the Qur'ân the word of God?'[92] Smith describes this

---

[90] *Ibid.* This implies also an awareness of other traditions and their inter-relatedness, cf. his notion of 'a history of religion in the singular' (*WT*, ch. 1, see also Chapter 2.6.1 above), though this is not the focused matter at this place. Thus, the argument is also possible that 'the wording of the Qur'ân may well be seen as *an advance*' in the meaning 'spiritual advance over preceding scriptures,' Smith 1991b, 185, 190f (emphasis mine). Smith argues based on the work of the Jewish scholar James Kugel that the Abraham story and myth/function is already present in the Qur'an, whereas the role of Abraham in the Jewish and Christian traditions is first developed after the genesis of their scriptures and the written stories of Abraham, 185ff.
[91] Smith 1991b, 183.
[92] Smith 1967/1981p. Subsequent references in the text refer to this study.

study as 'my first public appearance in the field of theology (as distinct from Islamics or comparative religion).'[93] Sticking with his general rule, the lecture was not published before it was tried out on a Muslim audience.[94]

First of all, Smith sees the question of whether the Qur'an is the word of God as 'a question on a matter of ultimate seriousness' (283). The word of God 'is or ought to be humankind's crucial concern,' even for the secular historian (285f). Yet, the question is both a threat to Christians, who never asked the question but only took the answer 'no' for granted, and to Muslims who only answered the question with 'yes' and who never asked the question in public (290). Smith therefore considers all traditional understandings of this question to be unsatisfactory, which applies as much to the 'no'group as to the 'yes' group (283ff). The seriousness of this is clearly stated by his descriptions of the two: whereas the former has been ignorant of the 'no small band of eccentrics that holds this book to be God's word,' the people of the latter 'have been willing to die for it.'

Smith sees this dichotomy as representing a major theoretical problem, one of theoretical incoherence (294). However, he hopes to get support from 'those whose 'yes', and ... those whose 'no', to our question is reasoned and sincere' (287). As an untiring academician,[95] he sees it as 'an intellectualist imperative to construct a theoretical answer more comprehensive, coherent, and unifying than the traditional ones' (295). The theoretical problem can be stated thus: 'How is one to rationalize the divergence, to conceptualize it, to interpret it intelligibly?' The major inducement, however, seems to be a belief in the unity of knowledge as well as in the unity of mankind (298f). Consequently, Smith 'cannot see how in principle any answer to our question can be truly adequate for a Christian unless it were also and simultaneously truly adequate for a Muslim' (299).

On the one hand this may be interpreted as an example of his vision of a global community that also relates to his notion of corporate critical self-consciousness.[96] On the other hand this raises vast questions

---

[93] Smith 1967/1981p, 282, = the preface to its reprinting in *UI*. The 'public' was the audience of the Taylor Lectures, Yale Divinity School, 1963.

[94] Which took place in India in 1964. The lecture was first published in Smith 1967b.

[95] Cf. once more the preface of this article, 282: 'I as an intellectual in the modern world have always as my primary obligation and final commitment my loyalty to truth—subject to test of my fellow intellectuals, who constitute, of course, the primary audience of every thesis proceeding out of a university.'

[96] See Pruett 1990. See also Smith 1992, which is an article that attempts to raise theological questions, but where 'our fundamental problem ... is that of sharing, rather, *human* experience,' 58.

within the understanding of truth. It is therefore quite unsatisfactory that Smith ends his theoretical elaboration here. The initial question, which served as a point of departure, seems therefore to have been left unanswered by Smith. Yet, Smith sees the reward to be that the question has become 'an open question' where the answer has to be discovered; a question which is 'no longer simple, but has to be understood' (300). For this question, Smith gives in the end no help. What remains is the humane and pragmatical truth of the Qur'an, for humans. One may of course suspect Smith of leaving this question for the same reason that he does a definition of faith and a reference for cosmic truth. If so, the answer is simply: transcendence.

3.9 Particular Similarities and Differences related to Form, Meaning and Effect

I have now explored Smith's development of a general theory of 'religion', as well as the relation of this general theory to his interpretation of various aspects of the Islamic tradition . Regarding 'self-understanding', one of the key issues in this study, the examination of Smith has proved that a 'normative theological framework' is present by Smith. One may ask whether this framework is a Christian one. That is a question that has to be raised in Smith's case. On the one hand it seems that Smith's Christian background has informed him significantly, not least his view of Christ as a moral impulse for approaching global religious diversity (cf. his notions of 'faith' and 'world community'). Christ serves also as channel from transcendence/God towards humans, that is, as providing faith for humans. Christ is, however, not regarded as an exclusive vehicle for faith. Lastly, at some places it seems that distinctive Christian language is employed in order to depict features/phenomena in the Islamic tradition and community (cf. what I have called revelational and incarnational language).

It is, however, seldom that distinctive elements from within traditional Christian vocabulary and doctrines are held together with comparable Islamic features/phenomena, though this does occur within his writings. In this chapter, therefore, I will draw the attention more explicitly to these, what I will call 'similar externals.' This may in particular illustrate what his general theory means when it comes to concepts and issues that one would expect him to treat in a comparative approach to the relation between the faith(s) of Muslims and Smith's own faith, the Christian.

In a study on Muslim-Christian relations,[97] which in a temporal

---

[97] Smith 1959/1981m. Further parenthetical remarks refer to this study.

sense closes the circle from the first chapter of my exploration of Smith's writings[98], and as a consequence of his personalist approach, Smith highlights pragmatic matters. Instead of asking: 'whether or how far a given phenomenon in one religious tradition is itself similar to or different from an apparently comparable one in some other tradition,' Smith asks: 'whether or how far *its effect* on a worshipper is similar or different' (233). The problem of only tracing similarities and differences on the level of 'data', according to Smith, is that 'similar data may, on inquiry, elicit differing responses in distinctive contexts; and differing data, similar responses.' This is certainly not a very radical methodological consideration in religious studies. It is, however, more distinctive when Smith makes 'its effect' a principle when he opts for putting emphasis on the 'effect' and the 'response.' His concern is with the 'personal involvements or interaction with ... [religious] objects and symbols' (233).[99] In that regard, the 'distinctive contexts' will both provide a place for the 'effects,' as well as the possibility of turning the similarities on the level of phenomena into differences on the level of effect/'role of.' Let us now see what kind of results Smith obtains in the Muslim-Christian instance.

Smith's point of departure is a criticism of the assumed optimism of designating similarities or differences in religious regards. In a rather bold statement he asserts:

> The most sophisticated student can only with difficulty, if at all, designate precisely what the similarities are or even formulate satisfactorily the differences (234).

Parallels, according to Smith, 'are at best only approximate.' On the other hand, on a fundamental level, although elusive and in spite of differences, there may be substantial comparability (*ibid.*). Based on this comparability, which implies that the differences are only partial, Smith sees possibilities for dialogue between persons of different traditions.

In the academic realm, however, he sees a responsibility for 'comparative religion' to construct 'concepts and intellectual analysis by which divergent religious traditions may become mutually intelligible.' This statement has as its subsequent rule, which I have given due attention to previously, that any statement about religion should be 'cogent in at least two traditions simultaneously' (235). Smith sees this rule as both an

---

[98] One will see that there are clear overlaps between Smith 1959/1981m and *CR*, which is a study that was published the same year, regarding his general comparative considerations.

[99] Smith locates this 'orientation' as distinctive for the Harvard 'school'.

ethical requirement as well as a criterion of intellectual success (236). Furthermore, a statement on religion made by a comparative religionist should not only be cogent to those religious traditions involved, but also 'to the academic mind whose commitment is solely to the truth' (236). Smith thus establishes a tripartite criterion for studies in comparative religion. Consequently, in the Muslim-Christian instance a reasonable application will be that: any comparative statement has to be simultaneously cogent to a) the Muslim tradition, b) to the Christian tradition, and c) to a philosophical understanding of truth.

As a rather shallow example of what this might imply, Smith contends that a common held opinion by Muslims and Christian students of comparative religion, is that Christianity and Islam are comparable. On 'a more advanced level of scrutiny' Smiths maintains that 'the similarities, which undoubtedly exist, perhaps lie in rather unexpected areas' (236). It is this latter contention he seeks to substantiate his survey of Christian-Muslim 'elements.'

One of Smith's presuppositions is that the only one God 'deals with man wherever He may find him as best He can, despite or within the limitations of the variety of religious forms' (237). To this Smith gives a corresponding criticism of the opinion that 'the different religions give differing answers to essentially the same questions' (236). As we have seen, Smith sees the divergences to lie rather in asking different questions than in some kind of a common core.[100] Hence, it is not meaningful to compare apparently similar data in Christianity and Islam (Bible/Qur'an, Jesus Christ/Muhammad, churches/mosques, etc.). At least one has to 'collate, expand, and reflect' on the similarities. This emphasis on meaning and function is examined by enquiring into certain issues and terms within the Christian and Islamic traditions, which is quite illuminating for his methodological considerations above. Some of these points of comparisons will, however, reiterate parts of what we have previously 'thematized' in his writings.

Smith starts by giving attention to the term 'the will of God' (237f). The Christian and Muslim usages of this term, he says, refer to 'different concepts.' Whereas the Christian meaning (e.g. in *Our Father*) is 'an aspiration towards seeing mundane affairs accord with a higher pattern [i.e. that of God],' parallel to the position and function of *shari'ah* and *islam* in Islam (!), in Islam, on the other hand, 'the will of God' 'is not what man should do but what God does do' (238). Therefore, 'for Muslims

---

[100] Yet, related to his strong unitary perspectives of 'history', 'faith' and 'transcendence', although perhaps not uniformingly!, one might however dispute this assertion. For a strong criticism of Smith at exactly this point, see Heim 1995, ch. 2. This issue will be pursued in Chapter 7.

... man can disobey God's command *[amr]*, but cannot contravene His will *[mashi'ah, iradah]*.'

Smith continues this kind of elaboration by an inquiry into the widely held, and approximate ('obviously not absurd') opinion that the Qur'an is to Islam as the Bible is to Christianity (238). By closer investigation Smith finds that a better statement would be that 'the Qur'an is to Islam as the person of Jesus Christ is to Christianity' (239).[101] Smith holds that 'the central focus of revelation [in the Islamic system] is the Qur'an' (239). On the side of Christianity, the Bible is the 'record of revelation, not the revelation itself.'[102] He sees compelling evidence of what occurs in making certain parallels between the two due to the fact of the 'Muslim misinterpretation of the Gospels apparent in the view that God revealed them to Jesus (cf. Qur'an 57:27).' Instead of this, the better parallels may be located between, for example, the Gospels and Hadith, and between the Qur'an and Jesus Christ.

One result of comparing these traditions thus is that 'in both traditions salvation is by faith—faith in God and His revelation' (240). The difference, however, is that Muslims have faith in 'what Muhammad brought' whereas Christian have faith in 'God and Christ, which means 'living in Christ' and ... participating in the Church.' Since what Muhammad brought was 'a moral imperative,' faith in the Islamic instance means 'aligning oneself actively with a moral orientation.' In this respect, Smith also gives attention to the question of 'mediator' between God and humankind. Though he is hasty at this point, he finds that in the Islamic tradition, as in the Jewish, righteousness is the mediator as it is in the Christian faith. Smith distinguishes however between social salvation by righteousness, and personal salvation by faith in righteousness (240). Nevertheless, Smith asserts, 'at least in Islam,' that salvation of sinners is available not only through Christ, but also, in principle, also 'through a law.' Thus, 'revelational differences', as he has put it otherwise, do not seem to matter decisively. The reason for this may be that both 'social' and 'personal' salvation can be included in his view of human/mundane truth and, correspondingly: human/mundane salvation, albeit this is not explicated at this point.

An important point for reflection, and of importance for this study, is Smith's elaboration of the relation between the role of theology in Christianity and the role of theology in Islam (*ibid.*). Smith says that

---

[101] A further parallel mentioned by Smith in order to illustrate his point is: Muhammad corresponds to the role of St Paul/St Peter, especially for Roman Catholics.

[102] Without forgetting that this discernment not always has been clearly conceived by Christians, Smith qualifies his statement by 'which has perhaps been more firmly grasped in Christian thought recently than was always the case,' *ibid.*

theology has always been central to Christians, not least because of the Greek influence on early Christian development. In addition, Christians have assumed this to be the case in other religious traditions as well. Yet, for Islam, theology is not the decisive expression, which is the law.[103] Therefore, 'law is to Islam as theology is to Christianity' (241). Smith also reverses this order and finds the Christian equivalent to the role of theology in Islam to be:

> Theology *('ilm al-kalam)* is to Islam as *philosophy of religion* is to Christianity: a serious, often brilliant discipline for those who are concerned with it, useful as apologetics, but peripheral to the main development, dispensable, and even suspect (241, my emphasis).

Given Smith's preference for 'faith' over 'belief' and 'theology', no wonder that his sympathy does not lie in this field.[104] As one will discover later, a disinterest for law is also the case for Cragg, yet for other reasons. Cragg's interest in theology in his Christian theology of Islam, however, does not coincide with Smith at all.

Smith also gives attention to the relation between church and mosque. He maintains that the mosque is more like a chapel. The mosque repudiates priesthood and has as its primary function the 'conventicle-type worship' (*ibid.*). The church, on the other hand, aims at representing also a 'temple-type cult,' in addition to its features from the synagogue. Another characteristic, is that a local church is church only insofar as it

---

[103] Smith follows Bergträsser at this point, cf. *ibid.*, 241, n 9: Smith quotes Bergträsser extensively another place: 'Das islamische Recht, in seinem weiteren, die Regelung des Kultes mit umfassenden Sinn, ist der Inbegriff des echt islamischen Geistes, die entscheidendste Ausprägung islamischen Denkens, der Wesenskern des Islam überhaupt,' Smith 1960/1981e, 88, which is, if one ignores its idealist language, not a very controversial suggestion. Yet, Smith's conclusion is that even *shari'a* has not been a central concept in Islam, though it may be the decisive expression of the law. Cf. note 104 below

[104] That does not mean that *shari'a* has not been addressed, see e.g. Smith 1960/1981e. Interestingly, in this study which he finds to be of greatest impact for Muslims themselves, in particular in revising their understanding of *shari'ah*, his emphasis is on the *verbal noun (shar')* which makes him see *transcendence* more clearly, as the 'conceived *and felt* ... moral obedience/disobedience to God,' *ibid.* 99, because God is to be seen the subject of the verb, *ibid.* 87f and 98: '*Shar'* is a *masdar* ... referring not to a system, a law, but to a process; not to an entity, but to an activity. *Its subject is always God.* It refers to the process or act of His assigning moral quality and moral responsibility to human life,' 98, emphases original. This certainly resembles Smith's study of concern here, cf. point [1] immediately above.

has a formalized sanction of the wider and total community of Christians. Yet, the latter is more or less derived from the former, according to Smith. Anyway, there is some overlapping between the two.

Smith also compares the Islamic idea of *huda* (guidance) with the Holy Spirit in Christianity (cf. John 16,13) (242f). Smith sees in the idea of God as *al-Hadi* (the Guide) an expression of how the doctrine of *ijma'* should be understood:

> God's active (and in some sense redemptive?) dealings with man are not confined to His erstwhile initiative in overt revelation. His mercy and grace in His moves to bring men to obedience and hence communion with Him, though climaxed historically in His sending the Qur'an, are yet a continuing process (242).

For this reason, Smith sees the Spirit and *al-Hadi* as close parallels.

A sixth parallel is one between the doctrine of the Trinity and the 'ninety-nine names' of God in Islam (243). Smith does not maintain a parallel of content, but of relationship, for example in the formula: 'They are not He nor are they other than He.'[105] Smith is aware of how shocking this might be for even a liberal Muslim, but insist that his suggestion may have bearing on any attention to deal with 'the relationship of God to His qualities.'

Another concern is that of the chronological relation between Islam and Christianity. Smith rejects the Islamic critique of Christianity's lack of recognition of the Prophet. For Muslims, there are similar problems in relation to accepting, for example, Ghulam Ahmad and the Qadiyani Ahmadiyah movement.

Smith also suggests, as a 'bold and provocative speculation', that there might be an 'analogy between the significance for a Christian of the Eucharist and the significance for a Muslim of memorizing the Qur'an' (244). Smith assesses this to be an 'interesting and instructive' issue, though it may not be a valid parallel. It is important that this 'speculation' is derived from the aforementioned parallel between Christ and the Qur'an that has been 'vigorously born in upon me in subsequent discourse with both Muslims and Christians.' Smith sees in the parallel of significance (of Christ and the Qur'an), an expression of 'Divinity to have taken initiative to 'come down' into our mundane world' (244). He paraphrases formal

---

[105] Smith quotes at this place a statement of al-Taftazani's in his commentary of Nasafi (*al-'Aqa'id*), *ibid.* 243, n 13. See also Chapter 5.6 for Cragg's elaboration of the ninety-nine names related to his discussion of common prayer between Christians and Muslims.

Muslim doctrine by saying that the pre-existing and uncreated Qur'an is for the Muslim 'the one tangible thing within the natural realm that is supernatural, the point where the eternal has broken through into time.' Thus the *hafiz*, the 'memorizer' or 'apprehender' of the Qur'an,

> has interiorized [the *meaning* of the Qur'an] in a way that could conceivably suggest to a Christian some analogy with what happens when a Christian in the Communion Service appropriates to himself the body of Christ Who in this case is the mundane expression of God, the supernatural-natural, the embodiment of eternity in time (244).

One is certainly again[106] reminded of the two competing formulas *finitum capax infiniti* and *finitum non capax infiniti* at this place, the former being the Lutheran position and the latter being the reformed (Calvin) one. The very crux of the matter is whether eternity only breaks through time, or that time, in this respect, is the shape of eternity. On the Christian side this has been a salient issue within the understanding of the Incarnation and of the Eucharist. It is noteworthy that Smith uses once again a clearly incarnational language at this point ('embodiment', 'supernatural-natural', 'mundane expression of God'), although this does not alter his stance regarding the Lutheran/Calvinist alternatives above.

Smith ends his comparative study by posing the both obvious and intricate epistemological question to whether one could possibly know whether the significances of the Qur'an for the *hafiz* and the Eucharist for the Christian are comparable. He ascertains that both Muslim and Christian communities are at loss both to explain what their own experience means to themselves, and how an alien one should be assessed. Smith speaks of ineffable intangibles (245). In the case of the apprehension of the Qur'an and the reception of the body and blood of Christ Smith concludes that there might perhaps be less in the analogy than when he first thought of it.

To conclude: As one may have noted, Smith is more comfortable using the idea of analogy than that of likeness, similarity or, for that sake, identity. What is also clear is that Smith emphasizes the meaning, effect and significance rather that on 'the outward form' (246). Therefore, within such an understanding, neither similarities nor differences are as great as might appear at first sight. At this place, Smith also resonates with some features of the method and hermeneutics of the one we are about to start

---

[106] Cf. note 44, p. 40, and 103, p. 83.

examining: Kenneth Cragg. Again, this is so despite their divergent ways of substantiating their comparative theologies.

3.10 Interim Conclusion

In an early article on the development of 'islam', Smith finds a certain ambiguity within the usage of this concept in the Islamic history. This ambiguity relates to the difference between Islam as the active, personal faith on the one hand, and Islam as a transcendent ideal for Muslims as well as an historical phenomenon for outsiders, on the other. Smith identifies in this an historical development from an original personal piety, via an ideal religious system, to an emphasis on Islam as an external mundane religious system, reaching finally to a description of the civilization through which it was expressed. In Smith's view, the dividing line is thus not to be drawn between insiders and outsiders, but within the insiders, the Muslims, as a differentiation between personal and objectified aspects of Islam. This study impacted both upon his understanding of Islam and the general problem of understanding religious matters both from the inside and from the outside.

In a separate chapter in *ME* Smith aims to discover whether Islam fits into his overall thesis of a reification process: away from a pristine personal religiousness, especially influenced by the Western impact upon the rest of the world. The Islamic case is intricate because the Muslim use of 'Islam' as a self-description as well as designating an entity. Moreover, also the awareness of one concept (*din*, pl. *adyan*) for both a personal religion, a religious system and a plurality of religions seems to make the case difficult for Smith (the Sufis being the exception). Smith finds however that certain external pressures in the Arabian environment determined the reification of Islam from the very beginning. Also in the modern times (19th century onwards) Islam has turned to the notion of Islam as a religion, presumably by the demands of apologetics. Yet, at the same time, Smith also discerns another line within Islam and the Qur'an that worked against this, emphasizing personal faith as a fundamental and transcendent orientation and activity. In this respect, what Muslims are specifically makes them generically the same as other groups. Smith finds evidence for this personalist orientation 'with transcendent overtones' in the Arabic language used in the earliest time of Islam, and in the usage of 'islam', 'God', *iman* and *mu'min* in the Qur'an. The logically, structurally, and Qur'anic-corresponding preference of verb and verbal forms over nouns draws the attention to faith as an active quality willed by God, and not to Islam as an abstract system.

Consequently, although Smith sees Islam as an intricate instance being the first and most reified of the various religions, he still sees it as an illuminating one. Yet, his interpretation of Islam seems to be strongly determined by his desire to gain support for his general hypotheses from this part of the world's religious history.

In a contemporaneous but more popular version of these insights (*FOM*) Smith's particular concern is how Muslims' faith may be approximated through the *Shahadah*. Smith sees in this 'creed' the expression of the *coherence and simplicity* of Muslim faith, particularly related to God's *tawhid,* and opposed to *shirk*. At the same time Smith recognizes *Shahadah* as a symbol, playing a similar role to that of the Cross for Christians, also in modern times. He also stresses its role as presupposition in opposition to 'belief' in its modern meaning. His inquiry into *Shahadah* thus leads Smith to an awareness of the distinction between faith and belief. Smith also recognizes the second part of the creed— Muhammad as the *rasul Allah*—yet only due to his function, not to his status, which makes him more like St. Peter and St. Paul than Christ in his bringing witness to the central event (the Qur'an). Smith also maintains that *Shahadah* shows us that religion is not primarily human beings searching for God, but God Himself acting and speaking to us. Consequently, man's task is that of response. At this point Smith's account resembles very much his own Protestant faith. Finally, Smith perceives a difference between Muslim and Christian concepts of revelation (the Muslim: *from* God of what is *right*; the Christian: disclosure *of* God and of what is *true*), yet without giving this 'revelational difference' weight in his development of the Muslim-Christian relations.

A decade after these studies of the Islamic concept of faith, Smith contends that they were dramatic not only because they forced him to discern more clearly between faith and belief, but that the very foundations of his Christian theology and the philosophical question of truth were at stake. The interpretation of Islam thus contributed to a rethinking of both his Christian and academic self-understanding. These matters are elaborated in his studies on faith and belief in the Qur'an (Smith 1974/1981f, and the chapter on Islam in *FB*), which are matters of direct impact upon the approach of our study. Smith follows his general pattern from *ME, BH* and *FB,* maintaining that faith and belief are different, and that belief in the modern form is not what religious persons are really about. In the Islamic instance Smith finds that the notion of belief is wholly alien to the Qur'an, for what he calls good reasons. The 'good reasons' are *inter alia* that the Qur'an is occupied with the matter of faith, that is, the right response and commitment towards God. Smith makes such observations based on precise and untiring investigations into words and groups of words in the Qur'an. Smith finds therein that faith and belief do not only represent two differing approaches to knowledge ('recognition' and 'awareness', viz. 'believe (wrongly)'), this difference also represents the difference between anthropocentrism and theocentrism. Faith is thus ultimately enabled by God's merciful action to salvage us from what Smith calls our epistemological bewilderments. Thus, the support which Smith finds in the Qur'an for his faith-belief concepts, is interpreted in distinctive Christian terms, which of course develops linguistical relations between his Christian self-understanding and his interpretation of Islam. Such relations are particularly enabled by what he sees as a strong relation of convergence between Christians and Muslims in respect of faith.

This is, however, not only the case in the Qur'an. Smith also sets off to elaborate on faith in the Islamic tradition. In the commentary of Taftazani on Nasafi which has played a decisive role in Smith's life, Smith finds something 'humanly true' in his work, namely his notion of *iman* related to *tasdiq*; *iman* as a personal appropriation of truth. Thus Smith relates *iman* to the Islamic notions of truth; *haqqa* (related to truth as real/Real) and *sadaqa* (related to truth of persons), which he sees as aligning with the Islamic and Qur'anic 'drama of decision.' Smith sees this as a salient case of human beings becoming moral and true persons by aligning to (the) reality by their human behaviour. Smith sees therefore *tasdiq* as a cosmic human quality that recognizes truth as well as 'existentializes' it. As such, *tasdiq* should not be translated 'believe' in the modern sense, but as a qualifying of 'faith', namely as sincere and active, ultimately resembling the nature of God's activity. Such a faith is, however, not an Islamic faith, but a human faith. Hence, *tasdiq* merely denotes the form and nature of this quality, not its content. This fits certainly in Smith's general thesis. On the other hand, Smith seems to be more sympathetic to this Islamic sense of faith: what one does with what one recognizes as true or what kind of person one is or wants to become, than to what he assumes to be the Christian position: 'believe, not yet to know,' and further: only on 'this side' of knowledge, not beyond. Consequently, Smith's understanding of *tasdiq,* and consequently of *iman*, turns out to be a matter within his self-understanding, in this case supported and helped by Islamic theology (*kalam*).

Another approach to approximate the meaning of faith itself concerns the notion of *arkan.* To conceive this is important as faith is the final criterion for the right relationship between God and humankind on the human side. Based on a traditional formula where *arkan* is mentioned in a definition of faith, and furthermore, because notions may be ambiguous within Islam, Smith argues for the meaning held by a minority of Muslims, namely that *arkan* does not mean 'the pillars of Islam', but the limbs of the body. If so, Smith also asserts that faith should be connected to deeds (*al-jawarih*). Yet, throughout history the meaning of *arkan* changed from 'limbs' (in *kalam*) to 'the pillars' (in *fiqh*), which Smith sees as a development from pious acts to 'handy and in some way obvious illustrations of pious behaviour.'

A significant contribution of Smith regards the Qur'an, its true meaning and its role as God's Word. By a so-called non-reductionist approach, which attempts to integrate as well as transcend previous Muslim and Western readings of the Qur'an, Smith finds that: a) the Qur'an has served different people differently, b) it has served the investigator and observer, and c) today one should acquire an historical self-consciousness about this from all parts. Aiming at the latter, Smith contends that one should recognize the Qur'an as God's Word. On the other hand, he concentrates in practice on the human meaning it has had as scripture, and still has, that is, as a human activity. Looking at its function and role, the Qur'an has played a major role. Yet, this view immediately connects his particular approach of the Qur'an to the role of Christ and the work of the Spirit. The language he uses for this is utterly theological with Christian features: it resembles the way revelation, the Incarnation, the Eucharist, and so forth, have normally been described in Christian circles. Smith's comprehension of the Qur'an as scripture seems therefore to draw Smith's argument closely to a distinctive Christian self-understanding. Hence, the fact that he labels this approach an historian's findings seems to be somewhat simplistically stated.

An important point in Smith's description of the role of the Qur'an is how every Muslim has attempted to attain a best possible interpretation of any particular verse of it and thus always seeks to advance upon previous interpretations in order to secure its plausibility and coherence for Muslims who struggles with pressures and problems in their lives. Hence the true meaning of the Qur'an is the total meaning that can be established as the solid historical reality of the continuum of actual meanings over the centuries to actual people.

To see it this way is presumably as challenging for Western scholars with a distorted notion of history, religion and language, as it is for Muslims. This becomes especially acute when the question of the Qur'an as the Word of God is brought to the comparative 'table.' Smith's concern, based on his view of a unity of knowledge and of humankind, is to give a comprehensive and synoptical view that may contribute to solve the problem of theoretical incoherence where the one group answers 'yes' and the other 'no'. At this place Smith echoes his verification principle from *CR* (and later *WT*) when he asserts that what may be true for

Christians at this issue must also be true for Muslims. In the end, however, Smith does not offer a solution except leaving the question open.

In a last chapter I have drawn attention to how Smith compares 'similar externals' in the Islamic and Christian tradition. The way he compares meaning, function and effects of traditionally conceived similarities and 'similarities' that seem similar but are not, is illuminating for his previous arguments (for example his verification principle and his notion of truth). Within these comparisons Christ connected more closely with the Qur'an than with Muhammad. The mosque is conceived as closer to a chapel than to a church, and the memorizing of the Qur'an is equated with the Eucharist, and so on. Smith calls this a comparison of analogy rather than of identity or similarity. In this, Smith resonates with the hermeneutics and methodology of Kenneth Cragg, despite their divergent theological positions, especially obvious in how Cragg renounces Smith's distinction between faith and belief.

4

KENNETH CRAGG'S INTERRELIGIOUS HERMENEUTICS

4.1 Introduction

I will now examine Cragg's general approach to interreligious relations. Of particular interest is how he develops concepts that can be seen as expressions of a characteristic approach to self-relating and self-change. To speak of a general approach as distinctive from one that is focused on Islam in particular, is, however, difficult in the case of Cragg. On the other hand, it might be possible to distinguish between material in Cragg which on the one hand is predominantly conceptual and general, and on the other material which is concerned with concrete issues in Islam, even when these 'levels' occur side by side. In this respect it will prove illuminating to have a closer look at his writings in order to discern which parts of it will be of particular interest for the present study.

Cragg's authorship spans a range of themes, though not in any encyclopaedic way.[1] This applies both to his approach to Islam and to his elaboration of the Christian faith. In addition, one may also discover a

---

[1] Cf. Lamb 1997, 168, 172f. Cragg is mostly concerned with the Qur'an and modern Muslim thinkers and most notably leaves out *historical Islam,* most aspects of *shari'ah,* as well as eschatology. See also Hoover 2000. His concern is with Sunni Islam, in particular modern voices, whereas Sufism and particularly Shi'a Islam have been less addressed. Regarding Sufi, his compilation of Sufi (and qur'anic) material in *WSuf* is one exception. One of Christopher Lamb's strongest criticisms against Cragg is that his selection of what he engages in Islam makes him develop an *idiosyncratic* view of Islam where the Muslim inclination towards *orthopraxy* over *orthodoxy* is disregarded in an incoherent way, *ibid.* 168 and 172f. See also Kerr 1981, 157, col. 2, for the Islamic concentration upon 'the systematization of moral guidance through the *shari'ah* rather than upon 'theology' in a more abstract sense.' On the other hand, Lamb sees Cragg's approach as theologically thorough, and which offers 'coherent and biblically-grounded Christian theology of interfaith relations,' *ibid.* 172.

Moreover, Cragg became regarded, eventually in the 70s, as a 'major figure in the academic teaching of Islam,' so Sidney Griffith, Griffith 1994, 29. This assessment is based on the appearance of his Islamic/Qur'an studies, introductions and textbooks in the late 60s and early seventies (*HI, IW, EQ, MQ*). See also Slomp 1990. Some of these studies of Cragg, and others, are still in use in undergraduate course introductions to Islam. The backside of this is, as observed by Griffith (Catholic),

4 Kenneth Cragg's Interreligious Hermeneutics

consistency throughout his works, though certain developments are discernable as well.[2] Yet, for instance, the purpose and temper of, for example, his dissertation can still be conspicuously discerned in works in the 90s. Thirdly, although one may see a certain development in the range of themes that are comprehended across his authorship, he seems to *reiterate* particular themes at different stages. Some of his publications from the latter part of the 90s, for example, may at first glance seem to be a mix of very different interests. But a closer look reveals that all these themes are comprehended at least partly in earlier stages of his authorship.[3] It must still be said that many of his studies comprise a range of themes. The obvious advantage of this is that it makes possible a broader approach to the issues he handles. The problem is that one often gets the impression that many of these themes are neither handled in their depth nor with sufficient logical stringency. Nevertheless, a brief listing of themes that

---

that it may be problematic, both for Christians and Muslims, that Cragg concentrates (as a Protestant) on the Qur'an in a *sola scriptura* way, that is: his language has 'the ring a New Testament scholar about it,' and thus leaves out the traditional exegesis of it, *ibid.*, 30.

[2] Whereas a (epistemological) shift is easily discernable in Smith's writings, this is not the case in Cragg's. The reason seems to be that it is his encounter with the Middle East that entailed a 'sifting of meaning,' cf. note 81 below. Because his D.Phil. thesis and other studies are written *after* this stay in Beirut, one might say that a shift, at least in respect of the 'meaning of Christian mission,' took place *before* the start of his production. It might have been possible to discover this shift by examining earlier minor writings before his departure to Beirut in 1939. Nevertheless, I have not made this a priority. From his 'Christian story-study,' *FLN,* it seems however that two factors impacted upon him after having experience a kind of 'ecclesiastical redundancy' in the first years in Beirut and Gaza, 1939-41: The one was his relation to the Bishop in Jerusalem, Graham Brown, the other was his time at American University of Beirut (AUB), 97. These two impacts merged in the establishing of the St. Justin's Hostel. By no accident, it was Justin Martyr, the prominent Christian philosopher, who was 'canonized' and made a patron, symbolizing also Cragg's affiliation to Beirut and AUB.
Another point is that his sifting experience in Beirut came to expression in his thesis, 1947-1950, and then, as an extension of both his commitment to Beirut and his thesis, in his time at Hartford, 1951-1956, where, *inter alia, CM* was produced. In short: A theological shift occurs in Beirut and is developed in studies from the time in Longworth and Hartford.

[3] This is especially the case with *CM* which contains both political history (ch. i), social history (ch. viii), rudiments of interreligious hermeneutics (ch. vi), Islamic history/phenomenology of Islam (chs. ii-v), not least Christian apologetics related to the Islamic meaning of the 'call of the minaret' (chs. ix-x), and, lastly, practical considerations for missionaries in Muslim dominated countries (ch. vii, about the role of language and literature; ch. viii, about the full notion of 'salvation' including 'health'; and xi, about the question of quality and quantity in missionaries in Muslim dominated countries).

have occupied Cragg throughout his authorship may be classified this way, yet with a great deal of overlap, and only drawing from his monographs[4]:

   a. Christian mission and relations to Muslims and Islam, including religious/theological, social, political, economical and technological issues (e.g. *ITC, CM, SM, MC, JM*). This emphasis comprises the vast majority of his works. More distinct issues may be discerned in subsequent paragraphs below.

   b. General studies in Islamics ('Islam from within'), where the relation to Christians and Christianity is less emphasized (e.g. part II of *CM, HI, IW, RMH*), or in a 'study-programme' way postponed for the reader's response (*DR*),[5] and inclusive translations of and studies in the content of the Qur'an (e.g. *MQ, EQ, PM, RQ*)

   a. Works related to the modern Islamic world and its Muslim writers (*ITC, CCI, PF*)

   b. Works with an emphasis on religio-political issues: of the Middle-East, in particular the situation for Arab Christians (e.g. *AC*), the Jerusalem question and other 'Israel' issues, for example Zionism (e.g. *PAL* and *TYJ*), and various issues that challenge Western Europe, especially the United Kingdom (*DF)*

   c. Christian mission and relations to religions other than Islam, particularly Judaism and Buddhism, but also Hinduism and African religion (as chapters in e.g. *CWP* and *CFs*), including two comparative studies in Christianity, Judaism and Islam (*PM* and *WWd*)

   d. General interreligious studies (e.g. *CWP, COR, CFs, MG, TT*)

   e. Christian mission and relations to the modern Western world, especially related to 'secularism' (e.g. *SEG*), and 'humanism' (e.g. *GHT*)

   f. Studies in the genesis and development of, and response to, Christian teaching (*PP, DC, ECF*)

---

[4] Which excludes: articles, pamphlets from his missionary activity/study programs in the Middle East, as well as translations of Arabic works by other authors (Muhammad 'Abduh, Muhammad Kamil Husain, Taha Husein).

[5] The questions to the reader following every chapter direct the reader's attention to the relation between the understanding of Islam presented in the study and the Christian response based on both theological ideas and Biblical passages. This study is based on a collection of Christian studies of Islam that was prepared in connection to the Study Programme of the Near East Christian Council 1956-59 (see Biography and References). The questions reveal a distinctive *apologetic* approach to Islam studies, see e.g. two of the general but representative questions on p. 29 immediately having presented 'the Muslim's worship' (11-19): 'What perplexities or criticisms does Christian worship arouse in the average Muslim? How do you meet them?' The purpose of these studies were 'to serve and equip the Christian communities for adventures of ministry and expression towards their fellow men in Islam,' 5.

g. Poems, either of his own collection (*PWC*), or collection of poems and prayers 'common' to Muslim and Christians (*CP*), or Sufi prayers (*WSuf*)

h. Theological auto-biography (*FLN*) and 'Islam-biography,' of Oxford, (*IAS*)

When it comes to *interreligious hermeneutics* Cragg's considerations about this are scattered. They are often to be found in introductions to articles and works, but also in connection with topical elaborations. Another issue to be aware of, which probably requires more of the student, is that Cragg writes in a rather distinctive imaginative manner. His style is not strictly logical although he often deals with philosophical questions. Yet, there are some works that have a broader discussion of interreligious issues, also from a quite general point of view. In this regards *CWP, COR* and *CFs* deserve special attention (cf. f) above). Reading these studies carefully, one will discover a range of rudiments that may serve the reconstruction of a fuller interreligious hermeneutics. Whether such a reconstruction at the end can be recognized as coherent and consistent will be discussed below. My primary concern here is how Cragg develops a hermeneutics in order to establish a systematic relation between, on the one hand, his interpretations of religions in general and Islam in particular, and his Christian self-understanding on the other. An attempt to answer this question will be undertaken by examining selected works, from his dissertation (1950) to *CFs* (1986).

4.2 Modern Muslim apology and Christian theology and mission: completion by criticism and recognition

Cragg's huge dissertation[6] (855 pp. + appendices!) from 1950 seems to shape his entire authorship in several ways. Already in this study there is present an impressive interest in modern and contemporary Muslim intellectual activity ('modern Muslim apology'),[7] an overview of the relation between religion and political/social issues, and the implications for Christian theological relevance and mission to the Islamic world under its

---

[6] *Islam in the Twentieth Century: The Relevance of Christian Theology and the Relation of the Christian Mission to its Problems (ITC)*. Parenthetical remarks in this chapter refer to *ITC*. The use of I/II refers to the fact that his dissertation is divided into two parts.

[7] Most interestingly, in his survey of related research, Cragg accuses Wilfred Cantwell Smith (*MI*, 1943/1946) for lack of sympathy for 'actual Islam' as distinct from a

'apologetic leadership.' The study ranges from critical encounters with significant Muslim modernists 'outside the Arab Muslim mind'[8] (such as 'Abduh, al-Afghani, Muhammad Ali of India, and Sir Muhammad Iqbal) to suggestions of Muslim-Christian 'cells' for theological co-operation as a part of 'plans for Christian action.' In sum this initial work of Cragg may be characterized as a fundamental and strategic study in Christian mission to Muslims.[9]

For the purpose of our study I will here only consult some selected parts of his dissertation. These will be drawn from the introduction, including his conclusions of the criticism he has made of modern Muslim apology (part I, ch. III), from the part on the missionary relation to Islam where he considers 'the problem of communication *from* Christianity' and 'the problem of communication *to* Islam' (part II, ch. V.1-2, my emphasis), and finally from his last elaboration on the 'theological relationships' (part II, ch. V.5.f).

4.2.1 THE 'CONVICTIONS,' 'HOPE' AND 'SPIRIT' OF CRAGG'S APPROACH

Cragg's D.Phil. dissertation rests upon, as he says, two convictions and a hope. The convictions are that:

> There is an intellectual and social crisis of great significance both to Muslims themselves and to the world at large, and that Christianity has had more prolonged experience of similar, intellectual and social obligations in the modern world which

---

potential Islam that he seems to be seeking, *ITC* 35. Cragg sees this as a subordination of theology to sociology. As I have mentioned in the introduction to Smith's works (Chapter 2.1) this study (*MI*) does not fit to the scope of our study and is socio-historical with strong socialists interests (which Cragg calls 'strong partisan bias'). Cragg maintains in a letter to me that he learned this 'focus which was on contemporary inter-apologias and times' from H.A.R. Gibb, Cragg 2000e.

[8] *FLN,* 110.

[9] That the study concerns 'fundamental' aspects of the relationship between Muslims and Christians is Cragg's own description, see II: 130. The use of 'strategic' here shall not be confused with what Cragg himself calls 'purely tactical aspects' (*ibid.*). I use the term to refer to a) one of his major aims with his study, namely to contribute to a *new* situation between Muslims and Christians, combined with b) his extensive use of church/Christianity and Islam as respectively subject and object, c) the missionary/apostolic role of the church, d) the emphasis on religious leadership by both Muslims and Christians, and e) his use of 'strategic' (e.g. II: 137). That he ends his study with a certain hesitance about whether Muslims will reply and the state of affairs change (II:278-280) does not weaken my use of this notion, rather the contrary.

has qualified it—given a basis of genuine fellowship—to serve contemporary Islam and its problems (i).

The hope is, most interesting for the approach of our study:

> That if a constructive relationship between the two faiths can be attained on these lines the old unthinking resistance of Islam to Christianity may give way and areas of understanding be discovered where the old antipathy will be overcome by a new readiness to consider Christ and His Church (*ibid.*).

Now, this relation between the intellectual and social crisis of Islam and its retrieval by Christianity is, despite Cragg's proposal for fellowship and removal of 'unthinking resistance,' not to be seen as a mere hospitable offer to help. Cragg sees very critically the intellectual mood of Muslim thinkers as 'seriously lacking in adequate awareness of what religious apology today really entails,'[10] he sees no progress and, therefore, no adequately realist attempt to redeem the intellectual and social situation' except by 'the great potential service of Christianity' (v) as a mitigating circumstance (561f), especially in terms of self-criticism (vi).[11]

Yet, this offer of help should also not be understood as an offer from somebody who aims to beat another religion, rather the contrary.

---

[10] See especially part II, ch. III, 530-563. Moreover, he sees this as relating to the *temper* of 'the Muslim mind,' characterized by preferences for emotional and practical satisfactions, indifference to intellectual quality, and more at home in the imaginative world than that of rationality and ideas (with reference to H. A. R. Gibb), 127. Hence Cragg sees his questioning of the capacity of the Muslim mind to reckon with the modern intellectual challenge as fundamental to his entire thesis, 128. Finally, this situation seems to correspond to the difference between theology and religion/religious life, 126-128. Ultimately, and understood as 'a *universal necessity* to religion of theology,' 'the worth and quality [of a religion], must in the end depend upon its *active theology*,' 128, my emphases.

[11] See also his retrospective comments on his thesis in *FLN*: 'This was why I was wanting to discover the *self-critical* Islam,' 108, and 111: 'The central question, it seemed to me, was whether Islamic *faith* and Muslim *life* were required to be in mutual *negotiation* at all' (my emphases). In this respect Cragg sees his thesis as an exposure of a Muslim 'self-satisfied' and 'self-exonerated' apologetics, *ibid.* 108. The personal inducement for his thesis seems to have been threefold: a) the way he had experienced in Lebanon how goodwill, hope, etc., was entangled in a 'crippling prejudice,' as enmities, suspicions, questionings, b) the resolute disqualification of Christianity at the very core of Islam and its finality, and c) his inspiration after arrival in Longworth by the Lux Mundi movement which had developed in the Rectory over several summers almost 60 years earlier (see note 82 below), cf. *FLN* 107, 111. Based on this Cragg saw very well both the possibility of 'con-spiracy' (breathing together!) and the problem of disparity, *ibid.* 111.

Cragg says that critical frankness should not be equated with an attitude of condemnation (562).[12] The reason for this is that Christian theology itself has had a long history of struggle after the emergence of the modern world. And, it is this experience it should mediate to Muslim apologists (563).

Yet, this is not a formal experience that could be transferred to Muslims merely by its structure, as it were. This is an experience of 'Bethlehem and Jerusalem' being satisfactory for the human needs of our world. Hence Cragg sees the church as potentially helpful because she is herself the result of, and bearer of the commission of God's unique but inclusive self-disclosure for all humanity. Thus, the church becomes 'the truth's inclusive relevance institutionalised' (22, my emphasis). In this way Cragg attempts to balance the interests of uniqueness and inclusiveness.[13] Yet, a consequence of this is that

> if Christianity be as it is claimed the tests that time and change impose on any faith will *pre-dispose it Christwards*. To share in their [the Muslim's] inward coming into Muslim consciousness must surely be a profoundly Christian, because a truly Christ-like, thing (23, my emphasis).

In short, g Given the nature of Christian beliefs, the crises which Muslims experience intellectually, politically and socially in the first half of the twentieth century will open them up towards the Christian message. For Cragg, this is ultimately a matter of 'a valid theory of development and change' (561). For Christianity 'as it is claimed,' one shall probably read here 'a readiness for self-effacement after the pattern of the Cross' so that 'the more men come to themselves to know their insufficiency the nearer they come to God in Christ' (24).[14] This ends his *confessio et defensio fidei*.

Now, Cragg is very aware of immediate reactions that may confront this 'spirit.' Yet, he contends, if this Christian 'interest' in Islam has to be disqualified one should reckon any serious study of comparative religion impossible. Cragg's final argument, therefore, is that his approach at this point should be justified as a matter of pre-suppositions (23). It seems

---

[12] Cragg's self-description of his critique of the modern Muslim apology is: 'frank but sympathetic,' *ITC* 126.

[13] See also Cragg 1966a, 171: 'And this sense of the cross is *inclusively unique* (not exclusively unique, which is something else) and does not deprive *other calvaries* of the place and travail it shares with them while remaining in all history *their representative*' (my emphases).

[14] As one may see, this interpretation of 'Christwards' resonates with Luther's *Christum treiben*. See also below, 4.2.2.

that Cragg is suggesting a close relation between examining the 'formative quality of religious beliefs' (21) and the religious or spiritual quality of the investigator himself. If this is to be maintained, as also Smith does, one cannot in principle exclude certain parts or purposes from the investigator (for example normative judgements). This does not mean that his method be regarded as arbitrary. Cragg, indeed, himself stresses the intellectual standards and 'proper academic safeguards'. The point is that 'spiritual purposes are finally rewarded according to their quality' (23).

Yet, what are these qualities? To what extent does Christianity have a theory of development and change that is superior to the Muslim modern apology? And, finally, how does he comprehend the possibilities of developing relations between Christians and Muslims?

4.2.2 'THE PROBLEM OF COMMUNICATION FROM CHRISTIANITY': ULTIMATE CLAIMS, GENUINE LOVE AND THE RICHER POSSESSION OF ONE'S SELF-UNDERSTANDING

Because Islam is coping, and Christianity has been coping with the same mental challenge (modernity), Cragg maintains that the Christian experience of this 'theological travail' must be 'somehow capable of mediation' (128).[15] This *capacity of mediation* is further justified for him by 'the knowledge' that a religion is part of 'the very order of God and man which religion in its entirety relates' (129). At this point Cragg presupposes an understanding of religion as a universal enterprise, namely 'the order of God and man'. It is most interesting to see that what may seem to be a rather harsh assessment of the Muslim capacity to cope with modernity ends up with an emphasis on *commonality*. Hence his notion of 'reciprocity' is the 'attempt to face the demands on one side [and, which] pre-disposes the response of the other' (cf. 'pre-dispose Christwards' above). Cragg sees this reciprocity as a possible disarmament of Islam's susceptibilities and inhibitions as 'the temper of the Christian approach is subdued to these demands of communication' (*ibid.*).

As one sees, this reciprocity consists basically of a set of needs on the Muslim side, which Cragg has discerned by his analysis of modern Muslim apology to the challenge of modernity on the one hand, and the

---

[15] If one compares *ITC* at this point with *CFs*, see below (4.5.4), it is possible to assert that the main characteristics of Cragg's authorship relates to the possibility of mediating between 'communities and minds,' in particular between Islam and the Muslim mind, and Christianity and the Christian mind, see *FLN* 126.

Christian remedy in respect of a successful experience with 'theological travail' in relation to the same 'mental challenge' on the other. Using a language of 'balance', this reciprocity is heavily asymmetrical. This is primarily mediation from Christianity, and not a Christian mediation of Muslim needs. Hence Cragg does not reckon this reciprocity immediately operative, but as a truth of the situation (*ibid.*).

Yet, this is not the whole picture. Considering 'the problem of communication from Christianity' (130-139) Cragg asserts that the Christian 'builder of bridges' (the 'priest' or 'pontifex'!) is tested seriously himself. The very issue is that '*self-expression* [of Christ in His fullness] to an 'other' is also a lesson in *self-understanding*' (130, my emphasis). Moreover, using the analogy of poets and authors (for example John Donne), Cragg maintains that: 'language has the power to make an interior experience explicit' (*ibid.*) and that

> The Church finds that truth brought o[u]t [to] bear on others learns more validly its own inward content and reaches a finer quality through the effort of communication. Its hearers draw out its full wealth (131).

This general view of the impact of self-expression upon one's self-understanding is, according to Cragg, nowhere more potentially beneficial and latent for Christian self-communication than in 'the exacting relationship with Islam' (131). As one sees, by a cluster of relational notions (relationship, communication, self-learning by self-communication, self-understanding by self-expression, etc.) the previously noticed asymmetry in this reciprocity comes out more as a real mutuality where the double-sided exchange is operative. Consequently, the church in its perceived hostility, resistance and misunderstandings on the part of the Muslim world

> may well find itself in *richer possession* of itself and in worthier trusteeship of its truths (*ibid.*, my emphasis).

I assume that this shall be interpreted qualitatively: that the church may discover its Christian faith in a better way than if it had not attempted to relate to Islam. This interpretation seems to be supported by another statement, which enlarges the perspective even more:

> Islam throws Christianity back, *in a way that is unique to it*, upon its most *distinctive* truths and its most ultimate *reserves of the Spirit* (*ibid.*, my emphasis).

Yet, how should this quotation be understood? What is clear is that the attempt to communicate something to Islam entails a *counter-move,* namely that it is thrown back to its own particularity, to its distinctively Christian doctrines. What also seems to be the case is that this is 'unique' as far as it would not necessarily have been the case without the relating to Islam. Thus Islam contributes to the formation of the Christian (self-) understanding of 'central matters.'[16] Certainly, not in the role of a teacher who helps a pupil to develop his or her identity, more by its function as contrast, of being awkward and exacting.[17] Importantly, what ultimately facilitates this Christian re-interpretation[18] is the 'reservoir' of what the Holy Spirit possesses. One might, therefore, say that whereas the hermeneutic observation is induced by the analogy of poetry and function of language,[19] the theological justification for this hermeneutical enterprise is based on a particular understanding of the Holy Spirit.

---

[16] This interpretation is confirmed in a letter from Cragg to the author dated 29 May 2000, Cragg 2000e: 'What I meant to say was that been attentive to what Muslims said about the Incarnation and the Cross drew out of one, as Christian, a keener awareness of what faith as to these truly meant. I think I understood what e.g. I had always meant by 'Christ died for our sins'[,] these elements of belief said by wrestling with how to take up, in sincerity, why Islam saw them as unwarranted or inappropriate to God. Open listenin[g] proved enriching because it demanded a redefining (not abandoning) of what was always held ... The Muslim perception— if heeded—had the potential to elucidate—and hopefully purify one's commendation of meaning ... Hermeneutics, thus, is not only 'domestic' attention to the text but also existing in interfaith discourse in hope of inner honesty.'

[17] See p. 136: 'That being so [i.e. the relation between love and truth], how *potentially enriching* to the Church the nature of Islam should be, with all its *awkward and exacting demands* on Christian communication,' my emphases.

[18] 'Re-interpretation' is not used here in any agnostic sense. It will be showed later that Cragg explicitly reserves his approach from an agnostic interpretation.

[19] See also *WWd* (1999d) for a similar approach at a late stage of his authorship. In ch. IX he speaks (albeit with a rhetorical question) of a *development* in respect of 'meanings, at first unrealized, that are legitimately located in the [sacred] text' by 'the receptive community' as found in Judaism, Christianity and Islam, 148, 141, 155. The immediate context is how 'ultimate literature' of prophethood, such as the Bible and the Qur'an, can be "sealed' for a forward empire of relevance' and thus be 'ongoing' in its finality, that is, to be 'quantitatively complete but qualitatively potential,' 138-141. In this respect, 'prophetic texts leave the issue and the decision to the *reader,*' 149, my emphasis. Hence, canonized texts are *bent towards the future,* 145. Perceived like this, Cragg maintains to preserve the meaning of prophethood far better than a 'crude 'futurizing' that takes prophethood avidly as mere 'foretelling," 141. On the other hand, some reading options will be illegitimate. One example of this can be found in his severe criticism of contemporary Zionism which he sees as self-congratulatory in respect of how 'chosenness' and the 'land-inviolability' are interpreted in the light of the 'rationalizing, and nationalizing, of Jewish experience.' Cragg sees Zionism as ignorant of (authentic) prophetic 'moral conscience' as well as its (self-)accusation of chosenness and

If this interpretation is valid, it not only compensates for his attitude otherwise in his approach; it also implies an awareness of what may be called the returning impact upon him who has something to communicate to an 'other.' As such, the relation between self-expression and self-understanding seems to resonate with the approach of my study (self-relating and self-change) as well as with and the meaning of *relatio*.[20] Whether the notion of 'pre-disposing Islam Christwards' thus may correspond to a post-disposing Christianity Christwards can only be decided by entering Cragg's further elaborations on the communication from Christianity and to Islam.

Nonetheless, Cragg draws attention to the possible temptation to compromise either doctrine or spirit. This corresponds to maintaining both the truth and love of Christ, an intellectual and moral concord, which is unlikely to attain apart from the Spirit (133). I take this to support my interpretation above, but also to support the case that his rather harsh ('frank') assessment of modern Muslim apologists should be seen as an expression of persuasion of truth, and hence a part of the work of the Holy Spirit together with, yet dialectically, attitudes of love (patience, humility, disavowing 'ascendancy', will to fellowship, mutual understanding and relation, etc.), for which his study is full of concern. This is what Cragg calls 'the dilemma of the Spirit.'[21] The solution is described thus:

> The more fully and emphatically we affirm Christ, the more searching become the moral demands of our theology in terms of our attitude and spirit, and the more exacting the burdens of its presentation to others (134).

This corresponds ultimately to the 'pattern of the cross,' to which any Christian mission should seek to conform if it aims at self-consistency (136-138). A consequence of this pattern, however, is that it both criticizes and recognizes the Other, in fact: also the church.

---

land-inviolability respectively, and thus not in line with the potential meaning of Hebrew prophethood, *WWd*, 142, 146f, 156-158. Cf. also *PAL* (written in 1998, the 50th anniversary of the state of Israel!), in particular ch. 11 ('The searchings of Reuben'), 186-203. Cragg is never as passionate as when he writes about (against) Zionism.

20 See Chapter 1 (Introduction), and 'relatio' in Lewis and Short 1887/1955, *A Latin Dictionary*, 1544f and 1554f.

21 Cragg makes at this place a critical remark regarding W.E. Hocking and his criticism that: because of the church's 'disloyalty in love' it should be disqualified in terms of its truth, particularly in regards of 'the unique claim and content of Christian truth' consisting of 'the Incarnation and Redemption,' 133f.

4.2.3 'THE PROBLEM OF COMMUNICATION TO ISLAM': ABROGATION AND INTEGRATION

Cragg dedicates one chapter in his dissertation to 'the problem of communication to Islam.' His purpose is not to see how the gap between Islam and Christianity can be bridged from the Islamic side, but from the Christian side to see how to 'anchor' the relationship on the Muslim side (139). A keyword in this respect is 'controversy,' which Cragg sees as an inescapable quality of the Gospel, 'the critical quality of the Gospel' (132), and thus also in relation to Islam (141, 145). Yet, this is not primarily a controversy between the church and Islam but, rather definitionally expressed: a controversy *of* God, in Christ and with his people (140; 145, with Islam). It follows that any Christian criticism of Islam is ultimately a critique on behalf of God, a theological critique. That this takes the form of a Christian criticism of Islam is an implication of the fact that the church is the bearer of the unique, Divine *sui generis*-initiative represented by the Incarnation and suffering of Christ (140). This does, however, not imply that the church is exempted from the same critique (141).[22]

This stress of controversy is not for the sake of controversy itself. The language Cragg uses is more informed by a dialectical notion of fulfilment and satisfaction. On the one hand he may say that completion of the 'aspirations' of non-Christians can only happen by explicit criticism, or that the Gospel fulfils by contrast rather than by similarity (140). On the other hand 'their valid hopes and desires' have to be 'actualised' (*ibid.*), as also their 'values' may and must be purified and conserved (141). His vocabulary proceeds along these lines when he introduces the relation of the Gospel to Islam.[23] This approach should be understood as a double, yet, unified activity. Cragg speaks of a 'double significance' that is 'an indivisible whole' (*ibid.*). Further, of a double relation (*ibid.*), a double call (142) and a double ministry (172).

The critical point, however, is that the potentialities on behalf of Islam will be rejected if the controversy is evaded. Hence to fulfil and complete Islam is to criticize it. Finally, Cragg uses the analogy of baptism to describe the confirmatory and critical activity of bringing the Gospel to non-Christians. As the 'regenerating baptism' is a baptism 'into new and

---

[22] See e.g. II:273 where both Muhammad and the church are contrasted to Christ in regards of propagating themselves in terms of prestige and power.

[23] More specifically, the dialectical pairs of notions are as follows: satisfaction–criticism, fulfilment–repudiation (140), abandon–retain, repudiate–enrich, repentance–faith, liberates–condemns, judgement–perfecting, criticism/ correction–satisfaction (141, 148), critical–confirmatory, denied–integrated/re-[e]nforced (142).

truer fullness,' and on the basis of what is mentioned above, one may conclude that Cragg on the one hand suggests a rather critical discontinuity in being a Muslim and becoming completed by the Christian Gospel, and, on the other maintains an affirmative continuity between the potentialities in Islam and the fulfilment of them in Christ.

Using the traditional tripartite scheme of theology of religions,[24] it may be maintained that Cragg seems to combine the exclusive and inclusive approach. How these are balanced is not easily answerable. Firstly, the criticism and completion are inseparable. Secondly, there is a consistent relation between them, a relation that entails a certain direction, namely from criticism to completion. Thirdly, in this 'move' the former seems to function as *means* for the latter. Hence it may be concluded that the inclusive relation between Islam and the church (as bearer of the Gospel) is primary to the exclusive function of the critical quality of the Gospel.[25]

As a Lutheran student, I think this obviously resonates with the relation between the second use of the Law (*usus legis spiritualis*) and the Gospel as understood in the Lutheran tradition. Whether Cragg's emphasis on continuity is compatible with a Lutheran view of the Law-Gospel relation will be assessed below (Chapter 7). So much can be said here, however, that within certain strands of the Lutheran tradition this is very much possible. What demands more effort to harmonize is what seems to be a dialectical function of the Gospel itself (for example p. 145: 'the contrasted character of the Christian Gospel'), and not between the Law and the Gospel.

One might however ask: What particular in Islam is then to be criticized and confirmed? Though we will enquire more extensively into this in the next chapter, an incipient answer to this will advance Cragg's argument further.

A basic assumption for Cragg's criticism of the Muslim apology of the former part of twentieth century is the reciprocity of 'movement [of any religion] Christward' and 'change making for deeper adequacy in the human situation' and, therefore, a correspondence between the demands and criticism of 'the times'[26] and the criticism of the Gospel (145f). This

---

[24] This scheme will however be criticized in Chapter 6.

[25] An evidence for this is a kind of language that neither operates with *totus-totus* nor with *either-or*, but with *partly-partly*. E.g. 171, where he describes the belief in the all-embracing God as one 'capable of being degraded' and as such 'capable of being perfected.' This follows the principle of 'not argue as if its abuse were its absence.' See also 172 where Cragg maintain that 'Muslim personal religion' can be related to the Gospel in its '*partial eclipse*, as well as for its *potential value*' (my emphasis).

[26] One might discover a certain trust in the change and demands of 'time' several places, e.g. 167 where Cragg asks (rhetorically?) whether 'the development of

double front of controversy with which Islam has to engage, is, according to Cragg, situated deeper than traditional matters of conflict. Based on the triangle of Christian criticism/demands of modern challenges/Islam, Cragg suggests that Islam lacks a Divine supra-natural quality and a radical human realism. In other words, there is nothing in Islam to compete with the redemptive love of God and the doctrine of sin as expressed and implicit in the Incarnation and Redemption (157f, 160). Yet, Cragg does not only see this proposal as a deduction of 'Christian prejudices' but as a 'crystallising of the lessons to be learned from Muslim apology itself' (155f). In the next major chapter (5) I will examine how his critique of Islam is developed at this point.

Nonetheless, the critique of the quality of Islamic theology and anthropology does not mean that Cragg excludes Islam and Muslims from any activity of God. In fact Cragg implicitly differentiates between the God in Christ *and* God the Spirit. Cragg sees 'deeply valid elements of spiritual insight and concrete achievement' in Islam that can be positively recognized as truth; true religious expressions. But true religious expression in Cragg's language means nothing less that an activity of God the Spirit (149). This does not imply that Christianity can be superseded or that Christ can be improved upon (149), only that there are elements in Islam that should be recognized as a result of the presence and work of the Triune God. As such they may illustrate and serve Christ (155).[27] Consequently particular issues such as the doctrine of God, revelation, the notion of 'human unity' and the all-pervasiveness of religion may be integrated in the faith in Incarnation and Redemption in spite of all disproportions and demerits (159-172).

We may, therefore, conclude that Cragg's differentiation within the Godhead makes possible a differentiated approach to Islam, spanning both exclusive and inclusive elements and relating both to different persons of the Trinity (Christ and the Spirit), as well as relating to a double, dialectical significance within one of the persons (the critical and completing quality of Christ).

---

time' may come to the rescue of the church in its dilemmas over communication to Islam. Whether this is an expression of a God-related *hope* rather than a belief in *progress* is a point of discussion. To me it seems that there is entailed a combination of the two in his approach, see e.g. 147 where he is very optimistic about a *settlement* of the 'controversy' with Islam.

[27] It may be here that the corollary for the use of the Spirit is to be found, i.e. the function of the Spirit as the *guide* and *interpreter* of Christ (John 16). One might wonder why Cragg does not introduce the Spirit as 'judgement over the world' (John 16.8-11) as criticism has been a major theme above.

4.3 The Call of the Minaret as formative clue and contrariety

In many respects *The Call of the Minaret (CM)*[28] is the popular version of much of the arguments in Cragg's dissertation, which is further simplified in *Sandals at the Mosque*.[29] It is also the result of his period as Professor of Arabic and Islamics at Hartford Seminary Foundation, Connecticut (1951-56).

Cragg's aim in *The Call of the Minaret* is to use the muezzin's 'call of the minaret'[30] in two-ways: a) In it to seek the clue to Islam assuming that the call is 'perhaps the best single epitome of Muslim belief and action' (viif), and b) from that clue to learn in order to dimension the Christian relation to what it tells. From such formulations one might expect the interpretation of Islam, in this case of what is assumed to be central to it, to determine how the Christian message should be presented to a Muslim audience.

Evidence for this interpretation can be found in the further part of the preface. Firstly, it seems unavoidable that the Christian must first come to an intimate understanding of Islam before he attains to an

---

[28] Parenthetical remarks in this chapter refer to *CM*. Since my attention has been directed to the development of Cragg's ideas, I have not used the revised edition of *CM* from 1985.

[29] This is especially the case in the relation between Islam-interpretation, Christian theology and Christian mission. See also his positive remark about his access to contemporary Islam through 'the apology of numerous Muslim writers', viii, which in a particular way connects the two works since the main part of his dissertation consists of a survey of 22 different authors, and journals and movements, related to their contribution to a 'modern Muslim apology.'

CM is also popular (and missionary) in respect of its 'strange case of stumbling into print'. In *FLN*, 118f, Cragg writes that *CM* originated in his time in the US, as a contribution toward 'focusing ideas' for a small group who met for Christian study of Islam in New York, of whom many had experience from ministry across Asia and Africa. Cragg saw his contribution as a reflection of the 'change of scene and temper' since Temple Gairdner's *The Reproach of Islam,* 1909. Jan Slomp calls it a 'rethinking and reshaping' of Christian missions to the Muslim world, and 'the programmatic quintessence of Cragg's theology of islam [!],' Slomp 1990, 171. See also Cragg 1981b and *MC,* 3, n1. After coinciding with several conferences it finally emerged, originally unknown to Cragg, on Oxford University Press, New York. Being reprinted several times in the past decades since it was launched, it is pertinent to call it Cragg's *classic,* in the same way as *ME* is Smith's classic. By no chance Sidney H. Griffith labels (!) *CM* as 'vintage Cragg,' Griffith 1994, 29.

[30] In Cragg's version: 'God is most great, God is most great, I bear witness that there is no god except God: I bear witness that Muhammad is the Apostle of God. Come ye unto prayer. Come ye unto God. Prayer is a better thing than sleep. Come ye to the best deed. [This phrase among Shî'ahs only] God is most great. God is most great. There is no god except God,' *CM,* 30f, Cragg's insertion.

authentically Christian relation to 'the Mosque and its worlds' (ix). The structural composition of both *CM* and *SM* supports this.[31] Secondly, Cragg seeks a result that goes beyond 'areas of conscious otherness' so that Christ can be known 'to the heart of the muezzin's faith' (*ibid.*). At least in spatial language, this implies an attempt to abandon distance in order to draw Christians nearer to Muslims.[32] Even when the perspective is solely of the Christian interpreting the call of the minaret (either to establish the meaning for Muslims, chs. ii-v, or for Christians, chs. vi-xi), the Islamic meaning of the call to prayer *has a dimensioning role in the* way the Christian relation and message is developed.

Another way of describing this aim is given by Cragg's purport to help the Muslim 'to become what he is' by shaping and defining the definition of Islam (ix). This is to be conceived as the large duty which combines 'the full measure of Islam' with a commitment to 'all meanings of Christ,' which Cragg sees himself summoned to. At first glance this programme may seem to be unduly patronizing. On the other hand, before we assess Cragg's approach as a whole, he deserves sympathy for his directedness in respect of taking his own religious position serious in relating it to Islam, as well as his concession of Islam as a dimensioning of the Christian relation, even if its apologetic form is striking.[33]

---

[31] The 'Islam expositions' (*CM,* Part 2; *SM,* Part 1, 'In Quest of Islam'), although Cragg resists to name them so, see *SM,* 19, which is partly understandable given Cragg's (imaginative) nuances not least in the making of the titles of his books, are placed before the chapters on the 'Christian response' or 'Christian relevance.'

[32] Cragg gives here also notice to the impact of Muslim friendships and associations upon this study. See also *SM,* 21, where Cragg criticizes a *secluded* theology and instead suggests a theology that is 'outward and relational' and which is on 'the frontiers of religions in their mutual existence.' This suggestion asserts to have the 'oldest and surest of Christian precedents,' that is: of the New Testament itself, *ibid.* See also my examination of *CWP* in 4.4.2 below.

[33] This is especially the case in chs. ix-xi. In my opinion, a quite fair description of this might be found in the characterization of Abrahim H. Khan, philosopher and Past President of the Canadian Theological Society, of Cragg's approach in *MC,* namely as: 'less of a critically cognitive undertaking and more of a hermeneutical enterprise with an apologetic intent,' Khan 1986, 189. What is highly debateable, however, is how Khan continues: 'and hence scandalous to Muslim appreciation of Muh?ammad and to an understanding of Islam,' and his strict dictum: 'that any such approach to dialogue, based on religious precommitments of any sort, is suspect, and unlikely to be reckoned as a serious critical undertaking in the academic study of religion,' *ibid.* With adherence to Khan's dictum such different theologians as R. Panikkar, H. Küng, S. Samartha, M. Borrmans, L. Newbigin, and P.F. Knitter are also disregarded (most notably, not Kierkegaard and Tillich!), *ibid.* 189; 196f; 202, n 35. This raises of course the question whether his critique is somewhat large-meshed. In my opinion, to confine 'academic studies of religion' thus, hinges on an objective-critical, anti-ideological academic ideal ('the citadel of academic objectivity'; 'the line of scrimmage between scholars and gurus,' 199) that does

Yet, how are the aims of the preface realized in the rest of the book? As I mentioned above,[34] interreligious questions are particularly treated in ch. vi ('Mosque and Meeting'). Cragg's point of departure is that the mosques are meant to 'gather'.[35] Cragg takes this to mean a serious invitation also to Christians: to meet Islam. Yet, this coming together does not mean to give up ones religious loyalties, rather the contrary. Describing how an (Arabic-speaking) Christian immediately will associate what he hears in the mosque with what he knows about Christ, Cragg concludes, 'one cannot have a religious relationship which begins by neglecting the religious criteria [of one's own]' (177). Hence any relation between Christian and Muslims includes for the Christian a normative relation to what Christ and church means, as also the Muslim, on the other hand, has to evaluate for himself and his community what a meeting with Christians may involve. Moreover, this is the only way of facilitating the meeting with the hospitality it deserves. The guiding principle seems thus to be that essential loyalty abandons mutual exclusion.[36]

This might on the one hand appear to be undermining the capacities for interreligious relations. However, Cragg's point is to stress his contention that this meeting represents a 'mutuality of significance' so as to show the supreme difficulties of 'meeting'. In this latter point it can be shown that Cragg's direct and scarcely disguised approach may be regarded as hermeneutically apt. In his study of how different religious traditions relate to religious 'strangers', or 'aliens', outside their own 'system', Andreas Grünschloß concludes that the aim of being open and

---

not fully recognize the importance of hermeneutical studies in the fields of religion where, of course, 'precommitments' are inherent and inherently important. That religious commitments 'are assumed, and not critically investigated in the same manner he has investigated Muhammad,' *ibid.* 190, should not exclude Cragg's approach from any academic activity, that is: as a hermeneutical endeavour, especially not as theological, as is the concern of the present study. Most interestingly, on the other hand, an awareness of this seems to be included in Khan's article: 'Within theology such a study [i.e. Cragg's study] is not without some merit, since it can prove to be a strategy to find out *where one is theologically, how one understands oneself in the world,*' 193, my emphasis. This comes very close to the approach of our study.

[34] See note 3, p. 147.

[35] Cf. the meaning of *jami'a*, as one of the Arabic references for 'mosque', 176.

[36] At this place Cragg resembles later thoughts of for example Hans Küng, see e.g. Küng 1991 *passim,* especially when Cragg proceeds with rhetorical questions like: 'Does the co-existence of peoples require the co-existence of religions?' and: 'The diversities of religions may in fact have contributed to the disunity of men' (180f). The justification of Cragg's demand here is not to be sought in a conformation to external pressures, but in *anthropology*: 'It is rather the obligation of their nature [i.e. of the religions] and their ancient sense of the metaphysical oneness of humanity' (181).

self-limiting towards the other, and simultaneously keeping one's loyalties to particular perspectives and commissions, easily ends in *aporia* as regards of competing with each other.[37] Whether it may be feasible to retrieve this difficult situation, is another question. At this place I only want to stress the seriousness of it.

One might also support Cragg's view of the role of one's own self-understanding for any 'true mutuality' or 'spiritual communication' (175) by means of the notions of 'prejudice' and 'fore-meanings' and their important role in any understanding, as understood in the hermeneutic tradition, for example in Gadamer.[38]

Basically it can be said that Cragg establishes a hermeneutic situation consisting of the Christian who is called to interpret Islam and express his faith in Christ for Muslims on the one hand, and 'things Islamic' that represents an exactingness to the Christian interpreting mind and spirit on the other (178). Whereas the former represents the moral obligation to 'care about Christ,' the latter perceives Islam both as 'contrariety' and 'clue' (179). The latter of these deserves some attention.

Islam is to Cragg 'a harsh world' (178). Yet, because much of the harshness is well intentioned, it has to be transcended. To state it another way: Cragg assumes that Islam misunderstands when it relates to Christians and Christ. Once again, this might at first glance seem both undue and harsh. Yet, on second thoughts this may represent a valuable hermeneutical observation. In his xenological study, Andreas Grünschloß draws attention to the role of 'mis-understanding' in the work of Schleiermacher.[39] In Schleiermacher the role of mis-understanding in respect of hermeneutics is more fundamental than understanding ('daß sich das Mißverständnis *von* selbst ergibt'[40]). Hence any attempt to understand the Other should continuously deal with non-understanding. Because of this non-understanding one is requested to re-orient Oneself, understood as an interior movement of inquiry, keeping the original direction of attempting to employ an understanding of the Other. Grünschloß interprets this as a possibility of discovering *(Entdeckung)* the Other by uncovering *(Ent-*

---

[37] Grünschloß 1999, 269.

[38] Cragg reveals a developed sense for this in a somewhat later study, *DR*, 6: 'Will it not be sounder, not to say more feasible, if we confess our interests, take conscious control of their 'prejudice', and by discipline and hope release their potential assets of affinity, humility, perception, and involvement?'

[39] Grünschloß 1999, 295-299: 'Der 'Mißverständnis' als hermeneutische Grundsituation.' Grünschloß refers to Schleiermachers *Hermeneutik* in two different works: *Hermeneutik und Kritik. Mit einem Anhang sprachphilosophischer Texte Schleiermachers,* hrsg. und eingel. v. M. Frank, Frankfurt 1977; *Hermeneutik,* hrsg. v. H. Kimmerle, Heidelberg ²1974.

[40] *Ibid.,* 296, my emphasis.

Deckung) that of One's own, which until then had been covered *(Deckung).*[41]

One may, however, ask to what extent this emphasis on what happens to Oneself in interpreting the Other is really engaged in Cragg's approach. The 'mis-understandings' seem to be more in the possession of Muslims than of Christians since it is the Christian message that is misunderstood, and is that which he seeks to make plausible for a Muslim audience (after all). Furthermore, when Cragg faces the phenomenon of 'opposition' (274), the interpretation of it is that it signals that Christ is relevant for Muslim, that is: Muslims are at least not indifferent, whereas the remedy is to subdue the obstacles to the 'master-purposes' by delineating Christ more deeply. But again, all this is compelled by Muslim objections.

At the same time Cragg employs a language of capacities that makes his own self-understanding dependent on the Islamic capacity of accepting 'what is worthy of all acceptation' (274). This sticks to a general belief that 'the language of God in Christ' is not beyond anyone's understanding. This again relates to the work of the Holy Spirit who is seeking 'his clues in all areas of life.' Ultimately, however, this has to do with the universal Christ. Cragg does not employ a well-developed doctrine of the universal Christ. Yet, what he says is that 'the ruling concepts of Christianity,' understood as the human being the vehicle for the Divine, and where God and man are in living relation, 'necessarily recur ... in articulate [or] ... inarticulate, form in the religious faiths of the world' (183). This is to say that the structures or themes of the Incarnation, where God uses the human as his vehicle, and of Salvation, where God and man are in living relation, are to be found throughout the world's religions. This is further conceptualized as a 'mutual transaction of expression'. Hence the Christian 'self-relating' to other faiths has to be continually open to discoveries of clues to an understanding of Christ. Using the analogy of the rewards of ecumenical work, Cragg therefore says: 'it takes a whole world to understand the whole Christ' *(ibid.).* This shall not be understood as rudiments of a universal history of revelation but as an explication of the truth that Christ is *relevant universally.*

The same line of though can be discerned in a contemporary article.[42] In this Cragg offers some considerations that resemble those of the *Call of the Minaret.* It may also be maintained that these are continuous with positions he holds later on in his authorship. This article about an adequate Christian relation to the Qur'an is

---

[41] *Ibid.,* 298.
[42] 'The Qur'ân and the Christian Reader. I', 1956a. Parenthetical remarks refer to this study.

an attempt to consider some of the deeper attitudes of the
Quranic religion and the characteristic convictions of the
Christian mind as these are derived from the New
Testament (61).

A reasonable interpretation of this citation, seen through the article as a
whole, is: a) that Cragg wishes to go beyond the traditional, confrontational,
and closed Islamic way of expressing itself, towards a deeper and more
open understanding of Islam, which he himself should enable, and b) that
this has to be done in a certain *mutuality* with the Christian self-
understanding as it is expressed in the New Testament scriptures. This
interpretation implies that a. and b. should be held and thought together.
Yet, what kind of relation is to be presupposed here? To answer this one
has to ponder another quotation that employs the notion of truth:

> Truth is not simply a matter of propositions to be proved,
> but also, and oftener, of perceptions to be purified (62).

In this context 'perceptions' means the qur'anic world of meaning, which
should be explored by Christians. The aim, however, is most interestingly
expressed as: '[to] repossess our Christian convictions with a new
capacity of interpretation' (62). Or, stated in a similar way, this is

> far from being a proposal to find proof-texts in the Qur'ân
> for Christian quotation . . . Rather it means an openhearted
> effort to understand the meaning of Christianity in the light
> of the fullest reckoning with the ruling themes of the Qur'an
> (63).

At this place one may say that 'oneself' becomes more deeply employed
in Cragg's interreligious hermeneutics, that is: it is not only Islam (the
Other) that is comprehended in his studies in the Qur'an. The Christian
reading of the Qur'an is thus not solely a matter of bringing Christ to
Muslims in an understandable language. It also includes, by the
interpretation of particular elements in Islam, an opportunity to repossess
one's own self-understanding: the Christian faith. Hence, understanding
Islam enables a deeper understanding of the Christian faith. This should
not necessarily be understood as an entirely new interpretation, but rather
as what Grünschloß calls 'un-covering' of previously 'covered' areas of
Christian faith. Hence it must to a certain extent be justified to speak of
Islam, be it the call to prayer or the Qur'anic world of meaning, as a
formative context for a Christian reformulation of one's self-understanding.

4.4 The Open Faith and 'the Sanctuary of Incorporation': A Theology of Religious Pluralism 'in Proceeding' and 'in Christ'

4.4.1 SALUTATION AND SELF-GIVING

Another important book in respect of the development of Cragg's interreligious hermeneutics is his *Christianity in World Perspective (CWP)* from 1968.[43] In this study he develops both more open attitudes towards other religions as well as a more explicit exegetical and theological justification for Christian relations to these.

The relevance of *Christianity in World Perspective* for the present study is particularly located to Cragg's elaboration of 'a Christian theology of the religions' (70) and 'a theology of religious pluralism' respectively (65). Cragg sees such attempts as inevitable if the Christian faith is to be maintained as universal and world-relevant (65). He even suggests an 'inter-religious responsibility' (*ibid.*).

Cragg takes religious plurality as a fact. And this fact has a certain impact on how the Christian may relate to other religions. Cragg maintains that religious plurality[44] has to be recognized as a matter of contending a distinct truth in a certain environment of alternative approaches to human life:

> There can be no true claim to a Christian distinctiveness that ignores the actuality of divergent and alternate interpretations of human experience or lives by deliberate isolation from their significance (65).

Already we find a clue to a systematic relation between Christianity and other faiths, namely as far as the Christian expresses a truth claim it cannot be reckoned with in absence from parallel claims of other faiths. Other faiths are 'significant' for the Christian one. The other side of this is that

---

[43] Especially ch. 3 ('A Theology of Religious Pluralism') and ch. 2 ('New Testament Universality: Precedents and Open Questions') are of particular interest for our study. Subsequent parenthetical remarks in the present chapter refer to *CWP*. Regarding Cragg's Islam interpretation, also ch. 5 ('Christian Creed and Islamic Worship') will be relevant, especially in the light of the general interreligious hermeneutics and theology of religious plurality he develops.

[44] Cragg seems to use pluralism and plurality almost interchangeably. There is at least no consistent differentiation of the use of 'plurality' and 'pluralism'. Evidence for this is implied in his use of for example 'a theology of religious pluralism' (65 and the title of ch.2). If pluralism was reserved for theological, ideological or theoretical purposes, and plurality for mere description, this should have been rendered 'theology of religious plurality'.

4 Kenneth Cragg's Interreligious Hermeneutics

Cragg also seems to suppose some kind of truth outside the Christian faith. Hence, his chapter on a theology of religions attempts

> a Christian salutation in contemporary terms of those outside Christian community of mind and worship—a salutation that must include, as all greeting does, a worthy cognizance of the other and a ready giving of oneself in and with the world, without exoneration of will or exemption of spirit (64f).

In this somewhat dense quotation basically all of his theology of religions is present. First, and not to be underestimated, his language of salutation and greeting should be mentioned. This is more unconditionally expressed here than in his earlier studies. This emphasis is reiterated in his later studies.[45] Secondly, also a kenotic motif is present ('giving of oneself in and with the world').[46] Thirdly, one finds also a deliberate reference to 'mind and worship.' As will be shown below, this relates to Cragg's emphasis on 'worship' over 'creed' (75), which is related to his distinction between the creative and adventurous mind on the one hand, and the custodian mind on the other (73f).[47] Finally, his mentioning of the 'cognisance of the other' resembles

---

[45] See e.g. *COR* and *MG*. Even the mere indexes of these will show this concentration.

[46] For a retrospective discernment of what he aims to denote by the *kenotic* features of his theology, see *FLN,* his 'Christian' autobiography, 302, n 8. His contention is not that of "emptying' (e.g.) a vessel of its contents, so that nothing remains. It is a divesting of what might normally be assumed to belong to a status so that standing, or dignity, or privilege, *might* seem to be no longer possessed but are in fact more superbly fulfilled.' Cragg, most interestingly, refers to the King in Shakespeare's *Henry V,* where the king leaves aside his crown and take on a borrowed robe and goes among his soldiers. On the rhetoric question whether the king is still 'royal' and 'kingly' or less so, Cragg answers: 'more so'! Further, and connected to a story in Isaac Walton's *Life of George Herbert,* where a usually well-groomed poet arrives to a music session all muddied and bedraggled, having helped the peasant whose animal had fallen down in the road, Cragg states generally that: 'There are some dignities that exist only to be laid aside e.g. that of shepherd or friend. They cannot be what they are and be self-preserving, self-immunizing. The Christian faith is that it is this way with God, with 'God-in-Christ'—and Jesus is the proof. The divine is not self-economizing, but self-expending. This is *kenosis.'*

[47] This does, however not exclude him from using 'custodians', for example 'of faith', in a neutral sense, see e.g. *CWP* 43, 83, and *WWd,* 155. Nevertheless, 'custodian' seems to qualify, if his works are seen together, the unwilling attitudes within Christianity and Islam which resist any rethinking of their 'dogmas' (which are also predominantly negatively used). This allows him to establish not only a critical perspective on Islam, but also on his own Christian faith, or more precisely: his Christian background. This point is not always recognized by reviewers of Cragg's works, see for example Khan 1986, 190.

the awareness for 'alternate interpretations of human experience or lives' as quoted above. This implies a

> *capacity to feel with* the reactions and impulses of every texture of belief and unbelief and to *possess*, not merely as assessors, still less as aliens, but as companions of mortality, the world of their fears and sanctities (73, emphasis mine).

These are very strong expressions of interreligious attitudes. In these are not only embedded senses of sympathy, empathy, respect and *convivencia*, to use some of the descriptions of different levels of intercultural approximation used by Theo Sundermeier in his 'Xenologie,'[48] but an attitude of responsibility[49] and of common possession. Interestingly, Cragg explicitly abandons the use of 'assessor' and of 'alien.' This is also underlined by his notion of 'a ready giving of oneself in and with the world' above. In sum: Cragg's interpretative venture to relate to other religions is an interreligious responsibility given from the relevance of the Christian faith. In this activity his *fate* as interpreter will be identical with that of those he attempts to relate to and understand. Or better, and presumably implicit in the statement above: In this endeavour the Christian interpreter shall give himself in analogy to the *self-giving* (*kenosis*) of Christ.[50]

---

[48] Sundermeier 1996, 155.

[49] See also *ibid.*, 66f: 'The need is to search for the positive meaning of this awesome human responsibility of faiths other than our own and of the providence that entrusts it in such critical plenitude of precious folk, of mouths and minds of millions.'

[50] In this light shall, presumably, also his humble presentation of the future of Christianity 'losing ground' and the 'post-missionary resilience' of other faiths (65-70), be read. As one will discover below, this belongs to the consequence between the kenosis of Christ and the kenosis of the church. As one also will see in my exploration of Cragg's writings below, divine kenosis starts already in the creation. To complete a Trinitarian picture of Cragg's teaching of kenosis, he also maintains the kenosis of the Holy Spirit: the omni-active, yet hidden, Spirit. One may therefore outline a *kenotic line* in Cragg's writings, consisting of *inter alia*: Incarnation, life and death of Jesus, the activity of the Holy Spirit, and the self-expenditure of the Christian and the church. This is what he in an interview with me called a 'Gethsemane from age to age,' Cragg 2000c. See also note 46 above, p. 167, and note 148 below, p. 211.

Cragg belongs in respect of his kenotic Christology undoubtedly to the tradition of what Rowan Williams describes as an 'incarnationalist concensus' within the Church of England, see Williams 2000, 225-229. Prominent names here are at a first stage the seminal nineteenth-century thinker F.D. Maurice (1805-1872), whose attitude towards other religions also influenced Cragg, *FLN,* 52. See also Cracknell 1995, 41f, for Maurice's positive appraisal of Islam. Secondly, the movement and members

Cragg's normative point of departure is the notion of hospitality. This is not an utterly unfounded term but is seen as one that is 'surely the closest of all analogies to the meaning of the Gospel,' both in 'its actuality and potentiality' (71).[51] According to Cragg, what he calls 'the will to inclusive relationship'[52] is the "perfectness' of ready hospitality in God' (64). In line with this is also the very beginning of the chapter of concern to be understood, that is: his quotation of the 'if you salute your brethren only ...' of the Sermon on the Mount (Matt. 5.47). In other words, his embracing of other ways is intimately related to the very core of his Christian faith, that is: relation is *self*-relating. Consequently Cragg introduces Christianity as the open faith (*ibid.*).

4.4.2 THE OPEN FAITH: THE CREATIVE AND RISKING MIND, AND THE SPIRIT IN PROCEEDING

One might, however, ask how open this relation to other faiths can be. Is it still possible to retain a kind of evaluation of other faiths from the Christian point of view? An answer to this is given in *Christianity in World Perspective* in three different ways. One negative: what Cragg reckons as illegitimate approaches to other religions. Then, a positive

---

of Lux Mundi should be mentioned (1889, cf. note 11 above and note 82 below). Cf. also Gore 1890b, whose article got most publicity after the launch of the *Lux Mundi* essays, and which contained a reference to a divine kenosis. This article has had some influence on Cragg, *FLN,* 46. Rowan Williams maintains that this incarnationalist consensus, which was also sacramentalist, is marked by a concern for 'all material existence to be potentially charged with the life of God,' Jesus as the 'bridge between human and divine society,' and hence 'a powerful polemic against the Church's withdrawal from the public square,' *ibid.* 225. Modern theologians outside the Anglican community who fit and develop this consensus are seen in J. Moltmann and Eastern Orthodox tradition (Lossky, Zizioulas). Williams also refers to sound political criticism of a tendency of a too easy identification of human patterns (state and family) with the Trinitarian relations, as well as a critique of the incarnationalist consensus as an abstraction from the *story* of God incarnate. The latter has also been posed against Cragg, see note 113 below. Williams' latter critical point will be employed in my constructive criticism of Smith and Cragg in Chapter 7.

[51] See e.g. p. 47 where hospitality is seen as a measure of the universal mission of the Apostles: ' ... breaking out of Jewry into *Gentile hospitality*' (my emphasis). See also *ibid.*, p. 54: 'a hospitable and transforming Gospel,' where the context is almost the same: The universal Christian mission and the debt of the Gentiles to the Jews, symbolized by the gift of Paul to the 'saints' of Jerusalem, a 'splendid precedent and a deep sacrament of unity.'

[52] He might be alluding negatively to Nietzsche's *will to power* here. Cf. also Cragg's 'will to actual encounter', *ibid.* 80.

way where he gives theological reasons for preserving the Christian faith as open towards other faiths. And lastly, his agnostic solution to the ultimate questions of the status of the other faiths in the light of the Christian faith.

His listing of negative attitudes relates finally to what is pertinent in the light of Christ and the relevance of Him to the world:

> There can be no acquiescence true to Christ in a theology which is content to see the Church in complacent immunity from mankind, contentedly exclusivist, dismissing the big world as a proliferating irrelevance (66).

Related to this are several 'temptations and problems.' On the one hand: The pitfalls of 'easy sentimentality', of 'obtuse assertion of identities where distinction is urgent,' 'appeal to goodwill that disqualifies itself by bad faith,' 'superficial neutrality that evacuates issues of their real essence' and thus 'saps the integrity of the mind that moves within them' (70f). On the other: 'Militancy that makes exaggerated claims, the aggressive fear that forecloses[53] finer possibilities or invokes the menace of relativism and too readily levels charges of syncretistic disloyalty' (*ibid.*).

Based on these listings one may expect Cragg to place himself in the safe 'realm of the middle.' If so, that means that he aims to avoid neutrality but not truth claims. Further, that he wants to avoid relativism and syncretism, but not a 'finer possibility' that might seem to resemble both relativism and syncretism. This can possibly be confirmed by what he calls a 'truer loyalty [to Christ] by taking larger risks' (74), since unrisking minds will entail diminished meanings.[54] A sense for syncretism can also be seen as consistent with such wishes, which points to Cragg's

---

[53] Regarding the central negative notion of 'foreclosing' at this point, see also his criticism of the relation of John Henry Newman towards the 'mother Church' (i.e. the Roman Catholic Church) in *CFs:* 'To adopt it [i.e. Newman's desire to be wholly submissive to and ruled by 'the authoritarian faith'] would simply be to refuse all cognisance of pluralism and so opt out of this world,' 316.

[54] Cf. *CFs,* 328, where Cragg sees Peter in Acts 10 and 11 as an example of how one successfully may take risks outside one's boundaries of familiarity. Cf. also his later *WWd* where he more generally (in relation to all Semitic faiths) states that 'only by a patient sufferance of *risk and jeopardy* may it [the after-life of Semitic prophethood after having become 'completed'] take an onward course,' 143, my emphasis. This belongs to 'the nature of imaginary,' *ibid.* 151. This has lead Christopher Lamb to describe Cragg's work as 'guided more by artistic than logical consideration,' Lamb 1997, 173. As far as it goes, this is right. Yet, it is possible to make a quite positive esteem of the role of 'imagination' and 'images' in theology, see McIntyre 1987, 159-175. John McIntyre, who at this point is dependent on J. Baille (and on a (self)criticism of Reformed theology!), maintains in his 'analytic

suggestion immediately below.[55] A detour to his notion of New Testament 'precedents' (ch. 2, *CWP*) may support this interpretation of Cragg.

Cragg sees in the New Testament encounter with other cultures, particularly the crossing out of the Jewish borders to the Gentiles, precedents to how the church should relate by and with the Gospel to other faiths. Included in this precedence is a creative venture to vocabulary transactions and trans-language initiatives (55). Drawing upon such key examples as the borrowing of λογος, μυστηριον (*ibid.*) and κυριος (58f), as well as the involvement of the Gospel with 'the cultic reference of all men' in the Eucharist (59) and Paul's address at the Areopagus (60), Cragg maintains that the New Testament creative and risking mind is perhaps not so un-syncretistic as some might want it to be, though Cragg denounces the very use of 'syncretistic' about these matters as 'perverse' (57f), presumably because he sees the very pattern of the Incarnation in the way the Spirit with its 'Scriptural energies' accomplishes and completes definitively[56] the Canon of Scripture (56). For Cragg, therefore, the dread

of imagination' that imagination has a *range* of functions that in my mind are quite pertinent to mention if one is to judge Lamb's criticism and understand the nature of systematic theology properly with regards to imagination. These functions are: to be perceptive, selective, synoptic/integrative, creative/ constructive, interpretative capacity, cognitive (!), emphatic, communicative, contemporanizing ('past/future-as-present'), conspatializing ('make the absent present'), create 'our-world' (cf. I. Murdoch), and to be ecumenical. For myself, I find almost all of these suggested functions of systematic theology to fit a description of Cragg's interreligious hermeneutics. This will become clearer as this study proceeds but is already at this stage observable.

[55] See Martin 2000, 279. Implied in Luther H. Martin's characterization of 'a syncretistic field' is a challenging of 'authorized religious truth,' 'normative theological views,' which can be seen as a partly parallel to Cragg's antipathy towards closed, custodian-like minds.

[56] The use of 'precedents' should not be interpreted as leaving out the normativity of the Scripture of which e.g. Jan-Martin Berentsen has accused Cragg for doing, Berentsen 1994, 90 (his critique relates to *COR* but is equally applicable to *CWP*). The precedents of both Christ and the apostles in the New Testament are otherwise seen as 'definitive' (47, about Jesus' Messiahship), as 'ruling' (51), about the universal importance of Paul's bringing the Gospel from the Jews to the Gentiles), and the interpretation of 'that which we have heard' (59) takes precedence as unique and, therefore, irrepeatable (56).

That Cragg also characterizes New Testament precedents as 'important' (the 'vocabulary transactions', 55), 'splendid' (the gift of Paul to the Christians in Jerusalem, 54), and 'magnificent' (62) does not rule out the normativity of the New Testament as a 'venture of interpretation'. It only makes the understanding of its normativity more dynamic, differentiated and more tightly connected to the events of which it records and interprets. Cragg would probably have added: more incarnate. This is pithily formulated in his warning about the authority of the Scripture becoming inflexible when it is only recognized in its decisiveness, and not also in its exemplarity (62). This becomes particularly acute since the world of syncretism is more suspicious than the fact of it, as similarly the 'paralysis with dogma [is] always worse than risk for it' (58). Based on the precedents of the New Testament as both example and authority, Cragg sees the Christian task to accomplish the same kind of creative trusteeship (56). In this respect one might describe Cragg's 'supreme context' as effective communication.[57]

This becomes even clearer when Cragg presents his constructive theological statements about other faiths. As we have seen in earlier writings of Cragg, when it comes to the theological assessment of the Christian relation to other religions, his notion of the Holy Spirit is activated. That is also the case here as he sees the 'mystery and burden of the plurality of religions' as a supreme test of the meaning of the Holy Spirit (71). This is then interpreted in the light of what follows after 'I believe in the Holy Spirit' in the Apostles' Creed (that is: Lat. *sanctorum communionem*), which Cragg chooses to translate as 'the communion of holy things' (*ibid.*) and 'participation in holy things' respectively (*ibid.*, n1). In this notion of the Holy Spirit related to 'hallowing relationships' Cragg consequently sees a wise clue to a right confession of the belief in 'the holy, catholic Church.'

A keyword here is *relations*. For Cragg there is 'spiritual content' between religions that 'inter-penetrate and co-exist' (74). He therefore abandons the use of 'non-Christian' because of its expression of the temper of 'the custodian mind.' On the other hand, the developing of relations and communication is for Cragg not only a matter affirming kinship but also a logical consequence of ensuring a truth that is a received truth (74). The urge to communicate is therefore grounded in a fact that what is to be communicated has already been communicated to the Christians themselves.

---

changes and that much of the geographical world outside the Mediterranean is not included in the New Testament world.

That Cragg is careful and deliberate in his choice of different characteristics becomes clear in his assessment of Paul in Athens (Acts 17) as 'an important, if not definitive, passage of New Testament precedent' (60). The reason that it should be definitive seems again to be dependent on whether it resembles the way Jesus faced resistance and ignorance on his way to the cross, particularly in the light of the fact that Paul's address was never finished and that he experienced a 'travail.' Seen also in the light of how Cragg compares Jesus in Gethsemane with Muhammad in Mecca in his writings (see Chapter 5, e.g. 5.2.1), it is reasonable to understand Paul in Athens as 'important, if not definitive.'

[57] Cf. 1957b, 241: 'Our business in Christ's trusteeship is not merely to present facts, albeit incomparable facts, but to travail until Christ be formed in the hearts of men and until an understanding of His meaning conceives and grows in their souls [i.e. of the 'non-Christian world'].' This critical article was presented in *International Review of Missions* within a debate on H. Kraemer's book *Religion and the Christian Faith*. For his criticism of Kraemer, see below.

This is not to be seen merely as a matter of communication theory. This is far more a theological matter. Using the example of Christ, Cragg aims at establishing a distinction between self-possession and self-oblation, which is similar to the distinction between 'doctrine'/ 'creed' and 'worship'. Cragg understands thus the Incarnation as 'glory self-expending' and the Crucifixion as a rejection of the principle of self-preservation (75). As the religions have in their heart 'an obligation of yieldedness and of surrender,' they exist for "consecration' to the ultimate'—that is, sacrifice and worship—and not for the sake of creed. With an implicit resemblance to Cantwell Smith's distinction between belief-faith Cragg concludes by saying that:

> Seen from the standpoint of beliefs, faiths appear, substantially, as ends in themselves: seen from the perspective of worship they are themselves for ends beyond them (75).[58]

Cragg sees therefore a paradoxical mystery between guardianship and what should be guarded: the self-oblation. And, importantly, he refuses to surrender either side of the paradox. To see how he manoeuvres between the options of this paradox it is very instructive to explore how he relates critically to major scholars of theology of religion, such as Arnold Toynbee, and in particular Hendrik Kraemer and Karl Rahner, but also John Hick and W. E. Hocking.

4.4.3 EXCLUDING EXCLUSIVISM FROM WITHIN: *PRAEPARATIO EVANGELICA* AND THE RELATION TO TOYNBEE, KRAEMER, RAHNER, HICK AND HOCKING

Cragg criticizes first Toynbee's[59] invitation of the Christian faith as to

> forego exclusiveness in such a sense as to jeopardize that the very presence, for religious reckonings, of those dimensions which the Christ of the Gospel embodies, and which doctrine 'holds' and receives, and so allows to be

---

[58] Note that the parallel pairs here are 'belief-worship' (Cragg) and 'belief-faith' (Smith). Cragg's use of 'faiths' parallels Smith use of 'cumulative/religious traditions' and not Smith's 'faith' which is a personal quality. One may also say that Cragg's use of 'ends beyond them' parallels Smith's use of 'T/transcendence' and 'transcending'.

[59] (1889-1975), historian. Cragg refers to his *An Historian's Approach to Religions,* London 1958, and *Christianity among the Religions of the World,* London 1956. Cragg has elaborated more of Toynbee's interreligious ideas in *TT,* 222-241.

received, in expression and recognition (75).

It is indeed Cragg 'The Guardian' we listen to here[60] and the quotation can mean either of two things: Either that it is right to maintain exclusiveness on behalf of the Gospel, or that exclusiveness should be jeopardized but only from within an understanding of what the Gospel embodies. Arguments for the latter will be given implicitly in what follows.

Cragg argues firstly for maintaining 'the very tension' by which Christian theology is constituted (76). Secondly, he asserts that hospitality needs a 'home of faith in which to practice hospitality' (*ibid.*). Having this home of faith it is possible by 'the Spirit of love in Christ' not to possess the doctrine of hospitality exclusively, and still by 'the Spirit of the truth of Christ' to affirm it with fidelity.[61] This is what Cragg calls the 'sanctuary of incorporation.'

Within this metaphor of a house, the uniqueness of the Gospel is entailed both in its function of control and clarity as well as in its openness.[62] In other words, which also connects this with his reference

---

[60] Cf. also *ibid.*, n1: 'There is still ... the dilemma of doctrine as the guardian of the very meanings by which it learns that guardianship requires self-oblation.'

[61] For a parallel of this pair of 'Spirit of the love of Christ' and 'Spirit of the truth of Christ' where the love and truth of Christ are held together by the Spirit, see *ITC*, II: 130, and p. 156 (4.2.2) above. There, the point is made that doctrine and morality cannot be separated, and that the unity of love and truth, morality and doctrine, is ultimately to be found in the 'pattern of the Cross'.

[62] See p. 46 where Christ's *openness* to God and men is presented as the 'final reason' for His 'proceeding on a *contrasted* understanding [than the Messianic expectations of the people and even of the disciples, 43-46] of the mind of God' (my emphasis). Interestingly, when Cragg translates this 'openness to God and men' by 'dogmatic form,' it comes out as the orthodox 'Son of God.' Yet, this shall not be interpreted primarily as a matter of status but as of 'a *quality of identity* with the Divine nature, of *attunement to* the Divine will' (my emphasis). This corresponds also to his preference to 'how' (i.e. how Messiah 'had been') over 'who' (i.e. who people 'knew him to be'), although the two are inseparable for Cragg indeed (*ibid.*).
Moreover, Cragg makes at this place a connection between the universality of Christ and the radicality of God's purposes represented by the universal redemption and not restricted to, for example, national liberation. On the other hand, and as an argument for my interpretation of Cragg's relation to 'exclusivism', Cragg correlates the partial and imperfect to the exclusive in respect of which possible ways the Messiahship of Jesus could have taken (*ibid.*). Hence the universality and inclusiveness are finally matters of the *extent and depth of God's redemption* in and through Christ, and correspondingly: of how *human nature* is depicted. Or positively stated: 'The new sense of the person, the sense of *men as men*, not as Jews as Jews, or Greeks as Greeks, ... is the most remarkable achievement of New Testament religion ... a genuine *oikumene* of men' (62, first emphasis mine). This correlates to, now in a gender-neutral language, what he in *MG* while contrasting 'some "transcendental unity of all religions"' calls the *existential mundane unity* of 'the mystery of individuation', that is: of 'me-ness', 152.

to the Apostles' Creed: communication is nothing if there is no communion. At this place the relations to Cantwell Smith are evident as well (e.g. 'world community').

By a reference to an illuminating poem by Robert Graves[63] where Graves most illuminatingly describes the mind and pattern of the *apologist* and the *sceptic* respectively, one might ask whether not some of the apologist Cragg (for example of his dissertation) has turned out to become more of a sceptic.[64] If one compares the poem with his distinction between the custodian mind and the creative and adventurous mind above, this appears to be a reasonable view. On the other hand, genuine openness was certainly a part of his thesis, for instance in his identical emphasis on the openness as neither tactic nor strategy to 'help the case' (77).[65]

At this place he alludes implicitly to E. Brunner when he criticizes approaches that seek to establish 'points of contact'. While he pays no attention to Brunner, he pays Kraemer some.[66] How this is done is important because it shows where Cragg draws the line between himself and other Protestant, evangelical and missionary strands.[67] One of the things in Kraemer to which Cragg is most allergic, is the sense of having to be 'correct' about the issue of religious plurality by stressing the 'non-derivative, primary, original "given Christianity" ... "the Person of Jesus Christ"' (77). Cragg sees Kraemer's approach as a 'Divine absolutism in Jesus Christ' where he

---

[63] 'In Broken Images,' *Poems*, 1926-1930, London 1931, 40.

[64] *Ibid.* 77. The antithetic pairs of characteristics are: 'thinking and trusting in clear images but becoming dull' vs. 'thinking in but mistrusting broken images but becoming sharp', which results in 'he [i.e. the apologist] in a new confusion of his understanding' vs. 'I [i.e. the sceptic] in a new understanding of my confusion'. Considering what follows in Cragg's argument it is hard to avoid identifying Cragg with the sceptics.

[65] See footnote 9 above.

[66] Cf. Brunner's 'Anknüpfungspunkte' in his work *Natur und Gnade*. This point, however, is also taken up in relation to Kraemer, see *COR*, 72. Most interestingly, Cragg shows a 'rhetoric' sympathy in *COR* for the 'father' of the dialectical theology: Karl Barth. Based on a passage from Barth's study on Romans, Cragg asks whether his insistence on a totally 'given' truth, albeit 'exempt from liability to relate to reason or to otherness in stating itself, and quite independent of other religions as criteria either of its meaning or its authority, *is really the dogmatic form of an overwhelming experience of grace and is to be appreciated, indeed saluted and celebrated, as such?' COR,* 70f, my emphasis.

[67] At this point, David Kerr sees Cragg's approach as delineating the lines of approach in which he would locate the World Council of Churches (WCC, e.g. 'Christian Presence and Witness in Relation to Muslim Neighbours,' Mombasa, 1979), whereas Kraemer is located to evangelical mode (e.g. the North American Conference on the Evangelization of Muslim, Colorado Springs, 1978), Kerr 1981, 152, col. 2.

reduces the content of all other faiths to incidental traces, not essential elements, of what God has decisively chosen to vouchsafe outside them (78).[68]

In other words: There is no significant relation between 'other faiths' and the Christian.

Against Kraemer's doctrinism and aversion to 'mystery', Cragg claims precisely the opposite: to see the commendation of the revelation of God in Christ as 'moving, by travail, in significant community with men' (79). By this 'significant community,' the 'mystery of the Gospel' may be related to the 'mystery of things', that is, the mystery of the human existence, and the 'intentions' of the religions to what the Gospel 'intends' (87).[69] Cragg does not see that Kraemer's attitude enables this. In short: No true venue for 'mutual possessions in the spirit' and 'genuine openness' is possible for Kraemer and his likes. Despite the fact that both Cragg and Kraemer hold to a christocentrism in their theology, their approaches and attitudes towards other faiths are so dissimilar that Kraemer turns out to be *the* negative background for the development of Cragg's position.[70]

---

[68] See also his ironic and implicit critique of many strands of Protestantism (e.g. Lutherans, and probably also many Anglicans): 'We allow the relative value of natural reason, natural law, religious aspiration, the instinct of worship, and whatever it else be, so long as it is clear that these are broken lights, or streams feeling their way towards the tidal estuary where the waters of revelation flow powerfully in to make the river of truth' (79f).

[69] At another place, analysing Paul's address on Areopagus (Acts 17), Cragg sees Paul's affirming the *identity* between the God of its *intention* [i.e. of the text from the wayside shrine] and the God *of the Gospel, ibid.* 61. Cragg sees the issue as a disowning of the predicate ('unknown') of the Athenian God, whereas the 'Divine 'subject'' remains constant. The structure and impact of this assertion, it can be claimed, is *implicit* when Cragg in *CWP* sets out to interpret other religions based on the principle of interpreting them from their *intentions*, 86.

[70] This is reasonable given Kraemer's *The Christian Message to the Non-Christian World* (1938). The fact of *correspondence* between Cragg and Kraemer is, however, stunning if one reads works of the later Kraemer, e.g. Kraemer 1960 (which has been elaborated in his *World Religions and World Cultures: The Coming Dialogue,* 1960). Let me also quote a passage from one of his articles in *MW* (after the time of Cragg's editorial position) which can easily be perceived as entailing Cragg's approach: 'The time of Christian missions in the Muslim world ... is, as far as I see, *passed* in the post-colonial era. A radical rethinking and reshaping is therefore imperiously demanded ... [which] has to be disengaged from all former conceptions ... The past, age-long relationship of antagonism ... has turned into the *possibility* and *necessity* of a new relationship of mutual interdependence ... and of genuine human encounter and open dialogue ... The deeply humble fact remains that the Muslim world ... in its whole history has never had a chance to *see* the Christian Church as she is according to her true nature and calling,' 250f, Kraemer's emphases. This coincides, as far as I see, with Cragg's 'inducement' and 'spirit.'

Cragg's response, on the other hand, seems to be genuinely inclusive both by virtue and in respect of theology. Hence he refuses to see other religions only in terms of 'antecedent contact for evangelism' (79). He argues rather for a *praeparatio evangelica* (79), which he asserts can be affirmed sufficiently on Christian premises, although it should not be done too easily (79f). By this latter request, Cragg means at least four things (80f):

a. That other faiths should never be forced to subscribe to a *praeparatio*–understanding.

b. That the promotion of such an interpretation should be done in *humility, especially since Christ always comes into receptivity.*

c. That this approach does not exhaust the 'external significance,' and

d. That this approach is 'less than reciprocal.'

Again, it is important for Cragg to stress the aspect of self-criticism on behalf of the Christian and Christianity. This self-criticism is, however, not ungrounded as it seeks to apply to itself principles of which the Gospel evaluates 'all else' (81).[71] It is at this point, after the introduction of the *praeparatio* and the self-criticism that he encounters the famous ideas of Karl Rahner.

Cragg sees in Rahner a resourceful theological will more than a successful theology (81). What he particularly welcomes is the way he is 'banishing hardness of heart and pride in absolutist belief, and in mediating, on the personalist level, between custodians of faiths' (82). In other words: Rahner is, as it were, the 'anti-Kraemer'. On the other hand Cragg is reluctant to subscribe to all in Rahner's theology of religions. This reluctance is formulated in several questions. These are, however, formulated so broadly that one might wonder whether they are all seriously meant, or partly rhetorical in order to appear to be critical, or even to facilitate an 'interior dialogue' within Cragg's own mind. For example:

> Is there something forced about the whole picture [of Rahner]? or contrived? ... Could the notion be reversible, and we Christians be anonymous Buddhists, Muslims or Hindus? What if the 'anonymity' declines its perfecting? Is Christian silence a safer tack than Christian preaching? Are

---

[71] Cragg does for example not see the fact of 'the perversity of men' as any argument for his stressing of the relations. As the sin of men is a matter of moral failure, which 'compromises afflict in some measure all institutional religions,' there is no reason to claim that believers in any religion can be a 'merely external critics' (84). At this point he is more in line with 'readers of Barthian tutorship' than he seems to believe. In *COR*, 70, this point is however recognized.

the Christian premises of 'salvation' and 'Incarnation' too
partial as clues by which to regulate the whole plural scene?
... [A]re these ideas a stage in further adjustment of the
dogmatic to the empirical, a half-way house where orthodoxy
and sympathy are still in incomplete negotiation within the
Christian mind? Or could they perhaps make a true and
abiding Christian ground for mutuality, where openness can
both contain and orientate orthodoxy itself? (82f)

As one sees, some of these represent a rather common critique of Rahner's
'anonymous Christians'. Others seem to draw almost in a pluralist direction,
while others again might cover an interest in being explicit on behalf of
Christian mission.[72] The last question seems altogether to be the position
of Cragg, a middle-way between orthodoxy and mutuality, as seen in his
concern for both guardianship and relationships.

In *COR* he also introduces his relation to two other seminal
thinkers in this area: John Hick and W.E. Hocking. Whereas Cragg criticizes
Hick's 'Copernican revolution' and the premise that religions have been
geographically isolated until recent times,[73] he is more sympathetic to
Hocking's approach.[74] The feature of Hocking's position which Cragg
acknowledges is, most relevant for the present study, his idea of
reconception, which implies, in Cragg's paraphrase of his position, that:

each faith should strive to reconceive itself in the light of
the insights it discerned in other religions. For these related

---

[72] At the same time, after his encounter with Rahner, he contends very clearly that
concern for conversion very easily may end in a 'closing of ranks—and minds'
(86). Cragg's position is that the Gospel's 'capacity to shape crisis and demand
action is more rightly implicit in its content than explicit in our speech' (*ibid.*).
[73] Cragg's contention against Hick in the case of altering from a 'Christocentric'
(which parallels 'geocentric') to a theocentric (which parallels a 'heliocentric'
view), is that 'the earth is still lived on and, in that sense, earthly existence is truly
geocentric! Similarly, the Christian lives in Christo-centric meaning.' Cragg also
counters the latter point, the premise of geographic isolation in the past, by the
evidence that this did not in fact take place. Rather the contrary, diverse traditions
'have been interpenetrating, interacting spheres of faith through much of their
history and hardly any are explicable without reference to another,' *COR* 76. By
this statement Cragg resembles Smith's position, cf. Chapter 2.6.1.
[74] Which marks a certain shift from his more critical relation to Hocking in his
D.phil. dissertation, cf. note 21 above. Cragg seems to have got to know Hocking's
'admirable' philosophy thoroughly and 'urgently' the summer in 1943 when he
was delivering lectures on him, *inter alia*, at American University of Beirut, *FLN*,
98. Though a philosopher and not a theologian, Hocking has had a strong influence
on certain theological strands, see Tracy 1987, 452.

to the essence of all religions. Actual faith-systems all failed to embody these insights truly. But each might aspire to do so universally, by such reconceiving (*COR*, 76).

Cragg sees Hocking's position as attractive, humble and admirable. His acknowledgement of him seems particularly to be the case in Hocking's emphasis on religions which have 'travelled far in the path of self-understanding' as having a moral obligation to those who are 'less skilled in self-explanation,' so as to joyfully help them towards a 'new level of self-understanding' (*ibid.*). Though Hocking's 'spiritual chivalry' is likely to be read as a pluralist approach, Cragg asks whether not his idea of '[anticipating] for them what they mean, opening to them that larger room towards which they trend' can be read as an expression of a 'fulfilment-into-Christ' concept, where '"the trend" is our reading, rather than their nature' (*COR*, 77). At this point it becomes clear that his admiration of Hocking's spirit, does not imply an unreserved reception of his perception of interreligious relations. Rather the contrary, Cragg almost 'over-interprets' Hocking's position in his own preferred direction.

4.4.4 WHAT KIND OF POSITION?

After this examination, one might still ask what kind of position Cragg really represents. Cragg himself describes Rahner's theology as one that 'faces the right way' (83). Yet, he asks whether its conclusion is too tidy and systematized. For Cragg, neither the world nor the Spirit is that tidy and orderly (80). In line with this, he also asks whether the problem is too big for our theology, if not for our faith. His offer goes in a direction where one has to live 'imaginatively with unanswered questions,' 'being in uncertainties, mysteries, doubts,' as well as to live 'with loose ends of explanation' (83). This he calls with the English poet John Keats (1795-1821) a negative capability. Consequently he refuses to conclude with a theology of religions: 'The right theology of pluralism is the lack of one.' Yet, he immediately follows up with a 'hardly so,' because there is a theology of religions to be found 'in proceeding.' And what proceeds, is the Holy Spirit, 'in Christ, and with Him.' By this combination of Christology, pneumatology, and agnosticism, Cragg hopes to represent a required 'elasticity of mind' (85, Herbert Butterfield), which may contain expectations that the Spirit herself allows (85).

It is difficult to see that Cragg in reality eschews developing a theology of religions at this point, albeit not conclusively or systematically. Let me give several reasons for this claim. Firstly, Cragg stresses very much the pertinent attitudes of the Christian towards people of other faiths (hospitality, openness, responsibility). Secondly, these are not only liberal virtues by which peace and harmony may appear on Earth, and among 'alien' people, but inherently derived from the Gospel itself. As such there is at least a Christian interreligious spirituality or set of virtues that Cragg does not hesitate to formulate. Thirdly, when he attempts to formulate the theological consequences of this neither is he reluctant to criticize certain theologians of religions (Toynbee, Kraemer, partly Rahner). This negative positioning is not unimportant for that which is constructed on his behalf. Finally, he also facilitates constructive theological resources to justify the possibility of relations and communion in general, and recognition of a *praeparatio evangelica* in particular.

The sum of this is that, in spite of his many open questions and an ultimate agnosticism towards the biggest issues of theologies of religions, Cragg attains in *CWP* an *inclusive* theology of religious plurality that sees the *uniqueness* of Christ by the Holy Spirit as enabling certain *essential relations* to people of other faiths.[75] In addition, the issue of 'predisposing (other people/religions) Christwards' in earlier writings is somewhat softened in *CWP*, though presumably integrated in his idea of preparation. To back these conclusions one might quote him to the effect that within his 'sanctuary of incorporation' 'we learn it has no walls' (76). This is a rather bold way of stating an inclusivist intention. Yet, one might also ask whether it is this vision of the sanctuary without walls itself that, together with his affinity for elastic language, makes him evade the making of a more systematic theology of religions.

4.4.5 'THE OPEN FAITH' AND HERMENEUTICAL THEORY: SELF-GIVING BUT NOT SELF-CHANGE?

It may be rewarding to discuss his core concept of 'the open faith'. How is this openness to be characterized for instance in light of hermeneutical theory? As Anthony C. Thiselton maintains, 'openness' has been a central notion, especially from Dilthey to Betti, representing one important characteristic of interpersonal understanding.[76] Whereas the context in Thiselton's study is intertextual and interpersonal understanding, I see no reason for not applying this to the interreligious context of Cragg's

---

[75] Christopher Lamb is therefore only to a certain extent right when he describes Cragg's approach as 'evasiveness' and 'agnosticism,' Lamb 1997, 68 and 74. Nevertheless, and in some contradiction to this, Lamb describes him as 'one of the elder statesmen of what has become known as Inclusivism,' *ibid.* 171.

[76] Thiselton 1992, 33.

work, and our study, as long as interreligious relations may include intertextual or interpersonal aspects. Yet, for Thiselton openness should be connected to self-change, and, in the language of text-reader, that the reader must appear as an 'other' in relation to the text. In this respect he also quotes Hans Robert Jauss who in relation to his notion of a 'horizon of expectation' speaks about the impact of a text as a de-habitualization.[77]

Based on this, one might ask: is there in Cragg's understanding of openness the possibility of 'self-change', and of Cragg being the 'other'? Or: a capacity for expansion of, and of movement within one's horizon as in Gadamer?[78] What seems to be clear is that the openness Cragg claims, is an openness based on the openness shown by Jesus in the unique and inclusive event of His crucifixion. This event is decisive and exemplary for any Christian relating to other faiths. On the other hand, Cragg's openness also includes seeing in other religions clues to the reality and event of Christ, particularly stated by his concept of preparation. Yet, noting his metaphor of the sanctuary of incorporation one may contend that this seems to be more a matter of integrating the Other into the world of Oneself than risking one's self-understanding in the relating to the Other or seeing Oneself as the Other. Also, his notion of 'venture' and 'risk' for the sake of making the Gospel understandable for the Other is confined within the attitudes of self-oblation and self-expenditure which carries the aim of giving something to somebody.

In spite of all this, I think there is still an element of 'self-change' in Cragg's approach. His explicit and implicit emphases on self-criticism and self-risk entail the possibility of losing orthodoxy for the sake of communication. And, if orthodoxy is a representative for 'self', at least as some kind of an 'assumed original self,' change takes place indeed. Seen from this point of view, and if one applies the modest meaning of 'invention' that Thiselton traces back to Aristotle and Cicero, 'to search out leading concepts,'[79] one might say that Cragg is inventive both in respect of his own self-understanding (the precedents of Christ and the Apostles, especially Messiahship), and in respect of other faiths, that is, to find clues to the Christ-event, but also to interpret them according to their 'intentions'. This double qualification is exemplarily apparent in his admiration and extension of Hocking's ideas. Yet, I do not regard the radical notion of 'de-habitualization' as a proper description of this.

Cragg's own way of making this kind of intensification a theme

[77] Thiselton 1992, 33f. Thiselton refers to Jauss' studies *Towards an Aesthetic of Reception,* Minneapolis: Minneapolis Univ. Press, 1982, and *Aesthetic Experience and Literary Hermeneutics,* Minneapolis: Minneapolis Univ. Press, 1982.
[78] Thiselton 1992, 44, 46.
[79] Thiselton 1992, 61.

is, however, best seen, retrospectively, in *FLN*. The keyword here is 'negotiate' which he sees as 'a converse inside a self'.[80] This conversation seems to have been most prominently facilitated by the relation between 'faith' and 'life', in particular how he pondered the meaning of 'God in Christ' during and after his sojourn in Beirut, which he saw as the very intersection between Islam and Arabism on the one hand, and the legacies of Greece and Rome on the other.[81] Regarding the 'negotiation' of 'God in Christ', which took place in his time as Rector of Longworth outside Oxford after his sojourn in Beirut (1940-47), Cragg recognizes that he was 'inheriting a deep "negotiation"' from the 'holy party' of Lux Mundi and their dependency upon the Oxford philosopher T. H. Green.[82]

---

[80] *FLN,* 1. Cf. also *COR,* 5 where he sees his pondering the Christian significance of the world's other religions in analogy to 'Jacob at Peniel, wrestling with the angel for the meaning of his selfhood.' Interestingly, in an article from 1969, delivered to the Lambeth conference in 1968, Cragg stresses that his view of 'openheartedness' should not be seen as a ' "negotiability" of faith,' Cragg 1969c, 37. Though the terminology may differ from *FLN,* his view is consistent, see e.g. his subsequent statement about dialogue under the section 'The principle of spiritual transaction': 'Dialogue is, in fact, an attempt to understand such 'absolute' passages as 'No man cometh unto the Father but be me' (and indeed the whole gospel and nature of the Church) *more* responsibly, not less,' *ibid.*

[81] Cf. the title of the chapter on his time in Beirut onwards in *FLN:* 'The Sifting East.' Cragg paraphrases this as to be a sifting of meaning of the Christian faith 'within the transactions of culture and community to which inner loyalty had brought it,' 89. The whole impact of Islam is considered comprehensively in ch. 8 ('The Tribunal of Islam') of this autobiography ('Christian story-study'). Nevertheless, 'negotiation' was also experienced in a special way on his behalf during and after his three times of being found with a 'loved structure taken down' ('of such stuff are siftings made', 103), that is (see the Biography and References): a) The St. Justin's House in Beirut, which Cragg and his wife Melita established together with the Bishop in Jerusalem, and which had to close due to the Arab/ Israeli War in 1948, a year after the Cragg's had left for Oxford, b) the Archbishop Michael Ramsey's choking of the Central College of the Anglican Communion of which Cragg was the Warden when this event occurred in 1966-67, and c) the Middle-East and North-African churches getting its complete independency (the new Province of Jerusalem and the Middle East) from Canterbury which dissolved the Archbishopric and for that reason also the office of the Assistant Bishop, which was in Cragg's possession at that time. Whereas the former two happened because of 'tragic external calamities' and 'unhappy acquiescence by authority', the latter was seen by Cragg as 'a welcome attempt to heal Anglican 'unease in Zion," though it in his eyes did not succeed, *FLN,* 161. See chs. 4-6, *FLN,* for comprehensive descriptions of these events.

[82] *FLN,* 56. For Luw Mundi, see also note 50 above. Cragg refers to one of Green's letters to Scott Holland, one of the members of Lux Mundi, what he describes as a proviso: 'If you will allow your theology to think of it,' *ibid.* See also *TT,* the commented range of biographies of interreligious 'practitioners' of interreligious life and dialogue (H. Martyn, C.F. Andrews, C. Padwick, E. Wiesel, J. Parkes, A.J. Heschel, Isma'il al-Faruqi, S. Rushdie, Sala 'Abd al-Sabur, Asaf 'Ali Asghar Fyzee,

Cragg's notion of 'a converse inside a self' in *FLN* must be said to be a significant expression of a central hermeneutic concern, if not the most essential one. An anecdote shows it to resonate with the core of the philosophical hermeneutics of Gadamer. Jean Grondin tells, in his pondering 'the universal claim of hermeneutics,' that he once asked Gadamer what the universal aspect of hermeneutics consisted in, on which Gadamer answered: 'In the verbum interius.'[83] This point, however, is emphasized in *Truth and Method* only in passing, in a small chapter particularly concerned with Augustine's *De trinitate.*[84] Most interestingly, seeing Lux Mundi, Cragg and philosophical hermeneutics together, the point of departure of this chapter is the relation between the understanding of language and words on the one hand, and the Christian concept of Incarnation and the word as *reines Geschehen* on the other.[85] Gadamer regards this as an opening of a closed dimension in the Greek notion of language, namely how the inner word can remain word by being spoken externally,[86] or from the opposite angle by Grondin's interpretation of Gadamer: 'One can understand what is said only when one derives it from the inner speech lurking behind it,' namely 'that which strives to be externalised in spoken language.'[87] In this, most interestingly, a modest allusion to a kenotic Christology seems to be implied in Gadamer's treatment:

> Demgegenüber schließt die Menschwerdung Gottes, wie sie die christliche Religion lehrt, das Opfer, das der Gekreuzigte als der Menschensohn auf sich nimmt, d.h. aber ein geheimnisvoll anderes Verhältnis ein, dessen theologische Ausdeutung in der Lehre von der Trinität geschieht.[88]

In analogy to the Trinity the interior word can be said to neither diminish, nor alter, nor become exhausted by becoming external. Yet, this

---

R. Panikkar, A.J. Toynbee and W.C. Smith). Here, the central notion is 'troubled by truth' which connects the notions of 'trouble' and 'truth' in an interreligious context, that is: how one's own self-understanding (not only Christian) entails problems as one relates to people of other faiths, which includes themes close to 'self-converse': 'self-criticism' (14), 'self-interrogation' (11), 'self-examination' (13), and 'self-consciousness' (14). The point of relevance here is that *these are seen as inherent to and as a result of interreligious encounter.*

[83] Grondin 1994, xiv.
[84] Gadamer 1975E/1990G, third part, 2.b. (Ger. 'Sprache und verbum').
[85] Gadamer 1990G, 422f.
[86] *Ibid.,* 424.
[87] *Op.cit.,* Grondin 1994, xivf.
[88] *Op.cit.,* Gadamer 1990G, 422.

'inner word' is also characterized by process (*Geschehen,* cf. above) and perfection of the reasoning, as self-talk (*Selbst-Sagen*). This, according to Gadamer, can only happen as what is thought is first exported (*herausführen*) and yet simultaneously posed before oneself (*vor sich selber hinstellen*) in an inner self-expression (*Selbstaussprache*).[89] As far as I see, this equates the pair of event (*Vorgang*) and expression (*Hervorgang*), which is not to be seen as a process of change but as a realization (*Vollzug*) of understanding.[90] Gadamer sees this as not a temporal succession of thinking, but a spiritual event (Lat. *emanatio intellectualis,* cf. Thomas Aquinas), a contemporariness of word and formation of reasoning (*Intellekt*).

If Cragg's 'faith- and life-negotiation' is thought of thus, although the emphasis in Gadamer's elaboration is rather on the matter of extensification—the emanation of the word from reasoning—the case of intensification in Cragg's case should be justified from this particular hermeneutic point of view.[91] Without running the risk of 'psychologizing' or speculation, one should probably speak of at least two sets of inner words as regards of Cragg: 1) His inner words as educated theologically and spiritually before his missionary life in extensive contact with Muslims, and 2) his inner words before expressing in language how he conceived the relation between 'God in Christ' and Muslim faith.

An interesting test of Cragg's openness is to see how he interprets Islam in our next main chapter. For the analysis of this it may be rewarding to keep in mind what Gadamer calls 'the logical structure of openness.'[92] In Gadamer's hermeneutics this relates intimately to the nature of questions. For him of crucial importance is whether the questions enable one to open up an issue[93] *(Aufbrechen der Sache durch die Frage)* in order to come to a decision as to it. This requires basically:

a. Questions that entails a direction of meaning, that is, that they enable and aim at answers that are meaningful and thus function as keys to knowledge about the 'issue' *(die Sache)*.

b. Such questions presuppose a horizon of questions that represent a certain limitation and fixing of ones presuppositions and fore-meanings but thus gives the questions the direction they need to reach

---

[89] *Ibid.* 426

[90] *Ibid.* 428

[91] A statement which resembles Gadamer's view can be found in my interview with him 29 February 2000, Cragg 2000c, when he said: 'A faith which wants to be articulate is educating its content all the time.'

[92] Gadamer 1990[G], 368ff.

[93] For a discussion of the role of 'issue' in Gadamer, see Wetlesen 1983.

the answers. [94]

    a. Questions that are open and not only apparent *(Scheinfrage)*, that is: questions that open an issue and bring it into equilibrium *(in der Schwebe sein/das Gleichgewicht halt.)* in order to be judged *(entschieden)*.

    b. This combined matter of direction and openness is important to avoid distorted questions *(schiefe Fragen)* that are only open but without an intended direction, often covering questions that have not been posed.

Nevertheless, this way of perceiving hermeneutics comes very close to Cragg's expressed approach to Islam:

> In any event, no reading can be without presupposition. We cannot bring our minds and at the same time evacuate them. What matters is that presupposition should not be prejudice, or, if it be prejudice, be prejudice in the *right direction.* For too long, a wrong Christian prejudice has virtually sealed off the Qur'ân from attentive encounter or doomed it to barren neglect (*MC,* 119, my emphasis).

Whether his examination of Islam in fact brings what he promises in this programmatic statement, is to be examined in the next chapter.

4.5 Further Developments: Human Existence, Semitic Religion, the Christic Pattern, Cross-Reference and the Holy Spirit

Together with *CWP,* three other books constitute the main contributions of Cragg to interreligious issues in general: *The Christian and Other Religion (COR,* 1977a), *The Christ and the Faiths (CFs,* 1986) and *To Meet and to Greet: Faith with Faith (MG,* 1992c). Since these both reiterate and develop issues already handled in *CWP,* I will concentrate on that which in these works brings Cragg's arguments from *CWP,* and other previous studies, to greater clarity or more complex arguments. The issues at stake are:

---

[94] Gadamer 1990[G], 369. This relates to the distinction between 'das Fragliche' and 'Voraussetzungen, die feststehen,' *ibid.* See also Thiselton 1992, 44, who emphasizes the ambivalence of the 'horizon', between *limitation* on the one hand, and *expansion and movement* on the other.

—The common human existence as a clue to the Christian Gospel
—The Christic pattern, cf. the precedent of Messiahship in *CWP*
—The work of the Holy Spirit, and
—The concept of a 'cross-reference' theology as to describe the mediation of meaning between Christianity and other religions

4.5.1 THE RELIGIOUS CRITERION:
THE SELFNESS OF OUR SELFHOOD

I start with *The Christian and Other Religion*. The overall structure of this study is, briefly said, that Cragg starts with human existence and ends with the Holy Spirit, yet with an emphasis on 'God in Christ' in the middle of the book, which functions as an expression of the decisive criterion for the relation between Christians and people of other faiths.

However, Cragg deliberately starts with the 'man as the existential subject of all meaning.'[95] Here is, he claims, 'the single territory of our humanness' which he chooses to see as a 'common ground', a 'common denominator'[96], and even as 'the religious criterion' (3). Interestingly, as regards to his relation to Wilfred Cantwell Smith, he sees this as something 'more ultimate than *forms* of religion' (*ibid.*). Correspondingly, therefore, the singulars of the subtitle (The *Christian* and other *religion*, my emphasis) refer to a) 'The Christian' as a person and not as a classification, and b) 'Religion' as the 'felt and lived religious meaning'; the living commitment in contrast to the formal category or the system (xiif).[97]

Cragg's purpose is to sustain the decision to:

> move from within the human as in no way invalid for a wise theology and certainly as a congenial proceeding for faiths, both theological and otherwise, intending to converse (5).

---

[95] *COR*, xiii and 2. Subsequent parenthetical remarks in the text refer to *COR*.

[96] Cf. *SM*, for a first emphasis on 'common denominators of circumstance,' ch. 2. The *matter* is, however, already present in *ITC* and *CM*, cf. Chapter 4.2 and 4.3 above.

[97] The reference to Smith is explicit at this place. Though Cragg finds Smith's dictum that 'there are Hindus but no Hinduism' (*ME*, 62) too sharp, he obviously confirms Smith's emphasis on personal religious experience. Cragg's argument against this dictum is that Smith's emphasis on 'Hindus' as 'entirely peculiar to himself' runs the danger of 'complete atomism,' 120, n 1. Smith's replacement of 'religions' by, what Cragg somewhat imprecisely calls 'continuing traditions', only points to the fact that the religiousness of persons has to be identified by some kind of -isms, xiii. Cf. also Cragg 1980a, 10f, for this emphasis on the circularity of Smith's dictum, and Cragg's demands for 'something recognisably qualifying' of, e.g., 'Hindus.'

By this move he aims to go from human self-consciousness to the transcendent. The possibility to do so is related to an argument against Kant and what Cragg denotes 'cosmic illusionism.' Against Kant's suggestion of the impossibility of making statements of things outside our acts of comprehension (*noumena*) and the illusionist view that it is too pretentious for humans to make claims about the realities of religion(s), Cragg asserts that 'there is no meaning in deity, or reality, or the transcendent, that is not meaning for man. Irrelevance equals non-reality' (4).[98]

By this religious realism he hopes to create a ground 'where all our pluralisms meet' (3). Another way of stating this is by his understanding of the tight connection between anthropology and theology:

> As reverent theists we can be sure that we shall never be
> far away from a living theology if we are radically and
> honestly committed to the understanding of man (3).

This does not mean that one *has* to start with man, only that one *may* because any

> confident theism ... must in its implications be properly
> identifying man ... just as a true understanding of the human
> ... will be a large factor in theological conclusions (2f).

As Cragg opts to start with the understanding of the human, one may be interested in how he more concretely characterizes the human situation of his time. In short, and resonating with early works as *ITC* and *CM,* the features of what Cragg perceives as the 'broad aspects of our situation' with interreligious significance are:[99]

(1) The compound interest of human history (5-7). This cryptic

---

[98] Cf. also *WWd* where 'the sum of what theology must mean' is defined as divine manwardness, 'seeing that outside human relevance there is neither access to, nor significance in, the reality of God,' 118. This does, however, not confine God to 'things anthropic but only these can have conscious place in our theology,' *ibid.*

[99] This fivefold way of depicting important aspects of the human existence is not the only way Cragg structures his unfolding of the human situation. See e.g. Cragg 1980b ('Christianity as a World Religion') where he takes the opportunity to differentiate the 'world' (of the title) into: 1. The mortal world, 2. the natural world (the common exploitable order, the sacramental universe), 3. the common world (race and diversity), 4. the structured world (religion and power), 5. the 'graced' world (the world for the Christian of 'the transcendent as responsible live'). As one may see, there is a certain overlap between the two lists.

phrase refers to the 'old dilemma between man in his competence and man in his confusion' (5), the choice between construction and deconstruction, in short: the bewilderment of man by the (modern) cross-pressures of globalization, urbanization, economy, pollution, and politics. The main question raised by Cragg in this situation is: 'What is the ecology which can secure the inner city of the heart?' (6).

(2) The conscious cohabitation of religions and cultures (7-10). Cragg maintains that 'pluralisms'[100] are not new, but that they are conscious. At this point he certainly resembles the whole concept of Smith's 'corporate critical self-consciousness'. This is even more the case when Cragg talks about the fact of 'a period of universal history' and the cultural and spiritual interpenetration (7f). In this situation religious authority loses authority, and minorities seem to be more ambitious as to self-assertion (8). This is at least the experience and result of two centuries with mission (cf. the resilience of ancient faiths in Asia). Also the assumed static and communal assumptions of religious identity are weakened into 'some fluidity in faith participation,' although religious issues like this is of another nature than the buyer's market (*ibid.*). In short: 'Pluralism' is the condition and context of a Christian relevance in the world.[101]

(3) The preoccupation with the inner psyche (10-12). Cragg sees a correlation between psychology as 'the pool of Bethesda' of our day, and the turning of eastern religious accounts of the self into technique. The problem for religion is that meaning is reduced from an 'authentic possession' to an 'analysable condition' (10). In this situation our culture cannot contain ourselves (Eugene Ionesco) because we have no room in ourselves for it (10f). Against this 'loss of the self' Cragg maintains that: 'We must somehow accept the significance *of* ourselves if we are to find, and to fulfil, it *in* ourselves' (11). He sees this as applying fundamentally to all kinds of religion, namely: the acceptance of the will to be and to find final significance (11f).[102]

(4) The recession of religious assurance (12-15). For various reasons (intellectual, erosion of belief and practice, awareness of

---

[100] Cragg's use of 'pluralisms' is confusing. If one ventures to use such colloquial language, one should expect that it meant something like 'various theories about plurality/diversity'. Instead, it seems that Cragg uses 'pluralisms' to denote societies characterized by the fact of (religiously, culturally) diversities/plurality at a given time, what I will suggest to call 'plurality'.

[101] For another address of this situation, see Chapter 4.5.6 below.

[102] According to Cragg, also the Buddhist notion of *samsara* is likely to be interpreted thus: as a requirement of 'a life-thesis, a goal [i.e. *nirvana* as climax and not a forfeiture], with the interim obligation of compassion,' *ibid.* 11.

pluralism, the impact of material concerns) secularism and what Cragg calls 'irreligion' seem for many to be the inescapable future. Cragg, however, does not see anything embraceable by secularism. Instead he sees the danger of human autonomy being cut off from the will of God. Hence he sees Bonhoeffer's 'Before God and with God we live without God' as a neglect of the God-relatedness to which the biblical autonomy of man always was linked (14).[103]

(5) The argument between change and hope (15f). Cragg's point here is that 'religions themselves are not static' (15). This does not mean that they will make *total* changes, only that there will be disparity within their identities. All religions are 'in the flow of time and transition,' and of interaction. As one notes, this resembles almost identically one of the major assets of the world's religious history as conceived by Wilfred Cantwell Smith.[104] The feature of hope, finally, belongs to 'the sequence of generation,' the continual transmission and survival by renewal that 'forbids the hardening of the inflexible' (16).

Hence, Cragg establishes the human existence as a common ground for interreligious encounter: To relate to each other one must relate to the one and common human situation. This does not mean that all religious people are identical, only that each of them has to struggle with and ponder questions within the same world. Nor does it mean that this perspective is easily applauded by each and every religion. Cragg has obviously no problems seeing that, for example, Islam (and for that sake: the Bible) have another point of departure, namely as represented in *Bismillah* ('In the name of God the ...') Yet, Cragg contends that:

> Either way, man takes the stage. For the drama is about him and within him (2).

Another question is whether Cragg in this also runs the risk of projecting human measures on to the ultimate reality. Cragg's answer takes the opposite direction: 'If they [the human criteria] are inherently inappropriate the mystery itself would never emerge to concern our attention, still less our reservations of modesty' (4).

The human existence shall therefore be read as the context of that which Cragg conceives as the resolution this manifold situation; as 'the clue to its content of reference' (*ibid.*). The use of 'criterion' seems thus merely to imply that a theological solution of its inherent problem should integrate the features of the human situation intimately. Hence one must expect the dependence of the transcendent reality on the human existence of despair and wistfulness to be strong. Before we see how Cragg relates the two we shall first see how he in Chapter 3 of *The Christian and Other Religion* leads up to this by developing what I will call his 'modest theory of religion.'

4.5.2 THE DIMENSIONS OF RELIGION: EXPLORATION, EXPECTATION, ACCUSATION, PENITENCE AND ADORATION

As we have seen, Cragg claims a certain relationship between the common human situation and what Christianity offers. It is the latter part of this relationship (what Christianity offers) I will examine now. In Cragg's terms this can be depicted as the relation between the *scene* of the theatre and the empty space on the stage that has to be filled by someone. To draw on this I will attempt to see how he prepares the 'scene' before I consider the (ful)filling of the 'empty space.' This relates to what he calls the 'dimensions of religion,' that is, what I just called a modest theory of religion. Furthermore, these come to play for Cragg the role of comparative criteria. As his reflection over this is divided into 'the Semitic traditions of faith' (31ff) and the 'religions of the east, the monisms' (40ff), and since our study is predominantly occupied with the Christian-Muslim relationship, I will limit what follows to the former: his comprehension of the Semitic dimensions of religion.

Cragg's point of departure is his exposition of Heb. 4.13, of which he himself seems to be most inclined to the translation of *The Authorised Version*: 'Him with whom we have to do.'[105] It is particularly the expression 'have to do with' that he makes a theme, representing 'a measure of religion.' The question to be asked, however, is in what way?

The keyword he chooses for the exposition of this verse is *relevance*. Since 'relevance' has to do with 'relation', Cragg maintains that a *mutual relevance* between God and humans is expressed in the verse from Hebrews. This is furthermore to be related to the concept of *logos* which indeed is the term conveyed in this particular verse. Hence: 'God is the theme of a human *logos* for the reason that God has a *logos*-relatedness to our humanity.' Seen in the light of his idea of a *praeparatio evangelica* above, it is not very surprising that he employs an understanding of *logos,* although he does not elaborate on the background of ideas for this, neither from that of the Early Church nor of Stoicism.

---

[105] He also mentions more literal translations, that is: 'He to whom there is for us the word,' 'He to whom the word is ours,' 31. The Greek text reads, however: προς ον ημιν ο λογος. Another translation which he utilizes for another purpose is: 'Him to whom we give account,' *ibid.* 38. At this place ο λογος is interpreted as what one has to give an 'account' for.

What gains particular interest from him, is the pronominal aspect of this verse, that is: on the one hand the fact that the translation uses the third person, and on the other, the Jewish tradition which has taught us how to address God in the second person ('you'), a manner of expression which is neither alien to Islam yet with other kinds of idioms (32). The implications that this shows, according to Cragg, is how God is 'the terminal point of all our interrogation of life, all our wonder and puzzlement about who, and why, we are—God the addressee of man' (*ibid.*) Let us now see how this understanding of Heb. 4.13 is evolved into five specific aspects conveying how Semitic religion can be characterized as 'the measure of religion.'

    1. *Exploration*. Faith is to relate actively to the strangeness of the world and the enigmas of our own being (32). To believe that there *is* 'a word for us' implies a will to resist the unexamined life (33). What Cragg aims at balancing is 'search' and 'conviction': Both premature conviction and non-conviction exclude search for conclusions.

    2. *Expectancy* (34). Behind the notion of exploration lies the expectation of mutuality, that is: to have the questions answered. In other words, the search for the hidden God is induced by an invitation to be searched for. This dimension of religion becomes subsequently related to the whole matter of revelation:

> Expectancy, then, is what anticipates that which revelation (i.e. historical, within general, revelation) is understood as bestowing. It is wise to keep the link close between the two. For a deep credential of historical revelation is precisely the conviction that it concerns, illuminates, in a way answers, the questions which experience presents ... When meaning glimpsed becomes meaning confirmed, experience and revelation may be said to complement each other (34f).

Hence there is an intimate relation, yet not identical, between the expectations of humans and the 'historical' revelation understood as within the general revelation.[106] This presupposes that revelation is understood as 'apprehension' of something already existing. Put differently: This is the 'upturning of our face' towards God, which is the metaphor that Cragg claims underlies the first part of Heb. 4.13 (32, 35).

---

[106] This argument of Cragg resembles very much Tillich's method and theory of *correlation*. This is strengthened by Cragg's statement at the same page (34): 'We need not suppose a central cluelessness in a world so full of clues.' This is almost identical with the approach and formulations of Tillich, see Tillich 1994, 52.

Regarding the Christian and Muslim strand, Cragg says that in the case of the New Testament this is related to 'Christ crucified,' whereas it is connected to *fitrat-Allah* in Islam: the Qur'anic idea that God has 'natured' humankind (Surah 30.29/30).[107] Yet, the divine initiative will always have priority in the Semitic religions.

3. Related to this personal and answering God is also the dimension of human accusing, or theodicy (37). Cragg maintains that theism, particularly where the conditions of life are thoroughly investigated, paradoxically entails an 'authentic demand' for theodicy: expectation and desperation 'interdepend' (38). Ultimately, then, the demand for someone to solve one's situation strikes God.

4. Yet, the problem of attuning life to God may also turn in another direction: penitence. Given that God cannot be blamed for everything[108] and the human perceives itself as responsible for God, human beings have to perceive themselves as sinners. Otherwise the evil of our complex history is evaded or explained away.

5. The very climax of Cragg's journey of differentiation of the dimension of religion reaches its peak in the concept of adoration, which is the silence and 'awareness for the unspeakable, the light of the unapproachable' that can be found in *Magnificat* and *Takbir* respectively.[109] This dimension seems to convey the absolute meaning of 'the word that is ours' (Heb. 4.13).

By these five 'dimensions of religion,' the Semitic traditions of faith are exposed as far as the relationality between humans and God is concerned.[110] By a distinctive exegesis of Heb. 4.13 he has therefore elaborated on the concepts of 'relevance' and 'pronominality.' If we now proceed to his chapter on 'The Measure of Christ' we will eventually discover, related to the religious dimensions and criteria of the Semitic religions, that Christ appears as 'He with whom the word is ours,' and whom 'has taught us in the Word the language we may use,' which is the 'literacy' (in Christ) that may be 'learned and spoken in the common world'

---

[107] See also Cragg 1993b, 161.
[108] This corresponds to Luther's theodicy. Cragg relates at this point to another translation of Heb. 4.13, namely 'giving account for', see note 105.
[109] Cf. also Cragg 1981a, 33, where 'God is greater' (*takbir*) is introduced as 'The criterion of religion.' This criteriological interpretation of *takbir* should be seen in the light of the context in *COR*: As an indispensable element of a *Semitic* understanding of 'God' and 'religion'. For the understanding of *takbir*, see Chapter 5.5.
[110] See also Cragg's paraphrases of this 'fivefold voice': of search and desire (exploration), of hope and converse (expectation), of despair and quarrel (accusation and theodicy), of contrition and guiltiness (penitence) and of wonder and benediction (adoration), *ibid.* 39f.

(49). Thus, connections are developed to the last subsection as well as to an answer on the issue which this chapter took as one of its points of departure: the 'empty space' of the theatre.

4.5.3 THE PATTERN OF ENMITY AND THE PATTERN OF SUFFERING: THE LITERACY IN CHRIST LEARNED AND SPOKEN IN THE COMMON WORLD

Cragg sees his chapter on 'The Measure of Christ' as a possibility of self-exploration. Nevertheless, given the historical dependency of Christianity upon the Jewish tradition the self-exploration takes form of exploring a certain pattern of the Old Testament, yet being climaxed by Christ in the New Testament.

When Cragg takes advantage of the metaphor of the theatre, it is actually in order to make sense of Heb. 4.13 (cf. the previous subsection) and to develop the proper context for its understanding. Hence his initial step is to see the empty space on the stage of the theatre as a metaphor for 'the significance of the Old Testament' (51). Consequently, the answer that is 'expected' (cf. the first religious dimension above) is 'the Messianic action by the bearer of the Messianic identity' (*ibid.*). This double emphasis, on both 'action' and 'agent,' is characteristic for Cragg, which will become clearer as we proceed.

Cragg is aware that this starting point may seem arbitrary. Yet, his contention again is that one cannot start without presuppositions (51). Aligning to twentieth century hermeneutics this also implies that he renounces the possibility of attaining a 'God's eye view' where all religions are seen from within one single perspective. Cragg's perspective is the Christian one[111] as generated from the Jewish background. More important, however is his contention that, 'the point of departure fulfils itself in

---

[111] This raises immediately the question of *what kind of* Christian approach he employs. The most common label to be put on his Christian position is that of an *evangelical* Christian. See e.g. Griffith 1994, 29f ('clearly evangelical commitment to faith in Jesus of Nazareth as Christ and Lord'; 'modern evangelical Christian'). Yet, 'evangelical' is a highly ambiguous notion and, although I acknowledge this as a broad determination of his position within the Anglican community of churches, I maintain that this characterization has to be extensively modified and filled with content, as shown above and below, if not becoming entirely vacuous. An evidence for the demand for a more precise description is given in the ambivalent reception within evangelical strands, also outside the Anglican churches, of his suggestions. The impact on the Roman Catholic Church has been more significant, see Slomp 1990, 171, where his approach is often aligned to that of Louis Massignon who was influential on the notes on Muslims at the Vatican II's *Nostra Aetate.*

where it leads' (*ibid.*). This shall be interpreted thus: what Jesus offers vindicates the Jewish beginning.[112] Yet, how is this Jewish background to be described?

Cragg's approach to the Old Testament is ambivalent. On the one hand he sees 'the destiny of man' wonderfully summarized by the elements of creation (divine intention for and liability to the world), history (the wayward story included), land and people (based on exodus and election), particularly epitomized by the Torah which shows the 'down-to-earth, open-to-heaven, kind of real being', yet everything comprising 'the elemental factors in all human culture and economy', (52). Given this exemplary function of the one community, Cragg maintains the translatability of this to all people. On the other hand it belongs to Cragg's notion of the Old Testament that 'if the vocation was splendid, so is the venture grim' (*ibid.*): Hope is deferred, land and people are separated in exile, and the Torah suffers the stubbornness of its human partner yet still faithfully summoning the people to its purpose.

This conflict between the intention of God, particularly represented by the Law, and the human actuality gains significance by the 'meaning of the prophets' (53). Cragg sees in the prophets 'the mentors of the people under the Law, the steadfast remembrancers of the Torah, calling the nation back to its true destiny' (*ibid.*). Yet, inevitably this entails suffering for the prophets, and the enmity of the people is thus transferred from the message to the messenger. The main figure in this respect is Jeremiah, who will be addressed extensively later. In him Cragg sees exemplary that steadfastness incurs wounds and sorrow of heart. This is, however, not a matter of elusion as the prophet is not supposed to keep silent or abandon his words. The pattern, however, is defencelessness and proclamation of a pure word. This might in the end be the only means to loosen the descending spiral of enmity and hate. According to Cragg, this suffering is 'the hallmark of the love of truth' (*ibid.*). In all this, however, there is an important consequence drawn of Cragg, in short: the move from word and speech to personality, character and autobiography.

To return to the metaphor of the theatre: Cragg sees this tension between the intention of the Torah and the life and message of the prophets as represented it the hope of Messiah, corresponding to the empty place of the stage. This empty place is

> felt and interpreted from within the heart of that history, the
> place for the answer that satisfies 'within the conditions

---

[112] Cf. *ibid.*, when Cragg concludes: 'the Jewish expectancy holds, in the form of hope, all the vital elements of [the Christian] faith.'

that make its perception possible' (53f).

It is at this place that Cragg introduces Jesus. He admits that it may seem arbitrary to make Jesus so central to one's criteria but chooses to do so in order to see whether 'the whole question [whether Jesus is central] *can* be identified here.'

Cragg easily identifies Jesus to align with the pattern observed in the prophets of the Old Testament: By him word and personality, life and death, were held indissolubly together. In the confrontations Jesus encountered this pattern became even more evident as it was 'sharpened by the Messianic theme' (55). In him the 'Christic[113] pattern' appears as a climax of suffering, comprising 'the charisma of ministry, the forthrightness of the word, and the grace of character' (*ibid.*). At this place Cragg reaches the most decisive point of his Christology: the recognition of the divine Sonship of Jesus in point of history as 'love in suffering'. In Jesus, therefore, he sees the divine nature being expressed as well as the sin of the world being borne.[114]

---

[113] Cragg's use of 'Christic' is dependent on the Catholic (Hispanic-Indian!) R. Panikkar, see, e.g., Cragg 1993c, 186. Though Cragg develops his own distinctive version of this concept, he reveals strong sympathy for Panikkar's ideas in his seminal writings; *The Unknown Christ of Hinduism* (1964), and *Myth, Faith and Hermeneutics* (1970). His sympathy for Panikkar's 'open-ended-ness,' 'risk' and 'vulneralization' of God, which he finds to be biblically grounded, fits of course squarely into his own interreligious approach, *ibid.* 198f. Yet, one gets the impression in his careful exploration of Panikkar that Cragg is a bit less 'open-ended' than Panikkar. The crucial question is how 'open-ended-ness' may define its 'decisive origin.' At this point, see also Lesslie Newbigin's inquiry into Cragg's use of 'pattern' in his review of *CFs,* where Newbigin recommends a stronger emphasis on decisive *events*, Newbigin 1987. See also Newbigin 1989 for a similar point where he also develops his own position in close relation to Kraemer. Cragg's implicit response to that concern of the 'Christ-event' and not only 'Christ-principle' (Newbigin 1989, 328) can be seen immediately below. For a comparison of Cragg and Newbigin, under the heading of *feasible missiological approaches* in contrast to the 'liberal pluralism' of e.g. John Hick, see Wood 1996. Wood sees Cragg as one in the 'continuity' tradition after J.N. Farquhar, whereas Newbigin is interpreted in the light of the missiological position of 'radical discontinuity' most notably represented by H. Kraemer. Wood's point is that both Cragg and Newbigin contribute to an understanding of mission where neither the continuity can be total (*pro* Cragg!) nor the discontinuity absolute (*pro* Kraemer!), ii. Hence Cragg and Newbigin's approaches converge, *ibid.* 376.

[114] Cragg seems to be well aware not to deduct the nature of Christ from some principles or necessities. For him Jesus' Sonship is a 'reality in deeds' (56), hence Messiahship does not argue more that 'agency' (55). Consequently, Jesus is only 'Son of God' in a creedal sense if he was Son of God 'beneath the olive branches of Gethsemane, and in the darkness of Golgotha' (56).

Important here is that Cragg sees Jesus' ministry as a divine initiative (56). Jesus as the 'Son of God' is therefore not to be thought of as adoption, deification, or divinization. This issue is presupposed in the confession of 'Jesus is Lord', where

> the ' ... of God' which faith had earlier learned to say of men, of prophets, of wisdom, of will, could now be perfectly conjoined with the human because it had, indeed, been so conjoined in a history perfectly related to the divine mind (*ibid.*).

Cragg's emphasis is therefore on the fulfilled Sonship where God's will becomes one with the will of Jesus. Hence only 'God was in Christ' entails the 'Jesus is Lord' (*ibid.*). At this place the Resurrection 'celebrates and declares in the victorious quality of the love that 'bearing all things never fails' (*ibid.*).

The 'cosmic' consequence of this is that the Messiahship of Jesus presents the invisible as well as makes its perception possible (57). According to Cragg, therefore, 'the great empty place at the heart of history ... has been duly filled.' Keeping on with the metaphor of theatre, Cragg elaborates how this 'perception' of the invisible, that is: of God, has been made possible by the Messiahship. From seeing Jesus as the great catharsis of the world, he maintains that this and other cultic terms are both fulfilled and transcended by the Cross, which has been the perfect sacrament in history and by which power evil is redeemed. As such it is all embracing in the meaning of 'a universally accessible salvation' (*ibid.*).[115] And, moreover, as such the whole matter of theodicy (cf. point 3 in 4.5.2 above) is answered and made very distinctive:

> To have, within history, that event in which the full quality of human waywardness is present means that despair cannot

---

Cf. also Cragg 1993c, where Cragg phrases the significance of Christology as being 'the clue to what is real, a clue given from within the real itself,' 185. Hence 'the Christ event, the messianic action, substantiates the very nature of God,' 197. Cragg sees this as 'the best meaning we can give to the Latin, through the Greek, of the creedal phrase about 'being of one substance with the Father," *ibid.*
Cf. finally *COR*, 114f, where 'love in suffering' is said to be 'the heart of that divine nature' and where the Christic pattern 'becomes the criterion by which God himself is known.'

[115] His reason for emphasizing accessible is plainly not to override 'the precious freedom of the soul,' 57. His use of universally is to align to the fundamental matter of not giving ethnic preferences on behalf of the Gospel, 57, 60.

have further evidence for us beyond what we have already known . . . [and] the deepest theodicy is ours for the receiving (58).

But one may ask after this survey whether this development of the Christic pattern exceeds an intra-Christian way of describing fundamental aspects of an orthodox Christology? On the one hand, it seems clear that Cragg's use of 'pattern' in this context is primarily grounded in his intention to show the intimate relation between creation, human sin, the subsequent charge and suffering of the prophets and the culmination of both the suffering of prophets and God's intentions in the suffering and death of Jesus.

On the other hand, Cragg distinguishes between what is determinative and what is not (64). The former is obviously the Christ-event. The latter, however, is neither out of interest nor confined to the Christian tradition. This ('the human manifold') is seen as a resource by which the Christic can recruit for its interpretation. Because Cragg is aware that the determinate view itself 'owe ... to pagan cults, Greek mysteries and a Roman market of ideas,' he suggests that the 'human manifold' should be sought out also in his time. He therefore asks whether there are

> clear senses in which the questions, the anxieties, the stopping-points, the conclusions, and, properly, the symbols, of other men's faith-systems have elements that are already 'in Christ', and may, by us, be recognised as such? (64)

This question is directed towards an affirmative answer, which is implicit in his development of 'the saving mind' in Ch. 6 of *COR*. The keyword here is *mediation*:

> What matters, therefore, in the *mediation* of our faith to men is not, primarily, their assent to our *credo*, but their *discovery of its worth,* while the ultimate of our Christian duty is not to have our faith state itself like a theorem, but to *fulfil itself* like love (84, emphases mine.)

Since Cragg discerns distinctively between doctrines/formulations and the *meaning* of faith and religion (*ibid.*), it is possible to think of mediation of meaning between Christians with a 'saving mind' and humans of other faiths. This discernment resembles the discussion of exclusion and inclusion in *CWP*, or identity and identification elsewhere,[116] at this place with particular (and paradoxical) focus on 'in Christ':

> As a credal formula, 'in Christ' will require us to exclude: but as an ambition and instinct no exclusions will be possible (84).

As *COR* is a study in 'interreligion' (xiif), the saving mind, as derived from 'the mission of God in Christ,' is always looking for partners (84). In this way the most surprising relationships are developed as, for instance, with the relation of the story of the prodigal son (Luke 15) that Cragg utilizes to give *karma* a more radical sense 'than *karma* itself' and the deeper context of 'love which can halt and reverse it' by forgiveness (89). This is similarly done in relation to Buddhist *samsara,* namely 'to think savingly about ... human impermanence' (90). The Islamic instance will be covered in the next major chapter (Chapter 5).

Cragg's aim is to mediate between religions by exploring their human and their transcendent content. This is not, as sceptics may object, a 'one-way street' exercise in Christian prejudice, but a reciprocal enterprise:

> Its affirmatives are also interrogatives, its commendations open to interrogation. But realism must be reciprocal, offered and received (96).

At this point it seems that the mutuality in Cragg's interreligious position has gained a stronger feature. 'Saving mind' does not primarily mean 'saving from', but a

> spiritual regeneration which does not terminate what we are by identity but, rather, saves it in the newness of life (100).

---

[116] Cf. Cragg 1993c where he, in relation to a sympathetic exploration of Raimundo Panikkar's ideas, says: 'An immediate perplexity arises, namely, whether or how that sense of the Christic that is rightly identified as such in Jesus as Christ ... can extend and define outside the particulars that belong with it in him,' 198, my emphasis. By this Cragg aims at holding the identity of the Christic together with the eventual identification of it by 'other acknowledgements of the Christic made elsewhere with equal warrant,' *ibid.* Hence, extensification seems not only to be implicit in Cragg's approach but explicit as well. Provided that one sees the Christ-event as the generating point of departure, also the Christian community should be seen as an extension of the Christic, though it has to be perceived as 'inseparably with the one Christ event,' *ibid.*

This might appear to be unduly irenic and flourishing. His point, however, is to be taken as an important matter, namely: that to make Christ relevant to people of other faith is not a matter of alteration of identity but of completing it in a better fashion and of 'penetrating of meaning'. In other words: There is something to recruit from anyone who receives the commendation of Christ.

Not only are the affirmations more distinct here. Related to our questioning of the impact of the interreligious encounter upon Cragg's own position as present in *CWP*, it must also be said that the aspect of reciprocity is stronger in *COR* than in *CWP*. The relating to other religion entails, as in the quotation above, self-interrogation facilitated by the Other.[117] Hence I venture to suggest that there is in Cragg not only self-giving or self-commendation but also a potential of self-change. Cragg does not put it exactly like this, but given his elaborations on what it means to 'seek relationships and to hold criteria in Christ,' I find this to be a reasonable conclusion. The sum is, therefore, that what we have seen in *CWP* is developed further in *COR* in some respects. Regarding the theme of mediation I will now reconstruct how this point is argued for in *Christ and the Faiths (CFs)* from 1986, the keyword for his approach being 'a theology of cross-reference'.[118]

4.5.4. THE WAY OF THE INCARNATION:
A THEOLOGY OF CROSS-REFERENCE

The Christ and the Faiths (1986) is the largest interreligious work of Cragg in respect of dealing with diverse religious traditions.[119] That does not mean that it is more comprehensive in respect of depth than for example *COR*. The main difference, however, is that in *CFs* Cragg not only develops general interreligious perspectives, which is mostly the case in *COR*, but attempts in the main chapters to examine the crux of 'Christianity' from within certain other religious traditions.[120] What happens in the chapter on Islam, I leave for the next chapter on Cragg's Islam interpretation. Another characteristic is that methodological consequences are further clarified.[121] These are of course of particular interest since the interest of

---

[117] See also *LC*, 189, with regards to 'self-doubt' and 'self-search'.
[118] See also Cragg 1993c, which argument approximates to the major approach of *CFs*.
[119] Subsequent parenthetical remarks refer to *CFs*.
[120] The chapters and traditions are: 'God in Islam' (Chs. 2-4); 'Messiah and Jewry' (Chs. 5-7); 'Christologies and India' (Chs. 8-10); 'The Buddha and the Self' (Chs. 11-13).
[121] *COR* is, as the title reveals, more concentrated on the Christian as person and the challenges from the interreligious situation. It might be justified to call *COR* missiological or practical-theological, whereas *CFs* is more inclined to be a (conceptual) study in theology of religion.

our study at this place is still general. They are also of interest because Cragg at this place approximates 'other religion' further, a 'move' that gains almost a climax in the next subsection about the Holy Spirit.

In the introduction to *CFs* Cragg supports the increasing awareness of today, namely that

> Christian theology must justify its being 'Christian' by undertaking a theology of religion at large and incorporating this into its traditional responsibility for its own distinctiveness [that is, the theme of Christ] (ix).

This resonates with the approach of the present study in the following way: self-understanding must be self-relating. This claim is in *CFs* developed in connection with the concepts *bona fide* (ch. 1) and *bona fiducia* (ch. 14), embracing, literally, the rest of the book.[122] Whereas the former means 'good faith *in relationship*' (ix, my emphasis), the latter completes the former as the faith's 'content and substance, credally confessed and communally sustained through time and change' (*ibid.*).[123] The difference between the two might be described as the difference between how the faith on the one hand expresses itself in dialogue with and reference to people of other religions, and how the faith reflects systematically upon its distinctiveness and liturgically expresses its identity. Nevertheless, *fides-fiducia* should not be confused with the contrast between 'the creative mind' and 'the custodian mind'.

An implication of the 'faith in relation' is that we must concede: 'all [faiths] are options,'[124] and where: 'the interior convictions of each are in the external presence of all' (x).[125] This awareness of the plurality of

---

[122] In this case these chapters also emphasize the function of these concepts of establishing a superior framework of interpretation for material elements in the particular religious tradition, treated in the chapters between ch. 1 and 14.

[123] On p. 316 he defines it as 'the whole corpus of Christian doctrine and tradition which the *fides* in Chapter 1 possesses and fulfils.' The pair of words here parallels the pair of 'doctrine-personal' where *fiducia* equates to 'doctrine' and *fides* 'personal'. Cragg's point, however, is to emphasize the interdependence between the two: 'A theology cannot keep faith with contemporary challenge and play false with its past,' 317. At this place he supports L. Newbigin's understanding of religions as *'fiduciary frameworks'*. This is done deliberately in opposition to Wilfred Cantwell Smith who only sees the religions (the cumulative traditions) as a personal/participatory processes ('Islam is what Muslims say it is') and not carriers of a pattern, 344f, n 2 and n 4. Cragg's position is that the diverse 'ultimates' are 'not negotiable' (317). Yet, Smith is not the explicitly intended negative reference of this latter statement.

[124] Cf. p. 337: 'authority is ... competitive, ... absolutes alternates.'

[125] See also *COR*, xi, for this understanding of the religions as alternatives. The matter

religious options should, according to Cragg, proceed to address the matter of truth. What Cragg finds pertinent to make a theme at this place is the alternatives of 'truth for' and 'truth of' (*ibid.*). People may agree about the former, for example in the form of 'Islam is true for Muslims since faithful Muslims hold it to be true,' or in Cragg's form: faith-X is true (because 'by') X-faithful. This is of course a circular argument, in as much as it is the only truth people may accept. Despite the fact that the 'truth of' may be assessed as 'caught within' the 'truth for'-notion, Cragg asserts it to be a required theme of theology, particularly in the meeting of diverse faiths.[126]

In practice Cragg deals with truth in *CFs* by examining the problem of how different faiths understand themselves from within, and all other from without (xi). In short, the thesis pursued in the present study. Nevertheless, this problem he purports to surmount. One of the aims is to bring two different forms of 'inwardnesses' together, in relation, and at least to reduce the 'externality' of either to the other. Of particular interest, and that is the very project of the book, it is

> to see the several points of crux in Christianity from within the prescripts of four other faiths and in each case to interpret the one into the concern of the other [that is: of Christianity] (xi).

This is certainly nothing but extensification. His suggestion is that by going from a 'truth for'-thinking to a 'truth of'-thinking, that is, in the light of the criterion of 'in Christ', one might be able to solve the problem of understanding the Other merely from without its (the Other's) own prescripts. Cragg chooses to examine how central issues in four world's

---

of 'conceding pluralism' is examined in 4.5.6 below. The notions of 'internal conviction' and 'external presence' come close to Cantwell Smith's program of 'corporate critical self-consciousness'.

[126] For this distinction between 'truth for' and 'truth of', see *LC,* 189. Also, here truth of is 'included' in truth for since 'there is no agreed criteria by which we can affirm the truth *of* a faith.' There might however be areas where it is possible to agree upon verification and falsification, but not in respect of religious conviction. There, 'believing,' or better, and in accordance with Cantwell Smith, 'faithing makes it so.' Moreover, the 'shapes' of such 'faithing' should not require its exclusiveness or impose its own criteria upon others. Christian credentials of God do not necessarily have relevance to 'all and sundry.' Cragg sees this as a 'formula for constructive pluralism.' Nevertheless, by 'necessarily' Cragg finds missing in Smith's view the opportunity of a 'freedom of movement of belief,' that is: the point of mission, 240, n13. One might characterize this proposal as opting for a contest between genuine religious competitors in respect of giving persuasive credentials of God. Cf. also Chapter 4.5.6 below.

religions (*in casu* Islam, Jewry, Hinduism, and Buddhism) are deeply mediatorial of themes crucial to Christianity.[127] This central-central mediation resembles certainly features of his previous works. The terminology, however, is partly new. This regards particularly the concepts of 'cross-reference' and 'cross-reference theology'.[128] That which follows will address these particular concepts.

In the place where the concept of cross-reference is introduced (ch. 1, p. 4) the argument runs as follows: 1. Christ is *not* primarily anonymously present in the religions (as with Rahner), but is as prepossession known already by their own meanings. 2. These meanings and imagery are distinct from the New Testament understanding of his 'Christhood', through which Christianity exists. 3. The task for a cross-reference theology is, therefore, to bring Christ as understood by Christianity to the religions as they have understood him. This is by Cragg compared with the activity of translation.[129]

Thus, cross-reference means two things: a. To locate the cross-reference of a New Testament Christology within the plurality of expositions of Christ based on extra-Christian premise, and b. to translate from the normative context into those contexts which have not yet grasped the understanding of Christ in its fullness. In this, Cragg concedes other traditions the same right to do similar translation from their own prescripts, with for example Christianity as cross-reference, though their ability to do this will vary to a certain extent (6). Nevertheless, Cragg's contribution is a Christian one.[130]

In this way, the theology of cross-reference sets out to realize the concept of *bona fide*. It is a meeting between faiths that Cragg aims to facilitate,[131] not an all-embracing theological system, with which to examine in one operation the contemporary religiously plural situation, eventually in connection with a *tertium comparationis*. That Cragg renounces this is evident from his emphasis on that the *criteria* for a cross-reference

---

[127] Cf. also Cragg 1982b, 36 where the expressions employed are *inter alia*: 'vital to Islam,' and 'uncannily close to the features of our New Testament map.'

[128] The notion of 'cross-reference' is used already in 1985, *JM*. The approach of that study is: 'How should the New Testament significance of Jesus, 'beginning (as it does) from Jerusalem', look into—and seem from—those 'eastern sympathies' which Islam defines?' 2.

[129] At another place in *CFs* (12f) Cragg correlates cross-reference with the relation of typology between the Old and the New Testament scriptures.

[130] See *ibid.* p. 21 where he characterizes cross-reference theology as to be 'none other than the conscious, loving, tireless, hopeful trust of these referents [i.e. God, Christ, the Church] together and the patient interpretation of the theme of their consistency.'

[131] Cf. the title of his work from 1992, *To Meet and to Greet: Faith with Faith.*

theology must be brought from within each tradition (10). This corresponds to the fact that Cragg allows himself to use the criterion 'God in Christ'.

When I mentioned above how Cragg understands 'cross-reference', I did not elaborate on what he means by 'imagery'. Yet because the connotations to this are rather central to the concept of cross-reference, it might prove rewarding to unfold this further. In this respect the issue rather than the notions that matters. Cragg locates this imagery, which interprets Christ based on its own premises, in 'the data of their own experience and their verdict on the human scene' (5). This human world of experience is made central, a common denominator[132] (11), to all religious

---

[132] See also *ibid.*, p. 341. This openness towards the human wistfulness and condition, however, corresponds to a certain notion of the New Testament, *parrhesia*. In this regard Cragg cites 1 Tim. 3.13. The *theological* substantiation of this attitude is to be found in the *pattern of the Incarnation* (342).

Regarding the notion of 'common denominator' Cragg does not think of this that it may lead to a kind of common framework of reference. Where he deals explicitly with this (337-39), the answer is negative: There is nothing like a common framework of reference. Neither reason, nor wide dispersion/long persistence, coherence, capacity for realism, etc., can act as judging criterion to the question about, for example, authority, which Cragg regards as the perennial religious question (338). On the other hand, Cragg sees himself as responsible towards the whole human race. Consequently, it is not satisfactory to present one's conviction from solely one's own point of view, without relating it to external faith-systems. The solution which Cragg suggests is: 1. Evangelization within the pluralist framework, 2. to aim at best possible relation to the themes and built-in tensions of other faiths, 3. to put 1. and 2. in correlation to what we mentioned above as 'common denominator.' Hence, the solution is no objective frame of reference but an interaction between diverse perspectives in relation to a common situation.

The reward of this, according to Cragg 1977b, is that one avoids to 'Christianize' (cf. Bijlefeld 1967) other religion by the emphasis on the common world of life. Conclusively, he describes this as the 'sphere of our humility' and the 'arena of our relevance,' 175. Most interestingly, Cragg's comment of Bijlefeld's study at this place is very irenic, obviously seeing his own position as justified as not a neutral phenomenological, but as a 'committed, religious position' of 'a would-be expositor.' This self-characteristic is presumably one of the best descriptions of Cragg's approach towards Islam. See also *FLN*, where he reflects retrospectively on the several accusations of his 'christianizing' Islam: 'This was not the case. I was simply trying freely to possess the Qur'an in *all* its implications in a way that—as it seemed to me—Christians had long failed to do out of explicit distrust of its status or their sheer unfamiliarity ... Why is there no affirmative word to hold what 'prejudice' implies the other way—a word to suggest spiritual sympathy finding itself justified?' 116f. See also *MC*, 12f, where a similar argument is developed, that is: Cragg's approach as merely an effort to avoid 'incommunicado' between Christianity and Islam.

For a harsh critique of Cragg's Islam interpretation with regards to 'Christianization', see first Qureshi 1984, e.g. 203: 'To bear Christian witness is, for a Christian, an unquestionable right, even a duty. But to do so in the act of explaining Islam is suspect—Dr. Cragg is open to the charge of attempting not conversion but 'subversion.'' See also Grunebaum who describes Cragg's approach as 'veiled

traditions. The distance is thus not long to describe *cross-reference* in theology as 'a patient and perceptive ministry in human crisis' (7).[133]

On other places, Cragg describes this continuity of Christian and other faiths by means of terminology of sound and music, as resonance. He suggests that it is amazing how readily and pointedly 'Christian resonance' can be heard as 'transitions of meaning' in other religions (11). Yet, Cragg's point is that such resonance should not be silenced but transposed comprehensively into another 'key.' The issue is illustrated by how Pasternak's translation of *Hamlet* into Russian, and back into English, gains the same resonance or cross-reference in Stalin's world but with the distinctive Russian experience and reality as a part of the resonance. *Hamlet* is made relevant as 'the source takes on and takes up the pith of what it seeks out.' Or, as Cragg has it more generally:

> Unless what the other has is recruited, engaged, excited,
> no resonance will be heard (13).

This resonance is to be identified as cross-reference, where the process with the Christian meaning to other references is theologically identified as the way of the Incarnation (*ibid.*). Hence, this is not to be seen as a mere

---

apologetics,' which guarantees 'early obsolescence,' and as '[in its final judgement] dictated by the needs of his Christian audience,' Grunebaum 1970, 127 and 129. Finally, see D'Souza 1992, 66f, who sees Cragg's interpretation of Islam as 'in totally opposition to Muslim self-understanding,' and '[coming to the study of Islam admittedly] as a committed Christian. Filling in 'what is wanting' in Islam according to his own belief,' thereby ending up 'Christianizing Islamic concepts and ideas.'

The other side of this issue is a warning raised to him of not 'islamizing' the New Testament *kerygma*, see Griffith 1994, 33, who advocates historical Arab-Christian accomplishments to express their Christian faith in Arabic. The matter of concern is Cragg's disparagement of previous Arab-Christian endeavours to make 'God in Christ' understandable to Muslims without developing a distinctive Arabic theological dialect different from the Islamic Arabic, that is: 'a theology that thinks into Islam,' *AC*, 288. *AC* is particularly concerned with this challenge of the Arab-Christian minority.

[133] Cf. Cragg 1990, 177: 'Religions belong to humanness ... Religions ... cluster around crisis of existence and purport to order and interpret them ...' This resonates well also with earlier parts of his writings, e.g. *ITC* and *CM*. Evidence for the strong relation between *CFs* and earlier works can be found in Cragg 1966a, 109. At this particular place it is similarly the relation between the mediation of exploring the faith of the Other, the common human existence and the translatability of Christian meanings that is focused upon: 'We must venture relationships with existing faiths at every point of their assurance and perplexity, grounding ourselves upon a common human existence and our confidence in the translatability of the Christian meanings into their wistfulness and their convictions.'

method, or a 'dimension of communication' different from theology proper.[134]

As seen so far in this chapter, the whole approach of Cragg seems to be inclined to emphasize the continuity between what is distinctively Christian and 'the mental universe of other faiths' (342). Both the concept of cross-reference, and particularly that of resonance, implies a rather strong relation between the two. The question is, however, how harmonic this can be thought of. Put differently: does this approach integrate elements which neither resonate nor are relevant?

Let me put forward one example: The relation between Jesus before the crucifixion and Muhammad before *Hijrah* is a crux in Cragg's authorship.[135] In this context Cragg might say that: 'Christian theology is, therefore, not on alien ground in the territory of Muhammad's Mecca: it occupies it in *the contrasted idiom* of Jesus' (12, my emphasis). As one sees, both the continuity ('not on alien ground') and discontinuity ('contrasted idiom') are included. Most interestingly here, is the notion of 'counter-relevance' about the lack of correlation between the end of the suffering of Jesus and the similar end of Muhammad's rejection in Mecca.

Another feature, which I have already touched upon, is the pair of common-distinctive. As both notions are dealt with above, it is how what is common is related to the distinctive that is interesting here. At one place these are related paradigmatically:

> There is what is gratefully common in what is deeply distinctive (322).[136]

The context for this quotation are concepts like 'overlap' between the Gospel and the faiths of others, on the one hand, and the 'continuity' of Christian christology and Islamic prophethood on the other. As mentioned above, the crux for what is 'deeply distinctive' is 'Jesus as Christ'. Against this 'answer' all others will appear as 'questionings' (344). Cragg's point, however, is that the Christian understanding of Christ must integrate the meaning of other faiths, as any answer must take up and integrate the question that has been asked.

Cragg follows up ideas from previous work in *CFs*. This is particularly the case as to a conceptual clarification of how the religions

---

[134] See Cragg e.g. 1957b, 249, where Cragg criticizes H. Kraemer for this view (e.g.: 'Is it a tolerable position to argue that, while there are essentially no points of contact for what we mean, there are for what we preach?').

[135] See Chapter 5.5.2 below.

[136] A similar way of expressing it can be found in Cragg 1981a, 38: 'We cannot realize our common ground unless we discover the ground we do not share.' The question is whether this should be interpreted as an indirect statement regarding 'what is common is to be seen as element in what is distinctive.'

function as formative contexts for a Christian self-relating and self-understanding. In this respect the concept of cross-reference (theology) is introduced in order to describe the mediation of meaning between Christian and other faiths. This is particularly focused on Christ and the capacities other religions may have to understand him in their 'imagery'. In this, both elements of continuity and discontinuity play a significant role.

4.5.5 THE HOLY SPIRIT IN THE WORLD: REDUNDANT, UNEMPLOYED OR ACTIVE?

What can be perceived as the major theological substantiation of the relation between a Christian self-understanding and the understanding of Islam, in short, the justification for self-relating, is his conception of the Holy Spirit. This is particularly elaborated on in ch. 7 in *COR*.

Cragg's understanding of the third person of the Trinity is firstly connected to his understanding of 'being religious', of which he discerns three aspects in general.[137] These are:

1.   The impulse and prompting that initiates religiosity and religion. This 'prompting,' Cragg says, is personal, social, economic, political, creative, and artistic.

2.   The conception, reasoning and systematizing of religiosity that actuates being philosophical, mental, theological, scientific, ideological and imaginative.

3.   The expression or shape which associates or devises out of its partners, being active, cultural, institutional, liturgical, symbolic, physical, literary and spiritual.

---

[137] This consideration are in fact generated by a very telling passage from John Steinbeck's *The Grapes of Wrath* where a family, which has lost their grandpa, Wm. Joad, decides to bury him themselves, the cost and ceremony of the funeral being a too great challenge, *COR*, 103. Being a covert act and thus fearing the suspicion from the authorities, they decide to attach a simple statement of facts in a jam-jar. Having stated who grandpa was, how he died, that 'his fokes bured him becaws they got no money to pay for funerals,' they ask Casey, the derelict ex-preacher: 'Can't you stick on somepin from Scripture so it'll be religious?' It is the very last word in this question Cragg reflects on, in fact in the whole chapter called 'The Holy Spirit.' His question is: 'What, it is fair to ask, does the text add to the words of fact,' seeing in the deeds of the family a 'religiousness' which 'is already there' (in the mortal pathos, in the dignity of human courage, in the reverence for the dead, in the will to come clean, in the integrity that anticipates and cares about justification, in the patience of grief, etc.). And: 'With these, has the psalmist or the evangelist anything more to say?' Cragg returns later in the chapter to the Joad family (i.e. pp. 109f and 114) showing this to be an exemplary story of reference for his comprehension of the Holy Spirit in relation to 'other religion'.

By this understanding of 'being religious', Cragg sees the 'other religion' in all its areas of life and character, hoping that the Christian might be able to be the means of the Holy Spirit's 'presence and grace, his truth and hope and patience' (104). From this on Cragg carries on to elaborate on selected areas of a Pneumatology which may prove relevant for the relation to 'other religion'. These are: 1. The understanding of the work of the Spirit 'beyond the Scriptures and the Church' (place-inclusiveness), 2. The relation between spirit and form, and 3. A reflection on the 'time-inclusiveness' of the Spirit.

Cragg's elaboration on the question about the activity of the Spirit *beyond* and outside the church and the Scriptures (104) is, as in *CWP*, particularly concerned with the formulation of the Nicene Creed[138] about the Spirit that 'proceeds' (105). Cragg's position is the conception of an intimate continuity between the Father, Son and Spirit in the proceeding of the last named from the other two, which includes 'a continuum of energy and meaning whereby the Father is known in the Son and they are active, self-consistently, through the Spirit.' Hence Cragg translates 'proceeding' by 'truth in its own energies' (*ibid.*).[139]

The Spirit is moreover the one who is 'taking and opening the things of Christ.'[140] The second and third person of the godhead is thus inseparable. But if so, the question has to be raised about the work of the Spirit outside the church and the Scriptures, especially since Cragg does not seem to be happy with an identification of the Spirit and the church,[141] and recognizes at this point the possibility of reckoning with the Incarnation without the background of the Old Testament (106). This,[142] he suggests, will be very much a school of Christian faith, but far outside the prescripts of New Testament vocabulary and shape of mind. This is for Cragg a matter of perceiving the inclusive work of the Spirit; a universality of the Spirit necessitated by the partiality of all human witness, and necessitating

---

[138] And certainly also John 15.26.

[139] The point here is that the truth that comes from God is represented in the activity of the Spirit. Hence 'God in Christ' is the same as 'God in the Spirit'. This is Cragg's understanding of the Gospel, particularly the Gospel according to St. John.

[140] Cf. John 16.14.

[141] He seems (i.e. 'some will say with ...') to disagree with Hippolytus 'I believe in the Holy Spirit in the Holy Church,' COR 105. Cragg cites at this place Gregory Dix, ed., *The Treatise of the Apostolic Tradition of St Hippolytus of Rome*, London, SPCK, 1968, 21.17 and 22.1, i.e. pp. 37 and 38. See also Power 1989 for an examination of the relation between Spirit, church, and Scripture in the famous article of Charles Gore. Gore was one of the most influential members of Lux Mundi, see note 50 above.

[142] His illustrating example at this place is to reckon with the Incarnation 'within *brahmavidya* concepts of supreme union with the absolute and the tangle of those concepts with puranic ideas of many *avatars*,' *ibid.*

genuine partnership between them. Not perceiving the non-exclusiveness of the Spirit like this would be to surrender a Christ for the world[143] as well as giving preference to a static and archaic faith. If so, the Spirit would be either redundant or unemployed (*ibid.*). He might, therefore, suggest on behalf of the treatment of the doctrine of the Holy Spirit, with 'a friend of Klaus Klostermaier': 'Christianity is underdeveloped' (106).

Resembling his uneasiness about the 'custodians' in *CWP*, Cragg prefers the 'fountain that overflows' in favour of the cistern that 'contains.' At the same line he carries on: 'the pattern of the definitive Messiahship, has place for the unexpected and the disconcerting' (105). Most interestingly, Cragg sees a Pneumatology departing from the Gospel of St. John as fit to provide support for this statement. Yet, his inclusive understanding of the Holy Spirit must be interpreted as consistent with Jesus' word about 'the many things to say' and the pledge of the Spirit 'to guide . . . into all truth' (John 16.12f). Cragg's combined conclusion of the arguments about both the 'beyond-ness' of the Spirit as well as the 'Christ for the world' is that 'the very *finality* of the Gospel of Christ argues the unceasing and unfailing Spirit of God *everywhere at work*' (*ibid.*, my emphasis), what he in other words calls the 'the place-inclusiveness of the Spirit.' Cragg seems therefore to suggest a conjoining of the Spirit with what he has called 'Christic' rather than—in the form of identification—with the church.

The other aspect or element of 'being religious'— conceptualization and systematization—is connected to the relation between spirit[144] and form. This is to be understood as equivalent to the relation between 'meaning' and 'institution' (106). Connected to 1 Tim. 3.15 he asks how the relation between the two clauses, 'the church of the living God' and 'the pillar and ground of truth', is to be conceived? Is it, for example, possible to place an identifying 'is' between them? The issue at stake is certainly the same as above: Is there any truth to be found outside the 'church' as institution? That is, does 'God's house', i.e., the divine *oikonomia,* exceed 'church'?[145] The answers to these questions

---

[143] Most interestingly, his rhetoric question in this respects alludes to 1 Tim. 4.10: 'But can it be not so, if he is indeed 'the Saviour of the world'?' This connection of the finality of Christ and the universality of His salvation might be seen as crucial to any theology of religions, particular diverse kinds of 'inclusivism.' The end of 1 Tim. 4.10 ('especially those who believe') may also invite to this kind of discussion, that is: what about those who do not believe—in what way do they relate to 'the Saviour of all men' if this is not to be characterized as 'especially'?

[144] It should be noticed that Cragg at this place uses 'spirit' without capital 's'.

[145] My question here is based on how the first clause *(οικω θεου)* of 1 Tim. 3.15 should be related to the second clause *(η τις εστιν εκκλησια θεου ζωντος)* as to the scope of the third clause *(στυλος και εδραιωμα της αληθειας).*

certainly affect the doctrine of the Spirit. Moreover, if affirmed, this cannot, according to Cragg, be delimited to a matter of (inherent) identity. It should also entail actuality. Hence Cragg maintains, and this is characteristic for his whole 'economic' theology, that 'what it *is* ... in identity, it has to be in actuality' (107). To this being by becoming, and becoming by realizing the being (*ibid.*), the matter of the Spirit is central. At this place a resemblance to Smith's faith-belief distinction may be recognized, albeit—which is important—with another contrasting pair: what we could call 'is-ness' versus 'becoming-ness' (108):

> Here we apply it to the is-ness of the Church, of mission, of dogma, of the Christian thing, in their external forms. All these, like holy wedlock,[146] can only be what they are in their committedness as they become what they must. The Holy Spirit is never imprisoned in the verb 'to be', as it relates to them. There are no automatic guarantees in the Holy Spirit, no established creeds, codes, churches, symbols, which avail and achieve just by dint of being there, of being right in form, of holding fast and keeping going. All these forms turn unceasingly for their virtue on the vitality of the Spirit of life and love and power (108).

As one sees it is the vitality of the Spirit within the forms that is at stake here. This conveys, therefore, not the contention that spirituality is a formless matter (108):

> The initiatives of the spirit and the liabilities of the form can never be divorced and, for that reason, identity is never immune from ambiguity—or worse. All Christian relating to other religion is deeply involved here. There is no caring for spirituality that can ignore structures (*ibid.*).

So far Cragg is rather general in his considerations, although his reflection on the 'becoming of the Spirit' is to be regarded as highly substantial, if not the most substantial, to his interreligious hermeneutics. Nevertheless, the implications of these general and substantial remarks become more concrete in connection with the third element, the expression.

At this place he asks the question that only occasionally has

---

[146] Cragg compares the relation identity-actuality with how this relates to the nature of marriage.

turned up to the surface: Is the Holy Spirit active in the religions of today? Cragg answers this question affirmatively and opts for a 'time-inclusiveness' of the Spirit, in addition to the place-inclusiveness mentioned already. According to Cragg, the work of the Spirit is to be located *extra ecclesiam*, in the religions, and thus with regard to the actual reality. In this he does not want to be regarded as syncretistic (109), yet he regards himself as liable to attempt to keep the sight of 'all times within the framework of the one decisive event' (the Christ-crux of history) on the one hand, and 'a theology which lives that decisiveness within the present times' (the religions) on the other. This is what he calls a 'time-inclusiveness' of the Spirit. In other words, 'Our creeds and that human journey are what we have to hold together as Christians' (*ibid.*). In this, 'faith in the Holy Spirit is the only conceivable capacity.' As one sees, at this place Christ, the Holy Spirit and the human condition contribute to a 'whole,' which is Cragg's depiction of the world where the Spirit actuates the Christ-event.

One may however ask: what is then the particular contribution of Christ to people 'being religious' in the most authentic way? It is at this place most interesting to see how Cragg makes a list of how the religious, inclusive dimension makes humans 'whole,'[147] including 'the ability for a numinous humility, a radical worship, an open wonder, a gentle wistfulness' (111). What then is the Christian mission to such religiosity? Cragg's answer regards the availability of the symbol of Christ as a clue and sphere of association in order to make 'the mystery' luminous:

> It is so to live and relate that the symbol of Christ is always available to be the clue for the yearnings of mankind ... The calling of the Christian community is to be there with the Gospel as that sphere of association where the mystery is luminous (*ibid.*)

At this place Cragg maintains that the symbol of Christ is not a symbol among other symbols ('the rivers of calligraphy', the lotus-flower), but as the text of that search for expression (*ibid.*). It seems that 'text' here means something like an interpretation of all human living:

> Our ambition is to have these [the Christian symbols] always present to be the text of that search for expression which lies near to the heart of all human living, so that to

---

[147] Cragg implicitly takes advantage of an understanding of religion emphasizing the 'tying the part to the whole'-aspect, 110. He maintains that 'being religious' is not another 'relative' among other relatives, but 'is inclusive of all these,' *ibid.*

4 Kenneth Cragg's Interreligious Hermeneutics

feel, to suffer and to understand become one and the same
thing (111f).

Yet, what kind of interpretation is this? Could one think of other
interpretations which might serve the 'human living' as well as a Christian
interpretation? Cragg is rather vague at this point, which can be explained
partly by this being restrained to the level of 'being religious'. On the one
hand he explicitly rules out a language of contest, on the other he aims to
qualify the Christian symbolism as superior, although it contains a self-
critical element:

> Other faiths, to be sure, have their symbolism, and for these
> our reverence and our study. But, in the Holy Spirit, the
> Babe [Jesus as child incarnated], the Cross and the Eucharist
> are ours, not in vulgar competition, *yet articulate and
> present,* and always as an accusation of our own disloyalty
> (113).

It seems that Cragg is thinking in a category of articulation and actuality,
where symbolisms in diverse religious traditions may contribute more or
less to the illumination of the mystery of the ultimate reality. When he
says that this should not be perceived as a vulgar competition, it is
nevertheless likely to understand this as a kind of competition between
different religions. Given the premise that this reality can be approximated
in a range of ways, this conclusion seems to be inevitable. However, this
'kind of competition' may probably be best seen as a greatly deepening of
experience, ultimately in the divine kenosis from the time of creation
onwards.[148] As an example of this, the 'empty scene' seems to become
transformed into the Eucharist, in Cragg's words: a 'table for men' (Ps. 23),
where the bread and wine '[show] forth the Lord's death' as 'the point of
God's hospitality to the world' (113).

However, when he turns to talk about the 'Divine logic' (114f)
things become phrased more sharply. As seen above, 'love in suffering' is
what Cragg conceives as the 'heart of divine nature'. This is therefore the
criterion by which 'the partiality of all other means' can be judged and

---

[148] See e.g. p. 119 where he cites H. Wheeler Robinson, *Redemption and Revelation,*
1942, 295: ' ... the divine self-emptying from the foundation of the world ... The
believer is simply entering into a new and greatly deepened experience through
Christ and what God has been doing all the time.' This closes *COR*. See also note 50
above, p. 168. In addition to Wheeler Robinson, Cragg seems also to have been
informed by H. Bushnell, Hartford, in his teaching on divine kenosis. Though this
is primarily thought of in respect of Christ's death, one might say that Cragg has
expanded Bushnell's doctrine considerably.

evaluated, and thus this Divine logic may finally disallow all religions (cf. 2 Cor. 5.14). By this 'Cristic pattern' the only mean is given for the retrieval of the tragic situation of humankind (115). At this place there seems to appear a gap between 'other religion' and the Christic pattern. Yet there is still certain continuity between being religious and the Christic pattern, not least noticeable by his use of the term 'beyond'. Cragg contends that it is by the criterion of 'love that suffers' that the activity of the Holy Spirit through the Christians should be understood. Hence 'we' should

> interpret the world and its crises in terms no less costly and compassionate than those which took their Master to Gethsemane (*ibid.*).

What Cragg attempts to hold together here is: a. the autonomy of people of 'other religion', endowed by God the Creator, and b. that they may be moved Christwards in the freedom of their personal wills (116). The latter being in an important manner the responsibility of Christians ('it is the wills that are moved which move others'), Cragg concludes by referring to the statement above, that Christianity may be 'underdeveloped', not in its content but the reach of its disciples. Yet, this moving of the will to Christ is *grounded* in the 'ever-present, ever-patient, Holy Spirit, Lord and giver of life' (118). By the Holy Spirit, the relation between Christ's suffering and death and an authentic perception of humanity is conceived as according to 'the heart of God' and as according to 'the Divine logic'. Or even more precise, in Cragg there is a pneumatological relationship between Christ as in the Christian universe of interpretation, and the Cristic and incarnational pattern which Cragg suggests can be found within diverse religious traditions.[149]

4.5.6 UNDERSTANDING THE OTHER IN ITS OTHERNESS? CONCESSION OF PLURALISM AS A PREREQUISITE FOR MISSION AND A THEOLOGY OF CROSS-REFERENCE

Let us finally look at Cragg's article from 1990: 'Holding Faith and Conceding Pluralism: A Christian Position'.[150] This study is apt to profile

---

[149] Cf. also a far earlier reference: Cragg 1959, where this relationship is connected to the same problem of Christian communication as mentioned above: 'This human trust of the Divine Word makes *all-inclusive demands* for which our only sufficient reliance is *the Spirit*, who is himself Communicator, and *our only proper pattern the Incarnation* itself' (376, my emphasis).

[150] Cragg 1990.

and deepen the position of Cragg in this chapter.In addition, it uses also language that comes close to hermeneutical theory that I have adopted in my examination of Cragg's approach.[151] Finally, this chapter can be seen as a bridge to the next chapter about Cragg's interpretation of Islam (Chapter 5).

The article is written as a response to a paper delivered by Cardinal Jozef Tomko at a congress in Rome, 1988.[152] By this encounter Cragg presents nuances and proposals that are important for understanding his interreligious position. The point of departure for Cragg's response is his insinuation that the cardinal does not concede pluralism seriously. Tomko, he says, 'incurs the charge that we have not yet begun to live and think "plurally"' (174). What does this actually mean? An implicit answer to this can be developed as a detour of Tomko's argument, that is: as perceived by Cragg.

Cragg maintains that Tomko retains a '"singular" perspective', for example when he takes the 'salvation' as a 'premise' for relating to religious diversity (*ibid.*). According to Cragg, this notion is too strongly Christian and begs too many questions in its ambivalence and 'direction' in order 'to provide the context in which answers are to belong' (*ibid.*). One may really ask: But is not this a charge that one easily could accuse Cragg himself for? Nevertheless, be it as a clarification or a development, with a closer look it remains an important difference to be discerned between Cragg and Tomko, which, interestingly, relates to the Rahnerian notion of 'anonymous Christians'.

Cragg calls the approach of Tomko 'speculative' (175). Enquiring into things 'salvific' in the religions, one easily comes to ask about 'invincible ignorance,' 'intention,' 'anonymity belief,' and what is *intra ecclesiam* and *extra ecclesiam*. The problem is, according to Cragg, not the 'holding faith' but the not 'conceding pluralism' *de jure*, to admit others the right not to start from where we start, and to conclude differently. For Cragg this implies two distinct approaches towards other religions: Either to start with our questions based on our 'denominators,' or to encounter others '*within* their own questions' (*ibid.*). This corresponds

---

[151] Cragg 1990 turns out to be a comprehension of particularly ch. IX and X in Cragg *CFs*, 337-341. Cragg suggests here that truth is *de facto* pluralized by religious pluralism (339). By this he means that 'credentials are multiple' (*ibid.*), and that 'what we do with diversity will test what we do with dogma' (341). Religious plurality *de facto* (*not de jure!*) is thus inescapable for Christian theology that is understood as *bona fiducia christiana*.
[152] Tomko 1990: 'Missionary Challenges to the Theology of Salvation.'

to letting one's own perspective determine the understanding of the Other, or to take the perspective of the Other as the starting point.[153]

Cragg presents also an epistemological version of this argument, using the language of Kant:

> The Christian criterion of 'salvation' [i.e. Tomko's position] then ... 'phenomenalises' all that—could we 'reach' them— are the *noumena* of other faiths? We apprehend them only by our categories (176).[154]

Again we see how Cragg delimits his approach from a Kantian epistemology. At this place, not entirely, he implicitly also delimits his position from the way Gadamer emphasizes the importance of one's own horizon. Consequently, one might ask what kind of categories are to be engaged if not our own?

Cragg's answer is not easily available. Firstly, he stresses that 'All religions belong to humanness ... as having to do with the same, mortal wistfulness and finitude which belong to "this world which is the world of us all"' (177). This common situation has as its content especially the 'crisis of existence' that people purport to order and interpret. Whether a category of apprehension or not, this is at least an expression of a 'universal' by the interreligious situation.

His understanding of mission may give us another clue. In Cragg's vocabulary 'mission' is 'commendation'. As a translation of συνίστημι, the emphasis is placed on 'to set together, to constitute by aligning'

---

[153] An implicit support for this recognition of 'otherness' is found elsewhere, e.g. in *COR*, 21-24, albeit from an opposite point of view, where Cragg criticizes M. Buber's concept of *emunah* and *pistis* in his *Two Types of Faith*. Whereas Buber presents the Christian *pistis* as a conceptual faith, being propositional as well as argumentative, he commends the Jewish *emunah* as 'existence in fidelity,' meaning 'trusting in' and 'belonging with,' and 'counting on relationship,' cf. his personalism. Cragg objects that the case is that simple: 'Is there not a degree of believing *that* in any possibility of trusting *in*?' he asks, 22. He also sees an unbroken line from Paul, via Francis of Assisi, Luther and Kierkegaard, to D. Hammarskiöld where Christian experience has been the 'founding element.' Hence believing 'that' and believing 'in' are inseparable for 'a Messiahship we can identify within history.' Consequently, Cragg sees Buber as missing 'the reasons of the other's heart.' The context of Cragg's argument here, however, is 'the right courtesies' of mind as one encounter 'other religion.' In the *emunah-pistis* controversy he concludes therefore, that 'the very length of the misconceptions ... give us pause about ourselves.' Further: 'a potentially line-up of ideas has to be handled patiently' and 'only a resolute courtesy can begin to do so,' 24. This discussion with Buber has certainly implications for the relation to Cantwell Smith as will be shown later.

[154] The quotation marks within the quotation here and below refer to Cragg's citing of Tomko 1990.

(177f).[155] Mission is thus to engage with others *by consent*, not as developing a theoretical perspective, but as a 'commendation ... preoccupied ... *with them as they are*' (178, my emphasis). By this

> the 'commender' holds himself liable to *recruit that which, elsewhere, can 'acknowledge what he offers'* (*ibid.*, my emphasis).

Thus, the commender has something to offer as well as to recruit, but this cannot be done without consent and a deliberate acknowledgement on behalf of those it is offered to.

Now, what is the relation between the perspective of the human existence and that of his understanding of mission? Immediately after having presented the first perspective, Cragg speaks of the need to look for 'criteria' '*within* the orbit of the other tradition of religion' (177). Applied to the human situation as in *COR*, this is presumably done so to make the human horizon a point of departure for the further criteria that one brings from one's faith as to apply to the relation to other faiths. In other words, there is no self-relating or mission to other faiths unless 'criteria' within the other tradition are recruited. Hence the Christian faith is only relevant as far as it has been made relevant from within the other faith. This presupposes both a view of heteronomy[156] and of a certain openness in the religions. This is, however, to be found in the common life-world of 'waiting,' 'wondering' and 'wistfulness' (186). Only so is the otherness of religions respected, and only so may the genuine participation[157] and open mission meet (*ibid.*).

---

[155] See also *COR,* ch. 6 ('The Saving Mind'), regarding Cragg's understanding of mission. Interestingly, in 1964a, 305f, he contrasts his own position ('is there not at the faith's heart a central commendation in deed?') to Barth's position, citing Barth's commentary on the Romans where he claims that the Gospel 'does not expound of recommend itself.' Cragg's point is that the Holy Spirit may very well hand 'the problem back to us' as Christ 'proceeds through traditions, or habits, or trusteeship,' *ibid.* 306. At this point Cragg anticipates especially *CWP* and *COR*. Cf. also *CFs*, 79, where Barth is cited from his *Kirchliche Dogmatik*: 'God has no need for us.'

[156] Cf. Jürgen Straub in his 'xenological' study, Straub 1999, 72: 'Den anderen als Menschen wahrzunehmen, setzt voraus, ihn als reflexives, handlungsfähiges 'Subjekt' zu betrachten, ... also in der einen oder anderen Weise heteronom determiniert ist.'

[157] Cf. the prominent place of this term in Cantwell Smith's works. This point will be made a point of convergence between Cragg and Smith in the last chapter (Chapter 7.2.2). Note also how the chapter 'Call to Service' in *¹CM* was revised to 'Call to Participation' in the 1985-edition.

The programme in this study of Cragg comes very close to the understanding of comparative theology suggested by David Tracy. In an article on 'Comparative theology' in *The Encyclopaedia of Religion,*[158] he maintains, although preliminary, that comparative theology is

> any explicitly intellectual interpretation of a religious tradition that affords a central place to the fact of religious pluralism in the tradition's self-interpretation (447).

This concession of pluralism must, moreover, discern and interpret what Tracy calls fundamental questions of the contemporary situation (human problem, ultimate transformation, the nature of ultimate reality). By this he aims at developing a certain correlation[159] between tradition and situation, that is: between the traditional self-understanding of one's religious tradition (be it Christian, Buddhist, whatever) and the situation of religious pluralism.[160] This means, *inter alia*, that comparative theology should contribute to the (renewed) intellectual self-understanding of one's own tradition 'from within the horizon of many religious traditions' (*ibid.*). Yet, as far as it is theology, it must also address the matters of meaning and truth on explicitly theological grounds.[161] At a more conclusive stage of his article, Tracy may therefore define comparative theology as

> an academic discipline that establishes mutually critical correlations between the claims to meaningfulness and truth in the interpretation of a religiously pluralistic situation and the claims to meaningfulness and truth in new interpretations of a religious tradition (454).

---

[158] Tracy 1987. I will also use this article as a point of departure for Chapter 7.2.

[159] Both this and the previous fundamental questions evince a certain dependence to Tillich's theological vocabulary.

[160] *Ibid.* 453. Tracy does not seem to make any distinction between the terms 'plurality' and 'pluralism' although he is obviously aware of what such a distinction denotes. His emphasis on 'situation' would, with a more precise use of language, be better characterized by 'plurality'. For the distinction between 'plurality' (situation, description) and 'pluralism' (conceptional position, prescriptive element), see for example Berthrong 1989, 190. It seems to me that this distinction is quite consistent in works which aim at employing precise tools for studies on this area, see e.g. Dean 1995.

[161] *Ibid.* 454. Tracy also asserts that: 'Any theological attempt at comparative theology ... will interpret the results of history of religion's comparisons of various theologies by means of its own strictly theological criteria,' Tracy 1987, 446. This resembles Cragg's reiterated insistence on starting with Christian presuppositions.

As far as I am concerned, this makes the approach of Cragg even more perspicuous as a hermeneutical enterprise. This relates not least to how interpretation of the Other in its otherness has bearing on how one's self-understanding is impacted on. That these two correlate, has been pithily put by Richard J. Bernstein in another context, which also sums up Cragg's overall position and aligns it with the approach of our study:

> Perhaps the most difficult task in seeking to understand
> the otherness of the Other—especially other religious forms
> of life—is learning how imaginatively to extend, modify,
> and enrich our categories and genres of classification and
> description. There is no general method for achieving this.
> It requires *phronesis* and judgement which are, in principle,
> always open to criticism.

4.6 Conclusion

In this first main chapter on Kenneth Cragg I have aimed to reconstruct his general approach to the relation between 'self-relating' and 'self-change'. I have done this in connection with selected works, ranging from his D.Phil-dissertation (1950), via his classic (*CM*, 1956), to his major interreligious studies from 1968 (*CWP*), 1977 (*COR*) and 1986 (*CFs*).

In his dissertation, which is to be regarded as both an important formative source of his subsequent authorship as well as (in missionary terms) a fundamental and strategic study, Cragg reveals a rather direct way of relating and confronting what he perceives as to be representative for 'modern Muslim apology' of the 20th century. This at times confrontational line is basically based on his contention that Christianity has a 'prolonged experience' in dealing with certain social, political and intellectual problems that the 'modern world' has raised. His hope, however, is that the 'helping' of Muslims in this crisis may erode the old antipathy of Muslims towards 'Christ and His Church.' His aim is therefore ultimately to move Muslims 'Christwards,' which importance is given by the uniqueness, inclusiveness and relevance of God's self-disclosure in Christ. This theory of development and change is particularly informed by his contradictory notions of the 'pattern of the Cross' on the one hand, and the 'pattern of success' on the other (represented by Muhammad from the *Hijrah* onwards). His contention is that his preference of the former pattern may be justified as a matter of religiously normative pre-suppositions. The matter of self-reference is thus emphasized. In practice, however, Cragg comes out with a rather developed hermeneutic approach to Islam that makes both the systematic relating to Islam as well as the distinctive impact of Islam on one's self-understanding a theme. Thus, his dissertation contains attitudes to Islam ranging from an emphasis on asymmetry to emphasis on commonality and reciprocal self-learning. Theologically, these are partly based on the self-critical view of the real conflict as a conflict *of* God, *in* Christ, *with* his people, partly on the notion of 'fulfilment by criticism' which is based on a differentiation within the Godhead (between God the Christ and God the Spirit).

In *CM,* his classic and more popular study than *ITC,* Cragg uses the *adhan* (the call from the minaret) to seek the meaning of Islam for Muslims and from that to learn how to make Christ relevant to the heart of Muslims' faith. In this way Islam dimensions the Christian self-presentation. Cragg perceives this in terms of hospitality, of a meeting, where one's own essential loyalties may abandon mutual exclusion. By hermeneutical criteria this may be regarded as apt (the role of self-understanding, yet also conflict and misunderstanding). Though *CM* also reveals an ambivalence and asymmetry between the obstacles of Islam and the 'master-purpose' of Christ, Cragg also makes extensive theological developments in order to show how distinctive elements of Islam can be approved by Christians. This is particularly related to the work of the Spirit, the pattern of Incarnation and the universal relevance of Christ. Though the issues of self-change and re-interpretation are only implicit in *CM,* a contemporary article shows that Cragg is aware of these aspects.

In *CWP* Cragg develops his interreligious position into a distinct 'theology of religious pluralism.' In this work the open and integrative features of his approach become more dominant. Also with regard to theological justification it must be said that he is more explicit in *CWP*, and that he ventures more than previously. Cragg's contention is that Christian distinctiveness cannot be attained ignoring religious plurality: other faiths are 'significant' and they represent a 'responsibility' and common fate. Connected to this, one might recognize a certain 'tidying up' of his interreligious vocabulary, as well as an emphasis on how the Christian mind should be more creative and risking, given the New Testament precedents on this. These matters of attitudes are further substantiated by his theological elaborations on the 'open faith.' Cragg sees in the Christian faith a 'finer possibility' of a 'sanctuary of incorporation,' by which he aims to avoid relativism, syncretism and the foreclosing 'custodian mind' respectively. In this his conception of the Holy Spirit, which he maintains is being tested supremely in its 'proceeding' from the Father and the Son into the world of the religions, plays a significant role, not last connected to a modest doctrine of *praeparatio evangelica,* but also Christ, not least linked to how Cragg emphasizes self-oblation in interreligious relating. This study is also the place where Cragg positions himself within the discourse of theology of religions. Yet, although he criticizes for example Toynbee and Kraemer, and on certain points Rahner, he renounces making a final judgement on the relation between Christianity and other religions. This agnostic view is connected to a notion of 'negative capability', 'mystery' and 'elasticity'. Finally, I address the question of whether Cragg only represents the open faith as 'self-relating' and not 'self-change'. Based on hermeneutic theory I assert that there is built into his creative and risking approach an element of self-change, namely as renouncement of orthodoxy for the sake of communication.

This distinctive approach is further developed (and reiterated) especially in two major studies: *COR* and *CFs*. In these, various aspects of *CWP* are elaborated on in a way that expands and comprehends his interreligious hermeneutics further. The first theme that is elaborated is how human existence functions as a clue to the meaning of the Christian Gospel. Cragg thus asserts that to move from within the human to the distinctively Christian is a valid way. In practice this entails that any theological solution of the problems inherent in the human condition must integrate intimately the features of the same human situation. Cragg also develops a modest theory of Semitic religion linked to the terms of exploration, expectation, accusation, penitence and adoration. By these concepts he prepares the 'scene', which Christ subsequently enters, particularly in the form of a Christic pattern of suffering and autobiography, to which he finds definitive precedents in the Old and New Testaments. This pattern as recognized in Christ is understood as a divine determinate initiative, in which humans can recognize God. The very relation between Christ and the human experience across religions is particularly developed as a matter of mediation, given that there is what is 'gratefully' common in what is deeply distinctive. In his cross-reference (incarnational) theology Cragg comprehends how the problem of understanding the Other from without (externality) can be reduced bona fide, by themes deeply mediatorial of themes crucial to Christian faith. Finally, interreligious self-relating is substantiated by how Cragg sees the active Holy Spirit at work everywhere (place-inclusiveness) and always (time-inclusiveness). As such, this work of the Spirit is a school of Christian faith outside the prescripts of New Testament vocabulary and shape of mind, and also outside the church. This implies certainly that self-relating becomes intimately connected to self-change.

5

THE RELATIONS BETWEEN CRAGG'S CHRISTIAN SELF-UNDERSTANDING AND HIS UNDERSTANDING OF ISLAM

5.1 Introduction

We now turn to the specific relations that Cragg develops between Islam,[1] or the 'Muslim mind,' on the one hand, and his Christian self-understanding on the other. It must be said that in Cragg's opinion these are relations that connect central Islamic features in respect of the understanding of God and the Prophet on the one hand to central aspects of the Christian faith, in particular related to his understanding of the Incarnation and God's use of humans in His economy of salvation.

I will concentrate on the specific comparative parts of his authorship (*CM, SM, MC, JM, WWd,* plus a significant number of articles), that is, where he has both the Islamic and the Christian in mind simultaneously, as parts of a single argument. As shown above, Cragg's authorship also consists of studies that more specifically concentrate on comprehensions of Islam, the Qur'an and 'The House of Islam' *(DR, IW, HI, EQ, MQ, RQ, RMH,* see otherwise p. 122 (b) above). The relation between these and the comparative studies is that the latter results more

---

[1] I will often use 'Islam' and 'Muslim' interchangeably, or at least as complementary terms. Yet, in Cragg's approach there is an emphasis on 'the whole ethos of Islam' over a perspective of that of individual Muslims. That is not to ignore the Muslim as individual, rather the contrary: It is to avoid a 'personal evangelism' that ignores the way any Muslim is 'bound' to certain contexts, be it socially, psychologically or religiously, *FLN,* 94.

This relates to a personal sifting of Cragg's mind during his first time in the Middle East that was 'far from 'soft,'' *ibid.* 95. Also intimately connected to this emphasis, is his concern about relation and mutual communication, a concern that he repeats throughout his authorship, see e.g. *ibid.* 96. Lastly, this desire is interconnected with the point of moving from personal evangelism (as made a priority by the Lebanon Bible Institute) to 'a theology more responsive to perplexity,' *ibid.* 90. This does not, however, imply abandoning the missionary vocation, but a discernment of the 'diversity of gifts.'

A resemblance of this shift is reflected in his retrospection regarding the taking over of the editorial of *The Muslim World (Quarterly)*: Cragg sees this as a merge of his pastoral/missionary and academic inclinations, which he also contends fits to the needs of 'Islam itself,' *FLN* 116.

or less are integrated into the former, that is, his studies of Islam constitute the background against which the relations are developed. This is literally the case in for instance *CM,* where part 2, after a short part on 'Islam since 1945', elaborates central meanings of the *adhan*[2] for Muslims, before he (in part 3) ventures to interpret the Christian faith into this Islamic setting. Our main interest, therefore, is primarily in 'part 3s,' but as such also in 'part 2s' as they contribute to the understanding of the former.

In order to combine systematic concerns with a modest historical awareness, I will discern between a) earlier works from the 50s and early 60s, such as *ITC, CM,* and *SM,* b) some comprehensive studies in the Qur'an, such as *EQ* and *MQ* from the 70s, and lastly c) the two comparisons that relate Muhammad to the Christian faith (*MC*) or relate Jesus ('Isa) to the Muslim and the Qur'anic world of meaning (*JM*) respectively, from the 80s, as well as a comparative study on prophethood in the Semitic religions from the end of the 90s (*WWd*). Altogether these studies span a period of 43 years. Yet, there seems to be a consistency in respect of themes, as one will recognize in the next chapter, where the comparative studies on Muhammad (and the Christian) and on Jesus (and the Muslim) of the 80s are anticipated already in his dissertation from 1950.

5.2 Preliminary Description of Relations in the Earlier Works on Islam: How to Make the Christian Faith Relevant
5.2.1 TWO DISSIMILAR PATTERNS: THE SUCCESS OF MUHAMMAD AND THE CROSS OF JESUS

Cragg's approach to Islam is already in his dissertation (*ITC*) determined by what he conceives to be the divergent historical patterns of Islam versus Christianity, entailing almost a typological force, that is, 'the pattern of the Cross' (Christ) and 'the pattern of success' (Muhammad). As these patterns seem to sustain his entire authorship, it may be clarifying to have a brief look at how these are presented in his first major work.

Cragg sees the central point of comparison of Christianity and Islam to lie in the persons of Muhammad and Christ (II: 270). As a *tertium comparationis* Cragg chooses 'Antagonism and Suffering in the Economy

---

[2] That is, the muezzin's summons to prayer from the minaret.
[3] The emphasis on the Cross evolves into an emphasis on Gethsemane during his authorship. This can be seen as a consistent change due to his intimate relating of Christ and passive suffering from human evil and recalcitrance, but the decisive point is presumably the comparison with Muhammad in Mecca. The crucial point thus becomes his choice of suffering while he could have opted for another outcome.

of Truth and Righteousness' *(ibid.)*. This, he contends will make 'a particular and illuminating form of comparison.' Certainly, compared with this yardstick, the results must turn out as very different.

In the 'Cross of Christ'[3] Cragg sees an epitome of human sin, both in its historical form and in its nature, and of the redeeming love of God which motivates and fulfils the Incarnation. Christ is for him the one who relies solely upon the worth of his Word, whose silences are eloquent (136f), and where

> truth and love [are] behaving with utter self-consistency in
> a situation of evil and contradiction (138).

Hence Cragg sees the cross of Christ as intrinsic to both Divine Righteousness and human antagonism (270).

The picture of Muhammad is normally concentrated upon the *Hijrah*, 'the most formative event in the history of Islam' *(ibid.)*. However, in modern Muslim thinking there has been a tendency to be aware of Muhammad's sufferings and steadfastness against the hostility he experienced in Mecca by the Quraish. Cragg proposes therefore to set the event of Muhammad in Mecca alongside Christ on the cross (271). The result, however, is that Cragg sees the turn of Muhammad from suffering to sword, and to an ideal of religio-political order in terms of prestige and power, as distinguishing Islam elementally from the policy and purpose of Jesus in his 'fundamental otherness' (273f). For Cragg this is obviously a matter of spirituality versus material power. He therefore suggests that:

> Had Muhammad otherwise opted for a spiritual sanction
> alone, opposition would then have intensified into
> something like a crucifixion, or contented itself with a
> ridicule, as of something in which it sensed no political
> threat (275).

Most interestingly, Cragg sees this comparison as something 'most revealing and valuable,' by which the adherents of Islam and Christianity may be brought together into 'fruitful and vital relationship' (276). His lesson, therefore, is that any attempt to attain a common ground will eventually engage one with the integral difference which the comparison above has shown. This difference cannot be bridged by compromises, but may 'liberate those spiritual factors which can heal and convert and unify mankind' *(ibid.)*. Consequently, Cragg sees no immediate solution to the existing contrasts. He therefore ends his dissertation with the words: 'The end is not yet' (280).

5.2.2 FURTHER DETERMINATION OF MAJOR THEMES IN CRAGG'S INTERPRETATION OF THE CHRISTIAN FAITH TO MUSLIMS

The first major attempt to relate the Christian faith to Islam can be found in *CM*. As mentioned already, this study is mainly structured along a) an interpretation of the meaning of the call of the minaret for Muslims as an epitome of Islamic faith (Part II), and b) as an interpretation of the impact and challenge of this epitome for the Christian believer (Part III). Since the general hermeneutic considerations are already examined in the previous chapter, I will concentrate on the last chapter of *CM,* ch. X: 'The Call to Interpretation.' In brief, this is a chapter on how a Christian might interpret Christian faith and beliefs in selected parts (Christian scriptures, the person of Jesus Christ, the Cross, the Christian understanding of God, and the Christian Church and a Christian society) to a Muslim, given Cragg's interpretation of what the Muslim context and presuppositions are (Part II of *CM*).[4] Or more strongly emphasized: it is 'to rescue the word and discover the universe' of God's revealing love, in Christ' (273). I will not in the following present Cragg's interpretation of the call of the minaret for Muslims separately, but refer to it as I proceed along a selection of his interpretation of the Christian faith for Muslims.[5]

The Christian Scriptures

Cragg's understanding of the New Testament relates squarely to his comparative understanding of 'the word' in Islam and Christianity respectively. Whereas 'the word' in Islam means prophecy, the word in Christianity means personality. Hence, the New Testament scriptures represent a secondary word (272). The common point, however, is that 'it takes God to reveal God' *(ibid.)* It is only the approaches to this fact that diverge. Yet, the diversities become acute as soon as one maintains, as

---

[4] Most interestingly, this chapter (X, part III) was recommended very enthusiastically by a Muslim scholar in Ankara, Turkey shortly after it was published: '[Chapter X] deserves to be translated into the major Muslim languages and given the widest circulation. It [is] an earnest piece of writing ... with admirable restraint and beautiful passion ... ' Rahbar 1958, 44. The same author describes the *CM* as: 'Few books among Christian writings contain such acutely suggestive observations about Islam and its current outlook as 'The Call of the Minaret," *ibid.* 51. This is all the more interesting because, as Rahbar rightly notices, *ibid.* 40, it is avowedly written for Christians and from a Christian point of view.

[5] One might, however, ask whether he interprets the Christian faith for Muslims or, which I think is the primary aim, for Christians who minister in a Muslim-dominated context in order to make the Christian message understandable, relevant and reasonable. In short: To provide a *Christian apologetics* for Christian-Muslim encounter, 'apologetics' thus taken in a rather loose meaning.

Cragg does, that 'all presentation of Christ and of God must hinge upon the Biblical and, particularly, the New Testament expression' (275). The problem, however, does not primarily consist in language and textual translation, but rather an 'inclusive unfamiliarity' *(ibid.)* This seems to relate to a general scriptural distinction, regarding the origin of the Qur'an and the New Testament, between 'the Word of God to Muhammad immediately reproduced for men to hear' (the Muslim understanding of the Qur'an, 276) on the one hand, and the Word as 'a captured significance, a realized meaning' that as history is experienced and interpreted on the other.[6] Hence, the consequence is that whereas the Islamic revelation is governed by the principle 'man's abeyance makes it more assuredly God's,' the Biblical describes revelation as something that 'co-operates with human experience in order to complete and fulfil itself' (277). This difference becomes especially evident in the inclusion of the Psalms, the prophets and diverse historical material in the Bible, and only a little of this in the Qur'an. In these inclusions 'no attempt is made to hide their [i.e. the personalities of concern] shortcomings or minimize their frailty' (280). A conclusion is therefore that one has in the Bible a record, not only of God's salvific intention, but also of 'a measure of the humanity that God would redeem' (281), a fact that Cragg sees as one of the most important *and* difficult to communicate to Muslims. Via this exploration of the Christian scriptures for a Muslim context, Cragg hopes to have drawn the attention to the major questions involved, including the presuppositions (285), and not merely traditional controversies (corruption theories, earlier apologetics, idea of supersession, etc.) and exegesis, which he sees as hardly compatible with modern 'textual and other criticism' (283).

The Person of Jesus Christ

Cragg's proposal is a theology that includes Christology as inseparable from being theology, namely as 'the truth of Christ' within 'the truth of God'. As such, this will 'always be at odds with a theism that, in the name of divine unity, rigorously excludes one [Christology in this sense].'[7] Yet, a simple reassertion of the Christian doctrine of Christ will not suffice, according to Cragg, nor is the problem solved by taking a theocentric[8]

---

[6] Important here is the temporal order of the New Testament scriptures, that is, the 'evangel' recorded in the Gospels is experienced in the Epistles, and then finally written as Gospels based on this experience. This is, according to Cragg, the essential unity of the New Testament, 278.

[7] The quotation is taken from *FLN,* 111, but presents the same content as that which is found in *CM.*

[8] Written in 1956, Cragg is in many ways anticipating the pluralist debate of the 70s, which was particularly based on John Hick's proposal of a Copernican revolution,

approach. Rather the contrary: to be 'effectively' theocentric means to take Christology seriously (286f). Nor again can one emphasize the human Jesus solely, if one is not to 'fail Jesus Himself' (287). In addition to this, Cragg asserts that one would not do justice to the Muslim needs either if one left Jesus as a 'prophet-teacher' in Galilee.

Cragg's assertion that Christology is 'not an imposition upon facts but rather a conclusion from the facts' is important here. From this follows his proposal of beginning with the monotheism of Peter, James and John 'in Nazareth,' before one eventually ends up with orthodoxy[9] after having presented Jesus properly, along his own historic way, and along the way of the disciples' experience. In other words: 'Revelation of Divinity is also the revelation of humanity' (288).

Having done this, however, it remains to explain the faith about him 'from the Godward side,' that is, how concepts like 'the Father of our Lord Jesus Christ' (Eph. 1.3) can be substantiated theologically. Cragg's proposal is to relate this to terms which Muslims are familiar with, in particular related to the beliefs that a) 'He reveals' and that b) 'He is sovereign' (289). Most interestingly, having made these two beliefs a priority, which he sees as the central[10] 'clues in Islam to the interpretation

---

from Christocentrism to theocentrism, in his *God and the universe of faiths,* Hick 1973/1988. However, his context here is Islam.

Most interestingly, Cragg's emphasis on the interdependence of theology and Christology gains in the late 60s, the time not being insignificant considering the theological emphasis of WCC at that time, an emphasis on Christology as 'the indicative of God' over against a position that has 'retreated from 'theology' proper into 'Christology' and staked its absoluteness in Jesus as 'the man for others," Cragg 1969b, 387. Cragg sees this later position as both temporary and incomplete. This, however, does not mean that Cragg retreats from the social, political and economical challenges of contemporary theology. On the contrary, the present was perceived by Cragg in the late 60s as a test 'more than ever before in history,' *ibid.* 388. Cf. in this respect his contention that theology should not be tempted to become 'too small,' 'too proud' and 'too easy,' *ibid.* (and *passim* in that article).

[9] Cragg's use of 'orthodoxy' here and below is not defined, and used in a loose sense. One is, however, to understand it as a reference to a 'common, traditional Christology' which includes a strong belief in Incarnation, which is particularly the concern at this place, but also, otherwise, of redemption.

[10] This does not exclude other 'clues.' The most important criteria for the selection of clues, seems to be whether they may direct one *beyond* the sense of law, which he seems to find to be the major obstacle in Islam, towards, 'a deep sense of the Divine mercy and favor,' especially found in Sufism, 'forgiveness, renewal, and true piety,' *ibid.* 293. Yet, in spite of his sense for these 'aspirations,' he regards the Islamic perception of Divine mercy as 'unpredictable,' thus not assuring the faith of its believers, and not 'com[ing] forth to embody itself in a redemptive enterprise,' *ibid.*

of God in Christ' (292), at the same time he leaves out the themes of 'Divine Love' and 'the attendant mysteries of the Divine will'.

(a) Thus Cragg paraphrases first the Christian view of revelation which he equates with the Christian view of Christ, namely, paraphrasing Heb. 1.1:

> Against a background of interpreted history and into a concrete situation came a human life, a Personality, bringing into final focus and into unmistakable form the revelation of God (289).

The aim towards the Muslim audience in stating it thus, is that: 'It is our first duty that [the Muslim] should know what he rejects' *(ibid.)* This part of his interpretative strategy towards Muslims can therefore be characterized as a clarification of the doctrine of Christ in words understandable to Muslims. Though Cragg knows that the orthodox doctrine of Christ is rejected by Muslims, the doctrine may find 'some echo' in the Muslim idea that 'God reveals Himself by or in, Himself.'[11] Understood as 'Self-communication', knowledge of God will always be personal ('Who He is'), and not merely propositional ('that He is') (290). This parallels the difference between 'words, teaching, ideas, propositions' on the one hand, and 'the Word—experience, fellowship' on the other, which Cragg sees as the 'ultimate of revelation,' that which Christianity finds in Jesus, programmatically and technically[12] expressed thus: 'God in revelation is God in Christ' *(ibid.)* This exhausts also the meaning of 'God the Son', which is traditionally more problematic for Muslims,[13] although it does not exhaust the meaning of 'God'.[14] Conceived thus, the meaning of 'God the Son' gets a meaning and interpretation that can inhabit a Muslim world of meaning:

> It is the genesis and the ground of our faith that the One

---

[11] 290. Cragg does not, however, remark as to what he refers to by this quotation.

[12] In Cragg, 'God in Christ' serves as a *terminus technicus* for the Christian understanding of God's revelation. As such this may refer not only to the Incarnation, but also to Christ's life and death.

[13] Cragg is certainly aware of this and stresses that 'Son of God' excludes all paternity on the physical sense, *ibid.* 291. The 'begetting' of the Son is a translation of the 'will' of the Father by 'act.' As such God is 'at once revealer and revealed—the Father and the Son.'

[14] Cragg uses the notion of 'capacity' here: God does not exclude other capacities while he in his full personality uses the particular capacity of 'God in the act of revelation'. Cragg compares here the understanding of 'God the Son' with 'Beethoven the musician' and 'Leonardo da Vinci the artist', 290f.

Living and Eternal God has Himself undertaken to tell men
of Himself (291).

It is no accident that this could also be said of the revelatory 'telling of
God Himself' in the Qur'an, to which I will turn to below. What then of the
other Muslim belief, in God's sovereignty?

   (b) God's sovereignty or omnipotence becomes a problem in the
Muslim world of meaning as soon as one reflects upon the how of
revelation, that is, whether human life is involved in it. As bridging the
divine-human gulf is entailed in the entire notions of revelation and
religion, the Muslim option is that God's sovereignty is 'solved' by
intermediaries[15] (291). In other words: 'He does not bridge it of Himself.
He sends rather than comes. He gives rather than brings' *(ibid.)*. Cragg
perceives this position obviously as an *impasse*:

> Is an enterprise of revelation, in its most appropriate form
> for mankind, an act unworthy of God? Must He not be left
> to determine the steps of His own purpose and shall we say
> to Him 'Nay'? And if so, then we could never say that the
> Incarnation could not be. If it cannot be denied as a
> possibility, then any claims to occurrence cannot be ruled
> out in advance (292).

Cragg's claim is that God's omnipotence is 'most gloriously in operation
in Jesus Christ,' in particular because it succeeds to 'take action against
the empire of ignorance and evil in mankind' *(ibid.)*.

The Cross

As one must expect against a Muslim theological backcloth, the
understanding of Christ becomes highly problematic as one comes to the
end of his ministry. The obvious problem here is to turn 'resistance' into
'understanding' (294). What is unavoidable, according to Cragg, is the
need to 'affirm the Cross in the same spirit in which Jesus Himself suffered
it.' Since Muslims affirm the rejection Jesus suffered, Cragg asserts that
the 'Divinely arranged escape' is motivated dogmatically, not historically,
prominently in the presupposition that 'God will not, cannot, leave His
servants to suffer ignominy, nor allow their detractors a final triumph'
(295). As such, this certainly actualizes the issue of God's sovereignty in
a profound way. How to bridge this gulf to the New Testament records of

---

[15] That is, archangels and angels, prophets and teachers.

the event of Jesus' crucifixion? Again, Cragg sees in the Muslim position an *impasse*:

> If its culmination in Christ's being crucified is a subsequent invention (as it can only be if it is not fact), did the Church then invent the faith which made it, creating the history which in fact created it? (295)

This rhetorical question aims certainly at a 'hardly so' or 'of course not.' The more so, according to Cragg, if one also considers the faith of the first Christians in the light of their suffering and the belief in, not to say the experience of, the Resurrection (295f).[16] The very question Cragg sees the Muslim 'hypothesis' as an impasse to, is thus how one might explain the fact of Jesus' suffering, which he has found as a common fact in the two traditions of Islam and Christianity. By this, one might think that he steps slightly backwards in order to solve the whole question before it enters into full clash regarding the Cross (304). Yet, his characterization of the Muslim position is quite stark. In fact, so stark that his entire project of communication and developing relations seems to break down. In his view, Islam has 'robbed Him of Himself, transformed Him into an unrecognisable Jesus' and has consequently made God a '*deus-ex-machina* God.' That is:

> A God who turns the tables, opens the trapdoor, and confounds his foes; a God who deals not in the sure, if slow, processes of a moral order where love wins by suffering, but in arbitrary assertion of the inscrutable (297).

Having stated it that boldly, Cragg leaves any 'argument' as inappropriate. This correlates to what I called 'contrariety' above, and not 'formative clue,' in the previous chapter where also the general interreligious hermeneutics of *CM* are addressed.[17] At this point there is nothing left

---

[16] For his own part, Cragg sees the Resurrection as an *intrinsic victory* of the Cross which *seals* the redemption, see below. Hence his statement that: 'Because *He* dies *as* He did, He rose again,' 303.

[17] It seems, however, that Cragg at this place combines the two, that is, that *the contrariety is the clue*, 302. This is particularly the case with the relation between Muhammad and Jesus, cf. the similar approach in *ITC* above (Chapter 5.2.1). Whereas their situations are 'analogous' in respect of facing opposition based on 'prestige and pride,' the rest of their lives turn out to be contrasts. Cragg maintains *inter alia* that whereas 'battles in the early Islam are almost uniformly explained by Muslim writers as necessary to the survival of Islam,' Jesus 'suffered outside the walls [of Jerusalem]' and 'the Cross became His throne.' Cragg aims to set out this

but *clarification* and 'simple witness.'[18] An eventual recognition of the Cross is therefore to come only by the Holy Spirit, the 'Illuminator of the hearts' (303).[19]

Most interestingly, the 'explanation' turns the focus onto the relation between the Cross and 'its consequences for human life and character' (298). At this place the communication seems to have been retrieved again.[20] Cragg sees in the Cross the climax of the 'opposition of ungodliness,' which fact on a lower level Islam also admits. The Christian witness and faith, however, is that Jesus suffered the full length of the rejection, willingly,[21] and as the price of his loyalty to his own message. As one sees, Cragg turns to language of virtues (character, loyalty) when he describes the quality and superiority of the suffering of Jesus. His point is that there is a continuity and consequence between his message and his life, and that this shows us 'what men are' and 'what Christ is.' Having experienced rejection and opposition, the alternatives for Jesus were merely a) to withhold His witness, or b) incur its consequences. And, if b), the Cross represents 'what happens when a love like Christ's encounters a world like Jerusalem' (298).

This inclusive[22] expression of human 'wronging' is important to Cragg. Without seeing oneself within the 'revelation of humanity' entailed by the Cross, one will not be able to participate in the Cross as redeeming. Consequently, the (human) way the Cross came into being, and was carried out, gains an intimate relation to what and how the Cross redeems. Put differently, only by 'bearing' does the Redeemer 'bear away,'[23] and

---

contrast 'tenderly and without reproach.' Yet, against the accusation that may be posed immediately after reading this by Muslims (and Christians as well!), namely that the Christian church did not hesitate to step aside 'the pattern of the Cross,' Cragg asserts a kind of principle of originality: 'Faiths must surely first be understood in their architects, before they are assessed in their followers,' 303.

[18] This is not merely a matter of too big a controversy between the Christian and Muslim faith but correlates to the inexhaustive meaning of the Cross which will always 'defy a complete expression in theology,' 300.

[19] See also p. 302 where Cragg somewhat resignedly maintains: 'It may be best to wait for men to see it by its own light.'

[20] This becomes particularly evident when he refers to the *Shi'ahs* and their experience of sacrifice (cf. the stories of 'Ali, Hasan, and Husain) as a potential help to illuminate the Christian understanding of the Cross, 302. Nevertheless, this also makes Cragg confident that there is no parallel to the Cross.

[21] Cragg puts much emphasis on the Jesus' voluntary suffering and death. It is no 'sudden tragedy,' but a 'conscious choice,' *ibid.* 300.

[22] Cragg sees here Jerusalem as 'the prototype of all,' and the acts that lead to it as 'representative human sins': 'It was what the whole world did,' *ibid.*

[23] Cf. the one Greek term in John 1.29, $αιρων$, which Cragg maintains contains both meanings, *WWd*, 183, n 16. Cragg's use of bear/bore and bear/borne away, seems also to be induced by the Servant's Song in Isaiah 53, *ibid.* 113.

'forgivingness' as shown on the Cross, becomes 'forgiveness' (299). His words on the Cross express thus the inner nature of His passion: the Cross as 'a supreme deed of redemptive sacrifice,' driven by a quality of love which 'makes an end to evil because it freely takes all its consequences upon itself' *(ibid.)* And this love and act is ultimately *God's* own (300f). This is Cragg's theology of redemption.[24] It seems therefore pertinent to turn to the theme to which the interpretation of Christ ultimately points.

The Christian Understanding of God

This issue is certainly implicit in what has been exposed so far in connection with the issues of Scriptures, Christ and the Cross. Nevertheless, Cragg sets out to make explicit the 'full theological implications' of these themes (304). One major epistemological point that develops a relation between the previous 'themes' and *theo*-logy is that of the epistemological primacy, not 'in order of being', of the economy of God over the ontology of Him:

> It is simply that Christianity believes the Divine fullness to
> be known in context, in action, and in history, and that,
> therefore, thought on these may be the nearest and surest
> way to thought on God.

The theme of God should therefore be explored as a sequel to other topics, not as a source for derivation. But as a sequel, Cragg contends, we might gain knowledge of Him who Himself is a culmination of the knowledge of which He is also the origin.[25] As far as this is one possible Christian way of doing theology, the question remains, however, how the relation to Islam is to be conceived in relation to this understanding. In short, and on behalf of the (virtual) Muslim audience, Cragg relates this to: a) 'a misapplication of the criterion of simplicity', and b) 'a misconception of terms'. What is implied in his use of these?

Regarding the former, Cragg asserts: 'doctrines of God are not properly to be evaluated by the criterion of simplicity' (306). This is so, as

---

[24] Cragg seems to prefer the use of redemption instead of 'reconciliation' and 'atonement'. That 'to redeem'/ 'redemption' often has to be understood as interchangeable with 'atonement' is justified by the *terminus technicus* phrasing and ultimate meaning of 'redemption' as: 'to bear it [i.e. evil/sin] away.' This can also be substantiated by references where a synonymous use of repetition takes place, see, e.g., Cragg 1964a, 308 ('redemptive' and 'atoning').

[25] Cragg's point is to avoid making theology a mere 'afterthought,' that is, as reflection upon history and experiences. For Cragg, it is important to see any theological knowledge as facilitated by both the preceding origin of knowledge, and its proceeding towards its culmination in Himself, which, according to Cragg, resembles 'all personal knowledge,' *ibid.* 305.

far as one recognizes that literal simplicity (for example: 'God is One' and 'God is Love') does not necessarily imply abeyance or disavowal of thought. Hence, the criterion of simplicity should be resolved by the questions: 'How articulate is the simplicity?' and 'How adequately profound is the doctrine?' (307). In this respect, Muslims may in the end, if they get 'awakened,' consider the 'Christian extravagancies' as relevant.

The latter problem, of misconception, is approached by Cragg's contention that the Christian faith in the Trinity, or better, the faith in God *as* Father, Son and Holy Spirit, is a way of understanding the Unity of God, squarely within the Hebrew tradition (cf. Deut. 6.4). Hence, the Christian alternatives are not Trinity versus Unity, but Trinity versus atheism. Cragg's aim is to attain mediation and abandonment of travesties (308). Yet, how can that prove feasible related to this profound theological question? To answer this question, Cragg continues with his epistemological considerations, at this place on the relation between the experimental origin of Christian theology and its propositional form (309). If one looks to the origin of Christianity, he says almost laconically, one will find that

> The Apostles, and the Fathers, were not thirsting to multiply deities when in the historic faith they interpreted their Christian experience. They began, as Muhammad began, with God, with *Allâh,* One Sovereign, Creator, Sustainer, Provider, and Lord, ruling and revealing. ... They recognised that God sought man's sole worship and obedience ... They knew that human life stood under the law of God ... (309).

The mediatory point is that in all this the first Christians were 'akin to the Islam which Muhammad's mission constituted in the fresh enunciation of many of these truths' (310). Consequently, the God of worship and relationship, who overcomes darkness as well as distance, is 'God, as Muslims and Christians suppose Him' (310f).[26]

Yet, where the commonality between Christian and Muslim theology seems to lack, is when it comes to 'un-*islam*' (literally: non-submission), that is, humans' recalcitrance and waywardness. Cragg's first point is that a view of humans as free but rebellious is not inconsistent with a faith (Christian or Muslim) in the ultimate sovereignty of God, as long as this sovereignty is viewed as

---

[26] Cf. also *ibid.* 30f where he contends that in respect of *predicates,* the Muslim and Christian understanding of God may differ, whereas in terms of *subject of differing predicates* 'God' refers to 'the same being.' Cf. below especial my chapter on common prayer which relates to *CP* (and *AG*), Chapter 5.6.

a permissive will [that] allows and controls the situation in
which man's defiance can occur, and inasmuch as the very
possibility of the latter is implicit in the greater purposes of
revelation and grace (311).

The problem, however, is the matter of remedy for evil. Cragg asks: what if

the law that revelation sends down as the token and the
measure of the Divine will ... remain[s] permanently flouted?
Must not the revelatory purpose take cognizance of man's
legal and moral non-submission? (311f).

In response to this impasse, Cragg only sees one possibility: that God's
sovereignty is sustained by his redemption, prominently shown in
'Messiahship,' that is:

God intervening in history to put man right and to renew
the thwarted purposes of His righteous law.

Consequently, in 'God in Christ' Cragg sees 'the most formative element
in the Christian doctrine of God' (312).

    To complete the interpretation of the Trinity for 'use' in Muslim
contexts, Cragg also has to interpret the role of the Holy Spirit. Quite
interestingly in respect of his way of phrasing it, Cragg relates the Holy
Spirit to 'the experience [that] went further' by generating 'another fact,'
namely: a 'new unity among men,' consisting of 'new tasks of witness
and proclamation' on the one hand, and 'new joy and new release of
power and peace ... in *redemptive transactions* in the souls of men' on the
other (313, my emphasis). In this sense of a new fellowship in the Holy
Spirit where moral power was released, the connection with Christ and
subsequently with God was found:

This was so manifestly *continuous* with the earthly life of
Christ that man attributed it to the same source. It was so
evidently *of God* that it was recognized to be God's ... God
was evidently not only over men in creative sovereignty
and for them in redeeming love. He was also *in* them and
with them as an *abiding Presence*. 'The Holy Spirit
proceeding from the Father and the Son' (313, my emphases).

The doctrine of the Holy Spirit may resemble the way the Qur'an recognizes
God's relationship to man, that is, by His speech, messengers,

intermediaries, etc.[27] On the contrary, Cragg asserts, a God without relationships has nothing to do with theism, nor monotheism. Yet, what makes the Christian doctrine distinctive is that these activities are gathered and taken into its understanding of God Himself (314).

The 'experimental origin,' however, gained credal shape in formal definitions. Such are, according to Cragg, important as they embody the nature of the church's experience in order that all humans may enter into 'the same community of saints—and of mind' (315). In the Muslim-Christian context this means

> that we must strive to introduce the Muslim heart to the faith within the Christian doctrine by the same path that the Church itself followed *(ibid.)*.

In concrete terms this implies that 'Father' and 'Son' should be used analogically, and that 'God in Christ' represents the matter better than 'Jesus was God', which Cragg sees as far from the intention of the Fathers of Nicaea and Chalcedon (315f). On the other hand, Cragg reiterates his concern for the complex description of God's unity. In the analogy of 'human personalities ... the richest and most diversified unities within our experience,' Cragg asks rhetorically: 'If the order of ascending unity reveals increasing fullness, who shall say that the Unity of God is not the richest and the greatest of all?' (317). Entire transcendence is in the end 'a blank agnosticism'! In this, Cragg contends, and this is important for our study,

> the Holy Trinity only *carries further the truth implicit* in the Muslim faith in revelation and judgement (ibid., my emphasis).

Conclusively, the Christian *takbir* is not only to say 'God is most great,' but also 'because He has made Himself the Redeemer' (318). This peaks his 'Christian' interpretation of God for an assumed Muslim reception.

The Christian Church and a Christian Society

This is the last theme of Cragg's interpretation to Islam. I will simply note some elements in his argument which stress the theological argument outlined above.

Cragg sees the state-church issue as to be solved in direct connection to his anthropology and soteriology. Hence, as we should

---

[27] This view of the Holy Spirit seems, however, to play only an implicit role in his later writings.

discern between what man needs and what God gives in His grace, there is an ultimate distinction between church and state (325). The church is a unity of persons, a society within the society, built upon the idea of redemption and consequently on a view of man as wayward and sinful (324). As such, it is misleading to see, as Cragg contends some Muslims have done, the church to be in a position of disciplining and controlling Western civilization. Nor can faith be compelled.

The next point relates to the issue of expression. Cragg sees the church as expressing divine nature. As such, the ecclesiology is important as far as a discovery of the church entails a discovery of Divine intention. The emphasis on expressiveness corresponds essentially with the faith in the Incarnation (327). At this point Cragg also sees a link between Christian sacramental practice and the 'sacramentality' of Islam (328). Understanding sacraments as 'material expression and spiritual meaning,' Cragg finds 'clues' in the washing before prayer, the posture in prayer, the *qiblah* towards Mecca, the pilgrimage, Ramadan, and not to say the understanding of God's signs in the whole universe, clues which may enable Muslims to understand Baptism and Holy Communion. Most interestingly, Cragg wonders in this last part of *CM* whether this point may be rewarding in the future. As we will see below, this emphasis indeed becomes stronger throughout his.

For that which follows, it is quite impossible to cover thoroughly all issues that Cragg elaborates on in his Muslim-Christian 'mediating interpretation.'[28] I have therefore decided to concentrate on what I perceive as the most central and thorough issues. These are:

a.   The question of divine expression and how creation and humans can contain and mediate this

b.   The question of how God relates to humans

c.   The question of how God's omnipotence is realized in the events and biographies of Muhammad and Jesus

Between these themes there is a general increase of intensity and concreteness, from the search for commonalities in the understanding of creation and man, via the elaboration of human-divine association ultimately expressed in the Incarnation, to the peak where the different patterns of the personalities of Muhammad and Christ are made explicit and acute.

Nevertheless, all of these relations revolve round the major theme of divine-human interconnectedness, which might be perceived as the *tertium comparationis* in Cragg's approach to Islam. One will also notice that wherever Cragg starts his comparisons, he will almost always end up with the relation between Muhammad and Jesus. Hence, there will be

[28] *MC*, x.

certain overlaps between the three themes. The works I will consult are several articles from the time of *CM* onwards, and particularly the comparative studies from the 80s and 90s: *MC, (JM,) CFs* and *WWd.*

5.3 Expression and Experience: Sacramentality, Worship and Evil
5.3.1 EXPRESSION AND EXPERIENCE

I will start with a cluster of issues which focus on the commonality between Islam and Christianity. The relation of common concern, according to Cragg, is how humans may experience God and how God expresses Himself. In some ways, this chapter extends substantially the argument found in what may be called Cragg's religious anthropology and theory of religion (Chapter 4.5.1 and 4.5.2) by his attempt to develop relations between Islam and Christian theology.

An early and more general treatment of the issue of concern here can be found in the article 'The Divine Word in Human Trust' of 1959.[29] This article does not have Islam explicitly within its horizon. The reason for starting with it, however, is that it may provide us with a proper context for understanding of the specific Islam-Christian issues. The article has also a distinctive epistemological profile. It aims at elaborating the matter of how we may understand God in order to communicate this to others, with a particular focus on the Incarnation. The theme is interreligious, indeed. A fundamental assertion in the article is that:

> The Incarnation is God communicating. Our *interpretative trust* belongs within his *expressive* initiative (377f, my emphasis).

Consequently, in concrete terms, the relevance of God for the world is understood as a consequence of his self-revealing grace in Christ. It is this relationality between the human interpretative situation and God's self-expression that will be our concern here. Cragg's point is, that God cannot be thought of outside his relations.

The point of importance here is how this relationality is to be connected to the human life-world. This happens, according to Cragg, in human experience. This is the place of knowledge about God.[30] Christian

---

[29] Cragg 1959a.

[30] This is similarly expressed on p. 109, where the relevance of Christ is correlated to 'discovery' and not 'assertion.'

theology is thus definitions of Christian experience. (378f). The question is, however, how this relates to experience other than Christian. There are elements in the article that seem to affirm this, which relate to the aforementioned notion of 'clues.'[31] The general point is that Christ is anticipated 'in the bewilderments and frustrations of a world so rich in technological potential, so insecure in fundamental peace' (383). Because 'its clues are everywhere'[32] there is no reason to relinquish the presentation of Christ for the world.

According to Cragg, there are clues in the human life-world that point towards the Incarnation in the human life-world, given the meaning of Incarnation as the human situation where God reveals Himself. Cragg's assertion is therefore, that if we are to exclude God from a mundane 'intercourse,' we will also run the risk of excluding Him from his heavenly sovereignty. At this place the Muslim-Christian relation is doubtlessly hinted at. I will therefore proceed to another, late, part of his authorship in order to end up with an Islam-Christian resolution to the matter of expression-experience found in his article from 1959. This detour will use the Islam-section found in *CFs* (chs. 2-4) where one of the finest[33] developments of Cragg's understanding of revelation is to be found, in 'cross-reference' to Islam.[34]

5.3.2 THE SACRAMENTALITY OF NATURE AND THE CAPACITY FOR REVELATION

In ch. 2 of *CFs* ('Theologies of Magnificat') Cragg explores the main thrust of Islam, *takbir* (cf. *Allahu akbar*, or as Cragg prefers to express it:

---

[31] See especially Chapter 4.3.

[32] As note above (Chapter 4.5.5), Cragg qualifies and connects the work of the Holy Spirit to 'everywhere.' It seems reasonable, the authorship of Cragg seen together, to think of this as at least *one* of the backdrops for the understanding of the clues as being everywhere and having a direction towards the Incarnation. Another background seems to be an understanding of *imago Dei*: Based on the question whether one can *identify* the clues 'by which we have to 'test' His sovereignty,' that is, to give a Christian theological judgement about what divides the Islamic and Christian view of God's sovereignty, Cragg maintains that since God has given 'His image in ourselves,' it is possible to identify these clues, *MC* 158. In my opinion, there is no ground for playing the one off against the other.

[33] The reviewers of *CFs* have praised this work, see D'Costa 1987, Cox 1990, Cracknell 1988, Newbigin 1987. This is particularly the case of the sections on Islam and Judaism, but also his general approach, though there have been uttered some critical remarks and disappointments about his treatment of Buddhism and Hinduism, cf. Gabriel 1988, Lamb 1997, 161ff, Griffith 1994, 31, and Scott 1989.

[34] Subsequent parenthetical remarks refer to *CFs*.

'let God be God'[35]), in order to explicate important points of relevance for the relation between Islam and Christian theology. This can be seen as one example of a central concern, namely that commonalities are more likely to be developed in relation to doxology.[36] Cragg sees namely the cry *Allahu akbar* as a counterpart to the Christian *Magnificat*. Let us explore how Cragg unfolds this.

The first point is that *Allahu akbar* presupposes that there is something to be greater than (30).[37] This must be man, he says. God as greater than man, and man can only respond by submission. Cragg maintains that this premise presupposes what he calls the 'the annunciation of existence' *(ibid.)*. What does this Christian idiom (cf. the annunciation of Jesus to Mary by the angel) mean in Islamic terms? The connection Cragg makes to the 'annunciation of existence', relates to the difference between the divine attribute *rahmah* (mercy) and *taqwah*, which is the basic pious approach of a Muslim towards God (38). The inherent relation between these two is that of the reciprocity of the latter (*taqwah*) to the first (*rahmah*). With other words: Only divine mercy may induce Muslim piety.

The relation between these notions has traditionally been understood in terms of *wahy*, the revelation, that is, the Qur'an and Shari'ah. Cragg aims at exceeding this confinement of revelation. His contention is that God's mercy, *rahmah,* precedes revelation in the nature of, and on the earth of, man the steward. Through this, Cragg wants to develop a common theology of God's sovereignty (*Magnificat/takbir*) for Christians and Muslims.[38] Consequently, it is our relation to the 'annunciation of existence'—life as gift—that may lead us into a *taqwah*-relation to God. Despite his use of the double meaning of the story of Mary in the Gospel according to Luke (annunciation *and* rejoice, 39f), it is the commonality

---

[35] Cragg uses here Philip S. Watson's attempt to characterize the essence of Luther's theology in *Let God be God: An Interpretation of the Theology of Martin Luther*, London: Epworth, 1947. For this information I am dependent on Slomp 1990, 179. Cragg makes, *inter alia,* this notion equivalent to the phrase of 1 Cor. 15.28: 'That God may be all in all,' Cragg 1961, 128.

[36] See for example *MC* 109: 'Theology is always safest in doxology ... It may be that a sense of *community* in these areas will help us to care more wisely and duly for the questions that remain' (my emphasis).

[37] Cragg prefers otherwise to emphasize the *emphatic* form: '*Greater* is God' (my emphasis), which renders its grammatical form, see for instance *MC* 101f. Nevertheless, this emphatic form does not exclude a *relative* understanding, the 'completion of sense,' that God is greater than somebody, *ibid.* 102.

[38] Cf. his treatment of the Semitic religious traditions in Chapter 4.5.2. The fifth dimension was 'adoration,' which is to be realized in *Magnificat* and *Takbir*. It thus represents the climax of Cragg's (Semitic) theory of religion. See also the chapter on common prayer below (Chapter 5.6).

that he is interested in.[39] Both for Islam and Christianity it is the natural order that is basis and theme for the human praise of God. The goodness of the earth, the time and history, is the very reason for rejoicing in God (42). Cragg's consequent interpretation of this is, however, that human experience is sacramental *(ibid.)*[40] At this place we see a distinctive line back to the article on which we started this chapter, where experience and God's relationality were connected by the Incarnation. It seems that Cragg aims to apply this to his interpretation of Islam as well, that is, that the experiences of Muslims are sacramental.

The latter point relates intimately to the frequent use of *ayat* (signs) in the Qur'an. It is the view of the Qur'an that the world and life of humans are full of signs that point to the divine significance of reality. As steward, *khilafah*, man is not supposed to execute 'dominion' only, he is also endowed with the ability to sense and become aware of the 'mysteries.'[41] Humans are not self-sufficient but have their place in a reciprocal relation to God, that is, to fulfil their destiny as responsive beings. This is in particular the case in the sacramental meeting of *salat*, the ritual prayer, where the human body shows its dignity, devotion and humility towards God. This is, according to Cragg, the proper way of 'reading' the signs of life, *ayat*.[42] The contrary is that God dissociates with the world; that he is thought of outside of his relations to the world (42f).[43]

---

[39] Cf. also Cragg 1981a, 27f, 32, and *MC* 157. In *MC* also the impulse of theologies of liberation, *in casu* that of José P. Miranda, is acknowledged as a proper part of *Magnificat, ibid.* 157f.

[40] Cragg's notion of the sacramentality of nature is not exposed in his earliest writing. In retrospect he regrets that it was not elaborated on in his thesis because he sees in it 'a clear evidence of divine/human inter-relevance; crucial to a full mediation of either theology to the other see,' *FLN,* 112.

[41] Cf. also *MC* 105 and 107f. Both there, 112, and in Cragg 1961, 130, 'sex' and 'mystery' are seen together. This, however, does not exhaust the meaning of the mystery. *Ayat* seems to be primarily understood as tokens of God's presence. A similar approach occurs in Cragg 1998b, 250f, where 'holism', and particularly 'ecology', are mentioned as clues to 'Christian meanings,' in particular as mediating clues for Muslims via which they may perceive Incarnation and the 'sacramental principle' rightly (that is, like a metaphor, to 'recruit from one realm to convey another so that both are fulfilled,' *ibid.* 251).

[42] Cf. Cragg 1961, 130, where this 'perceptibility' is related to gratefulness (*shukr*) as the right relation to God. Cf. also how the corresponding name of God, *Al-Shakur*, and the phrase 'every patient and grateful one,' is linked with human attentiveness to the *ayat, MC* 100. See also Cragg's most intriguing comparison of gratefulness in the Qur'an and the gratefulness 'at the heart of the Christian sacrament [i.e. the Holy Communion],' Cragg 1959b, 248. This comparability is most interestingly with regards to the approach of the present chapter.

[43] See also the next chapter below, Chapter 5.4.

To sum up, this is what can be found as common between Muslims and Christians in their understanding of man. In theological terms this concerns the mercy of God in nature and history, which can be interpreted and responded to in a certain independence of the divergent revelations of the Qur'an/Shari'ah and 'God in Christ' respectively. Cragg is aware that by this sacramental principle he avoids a further identification of who this God is, which humans respond to.[44] This was indeed the presupposition for the isolation of the sacramental experience of the signs in nature and history. The question of identity is however treated in his next 'steps': ch. 3 ('The Capacities of Revelation') and 4 ('Zeal and the Lord').

An answer to this derives from his understanding of *revelation*. Yet, revelation, if it is to say something about who God is, would, according to Cragg, require something or somebody to contain and entail such an understanding. This is the meaning of the title of the chapter: 'Capacities of Revelation' (52). This leads us, therefore, to the issue of mediators, in the Islamic case: the understanding of prophecy.

What seems to be a major point for Cragg is to link his understanding of prophecy to his understanding of creation and the experience of its sacramentality (53). Consequently, prophecy is constituted by its being creaturehood:[45] Just as God has annunciated humans into existence, so the vocation and work of prophets presupposes an act of will on behalf of God. And, on the other hand, as the signs in nature point towards God, so also there is a 'capacity of revelation' in the prophet, because both capacities belong to the order of nature (54).[46] As far as 'prophet' and 'revelation' without capital letters are concerned, this is likely to be recognized as *common* for Muslims and Christians, and for that sake, for Jews.[47] Yet, instead of elaborating the meaning of prophecy, I will pursue the issue of expression and experience. A significant element in Cragg's argument is his distinction between the *will* and *nature* of God.

Despite the commonalities between Islam and Christianity as to revelation, Cragg sees a distinctive difference in respect of contents of revelation (ch. 4). Regarding Islam, Cragg perceives its emphasis to be on imperative and regulation, whereas revelation according to a Christian

---

[44] For a similar strategy, see my exploration below (Chapter 5.6) of how he resolves the issue of common prayer between Muslims and Christians.

[45] Cf. also *CFs*, p. 78.

[46] For prophethood as *ayah* (sg.), see *WWd*, 124. See also *ibid.* 40ff ('Prophethood and Language').

[47] Prophethood is the common theme of *WWd*, in which Hebrew, Christian and Islamic conceptions of prophethood are compared.

understanding has expression as its predominant feature (75). This correlates to the 'will'-'nature' alternatives in the way which follows: whereas the former represents God's will, the latter mediates God's love and nature.

For Cragg this entails 'differing dimensions of revelation, and of Scriptures ... present, contrastedly, within one common theme' (76). With Smith, revelational difference. In this way, Islam and Christianity are diverse variations, at times contradictory, yet on the same theme: God's relation to humans and the world. A necessary consequence of this unitary view of revelation understood by the notions of expression and experience, at this level of abstraction, is his contention that there is only one God and that 'Allah' is the same as 'God' as understood by Christians, although the predicates may differ.[48] This means that in the interreligious meeting of Muslims and Christians one may leave out the question of 'whether God' and concentrate on the 'how God.' One way of exploring the latter is to see how Cragg develops what I will call a 'radical anthropology', which in turn implies different answers from Islam and Christianity.

5.3.3 RADICAL ANTHROPOLOGY AND RADICAL RESOLUTION: EVIL AND FORGIVABILITY

To pinpoint the issue at stake: what happens when 'experience' turns away from the annunciation of our existence? Or, what happens if evil overshadows the sacramental experience of nature? It is with respect to these questions that Cragg develops a distinctive anthropology which makes the relation between Islam and Christian theology somewhat more fragile. Also related to this issue, there is a close relation between experience and expression, despite the way this is made a theme in quite different ways in Islam and Christian theology. Cragg's assertion is that experience, at this place understood as that which breaks the relationship with God and His intention with the creatures, should also be related to God if his criterion that God has to act in a relevant way to human existence and experience is to be met. Yet, what does this mean in respect of human 'wrong-doing'?

The predominant term Cragg uses for human deviation from God's intentions with our lives is 'evil.' He does not very often talk about 'sin,' less about 'guilt,' although both may be seen as inherent in evil.[49]

---

[48] See *MC* 124f.

[49] See *MC,* 135. It is also noteworthy to see how Cragg deliberately avoids 'salvation' as a *tertium comparationis,* see Cragg 1993a, 2. His argument is that this notion is too vague and ambiguous (against R.J. Jones, Jones 1992), and becomes occupied

Yet, what does evil consist of? Evil is first of all to be connected to the creatures since evil appears within the good and perfect creation. Hence, Cragg sees evil as deviation from the pristine creation, as 'the ultimate flouting of the creation's 'intendedness,'' which 'constitutes the crucial challenge to a divine order,' a 'tragic crisis of creaturehood.'[50]

This represents a threat to the sovereign God, who also turns out to be a vulnerable God.[51] According to Cragg, human perversity is a far greater threat[52] to God's omnipotence than idolatry, which is the perceived fundamental sin in Islam of 'associating' God with mundane things or persons (*shirk*).[53] When Cragg makes evil a theme, it is primarily the concentration on combating *shirk* he wants to remove the attention from, in order to focus on, in his view, a more profound problem.

Secondly, one has to distinguish between 'evil' and 'evils.'[54] *'Evil'* is more than accidental circumstances and unhappy events. Evil entails a dynamic that corresponds to 'a chronic 'wronging', in other words: a deliberate offence against what is right and good. Cragg finds that this meaning of 'evil' equates to the Qur'anic notion *zulm*. Hence, his

---

with questions that lead nowhere (e.g. 'Are there many who in the end will be saved?'). Most interestingly, Cragg shares this suspicion with a recent trend in theology of religions/comparative theology, namely criticism of the preoccupation with the tripartite scheme (exclusivism, inclusivism, pluralism) originated by J. Hick and Alan Race (Race 1983) and the issue of ultimate salvation, see e.g. S. Mark Heim 1995 and Grünschloß 1999, as well as Chapter 6 below. Cragg's delimitation relates, however, to the very intentions of his main body of works: to make Christ relevant for Islam and Muslims using 'Islamic reasons,' that is, by expanding the Islamic universe of meaning *from within*, towards acknowledgement of Christ. Cf. also Cragg 1990 (against Cardinal Tomko, Tomko 1990), particularly p. 186.

[50] Cragg 1990, 183f.
[51] Cragg connects the matter of idolatry to an understanding of God as vulnerable, that is, God permits humans to perform idolatry in His relatedness to them, see Cragg 1974, 130. The opposite of this is to identify God primarily with His 'imperatives'. There is no significant idolatry, Cragg asserts, where God is conceived as immune to humans. Although the provocation of such a statement is evident to Muslims, Cragg seems to aim at approximating Islam *as it is* to a Christian understanding of idolatry. This is clear when he says that he wants to take Islamic lordship 'in its own seriousness,' *ibid.*
[52] *MC*, 135.
[53] Cf. Cragg 1961,129, where *shirk* is called 'the supreme and fundamental evil,' cf. Chapter 5.4.
[54] Cragg 1966a, 108. The context of concern is what technology may contribute to, and not. Informed by the time it was written, Cragg maintains that technology may help us resolving 'evils', yet is helpless against 'evil', against which only the Cross will do. The pride of technology stands, according to Cragg, contrary to the humiliation of the Cross.

concept of 'Semitic 'evil.'[55] It is not unreasonable to label this understanding of evil as 'original sin' because his point is to emphasize what I will call the inevitabability of evil, or with his own terms: the intractability of human nature.[56]

So far Cragg has only addressed the general anthropological issue of human beings and evil(s). The whole matter seems, however, to become more acute when it comes to the perception of religious persons, or humans participating in religious communities. The crucial question here is whether religious activity may result in evils and evil. This problem is particularly addressed in a separate chapter in *CFs*: 'Zeal and the Lord'.

The keywords are 'zeal' and 'zealousness'. According to Cragg, this single phenomenon may contain two features in the Semitic religious world: On the one hand the zeal of people for God, on the other God's own zeal for humans: the 'zeal *of* God. Cragg's point is that these relate to each other. My interest here is, however, in the former: human zeal. Moreover, this human zeal is twofold: Firstly, the fight against idols for God's sake is a fight for justice and goodness. This fight is, in its non-violent form, necessary in order to maintain the claim of 'let God be God' in a world that has excluded Him and started to worship idols in the literal or reinterpreted sense. On the other hand, this zeal may turn out to become fanaticism. This happens, as Cragg describes it, when the mind becomes closed, and where hardness of the heart is utilized in order to combat all that threatens 'God'. This is particularly the case where religious communities connect themselves to ethnic and political motives. This is what Cragg calls 'the subtlety of evil,' and this is the paradoxical meaning of 'zeal'.[57] In short, evil in religion has the potential of being of the worst kind:

> We may well be farthest from God in the very pretence of obeying Him, that there is a demerit in all meritoriousness, that much penitence is self-congratulatory, that piety may often be a subtle form of pride. Religious rightness, in our own eyes, may, in God's eyes, be the utmost idolatry. *Allâhu akhbar* can never well be made to read *Islâmu akhbar*, or any other 'establishment' naming His name.[58]

---

[55] Cragg 1990, 182f. At this place the immediate context is a discussion of Buddhism. Cragg contends here that the counterpart of 'Semitic evil' is evil that is connected to transience, the rejection of desire, etc.

[56] Cf. Cragg 1961,135, where he also discerns between 'sin I do' and 'sin I am.' The latter he calls the *intractability* of human nature.

[57] See in particular *CFs*, 80-87.

[58] *MC*, 133. See also *AC*, 291f, where power and politicization are emphasized in this respect: 'It is religion itself that is most prone to harden and brutalize the claims of land and tribe and culture and nation ... Politicization of religious causes is not

In the case of Islam, Cragg maintains that this sense of evil, that is, religious self-accusation and self-interrogation, is not radical enough, and particularly, on the other hand: the remedy for it is not 'deep-going' enough.[59] This brings us to the quest for a resolution of evil. In line with the theme of the present chapter we my ask: What is God's expression towards human evil?

Cragg's first point is, again, that evil should be seen as within creation. Hence, everyone who believes in creation has to reckon seriously with evil as a problem. Moreover, if this view is correct, also the Creator is involved, if one maintains theism and not merely deism.[60] An answer to *how* he relates can be found, in anticipation of a more thorough answer, in Cragg's statement about evil as non-illusionary, that is:

Significance has to be retrieved by its very anguish.[61]

A crucial question is whether prophets and law, which Cragg sees together, can contribute to the resolution of evil. In more concrete terms, can the Qur'an and *Shari'ah* retrieve human existence that has already gone fundamentally astray? Cragg doubts it: 'Law will plainly be part of the answer, for it is necessarily part of the question.' His thought resembles Paul's understanding of the Law as giving knowledge of sin and proving its persistence (Rom. 3.20).[62] 'Do not' does not overcome evil in its fundamental shape, as perceived by Cragg. The problem is one of bad will and lack of will: 'Will-power among us is "won't-power."' Consequently, the Law feeds this won't-power more than it effects power of resistance for humans against their own 'won'ts'.[63]

The ultimate evidence for Cragg's view seems to be the very fact of *Jihad*. According to Cragg, the possibility of *Jihad* reveals that evil requires stronger instruments than reminding (*dhikr*) and education based on the guidance (*huda*) of the Qur'an, and consequently *Shari'ah*:

---

seldom the atrophy of religious conscience. Penitence becomes an irrelevance where power decides.' Cf. also *WWd*, 19, where he sees 'religion [as] a prime theatre of human perversity.'

[59] *MC*, 133. See also *WWd*, 19. It may be argued that it is the *resolution* of sin and evil rather than the awareness of it that is Cragg's concern.

[60] For Cragg it is important to stress the commonality in respect of a 'shared theism' between Christians and Muslims, see *MC* 136 and 145. In a certain way, this is the whole clue to his strategy of scrutinizing *how* God relates to humans and the world as a *present* feature of his being: 'Where we differ is about the divine involvement this entails,' *ibid.* 136.

[61] Cragg 1990, 183.

[62] *MC*, 155.

[63] Cragg 1990, 183.

The necessity of *Jihâd* suggests that what is wrong is something more than forgetfulness. Manifestly the reminder and the exhortation, calculated to correct it, do not suffice. The whole logic of Muhammad's career is that the verbal deliverance of prophetic truth fails of satisfaction and must therefore pass to the post-Hijrah invocation of power.[64]

Within Cragg's argument, this induces the conclusion that prophecy is insufficient. According to Cragg this is the place to introduce Christology because it is precisely at this place a Christian 'commendation' may be relevant to Islam. Nevertheless, I will postpone the introduction of Christology for a while and expose another area which gives rise to divergence between Christianity and Islam: The perception of forgiving.

That God forgives is certainly a matter in Islam. According to Cragg, if He does as the Qur'an witnesses of it, then he forgives effortlessly, that is, He forgives *who* and *as* he wants in his absolute freedom. This remains an inherent part of the Islamic view of God's omnipotence. Cragg shows his dissatisfaction with this understanding when it comes to the element of God's relationality. If God is relational, then his forgiving must relate to a (human) desire for forgiveness. This desire, then, must from its side be consistent with the evil that the forgiving addresses.[65] Cragg's point is that God does not forgive unilaterally if it is not desired by humans. This has to be so, Cragg, maintains, if God relates to the created world.[66]

Related to this matter, Islam appears as inadequate when it comes to that which Cragg calls 'the forgivability of man.' The notion of 'forgivability' is, however, not easily understood. A possible interpretation involves a simple connection to Cragg's aforementioned elaboration on

---

[64] *MC*, 155. It is mainly related to this matter that Cragg draws the attention to the *distinctiveness* of the Gospel, which is incompatible with 'the original assumptions of Islamic *Jihâd*,' *ibid.* 141.

[65] Cragg 1966a, 114. Cf. also *CFs*, 91 where Cragg in connection to a quotation of John Macquarrie asks whether the divine being is of such a character that it redeems the human question for mercy.

[66] Most interestingly Cragg concludes negatively in respect of Islam and draws a parallel to the assessment of the relation between the New Testament and the Qur'an. The following citation makes explicit the difference between those two in respect of integrating human 'experience' into its 'expression': 'The New Testament is thoroughly participatory in nature. It embodies the experience it narrates ... ,' whereas in the Qur'an, 'the experience is not taken up into its text,' Cragg 1982b, 27. Nevertheless, according to Cragg, this tension corresponds rather to an *internal* tension within Islam between the relationality of Creation and parts of Prophecy, as well as the non-relationality of God's forgiving, but also the Islamic perception of the origin of the Qur'an (*wahy*).

forgiving, namely, that forgiveness has to be desired by humans[67] and thus be connected to the actual evil that is in need of it. In addition, it has to correspond to God's holiness. Related to the latter, it is not at all self-evident that God forgives effortlessly. For this understanding of 'forgivability', Cragg's understanding of the Cross provides a clue, because it is at this place that the Cross has been 'planted' and thus has its proper place, as man's 'forgivability'.

This exploration may gain some light from other studies of Cragg. Relevant passages will be where notions like 'the Cross is an answer to ...' occur. There is a similar expression to that mentioned above (where the Cross has been 'planted') in an article from 1980.[68] Cragg describes negatively the Qur'anic understanding of forgiveness: 'The forgiveness of God has no pledged pattern, no saving 'rendezvous' at which man by repentance may dependably encounter it and know he receives it. It is just such a 'rendezvous' that the Cross affords ...' (204). If thus interpreted, it points towards central features of an 'objective' doctrine of atonement, like the best known version (there are other versions also) in Anselm's *Cur Deus homo*. If so, the element of 'forgiveness desired' becomes less prominent.[69]

The Cross, according to Cragg, epitomizes man's deeds, and consequently also man's evil.[70] This is what he calls the representability of the Cross.[71] The surest charge of the Cross emerges from any attempt to particularize it, that is, to blame He whom we crucify. Yet, in this, Jesus becomes a representative for the whole human race, or as John Baldwin has it: 'It is the innocence that constitutes the crime.'[72] The Cross is thus not primarily a doctrinal claim, but 'a human awareness accessible in its own right.'

Using this, Cragg aims to be an 'interpreter of man,'[73] particularly in his contention that: as evil is inclusive, so also is absolution in the

---

[67] Human beings are not saved against their wills, *COR,* 95. Cf. also *CFs,* 90f: 'Divine being has such character as to await man's will to love.'

[68] Cragg 1980a.

[69] Yet, not totally overshadowed, see Cragg 1971, 18f. The human will remains a central and strategic feature of Cragg's Christian relation to Islam. This reference supports, however, our understanding of the *how* of forgiveness.

[70] Cragg 1990, 185. See also Cragg 1966a, 112, and Cragg 1993c, 193, for the question whether the Cross is 'overloaded' in respect of epitomizing too much of humans' evil and tragedy. This question regards explicitly the Holocaust. Cragg's answer is that the Cross should primarily be understood on the background of the disciples. It is, however, his contention that it is still possible to read in retrospect all other sin and tragedy in the light of the Cross.

[71] Cragg 1966a, 110.

[72] Cragg 1966a, 111.

[73] Cragg 1966a, 111. Cragg alludes at this place to Kamil Husain's *City of Wrong*

shape of a cross.[74] In the Cross we have, Cragg asserts,

> manifestly, a climax of an expression of evil arising in and
> from a context of encounter in which a teaching undergoes
> rejection and, so doing, may be said, truly, to bear the evil,
> but is seen to bear it *in such fashion as* to 'bear it away'.[75]

When Cragg makes such a statement on the *modus* (fashion) of
the bearing of evil of the Cross, it is in order to say that:

a. Evil has been resolved
b. Evil has been resolved adequately
c. Evil has been resolved adequately outside the range of
humans and prophets, by Christ

In my view, Cragg's approach qualifies to be labelled an objective
doctrine of atonement, yet in another fashion than the construed,
apologetic form of Anselm.[76] Evidence for this conclusion can be found in
an article[77] where Cragg concludes simply as follows on the question of
what costs human freedom, which is fundamental for Cragg, has required
of God: 'His being 'in Christ' reconciling a world.' Most interestingly in
respect of our point of departure for this chapter (experience and
expression) Cragg summarizes his view in the same place, quite pithily:

This love is the shape of omnipotence in its mode of relation

---

(translated by Cragg 1958/ 1964, originally: *Qaryah Zalimah,* Cairo 1954), which
is a Muslim's imaginative interpretation of the meaning of Good Friday. Cragg's
point is that the meaning of the Cross is perceivable outside a Christian faith. In
MC, 132, the point is that this book of the Muslim Husain makes evident that
there are modern strands in the Islamic tradition that represents self-accusation
and criticism of reliance on power and political measures. The absence of self-
interrogation which Cragg finds in Islam, is thus not complete. His critical question
to Husain is however whether the Cross has 'only to do with a pattern of disobedience
to conscience?' or 'do we need an inward re-making?' that is, redemption, Cragg
1956b, 236. For more on Husain, see ch. 8 in *PF.*

[74] Cragg 1966a, 112.

[75] Cragg 1990, 184, my emphasis. For Cragg, 'only the trust that does not capitulate
to wrong and evil lives towards salvation,' *WWd,* 81. Hence, Jesus' attitude towards
evil and suffering is *active* and *willed.*

[76] This reference to Anselm could probably have been developed further. Regarding
methodology, Cragg's interreligious approach, to Islam in particular, can be seen as
a version within a *Credo ut intelligam*-framework because of the strong determining
role of his Christian faith. At the same time, given that the self-relating means
self-change, one might suggest the rephrasing of Anselm thus: *Credo ut intelligam
et referam.* What this phrase misses is the reciprocity of the relations for the
reinterpretation and reformulation of *credo* which is central to Cragg.

[77] Cragg 1990, 185.

with the creaturehood once for all willed into freedom and
so only restored from evil by bearing of that which the
cross epitomizes as, concurrently, the deed of men, the way
of the Christ and the self-expression of God.

In a less condensed form this means:

    a.   The sovereignty of God has its shape of relation in the person of Christ

    b.   The creation as the place for evil and redemption

    c.   Redemption as bearing away once for all, and the contrastive counterpart of the endowment of human freedom as far as it comprises all human evil

Seen together, the relevant chapter in *CFs* could be re-entitled: restitution of the human sacramental experience by the zeal of God.[78] The 'way of Christ' is nothing else but 'the self-expression of God'.

To sum up, the bearing of this chapter is that Cragg develops a strong theological relation between Islam and Christian theology in respect of the understanding of creation, nature and man. At one, lower level there is an Islamic-Christian equivalent relation between God's expression and the experience of humans, that is, a sacramental experience both in respect of nature and messengers/prophets. Yet, Cragg finds that the Islamic and Christian traditions divide over the issue of how radical human evil has to be perceived. Consequently, also the remedies for it remain different. This becomes evident in the matter of forgivability. The notions of 'expression' and 'experience' have proved helpful for clarification, on this point, of the relations between Islam and Christian theology. The result is different relations in respect of different issues, probably to be seen as occurring on different theological levels.

One way of holding the continuities and discontinuities together, is indeed best expressed by Cragg himself when he states, that by the Cross God does not become smaller, but 'differently greater.'[79] This claim is, however, predominantly related to his understanding of prophecy in correspondence with an anthropology of 'more radical despair and hope.'[80] I will now explore how Cragg develops his understanding of Islamic prophecy and the Christian view of 'more than prophecy'.

---

[78] For this interpretation of the 'zeal of God', see *CFs,* 77. Cf. also Cragg 1961, 131 where Incarnation is conceived as 'God as his own sign.' By this, Cragg develops an intimate connection between *ayat* in nature, on the one hand, and in the history of the condescension of Christ into the world. At the same place Cragg paraphrases this as 'expression of the eternal.' Consequently it appears to be an indissoluble correspondence between the notions of 'incarnation', 'sign(s)' and 'expression'.

[79] Cragg 1966a, 114.

[80] *MC,* 134.

5.4 Human-Divine Association and Dissociation: the True Meaning of Shirk and Tanzil

It is possible to continue this focus on expression and experience by directing attention to two concepts which Cragg employs in order to interpret pivotal parts of the Prophet's experience, especially during his activity in Mecca. These concepts are the antonyms 'association' and 'dissociation'. Linguistically, the terms should be clear enough: Whereas the former denotes that which is connected or related, the latter denotes things that are disconnected, divided or divergent.

As we explore how Cragg uses these terms, we will see that the relation between Christian theology and Islam is a by-product of his main elaborations, which is how the divine relates to the human in Islam. Though Cragg's approach is once again concentrated on the divine-human relationship in Islam, the material he engages is somewhat different from that of the previous chapter. In this chapter I will concentrate upon Cragg's interpretation of: a) the Prophets critical engagement with idolatry (*shirk*), and b) the Islamic understanding of the origin of the Qur'an (*tanzil*).

As early as an article from 1956,[81] Cragg reveals a distinctive approach to which he frequently returns later. The objective of the article is to ponder how Christians may understand the Qur'an comprehensively. Most interestingly for the problem pursued in the present study, Cragg contends that an answer to this may in turn enable a renewed understanding of oneself, that is, of the Christian faith (62).

According to Cragg, in respect of any comprehensive understanding of the Qur'an, *shirk* will gain a prominent place (63). *Shirk* is for him the very point of departure if one is to grasp the passion proper to the Prophet's preaching. It is this Arabic term that Cragg translates by 'association'.[82] What is it, then, that is being associated with God? In brief, *shirk* is what occurs when items of creation are ranked alongside God[83] or 'esteemed in any sense as capable of the functions and prerogatives of God' (63). The whole enterprise of *shirk* is a human activity,

---

[81] Cragg 1956a, 'The Qur'ân and the Christian Reader. I.' Subsequent parenthetical remarks refer to this article.

[82] There is nothing spectacular about this translation since this is one of the common ways of translating *shirk*. Yet, when Cragg later aims to give it a *positive* meaning, he runs immediately into a very sensitive area of Islamic self-understanding. See also Akhtar 1990b, 254, who translates *shirk* by: "to associate the true unique divinity—Allâh—with one or more false ones' thereby compromising Allâh's uniqueness,' and *mushrik* by 'associationist', denouncing the traditional translations of 'idolatry' and 'idolater'.

[83] *MC,* 111. See also D. Gimaret, *EI,* 9:485, who lets *shirk* denote 'nothing other than the man giving himself someone to worship in addition to God.'

and occurs when people locate their worship to places, items and persons instead of God. Cragg sees this as the classical formula of Semitic idolatry, exemplarily illustrated by the dance around the Golden Calf, Exod. 32, and Rom. 1.18-25. Mecca before Muhammad seized it appears also as a similar context as it was known as immersed in polytheism in the fashion of goddess cult, fertility and astral deities,[84] not least connected to the sanctuary of Ka'bah.[85]

However, Cragg makes an attempt to modify this understanding of idolatry in regards of what actually happened in that which was perceived as idolatry. He makes it a point that this form of idolatry did not identify the stones, natural phenomena, fertility agricultural and ethnic, stars and seasons, etc., with God himself, albeit he was partly localized to these.[86] A way of phrasing this was that God made Himself manifest in this way, without being exhausted by matters of place, events and items.[87] Or simply, that

all these are inside the Creator's creation and the benison of creaturehood.[88]

---

[84] E.g. al-Lat, al-'Uzza and Manat, see surah 9.

[85] Most interestingly, Walther Björkman in his article on '*shirk*' in *EI¹* (vol. 4, 1934, 378-380) claimed that words of the root *sh-r-k* were not included in the most ancient suras; the Meccan surahs. In *EI* (new edition) Gimaret disclaims this and attempts to give reason for the view that also the earliest surahs (e.g. 68.41 and 52.43, where derivations of *sh-r-k* occur) refer to the *matter* of shirk, supported by Weil and Nöldeke, although the term itself is missing (only 4 times in the Qur'an at all!) 'in those *sûrahs unanimously* accepted as the earliest,' *EI*, 9 (1996), 485. Gimaret also draws the attention to the fact that the traditional chronology of the successions of surahs in the Qur'an is not self-evident. The 'matter' in the Qur'an, and in Islam as stated in *Shahadah*, is that 'shirk, by definition, is contrary to Islam, since the first article of faith of the Muslim is precisely the denial of all associationism, the affirmation of the single God,' *ibid*. 486. That does not mean that Islam has been inherently univocal at this point, cf. the reciprocal accusations between e.g. Sunni theologians (whose recognition of the voluntary human act, so the Mu'tazilis, results from an association between God who creates and man who acquires) and the Mu'tazilis (that they attribute, so the Sunni theologians, a power to man comparable to that of God), *ibid*.

[86] Cf. also *CFs*, 81: 'One can have the arts without idolatrous reproach and one can be irreproachably free of them and still not have worship.'

[87] Wolfhart Pannenberg develops an identical argument in Pannenberg 1988, 198: 'Das Kultbild des Gottes will ... gerade die in den gewöhnlichen Formen der Manifestation der göttlichen Macht verborgene Eigengestalt der Gottheit sichtbar machen.' It is therefore precisely the *difference* between divine reality and the images that is being emphasized in, for example, anthropomorphic representations. Pannenberg is at this place dependent upon a study of Hubert Schrade (*Der verborgene Gott*, Stuttgart 1949).

[88] Cragg 1998b, 242. A similar argument can be found in Carl Heinz Ratschow: 'Gott

Consequently, the Prophet's reproach of this cult starts with a denial of the existence of the deities before he abandons the cult, not the contrary (64).[89] This is the proper background of the first part of the Islamic 'creed,' *shahadah*: *La ilaha illa-Allah*.[90] The uniqueness and exclusiveness of God are nothing but the contrarieties of idolatry, *shirk*. So far, Cragg has merely attempted to paraphrase, although it is a good re-phrasing,[91] the 'interior' Islamic understanding of what may be perceived as the most fundamental issue in Islam: The relation between God's unity, *tawhid*, and the opposition of *shirk*.[92]

The point where Cragg seeks to advance this interpretation of *shirk*, which he seems to affirm in principle,[93] is where he asks whether the qur'anic disqualification of any association (*shirk*) of God with mundane things must necessarily lead to a corresponding dissociation of God from humans as such (65).[94] Cragg's answer is definitely No! Quite the contrary, he maintains that

> the anti-idolatrous devalidation of 'association' must not
> be extended to disavow the Divine participation in the
> human for purposes that are worthily Divine *(ibid.)*

On the other hand, Cragg sees an immediate risk in dissociating God, that

---

bringt da Geschehen der Welt zur Gestalt, besorgt und vollendet es per res secundas—das sind Mächte, Kräfte, Vollmachten und Vermögen naturhafter wie geschichtlicher Art.' However, 'Die anfechtende Verborgenheit des Welt-Waltens Gottes wird erhellt und vergewissert von Wort, Werk und Person Jesu, den Gott als Heiliger Geist heute wirksam sein läßt. Ergo sind die Religionen im Urteil des christlichen Glaubens Teil des Welt-Waltens des dreieinigen Gottes—den Menschen gegeben,' Ratschow 1979, 122.

[89] For the correspondence between *essential non-existence* and *practical-political existence*, see *CFs*, 33.

[90] *There is no god but God (Allah)*. The use of lower-case and capital letters here is deliberate—*and* essential.

[91] Cragg's reconstruction of Islamic faith and the content of the Qur'an has been praised not only by Muslims, but also by Western 'Orientalists'. For this, see various reviews of for example *CM*, the classic in this respect (part II): Rahbar 1958, Schimmel 1962 and 1985 (*MC*), the most affirmative—and critical—of Wilfred Cantwell Smith, Smith 1957b, and Watt 1957. See also further: Scherer 1960 (*SM*), Ayoub 1987 (*JM*), Parrinder 1984 (*MC*), Race 1984 (*MC*), and Smart 1970 (*PM*).

[92] Cf. *COR*, 93: '*Shirk* is the antonym to *islam*.'

[93] Based in particular on the counterparts and precedents of the Old Testament, e.g. Elijah's fight with the *ba'alim*, 1 Kings 18.21ff.

[94] Another place, Cragg localizes the origin of the dissociation of God to *prophecy*, cf. *CFs*, 32: 'This distinctive prophethood of divine unity ... entailed a rigorous dissociation *of God* from the human realm' (my emphasis).

is, by 'misnaming' things of time and nature as powers in their own right.[95] To avoid this, these 'things' should be 'truly associated' with God, because 'God is our adequacy' (cf. Surah 3.173).

This in turn, enables Cragg to *rephrase* the problem of *shirk* in order to partly affirm it: Can God properly associate with certain human instruments if these are not being made items of worship/idolatry (*shirk*)? Cragg affirms this and contends that the Islamic conception of *shirk*

> cannot conceivably imply that the Divine Lord 'associates' Himself with no agencies or calls no times, people or places into participation in His purposes (64).

The keywords here are 'agencies' and 'participation' since Cragg aims at proving an instrumentality within Islam which implies a relatedness of God to what is human, in particular with his messengers and prophets.[96]

---

[95] *MC,* 111. It is also interesting to see how Cragg's elaborates on the *modern* meaning of *shirk.* His point is that idolatry is not an anachronism confined to the environment of Muhammad. Yet, this transformation of the concepts into modern times runs the risk of making too easy renderings of *shirk, cf. CFs,* 81: 'The busy iconoclast is liable to find the obvious idols and miss the hidden ones.' The identification in *COR,* 94, however, is that of *human power-structures that have been absolutized.* Cf. also Cragg 1961, 129, where *shirk* is formally defined as *false absolutes.* Cf. further 1980a, 198, as well as 1981a, 37.

Cf. here also Shabbir Akhtar, Akhtar 1990b, who says: 'That 'There is no god but God' is to impose an operative veto on oneself from attributing any *ultimate reality or power* to those ideals that enslave individuals and societies,' 259, my emphasis. Despite this obvious coincidence with Cragg where the meaning of *shirk* has gained 'a massive, perhaps illegitimate, extension of meaning,' a 're-interpretation,' *ibid.* Akhtar criticizes Cragg for being unaware of this kind of reservation when *shirk* is applied to modern times, 252 and 260, n 2. According to Akhtar, *shirk* is a religious concept which is not necessarily meaningful in a secularized society, nor can an accusation of committing it be raised legitimately to modern men. To me, this critique of Cragg seems on the one hand to lack convincing references to Cragg's works (Akhtar refers to *MQ*), cf. the citation that I just referred to in *CFs.* The striking point, however, is how Akhtar's and Cragg's approaches seem to convey an identical inducement: the demand for a rethinking of this central concept in a modern world other than the original world of iconoclasm and 'religious' idolatry. Nevertheless, Akhtar's suggestion of a distinction between *intentional shirk* (of the past) and *unintentional shirk* (of today), may prove helpful, *ibid.* 252, 258. See also Cragg's comment on Akhtar 1990b, Cragg 1991a, where he draws the attention to the qur'anic phrases of *min dun illah* ('to the exclusion of God') and *istighna* ('sufficing in-and-to oneself,' cf. surah 96.7), as well as his conception of the very meaning of *islam* ('letting God be God'), 124f. Thus, Cragg finds *shirk* to be 'more actual in the modern case of the 'God-ignoring' than of the pagan,' 124.

[96] Cf. Cragg 1974, 128. This participation is already implicit, according to Cragg, when Muslims ask about the meaning of the divine names, that is, meaning entails participation: 'If this is not so, all is silence,' Cragg 1980a, 200. See also Chapter 5.6 below.

Rewarding Encounters

Cragg claims that an 'involving of the Divine' in Islam is 'plainly inevitable' (67) because, without relations, the revelation, Law and the Prophet cannot be properly understood (65).[97]

Regarding the Qur'an, it is mainly its origin (*tanzil*) that concerns Cragg. This is probably one of the most prominent and delicate[98] questions in Muslim-Christian interrelations, and one that has not yet been settled.[99] Cragg's crucial question in this respect is whether the genesis of the Holy Scripture should be related to human instrumentality, or alternatively: that God is His own instrumentality. If the latter, do we, then, not deny His own right to be Himself and thereby excluding Him from acting in His freedom?[100] If the former, there being an instrumentality, should not these instruments be perceived as taking part in the mediation and shaping of the Qur'an? Is it not precisely this openness to such a divine freedom that must qualify as a proper 'submission'?[101]

There is certainly a range of opinions as to this within Islam (67). The Tradition, *Hadith*, maintains that Muhammad is nothing but 'a voice of crying,' or a pipe for the stream of its words and language. So also the mystic and great poet, Jalal al-Din Rumi.[102] On the other hand, one has the 'high' and 'remarkable prophetology,' although 'extravagant', not least in Sufi piety and philosophic speculation where propositions of Muhammad

---

[97] See, e.g., Cragg 1974, 128-132.
[98] Cf. the Pakistani Fazlur Rahman, who taught in Karachi, Durham, Montreal and Chicago, who had to resign from Central Institute of Islamic Research, Karachi and since Islamabad, in 1968 because of what he wrote in his book *Islam* (1966, ²1979). Rahman's view of the Qur'an is that: 'orthodoxy ... lacked the intellectual capacity to say both that the Qur'ân is entirely the Word of God and, in an ordinary sense, also entirely the Word of Muhammad. The Qur'ân obviously holds both, for if it insists that it has come to the 'heart' of the Prophet, how can it be external to him?' Rahman 1979, 31. This is, so far, identical with Cragg's position. No wonder that Rahman holds a significant place within Cragg's 'reservoir' of references. Where they differ, is particularly a) as to whether this qur'anic divine-human cooperation reveals only the will of God (Rahman), or also His nature (Cragg), *WWd*, 119f, and b) whether the 'political equation' of Muhammad after *Hijrah* was legitimate, *ibid.* 162. See also Slomp 1990, 185 and 188. See also *PF*, ch. 6, for Cragg on Rahman, in this regard particularly p. 91f.
[99] Nasr 1998, 219.
[100] See e.g. *WWd*, 135. A similar, yet contrary, problem regards the matter whether anything can be 'necessary' to God, cf. *CFs*, 79. Does God *need* His creatures, the prophets, or for that sake: a name for Himself? Cragg's point is, that as soon as God relates Himself to some of these, he becomes 'associated' with them.
[101] Cragg alludes certainly to the meaning of *islam*.
[102] Cf. Rumi's metaphor: 'out of their mouths the water comes and pours into the pool. All who are possessed of reason know that the water does not issue out of the mouth of a stone bird: it issues out of another place,' *MC*, 83. To this orthodox view belong also for instance Ibn Taimiyya and al-Shahrashtani, *WWd*, 126.

being a genius, pre-existent, uncreated, divine, the definitive Muslim, etc., were proposed.[103] Nevertheless, Cragg emphasizes what he conceives as the Qur'anic occasionalism,[104] that is, that the Qur'an is not exempted from being originated through events.

What he ponders is what this matter of place and time may imply for the understanding of *tanzil*.[105] In many ways Cragg reflects a historical-critical point of departure when he thus aims to go beyond the traditional Islamic way of thinking of the *tanzil* by considering the historical and other 'realities.' The crucial matter, however, is that he claims that he has not imported external criteria for judging this case. What Cragg employs for his alternative reading of the origin of the Qur'an, is internal evidence, that is, evidence that can be discerned from the reading of the Qur'an itself.[106] From this Cragg maintains, based on the Qur'an, that the statement 'that' God uses certain persons and events in His service must necessarily entail a 'how that?'

It is the latter he finds to be insufficiently and incoherently[107] pondered in Islam. This regards in particular the prophetic experience of Muhammad, *wahy*, while receiving the Qur'an during a span of 23 years.[108] If it had been properly treated, so Cragg, Islam would not have been able on its own premises to abandon the possibility of the Incarnation, that is, on the premises on which they repudiate 'litholatry and daemonism' (66). This means, however, that Cragg accuses Islam of traditionally having misunderstood *shirk*. Cragg's alternative Christian interpretation of the genesis of the Qur'an resonates with his understanding of the Holy Spirit[109] mentioned in the previous chapter:

Would it not be more worthy to think of the Divine Spirit

---

[103] *WWd*, 38f and 124f. Cf. also *MC*, ch. 4 and 5.

[104] Cragg translates the *asbab al-nuzul* by 'occasions of revelation,' *WWd*, 70. This is, according to a cardinal principle of qur'anic commentary, the first concern of *tafsir*, after grammar and textual parsing.

[105] 'Not to have these [the 'where' and 'when' of the Qur'an] is to be out of this world,' *MC*, 88. Further: '*Wahy* marches with occasion,' *ibid*. 91. Cragg attempts to open this 'gathering significance' to be even 'inclusive enough to take in a Gethsemane,' Cragg 1998b, 243.

[106] 'It seems strange in the extreme that Muslim theory about *Wahy* could so far diverge from the plain evidence of the Book itself,' *MC*, 88. The references he uses to the Qur'an are, *inter alia*, surahs 26.194 and 2.97, see *ibid*. 87. See also note 109 below.

[107] *MC*, 85: 'The question 'How?' must be absorbed into the dogma, and the mystery, of *Tanzíl* itself.'

[108] See *EQ*, further ch. 6 in *MC*, as well as chs. 2-4 of *RMH*.

[109] However, the activity in the citation below is meant to resemble the activity of the Spirit *as found in* surah 26.193f and 2.97. See also *MC*, 84.

bearing interpretatively and lovingly, unto revelation, upon
the realities present to the Prophet's soul, so that the
consequent disclosure, which condemns the false, unveils
the true and enforces the just, arises from the real travail of
those whom action involves? (68)

Otherwise one would have to affirm what Cragg sees as an Islamic principle
in this respect: 'The more an activity is divine, the less it is human.'[110]

It seems that his (strategic) aim of understanding of Muhammad
is twofold:

a) To facilitate Christian acknowledgment of the Prophet in his
'Quranic role,'[111] and from that to assess the 'wide areas *and* the painful limits[112]

---

[110] *MC,* 84. One of the correlations to this is the belief in Muhammad as *ummi,* in
particular where this is understood as illiteracy and hence supporting the *miracle*
of the qur'anic genesis. Cragg does, however, not translate *ummi* as 'illiteracy',
which he sees as having a doubtful historical foundation, but as 'lack of native
Scripture', *MC,* 86. See also *WWd,* 27 and 45. Hence he also understands *i'jaz* (the
matchlessness and inimitability of the Qur'an) as 'a veritable Arabicizing of
monotheistic faith,' *MC,* 86f. The contextual clue to this understanding is the role
'people' plays in e.g. surah 7.157f. The sensitive remark on behalf of Cragg is that
this 'does not diminish the Quranic story,' *ibid.* 87. His suggestion involves what
he calls a 'reverent realism,' *ibid.* 89.

[111] This phrase entails an important distinction as to 'time' and 'place.' Given the
evident fact of Muhammad being *after* Jesus in respect of time, it seems that
Cragg's reasons for acknowledgment of Muhammad as prophet hinge on his emphasis
on the possibility of Muhammad's mission as 'progressive by [criteria] of place
and culture,' although it might be 'retrogressive by simple time criteria,' *MC,* 92.
Muhammad's 'time' is then understood as 'immediate situations.' A counterpart to
this time-place distinction, is his preference for 'people' instead of 'religion,' and
'faith' instead of 'dogma,' *ibid.* 94. This resonates certainly his dislike of dogma
related to 'the custodian mind,' cf. above Chapter 4.4.1, but includes also an
explicit acknowledgement of Cantwell Smith's personalist emphasis, albeit he
'carries his case too far in distinguishing 'faith' from 'dogma' and 'being-in-faith'
from 'religion."

[112] These limits of kinship are particularly evident in Shabbir Akhtar's (British Muslim
modernist and philosopher of religion) energetic apologetics for a traditional
Islamic view of *tanzil* and *wahy* where he attacks Cragg's 'dynamic model' of
revelation, Akhtar 1991. Whereas Akhtar accuses Cragg of confusing genesis and
interpretation in Cragg's opinion that 'it is only because one sees the initiative in
the revelation as genuinely divine, that ... one wishes to know whether or not the
human recipient has a role' (so Akhtar), 98, Akhtar's own suggestion is to distinguish
between the genesis of the Qur'an and its *interpretation, which represents* 'the
effort of the human mind ... *after* the production and final delivery of the text,'
100 (he argues himself for 'the mechanical model,' 104). As an interpretation,
Cragg's approach is legitimate, although 'truistic,' and 'false, unnecessary, and
extremely pernicious,' 101. This distinction between genesis and interpretation is
obviously doctrinally driven by the claims for 'infallibility' and 'authority,' which

of a Christian kinship.'[113] This is for example the entire goal of *MC*.[114]

b) To approximate the understanding of *tanzil* to the Christian understanding of how God relates to the world, in particular the Incarnation

---

is based on the premise that 'fallibility' is intrinsic to 'human', and therefore entails an allergic against any 'partnership' between God and the Prophet's psyche, that is, the Islamic conception of *truth* makes it necessary to delimit the genesis of the Qur'an from any human participation. The 'time and place' matters that are so important for Cragg seem thus to lack any reference except the state of trance of the Prophet, which is literally 'nailed down' on p. 99 (cf. also Akhtar's affirmation of the 'axiomatic' about the Qur'an as 'the word of God *alone*,' p. 101). Hence, Akhtar characterizes Cragg's approach as 'entirely unmotivated once one intends to accept the authority of the word as truly divine and its contents as fully authentic,' 98. What Akhtar avoids encountering, however, is the element of possibility of truth in Cragg's approach, which is primarily an attempt to seek points of cross-reference in his approach of acknowledging the Prophet (Akhtar only refers to *MC* in this article, not *EQ* or *MQ*) from a Christian world of meaning, cf. below. This becomes evident when Akhtar asks rhetorically: 'If the doctrines be authentic [i.e. the 'religious doctrines of the Qur'ân'], why should we care about the nature of the prophetic experience?' That such a 'care' should allegedly only have an 'academic interest,' too clearly reveals Akhtar's disinterest in the interreligious 'offer' which Cragg has proposed. This attitude is, most likely, in Cragg's view to be aligned to the narrowness found across religious traditions, *in casu* in Islam. This is, however, the more surprising as Akhtar otherwise has acknowledged Cragg's approach in *MC* as 'sympathetic,' although 'marred by Christian theological preconceptions that militate against impartial inquiry,' Akhtar 1990a, 241, n 46. Given this ideal of 'impartial inquiry,' Akhtar places himself outside the scope of both Cragg's authorship and the present study. His accusation of the *incoherence* of the Incarnation and of the Trinity in *JM* seems to convey the same kind of ideal, which to me seems to be similarly impertinent given the role the relation between the Father, Son, but also the Spirit, plays in Cragg's authorship, *ibid.* 156f and 240, n 39. Akhtar employs an odd distinction between 'coherence,' which 'derives its impulse from an intelligible and indeed true metaphysical foundation,' and 'the rich moral potential of such orthodox Christian claims.' For a similar critique, see Khan 1986. Cragg's treatment of the relation between divine and human in the instances of Islam and Christianity can, and must, on the other hand, be conceived as a claim about the coherence of the Christian faith and the incoherence of the Islamic view of revelation, prophecy, anthropology, etc., yet possibly without the philosophical scrutiny Akhtar seems to require. More on this below. Most interestingly, though, being a lesson in interreligious realism, this encounter of Akhtar with Cragg does not exclude him from corresponding with Cragg, *ibid.* 236, n 25. Cragg also highly praises Akhtar as an example of 'mental labours obligating Muslims today,' that is, representing non-fundamentalists, *WWd,* 146, and 189, n 20.

[113] *MC,* 91. Cragg opts for the possibility of making a Christian verdict that 'freely perceives Muhammad's destiny with truth and by the same Christian discernment *takes issue with the rest*,' *ibid.* 142, my emphasis. This becomes crucial in respect of the relation between prophecy and sonship, *ibid.* For this, see also my chapter below (Chapter 5.5).

[114] See *MC,* xi.

understood as God's instrumental activity on earth, which he sees as the 'central mystery of all religious history—a mystery in which Islam's Qur'ân is also involved' (68).

To state it in this latter way is in fact to make what Cragg calls an 'adequate paraphrase' of the Incarnation, that is:

> To possess our terminology in the capacity to do without it.[115]

This can be seen as the linguistical expression of Cragg's general attitude towards Islam, which is also informed by a self-criticism on behalf of previous attempts to relate to Islam:

> We have been much too hopeless, much too dogged, much too dull, about our Christian theological relationships to the world of Islam.[116]

This approximation to Islam becomes evident when Cragg makes central the 'deep human experience under a directing sense of divine transcendence'[117] of the prophethood within the Qur'an on the one hand, and conceives the meaning of the Incarnation as to be 'the human expressibility of God' on the other.[118]

Another example of how he perceives and makes adequate paraphrases, in this case regarding the notion of the 'Son of God', may illuminate his whole approach to Islam:

> We mean that the power within creation and behind history discloses itself to us, out of its own freedom, in terms original to its own glory and realized in human personality within an encounter of word and deed, central to the whole mystery and tragedy of our human being as we know it in our hearts. 'Begets', 'sends', 'gives', are all, in their meaning, translations of this fact.[119]

Yet, this example makes it pertinent to proceed to the next chapter. How is this 'power within creation and behind history' to be related more comprehensively to 'human personality' and 'the whole mystery and

---

[115] Cragg 1974, 136f, my emphasis.
[116] Cragg 1961, 131.
[117] *MC,* 98.
[118] *MC,* 110.
[119] Cragg 1974, 137.

tragedy of our human being'? It is finally when we enter into the issue of prophecy and its travail that the former elaborations come to their full theological comprehension, namely in its discussion of which theology is most 'worthy'[120] of the Sovereign God. This is, however, intimately related to the two most salient biographies of the Muslim and Christian encounter: those of Muhammad and Jesus. It is here that the most important qualification of the relations between Islam and Christian theology is to be found.

5.5 Realization of God's Omnipotence: Takbir and Theodicy
5.5.1 PROPHETHOOD(S) AND 'LET GOD BE GOD'

What I set out to do here, is not merely to explore Cragg's understanding of prophecy as found in the Islamic and Christian traditions, but to see this issue in the light of his understanding of *takbir,* that is, his understanding of 'Greater is God' (*Allahu akbar*), as found in the call to prayer.[121] The most distinctive aspect of this call is its absolute comparative form, which is far stronger and more exclusive than its alternative superlative form (*al-akbar*). This matter, which by one term is called *takbir,* has already been mentioned above. I will now attempt to see how Cragg develops his notions of a 'theology worthy of God,' and of God as 'differently greater.' Both of these terms have been presented in order to develop relations between Islam and Christian theology. In this, the biographies of Jesus and Muhammad also become examples of different ways of expressing the sovereignty of God, *Allahu akbar,* or better, different ways of substantiating the faith in God as sovereign.

Consequently, Cragg asks for credentials for the doctrine of 'Greater is God.' In brief, he simply asks for a theodicy for the sovereignty of God. Yet, given Cragg's criterion that God has to be relevant to the human life-world and life-experience, one may wonder how this is to be thought of in Islam? Whereas I have drawn attention to the evil of competent humans above, another 'experience' is actualized in this respect, namely: fear, doubt, confusion and desperation.[122] What is the relation of God Almighty to humans, *in casu* prophets, whose self-perception is far from being that of self-sufficiency? This is nothing else but Cragg's pursuit of the fourth dimension of his (modest) Semitic theory of religion (cf. the

---

[120] I allude to ch. 5 in *RMH.*

[121] For this English rendering of the emphatic Arabic form, see *MC,* 101f, cf. note 37 above.

[122] Cragg 1981a, 32.

previous chapter) that is, human accusation, in this regard in respect of the interpretation of how this relates to God's omnipotence in Islam.

The matter is in fact twofold: a) how may human experience entail *takbir* understood as worship of God who is greater? And b) may any human experience appear as incompatible and problematic in connection to God's 'greater-ness'? Most interestingly, Cragg asserts that *takbir* presupposes humans who believe and worship.[123] This is the way God in effect becomes greater than others who fight for the human heart and mind. On the contrary, where the praise fades or appears as unjustifiable and groundless, God becomes dethroned. I will now examine how Cragg relates this intimately to his interpretation of Islamic prophethood, which in turn he relates to Christian theology.

The importance of prophecy is of course inevitable to Islam: 'As Islam sees it, there is nothing more than, other than, prophethood in the economy of God with humankind.'[124] To allude to the previous chapter: 'Prophets associate God with the world.'[125] Or, even stronger: The understanding of God cannot be divided from those He sends to the world in His place. There is nothing 'more than a prophet' in Islam,[126] and this relates in particular to Muhammad and his reception of the Qur'an. This can also be phrased positively:

> Everything that has do with God in Islam is finally within
> the context of the prophethood of Muhammad.[127]

If so, there emerges a connection that is highly interesting from a theological point of view: In order to understand God, we have to understand his messengers properly.

In all this Cragg makes 'prophecy in the economy of God' a *tertium comparationis,*[128] where human experience (travail, suffering) is

---

[123] Cragg 1981a, 29-33.

[124] Cragg 1993c, 194.

[125] Cragg 1981a, 28. Cragg sees the matter of association as included in the *copula* (and), or simply comma, between 'God' and His 'messenger' as stated in the *Shahadah.* See also p. ix, and in particular ch. VIII of *WWd,* which he describes as a 'theology of *Shahadah,*' 121. Cragg sees *Tasliyah* (the calling down blessing upon the Prophet, cf. surah 33.56) as deepening this truth 'devotionally,' namely that 'the reality of God is *credally conjoined* with the person of Muhammad as 'His messenger," *RMH,* 81, my emphasis, and *WWd,* 119 and 122.

[126] Cragg 1964a, 307, and 1993c, 194.

[127] *CFs,* 52.

[128] See the preface to *WWd,* ix: 'The final category, then, is the place of the whole [i.e. the measure of the burden of the prophets] in the economy of God.' Regarding prophecy as a *tertium comparationis,* cf. *ibid.* where Cragg states that his aim in *WWd* is to 'align prophethood in the Bible and in Islam in one denominator,' and

seen as crucial for the understanding of the role of the prophet(s) of Islam. This can be structured plainly like this:[129]

divine unity 1 *prophethood* 1 *prophetic personality* 1 *events/experience*

The importance of prophecy for Islam can therefore, as we noticed above, be stated thus: The significance of *islam*[130], and consequently the prophets, is ultimately dependent upon the understanding of God. If one asks about what this understanding of God really is, Cragg will again[131] refer to the term, 'Let God be God'. This is, he asserts, the common Semitic definition of the sovereign God.[132]

In this, he keeps the focus on both the doctrines of *takbir* and *tawhid*.[133] Cragg relates the historical context for the interpretation of these concepts to Muhammad's purification of and preaching against the Meccan idolatry. There, 'Let God be God' became a major vehicle for his combating *shirk* (cf. the previous subsection). In this historical sense, 'Let God be God' can be understood as the realization of God, more specifically in terms of '*to be* let be'. Only thus may humans recognize Him.[134] The question, however, is how it is possible to justify that God is the sovereign one which the Qur'an and Muslims claim and presuppose Him to be. In other words, the request for theodicy.

---

thus develop 'a theology of prophethood.' This use of prophethood as 'a deeply mediating theme' applies, however, differently to Christianity and Islam, as it represents 'the core concept of the Qur'ân' but only 'in part, of the Bible,' Cragg 1998b, 239. Cf. especially ch. VIII in *WWd*. Cf. also Chapter 5.2.1 above where Cragg in his dissertation uses 'antagonism and suffering in the economy of truth and righteousness' as a *tertium comparationis*. With other words: The consistency in approach between *WWd* (1999) and *ITC* (1950) is striking.

[129] I use '1' in the meaning of 'mutual dependency'. The 'graphic' representation is based in particular on Cragg 1998b, 243: 'That there is a clear logic from divine unity to prophethood and, no less clearly, from prophethood to personality, and from personality in prophetic calling to history and the concreteness of events, cannot sanely be in doubt.'

[130] Cragg 1961, 128. It is important to see how Cragg here and otherwise distinguishes between 'Islam' and 'islam'. Whereas the former is the comprehensive term, including its cultural and religious system with its history, the latter is often reserved for what it means to *be and act* as '*muslim*', in the sense not confined to 'Muslim' in the cultural sense but to their *human* way of being religious. According to Cragg, this distinction is important for what kind of relations one may succeed in developing between Islam and Christian theology. In fact, this is crucial for his notion of 'The 'Islamic validity' in being Christian,' Cragg 1961, 128.

[131] Cf. n 35, p. 237 above.

[132] Cragg 1980a, 197-199.

[133] The unity and oneness of God.

[134] Cragg 1980a, 198. Cf. also *CFs*, 34.

Or alternatively, Cragg asks, is his omnipotence of another kind? Cragg seems dissatisfied with a God who retreats partially, only being present on 'occasions.'[135] Cragg's request is that of critical inquiry: Who is God as perceived in Islam? How does he act? Are his 'deeds' credible? That there is a need for this kind of theodicy, is given by what Cragg sees as a Qur'anic inconsistency between the omnipotence of God, on the one hand, and the creation and revelation on the other.[136] A point, which resonates with previous observation in my reconstruction of Cragg's approach, is that the matter of theodicy is made a theme already by the creation.[137] Hence, Islam has to make credible, as well as identify, who God is in relation to the created world, humans included. Moreover, God's mercy, His *rahmah*, towards the world has also to be made a theme, especially for 'those it is meant for.'[138] This is the kind of theodicy and impasse that Cragg sets out to examine in relation to how prophethood relates to *theo*-logy. Or, as Cragg asserts in *CFs*: 'The divine is significantly at stake in the prophetic' (54). That is the backcloth for that which follows.

5.5.2 THE WATERSHED OF *HIJRAH* AND THE 'WEIGHT OF THE WORD'

As we noticed already in Cragg's dissertation from 1950 (*ITC*), Cragg conceives a distinctive difference between Muhammad in Mecca and Muhammad in Medina, after his *Hijrah*.[139] It is this distinction that

[135] Cragg *CFs*, 41. Cf. also Cragg 1980a, 202, where Cragg explicitly says that God's sovereignty is that point in Islam of which he finds most problematic. Most surprisingly, Cragg uses the concepts of 'deism' and 'divine absenteeism' to describe the Islamic notion of God. This is surprisingly because his constructive approach of relating to Islam is based on the view that Islam is theism and not deism, and thus in company with Judaism and Christianity. One reason for this intensified description of Islam, is that Cragg 1980a is a retrospective and personal article about his mission and relations to Islam. The fact that he has become disillusioned through his authorship and encounters with Islam, and thus has become a 'realist' (in effect: pessimist), is also evident in prefaces of reprints where his hope, yet often small, in what he had written, as well as a general hope for development of the Muslim readiness to consider the Christian 'commendation,' had faded. See, e.g., the preface of the reprint of *JM* from 1999.
[136] Cragg 1980a, 202. See also Cragg 1998b, 242f, where creation and prophethood are held together as comparable to the Christian notion of 'incarnation', because of the comparable 'divine/human situation creation itself contains and prophethood concerns.'
[137] *CFs*, 47, 74.
[138] *CFs*, 47.
[139] For the understanding of *Hijrah* as the point of the decisive change, see *CFs*, 12 and *WWd*, 71 ('pivotal both to the Book and the story'). To Cragg, the comparable crux of Biblical prophethood is *the exile, ibid.* 76.

becomes pivotal for Cragg's understanding of the commonality and contrast between Islam and Christianity, or better: between Islam and Christianity in their authentic origins.[140]

For the progress of my argument, I prefer to start with Muhammad's rule and organization of Islam after the *Hijrah*. In fact, Cragg does not draw much attention to this time. The reason for that is presumably that it may be difficult to keep affirmatively together with his desire for 'cross-references' or the like in his Christian interpretation of Islam. Muhammad from Medina onwards is mostly made a theme indirectly. Why this reluctance? Cragg's answer to this is simply, that whereas the time in Mecca was informed by his preaching against *shirk,* the time in Medina and the return to Mecca occur by the sign and structure of power.[141] This is the time of victory, success, pride and rescue from humiliation. The crucial Islamic point, according to Cragg, is, that if the Prophet failed also his message would. The fight of and for Muhammad is nothing else but the fight for his message, and all measures were permitted for a 'manifest victory.'[142] The seizure of Medina and Mecca in order to rescue the sanctuaries must also be read in this light: if the access to these was ensured by military means that would safeguard the worship and pilgrimages. Cragg even asserts that the Islamic obligation of submission in the end has to be realized by armed jurisdiction.[143]

Most important to Cragg, this provides the epistemological backdrop for his interpretation of the preceding time of Muhammad in Mecca. It was here Muhammad tasted rejection, humiliation and defiance. Against the ruling Quraish-clan he preached what was not acceptable: the oneness of God, social reformation, etc. The hostile reception of Muhammad, however, results in throwing him out. Or, as Surah 94.3 reads it, Quraish became a 'burden weighing down your back.'[144]

---

[140] This qualification becomes important because Cragg must defend his negative view of Islam based on what he sees as its inclination to use power in order to let the message and mission succeed ('manifest victory'), from accusations that Christianity in its historical proceeding did exactly the same. Cragg's argument is that *in respect of origin* the difference persists.

[141] Cragg 1982b, 37.

[142] This notion is used throughout *MC* but also otherwise, a term found frequently in the post-Hijrah Qur'an, *WWd,* 191f, n54.

[143] Cragg 1964a, 308. Cragg maintains that the connection between power and religion is a temptation for all religions. Cf. Cragg 1981a, 34, where this is shown in Christianity and Judaism. However, Cragg finds this to be *instinctively* present in Islam. The inherent problem, according to Cragg, is that this identification of God's and one's own power appears as if it anticipates and excludes God's judgement over oneself, Cragg 1964a, 308.

[144] Cragg 1993c, 194. Cf. also the title of Cragg's study from 1999: *The Weight of the Word* (*WWd*), cf. surah 73.5. *WWd* is precisely a study in how prophets carry their

Cragg utilizes also another epistemological tool for his interpretation of Muhammad in and around Mecca, namely that of a comparison with Jesus in Gethsemane. Cragg maintains that Muhammad in Mecca and Jesus in Gethsemane are comparable, or better: Muhammad's way from Mecca to Medina resembles Jesus' last way from Galilee to Jerusalem. Yet, this 'synopsis' is not univocal. Despite the commonality of resistance and suffering, the contexts of Mecca and Jerusalem differ distinctively, and most important: their fates entail quite divergent understandings of God. As such, their ways of facing suffering represent contrasted perceptions of their lives and missions. This aligns with what I referred to as 'contrasted idioms' at the end of the previous chapter.[145] This understanding has however implications for the understanding of the theodicy of God which I will pursue. This must however start with Cragg's understanding of the Hebrew prophets, which 'for the most part, knew exile, but not Hijrah.'[146]

5.5.3 *DRAMATIS PERSONAE PROPHETICAE:* THE REDEMPTIVE SUFFERING OF JEREMIAH AS MEDIATION BETWEEN OLD TESTAMENT PROPHETHOOD AND JESUS

The Old Testament plays a significant role in Cragg's attempt to develop interreligious relations to Islam.[147] The most significant reason for this seems to be that, a) Islam, as a matter of content, comes in many respects closer to the Old Testament world of meaning than to that of the New Testament, b) it is already possible by a comparison of prophecy in the Old Testament and in Islam to conceive patterns that bear upon and correlate to Muslim–Christian relations. His point is again that interreligious

---

'burden,' see in this respect in particular ch. I, although the whole book presents variations (vocation, personality, language, situation, conscience, suffering) on this theme. Cf. also Cragg 1998b, 244.

[145] Cf. *CFs,* 12. See also Cragg 1998b, 245f: 'Surely there is here a clear way through all the tangles of controversy to *something common* between Christianity and Islam, to be shared, *if only—*also—*to be found contrasted,*' my emphasis. Cf. *WWd,* 3: 'Only in positive terms can even negative conclusions—if we reach them— prove themselves necessary.' Cf. also *ibid.* 41 for the pair of 'common'/'contrast'.

[146] *WWd,* 20. It is crucial to Cragg that the Hebrew prophethood contrasts the Islamic prophethood and thus develops a Messianic pattern that achieves its climax in the suffering of Jesus, cf. also Chapter 4.5.3 below. Cragg also asserts that the relation between Islamic and Hebrew prophethood is a matter of different futurism: on the one hand *action,* on the other *hope.*

[147] One will find references to Hebrew prophethood, that is, Old Testament prophets, at various places in his writing. The most elaborated one, however, is *WWd.*

relations are not only matters of chronology but also of relations of content, in particular as contents are seen as dependent upon situations of origin.

Cragg does not treat the Old Testament comprehensively. What he does is to choose certain strands that impact upon his interreligious endeavours. One of these is his argumentative use of the traditions of prophets, especially those who are not included in the Qur'an.[148] And it is precisely the argumentative utility of this that informs his approach to prophetic matters. This can be easily discovered by a non-pretentious survey of which Old Testament prophets he draws most attention to, and of which play the most important roles in his argument. I think the following, rough picture will do some justice: The predominant one is Jeremiah,[149] then the 'servant' in (Deutero-)Isaiah (42, 49, 51, 53),[150] Ezekiel,[151] Hosea

---

[148] Cragg uses various series of reference to the Islamic mystical/puzzling exclusions: 'those who ... are Biblically supreme, from Amos to Malachi,' *WWd*, 71, 'most significantly of all—from Amos to Zechariah,' and 'the supreme prophets of the four great centuries from Hosea to Joel,' *ibid.* 143 (with the exception of Jonah, Arab. *Yunis*). This presupposes of course a historical dependency ('inter-association') of the Qur'an upon the Old Testament, which Cragg contends that even orthodoxy cannot have any quarrel with, *ibid.* 10.

[149] It is almost impossible to find a study of Cragg which omits Jeremiah. Just to make a selection, see for example: *CM,* 300; Cragg 1964a, 308; *COR,* 53; 1982b, 30; *MC,* 44f; *CFs,* 65.68; Cragg 1990, 184; Cragg 1993c, 194; Cragg 1998b, 239, 248; and *RMH,* 71. In his study in Semitic prophecy, *WWd,* the name of Jeremiah occurs on 38 different pages in the index of names.

[150] *CM,* 300f; Cragg 1982b, 30; *WWd,* 64f. Regarding its content and potential use for Cragg's christological 'strategy,' it is on the one hand surprisingly that he does not make more use of for example Isa. 53. I assume, however, that the reason for this is the *vagueness* of prophetic *identity* found in Isaiah 53, in particular the lack of speech and name and thus not obviously comparable with Muhammad. Cf. *WWd,* 22 and 64. I think this conclusion is reasonable given his parallel reluctance to use the story of Abraham's sacrifice of Isaac in Gen. 22 as 'a 'type' of Jesus' because 'we would have to know much more ... of the mind and attitude of Isaac,' *FLN* 251. The most important reason, however, seems to be that the personal suffering Cragg perceives in Jeremiah is the most grave and continuous he finds within the Old Testament prophethood, cf. *ibid.* 31-33. Nevertheless, when Jesus is compared with Muhammad, he seems to take over the features of the suffering and silence of the Lord's servant, see e.g. *ibid.*158. What is however *not* an argument for the servant not playing a prominent part, is its absence in the Qur'an. The absence of prophets in the Qur'an applies to several of the Old Testament prophets.

[151] Although Cragg sees Ezekiel as the most Islam-like prophet of Hebrew prophethood, because indications of verbal dictation, words as 'centres of power,' and some lack of personality (cf. Muhammad being the 'mouthpiece' of God's revelation), *WWd,* 35, 66f, he also sees him as contrasted to Muhammad and in line with the exile prophets, as suffering servants, *ibid.* 79.

and Amos, and in passing some of the other 'smaller prophets'[152], and, not to forget, the 'prophet-born' Psalms.[153] Cragg does also otherwise employ parts of the story of Job, due to his argument, cf. below.[154]

The prophet who plays the most significant role, Jeremiah, represents the inducement for Cragg's selection of prophet material for his Islam-Christian studies. This is to be derived from Jeremiah's role and logic of 'redemptive suffering' in person, implied by his preaching the 'words from God.' Cragg sees as

> the deepest truth about the language of Jeremiah ... the measure of prophetic 'incarnation' explicit in his whole long saga, his heart-travail and his personality in tension for, and with, Yahweh as literature-in-life, as 'truth through personality' (*WWd*, 66).[155]

The interpretation of this figure becomes therefore a hermeneutical key for understanding both Muhammad and Jesus. And, here is already present an answer to the question of relevance for our problem, namely: how this 'suffering role of personality in sentness'[156] is to be interpreted in relation to God.

A major point for Cragg is that prophetic suffering, although it occurred as a consequence of the people's resistance, happens on behalf of God.[157] In this meaning it is vicarious: for God,[158] but it is also 'almost as if' he 'replaces the entire people,' incarnating 'in personal burden the perversity of a world in the wrong.'[159] This relates directly to the role of the prophets in the association of God with humans.[160] No surprise, then, that Cragg emphasizes a personal view of prophecy, and not merely a verbal one:

---

[152] The most comprehensive use of the range of prophets is, again, found in *WWd*.

[153] Cragg interprets e.g. Ps. 56.8 as having a prophetic situational reference (the pleading of the psalmist with Yahweh to 'collect his tears into His flask'), speaking of a 'prophet-psalmist,' see e.g. Cragg 1998b where Cragg asserts that this psalm fits better the '*mise-en-scène* ... of a harassed and despairing prophet ... [that is:] far more exactly the burden of a Jeremiah,' 238f, 243. See also *WWd*, 34 and 182, n 5.

[154] For example *COR*, 41.

[155] For the use of 'incarnational' together with 'vicarious', see *WWd*, 2.

[156] Cragg 1998b, 246.

[157] Cragg 1993c, 195f, Cragg 1998b, 240, 242 (the prophetic 'on-behalf-ness for God').

[158] *WWd*, 19 and 129.

[159] *WWd*, 32.

[160] Cf. the previous chapter (5.4). Cf. *CFs*, 68. In this respect Cragg finds the divine-human association represented by Jeremiah unthinkable within Islamic prophecy. Hence, there is a difference of quality between Muhammad and Jeremiah. See also *CM*, 301 and *WWd*, viii.

What avails then is not the 'what' of the verbal but the 'how' of the human. We pass from truth in speech to something like truth through personality.[161]

Thus, the life of the prophets becomes 'a sacrament of meaning,' which he maintains to be an interpretation that must not be irresistible but, on the other hand, 'it cannot be excluded from what prophethood may entail.'[162] His argument, therefore, is not that prophecy has to be understood in the light of the Incarnation or the Passion of Jesus, but that the prophets' own experience points in the direction of the Incarnation and the Passion.[163] The rejection and resistance, which the prophets experienced, also entail another element: their insufficiency.[164] Cragg even holds that the *matter* of prophecy is their insufficiency, that is, human rejection and defiance point *beyond* the possibility and task of the prophets, to something 'more than' prophets, and consequently: something more than words alone.

It seems, therefore, that Cragg's exposition of the Old Testament prophets achieves a double heuristic function. On the one hand, a proper understanding of them implies an extended concept of 'prophet'. As such, some of the less flattering parts of Muhammad's life (Mecca pre-*Hijrah*) might gain some better esteem, at least in terms of significance. At the same time, the human response to the prophets, points to their inherent limitation, or even: their need for completion.[165] On the other hand, it is possible for Cragg to use this strategy in order to unveil sides of what he calls 'the mind of Jesus,' that is, the self-understanding of Jesus as 'sufferer'

---

[161] Cragg 1993c, 195.

[162] Cragg 1993c, 195.

[163] Cf. *CFs*, 65f. The terms used are: 'are' (versus 'say'), 'personal' (versus 'verbal') and 'autobiographical'. See also Cragg 1998b, 239f. The relation to the Incarnation is in *CFs* said to be 'kindred,' although Jesus is identified in a more 'ultimate sense' there. This 'ultimate sense' is normally linked to Jesus as 'Son' in Cragg's writing, His 'filiality' or 'sonship', see, e.g., 1964, 308, and *CFs*, 64 and 70. In this, there is a supreme *biographical* element: 'Prophethood has deepened into biography, 'the Word is made flesh,'" 1990, 185. In Trinitarian terms, this should presumably be interpreted, ultimately, as biography of the *God the Father,* cf. 1993c, 196, where Jesus is described as 'the divine portraiture in the human.'
Cf. also Cragg 1998b, where Cragg see the 'prophet-psalmist['s]' tears of Ps. 56.8 as 'pointing to a cross of His own at the heart of His creation.' The comprehensive relation between prophecy, incarnation and passion seems therefore to be *creation.* Cf. above, Chapter 5.3.2, where prophecy is seen as within creation (one of the capacities of revelation *in* creation).

[164] Cragg 1964a, 306. See also *WWd,* 75.

[165] See e.g. Cragg 1998b, 243f, where Cragg asks rhetorically in regards of the issues of 'the finality of prophethood' and the 'perpetual [human] rejection': 'If human history ever needed prophets, has the need ever significantly ceased?'

on behalf of God.[166] With direct correspondence to the approach of our study, the use of common factors in this respect may, according to Cragg,

search and refine the concerns our doctrines cherish.[167]

One of the results in this particular connection is that the relation between prophecy and the understanding of God becomes accentuated in a very distinctive way, in particular related to God's sovereignty. This deserves closer examination.

5.5.4 JESUS: THE CULMINATION OF VICARIOUS SUFFERING AS REALIZATION OF GOD'S *TAKBIR* AS LOVE

Having seen how Cragg conceives a similarity between the resistance against the Prophet in Mecca, the suffering of the Old Testament prophets on behalf of God, and finally the suffering of Jesus, I will now draw attention to the differences he perceives between them.

Cragg uses various constellations of concepts in order to elucidate the differences. One of these is the relation between sending and coming. According to Cragg, the Islamic notion of prophethood implies predominantly God who sends, yet does not come. This opens up for a concept of God as remote, retired, demanding, and thus, sovereignty without love.[168] Cragg's remaining point is, again, that such an understanding of God is inconsistent with a) the Qur'anic witnesses about God as Creator, b) the revelation and, c) prophethood. In connection with all these areas God is conceived in terms that reveal a closer relation to humans than the belief in *takbir* expresses.[169] These areas point to a God who comes, eventually understood in the light of Christ.[170] God's relation to humankind is therefore not exhausted by education and training but includes even 'suffering, as in a tragedy.'[171] The God who rules 'by the love that suffers and redeems' is therefore the same God who has taken the risk of human's ignorance by creating it with freedom.[172]

---

[166] Cragg 1982b, 30.

[167] *WWd*, vii.

[168] Cragg *CFs*, 69. In 1993a, 3, Cragg defines Jesus as 'God is 'come to.''

[169] *MC*, 136. This inconsistency corresponds to the difference between deism and theism. Nevertheless, Cragg labels the Qur'an as 'passionately theist,' *ibid.*

[170] Yet not exclusively by that meaning. 'Sending' and 'coming' represent *possible, yet diverse,* cross-references of creation and prophethood, *CFs*, 89-91.

[171] Cragg 1981a, 38f. Cragg claims this to be the 'map of things' of the Gospels, Cragg 1982b, 29.

[172] Cragg maintains that it would be impossible to believe in creation and God's 'immunity' simultaneously, *MC*, 136. Cf. also *CFs*, 78.

The difference between 'sending' and 'coming' is most strongly expressed by the diverse interpretations of the crucifixion of Jesus. This is certainly highly controversial in respect of the Islamic understanding of the sovereignty of God. This can be seen in Cragg's epitomizing of the Islamic reasons for rejecting the death of Jesus on the Cross, which include historical, but primarily ethical and theological reasons. These are:[173] a) Christ *did not* die on the Cross (historical). In Islam this relates perfectly to the divine protection of the prophets; b) Christ *should not* die (ethical). If he had, it would have spoiled any correspondence between God and justice; c) Christ did not have to die in order to make forgiveness possible, because God forgives effortlessly (theological). Taken together, the Islamic concept of 'omnipotence' escapes in this way the idea of a saviour and God who takes part in suffering and tragedy.[174] This can also be phrased in a way comparable to the matter of the present chapter:

> The will to rescue Jesus from the Cross is all part of that Islamic instinct to see almighty power not in a love that suffers, but in an arbitrary exercise of sovereignty.[175]

Cragg objects to what he perceives as the Islamic approach to power in this respect.[176] Regarding the historical aspect, Cragg maintains that the death of Jesus is one of the events in history that has been best attested. In general, Islam also 'needs' a connection between Jesus and history (12). As a prophet he belongs to history. What is rejected in Surah 4.156/157 is however not the intention to kill him, but the culmination (12f).[177] At this place Cragg parallels the Islamic 'strategy' ('They did not kill him, they did not crucify him. It seemed so to them') with the Docetics of the early Church, who also tried to safeguard Jesus from ignomity and suffering (14).[178]

---

[173] *JM*, ch. 6 ('Gethsemane and Beyond').

[174] Cragg 1980a, 205. Cragg 1971, 12ff.

[175] Cragg 1980a, 205.

[176] See Cragg 1971. Further parenthetical references refer to this article.

[177] For that which follows, see also *JM*, ch. 6, 166ff. Cragg sees the rejection of Jesus as a 'common ground' between Muslims and Christians.

[178] The crucial phrase of this verse, *shubbiha lahum* ('It seemed so to them'; *JM*, 170 (and *RQ*, 170): 'They were under an illusion that they had [i.e. crucified him],' parallels exactly the Greek verb δοκεω. Cf. also *JM*, 169ff, in particular 173f. That does not mean that he assumes a historical dependency between the Qur'an and the Docetics, although he assumes 'an echo in a Quranic verb' from gnostics and the Manichees, *ibid*. Cf. otherwise Cragg's view of a qur'anic 'adoptionism' (cf. surahs 17.11, 19.35, 19.92 and 39.4), *ibid*. 174 and 187, n 10. How difficult it is for Muslims to acknowledge the Crucifixion Cragg find to be evident in the most sympathetic study of M. Kamil Husain of the events in Jerusalem before and after the Crucifixion, yet putting the question of the Crucifixion itself into silence and the mystery of faith, see *JM*, 175.

Cragg charges the Islamic 'strategy' also at another point: why did the preaching of Jesus evoke such rejection and will to crucify? And: Despite God's plan to rescue Jesus from death, there is no evidence that Jesus in the Qur'an was aware of that (15). Consequently, Jesus (*'Isa*) of the Qur'an, confined as he is to the restrictions of Islamic prophethood, remains impotent but thus directs attention to the New Testament witnesses about Jesus as suffering and powerless.

This leads us to the ethical and theological aspects, which in Christ are united and which cannot be isolated from history and situation. For Cragg, ultimately, the historical alternatives—crucified/not crucified—represent alternatives about the nature of God.[179] Cragg starts, however, by objecting to the opinion that there is human evil that would be untouched if the reach of God's activity did not exceed the 'external' victory and success of the prophets:

> If there is only judgement then the world is doomed and
> God is defeated, and a defeated God is not the God we
> intend when we confess *Allâhu akhbar,* 'Greater is God'
> (16).

But what should the almighty God do with human antagonism?[180] Cragg's argument uses the notion of God's relationality as a backcloth when he characterizes the Jewish rejection of Jesus as 'a new level of rejection.' One might ask, then: new, in what way? Cragg's answer takes as its point of departure that it is new in so far as it implies 'a new level of relationship,' represented by the new *modi* of the Incarnation and passion of Jesus. Yet, in what way are these *modi* new? According to Cragg, the answer relates to what he perceives as the very matter of these events namely, that God shows that behind his law of creation is his love of creation.[181] Human recalcitrance cannot be forced but has to be transformed by love. Most interestingly, love is at this place thought of as the power by which its object may be endowed with a power over itself, which it otherwise would not have had:[182]

> When evil is borne redemptively, a *power* is released that is
> *remaking* the evil-doer.[183]

---

[179] *JM,* 167.

[180] Cragg 1961, 135. Cf. Chapter 5.3.3 above.

[181] Cragg 1982b, 30. The wordplay is of course deliberate. The premise for this distinction, again, is that Islam as religion has an inconsistent understanding of creation, cf. Cragg 1980a, 203.

[182] Cragg 1980b, 18.

[183] Cragg 1971, 17, my emphasis.

Based on this, the 'new level of rejection' should probably be interpreted thus: as 'God in Christ' discloses His love towards human beings, the opposition Jesus experiences in Palestine is not arbitrary suffering but a 'love that suffers,' and which cannot be isolated to Jesus the man but has to imply God Himself.[184] Consequently, the hardness of the people towards the 'incarnation of God's love' results eventually into the suffering of God.[185] The Cross has thus three *strands or agencies:*

    a) what men do in sin (the will to it),

    b) what Jesus suffers in compassionate love (the will for it), and

    c) what God wills in redemptive purpose (the will in it) (15).[186]

If held together thus, Cragg sees the Cross as epitomizing human evil.[187] This means on the one hand that man as evil is *necessary* for the suffering of Jesus.[188] On the other, this means that the Cross has a purpose and is thus not arbitrary (contra his perception of the Islamic view of God's power to forgive).

Yet, Jesus' suffering shows that the love of God has in the end to be connected to the understanding of redemption. If on the other hand man is seen as generally self-responsible, there is no need for redemption but education and guidance (*huda*).[189] If, on the contrary, redemption is

---

[184] In *MC,* 129. Cragg uses the parable of the vineyard (Luke 20) to illustrate the 'lifting of the whole level of relationship,' that is, 'that which 'fails' educationally must proceed punitively, *unless the 'lesson' has other resources of grace and long-suffering*' (my emphasis), the latter representing the Christian option, which is implied in the story about the landlord and his vineyard. The sending of the Son is thus seen as a new divine initiative of a new quality. For the issue of 'long-suffering' (Gr., New Testament, υπομονη), which is crucial here, see also *WWd,* 8f: "long-suffering', which overcomes evil, not by how well it resists but how far it surmounts and retrieves,' and 80: 'Only the trust that does not capitulate to wrong and evil lives towards salvation.' In the end, long-suffering seems to have its ultimate counterpart in divine *patience* and *grace,* that is, Christ's suffering is acknowledged by God, and the Fatherhood of God is activated as he is called upon from the depth of Jesus' suffering, cf. *WWd,* 137. According to this, Cragg sees an exchange 'if not of roles then of presence' between 'God in Christ' and 'Christ in God', *ibid.*

[185] *CFs,* 67.

[186] *JM,* 167. While accepting the first two parts, Muslims will deny the third, *ibid.* 168. On the other hand, the Christian interpretation needs the former two. Based on this, Cragg maintains that: 'This means a Jesus, in the Qur'ân, very like the Jesus of the Gospels, even if the Quranic 'Îsâ does not use the language: 'The cup which my Father has given me, shall I not drink it?" *ibid.*

[187] Cf Chapter 5.3.3 below.

[188] This interpretation is confirmed in Cragg 1980b, 18, where he says that the wound of Jesus 'arises directly out of the wrongness of the human context.'

[189] At this point Cragg sees the Qur'an as en expression of resolute individualism, Cragg 1982b, 38. A further element here is that Islam, by identifying its power with God's power, excludes itself from being judged, whereas Christ prepares God's judgement, *CFs,* 89.

perceived as 'sin-bearing,' the wonder of love appears as sin that is borne and saved. By this, evil also appears in a distinctive fashion as it comes to comprise not only wrong thoughts and deeds, but also suffering and pain.[190] Cragg contends that this evil needs a suffering of the kind Jesus offered because it entails both a suffering with and a suffering for.[191] Another way of stating this is that Jesus 'outloves' human beings, as 'transgressors,' in a way that they become healed.[192] Only so can the message of the prophet be confirmed, when evil is overcome by defencelessness and God becomes, paradoxically, the 'undefeated' one.[193] Hence, undefeatedness becomes the definition of sovereignty. Or, in other words, love as suffering becomes the superior power in terms of quality.

Yet, this is at the same time the revelation of something 'more than prophecy'—from within the estate of prophethood itself.[194] Jesus is the finalization of 'the vicarious principle'; he is the Son![195] Moreover, also the Resurrection has to be placed along this line, as the divine affirmation of Gethsemane, and the 'complete transformation of the Messianic theme':[196]

---

[190] *JM*, 181. Cragg sees the pain of some as the consequence of the guilt of others. He therefore speaks of a social supplement to the individualism found in Islam in this area, seeing persons as part of 'a human solidarity.' Evil is thus not merely understood as 'chronic wronging' (*zulm al-nafs*), cf. Chapter 1.3.3, but as a source of suffering and pain, also against God. Hence, the suffering of Jesus and the consequences of evil appear in one way as compatible.

[191] Cragg 1980b, 18. Cragg may also interpret this in *kenotic* terms, see Cragg 1993a, 3.

[192] Cragg 1982b, 37. His understanding of redemption as a deepening of creation, in addition to his distinctive selection of categories (retrieve, remake, heal, restore, etc.), points in direction of a concept of *recapitulation* not unlike the idea of $\alpha\nu\alpha\kappa\epsilon\theta\alpha\lambda\alpha\iota\omega\sigma\iota\varsigma$ conceived by Ireneus, cf. Cragg 1980b, 18.

[193] Cragg 1980b, 18.

[194] Cragg 1982b, 37. Cragg develops at this place a connection between education, suffering, and glorification. This correlates with his interpretation of Jesus as prophet, from being rejected to becoming redemptive in its fullest sense.

[195] See also note 185 above. Cragg seems to be consistent in his use of 'Sonship' as the 'more than prophecy,' see *MC*, 142. See also *WWd*, 2. A mediation between prophethood and Christ the Son can be found in Cragg's consent to John Skinner's description of Jeremiah: 'He breaks through the limitations of the strictly prophetic consciousness, and moves out into the larger *filial* communion with God,' *ibid.*, my emphasis.

[196] *JM*, 184. The Resurrection plays primarily the role of the difference between the completion of the common suffering of Muhammad and Jesus. Cf. also *CFs*, 12, and *WWd*, 136. The Resurrection is not very predominant in Cragg's writing. His 'centre of gravity' is without any doubt Gethsemane and the suffering of Jesus. Both the death and the Resurrection receive light (!) from Gethsemane. Cf. the last sentence of *WWd*: 'Their Easter took them [the fellowship of the prophets, the apostles, the Church] into the world where it is always Good Friday,' 166. This

The Muslim-Christian disagreement about the Cross has as one of its major elements the question about the possibility of God.[197] The way Cragg muses on this traditionally intricate matter is important because he develops a correspondence between God's greater-ness (*takbir*) and His unity (*tawhid*). The Islamic case is that of God's impassibility: if the sovereign God in any way would be capable of suffering, it would have been perceived as an immense threat to God Himself, that is, an external threat to his unity—in short, the threat of *shirk*. Cragg's question is how one as Christian may enter this issue without concluding likewise. Is suffering a threat against God's unity and sovereignty?

Cragg maintains that it is conceivable to think of divine passion, not as an external (superior) force of threat, which is rejected by the Christian faith as well,[198] but as suffering and travail within His own nature.[199] In Cragg's view, this turns the problem upside down:

> God would be denied His sovereignty far more radically if we denied Him, even for devout reasons, the power to make good His sovereignty against all evil by the outgoing, outdoing, majesty of love (*MC*, 138).

Consequently,

> to exclude the Cross of Jesus from the wisdom of God is not truly to believe *Allâhu akbar* (*JM*, 181).

For Cragg, this is nothing but God's freedom to choose His own strategy. And, why should we not ask where he realizes His intentions with the

---

fact became quite forceful for me when I heard Cragg deliver a sermon on Easter Vigil in Christ Church Cathedral, Oxford, 22 Apr 2000. When one would have expected the Resurrection theme (life defeating death, light overcoming darkness, etc.), again the overwhelming concern was suffering and 'bearing away [sin] by being borne [in person]', whereas the Resurrection only played a part as continuation and seal of the suffering, Cragg 2000b.

[197] *MC*, 138.

[198] Cf. *MC*, 138, where the "Articles' of faith' are mentioned in his respect. That does probably refer to the 39 articles of the Anglican Church, *in casu* article 1: 'There is but one living and true God, everlasting, without body, parts, or passions; of infinite power, wisdom, and goodness ... ,' although 'passions' is a rather ambiguous notion.

[199] For a more thorough discussion of God's passibility, see Weinandy 2000. Thomas G. Weinandy argues that it is ontologically wrong to say that God *is able* to suffer as if suffering was something external and accidental He took upon Himself. Weinandy's position is that it is wrong to say that 'God suffers', whereas God may react in a way that we may conceive as suffering, and which is in concord with His own nature.

creatures? Hence Cragg contends: Theism without theodicy does not succeed in maintaining itself as meaningful.[200] This is probably to be regarded as the background for the following decisive, christological statements:

> Christology is within theology ... Christology ... is the music of God in the key of humankind ... The Christ event, the messianic action, substantiates the very nature of God.[201]

According to Cragg, this equates explicitly to the formulations of Chalcedon that the Son is of 'one substance with the Father,' although Cragg maintains that 'one in *deed* with the Father' must have precedence over the former clause.[202] His point is that one should follow the Hebrew-prophetic track in order to develop the doctrine of Christ's relation to God adequately.[203] If so, one attains a distinctive, decisive understanding of God's *takbir*, namely that God's 'greater-ness' realizes itself by 'Christ crucified ... the power God.'[204] The theodicies are therefore answered on the Cross in that our recalcitrance and evil are present in the act of divine love in such a way that they cannot send us into utter desperation.[205]

---

[200] Cragg 1993c, 197.

[201] Cragg 1993c, 197. See also Cragg 1982b, 39.

[202] Cragg 1993c, 186, my emphasis. Cf. also *ibid.* 198: 'Let Chalcedon be interpreted in Gethsemane, the two natures in one achievement,' should also be interpreted this way, *ibid.* 198.

[203] The emphasis is thus on 'action' and not on 'status,' Cragg 1982b, 31, cf. the footnote immediately above. This resonates with how he relates divine ontology to divine economy, cf. his statement: 'The metaphysical Christology (if we may so speak), the Christology of definition and creed, lives only because of the actuality of the living, dying Jesus in the history. If we define our Christology at Chalcedon it is only because we learn it in Gethsemane,' Cragg 1993c, 186.
It is reasonable to affirm Christopher Lamb's observation that Cragg is more concerned with the economy of God than with ontological questions. See also p. 189, about *CM,* above. See also how Cragg criticizes *Islam* for being nominalist in respect of using the Names of God to denote divine action but not as characterization of His nature, *MC,* 103. The acute problem entailed in this, is that it becomes impossible to identify God with what the Names denote, e.g. 'God *is* love'. This relates certainly to the lack of divine-human relationship that Cragg conceives in Islam. It seems also that in respect of necessity, the 'inner divine meaning' has priority over ('as necessary to') divine economy, *WWd,* 117.

[204] Cragg 1980a, 206, and 1961, 130. Cf. also *WWd,* 115.

[205] *COR,* 57f. At the same time the theodicies are *disproved,* that is, the greatest theodicy becomes ours for the receiving of God's mercy. Hence, the proper attitude towards the divine initiative is gratefulness (*shukr*), the ultimate opposition to atheism (*kufr*), 1961, 130. Cf. also 1984, 139, but also *MC,* 139, where (*MC*) theodicy is seen as 'the fullest tribute to divine reality, the surest honesty in worship.'

The ultimate theodicy is therefore God's—'in Christ'. Cragg contends that the entire New Testament revolves round 'God in Christ' as the justification of God by the justification of the human race.[206] Cragg's contention is that God as interpreted by the Christian tradition remains consistent.[207] The fact that Islam does not see the need for this kind of theodicy shows all the more how differently Islam interprets God's relationality towards human life-world. To some extent, Cragg asserts that this Islamic attitude resembles even atheism.[208]

5.5.5 A LATE RETREAT?

As already mentioned, Islam after the *Hijrah* is taken as a complete contrast to the suffering and death of Jesus. This rather exclusive language seems however to have been somewhat moderated in his later works and studies. I find it pertinent to draw the attention to this at the end of this chapter on Cragg's interpretation of Islam.

In an article from 1998,[209] and which appears as a *novum,* Cragg acknowledges the common importance of Gethsemane and *Hijrah:*

> The central, and in measure shared [between Muslims and Christians], fact ... is that personality in a decisive piece of history [Gethsemane versus *Hijrah*] has been taken and understood as the predicate by which respondent faiths relate to God and God relates to them ... to use the simplest mediating terms—personality in travail in 'the path of God' was the context from which there came contrasted histories from which faiths took their perceptions of God (247).

This leads him to ask in 'good faith':

> Why ... this study of contrast, this perceived disparity between cross and Hijra, if from a common prelude of prophetic pain? ... Is there some hidden motive of sustaining,

---

[206] Cragg employs deliberately judicial language, which enables theodicy and soteriology to merge at this point, Cragg 1982b, 40f.

[207] *COR,* 58.

[208] Cragg 1982b, 40, where he maintains that atheism is essentially represented as 'not-God-ness', that is, in the Islamic *reluctance* to inquire into the apparent 'indifferentism' implied in the Islamic understanding of God.

[209] Cragg 1998b. Subsequent parenthetical remarks refer to this article. See also the contemporary *WWd,* 133, for a similar argument.

in a yet more subtle way, tensions and controversies we
ought—or thought—to have left behind? (249)

His answer to this is many-sided. Firstly, he emphasizes the general
hermeneutic insight that 'two great faiths serve to keep always in
perspective a characteristic accent, which, sensitively, the other needs to
heed' (252). In this he comes, of course, very close to Cantwell Smith's
notion of 'corporate critical self-consciousness'.

Secondly, he concedes the notion of power-structure as
inescapable, both in general but also in the case of its Islamic conception.
Because this is a quite new melody from Cragg, I choose to quote it in
length:

> If, as said, we cannot survive in a world where no love
> carries sins, a world where no one rejects violence or learns
> to be vicarious, a world where no one wills to suffer and
> forgive, a world where we cannot root these patterns in
> God Himself, in a word, a world without Christology and
> Christians in Christ, then too, we cannot well survive in a
> world bereft of power-structure, of the means to order some
> rule of law. If, in some measure, we have need of a faith born
> in Gethsemane, we may also salute a faith characterized in
> Hijrah (253).

What Cragg aims at, is a re-appreciation of the Hijrah, namely in terms of
an 'exodus' and a possible inspiration of liberation theology, as well as a
part of creation:

> It *[Hijrah]* signals that power is an inescapable dimension
> and just as creaturehood enjoys it in being managerial, so
> state-authority employs it in being protective, structural
> and governmental *(ibid.)*.

Consequently, he sees the mission of Muhammad in seventh century
Arabia as a possible 'benison of *Tawhîd* itself' *(ibid.)*. His vocabulary is
rather sanguine as he reads *Hijrah* as a pattern of 'emancipation, self-
help, venture and attainment of a goal.' Yet, this is certainly not a power
that escapes the risk of misuse and the 'spiritual price' of 'moral costs':[210]

---

[210] Cragg sees 'moral costs' as inevitable 'whenever arms take up a cause,' and 'spiritual
price' as required to 'pay both for the ugly things that require doing and in the
temptations of success.' For further direct elaboration on military means and
power instruments, which shows a certain sympathy for the pacifist position, see

Power will always pass into guilt, will always over-reach itself, always foul its ends by its means, and always tend to demand a false absolution in the interest of its own perpetuation (255).

Thirdly, he returns to the divergence of patterns of Jesus and Muhammad. The pattern of Christianity 'in its origin in Jesus as the Christ' has always been entirely different compared to the Islamic. This resonates with what I perceive as a consistent view of the difference between Christianity and Islam in respect of their origin. Yet, this time this difference is exposed as if the pattern of Muhammad (vindication by power) has to be balanced by 'another truth, a truth that Christianity has at its heart of its Gethsemane' *(ibid.)*.[211] This truth is, moreover, to be kept alongside the faith in power-assurance because such power-assurance will often end in a power-perversion.

Finally, as a consequence of this, Cragg seems to opt for a solution of complementarity,[212] albeit this is stated as a

---

Cragg 1992b. Cragg shows however sympathy for the paradoxes of both participating in warfare (contrary to the mercy of God) and conscientious objecting it (surviving (?) behind a shield of others' sacrifice which oneself disowns), 216. Yet, his major aim is to 'maximise all that can be recruited into hope and sanity,' 220, which in the Muslim-Christian case includes, a common 'sacramental awareness ... of the inherent hallowedness of the natural order and the mystery of entrustment with it,' of which clues are to be found in the Qur'an, *ibid.* In this he is also sympathetic to the pacifist, 'minority' stance within Islam, especially of the role of the 'private conscience' (in particular related to Muhammad Kamil Husain's works), 217. In these perspectives, both pacifism and 'peace-making and peace-guarding in the complex world' are possible options as long as *the independence of will* and 'let God be God' are maintained, 218, 220. The attitude to peace and war relates in the end therefore to how we think of God as humans. For a different version of this 'complementary' conclusion, and even with a certain displacement of the 'the centre of gravity' as shown here, see immediately below.

[211] Cf. *WWd*, 133, where the need ethics has of 'power' in politics for 'justice, righteousness, peace and order' (to avoid 'inter-innocence'!), is said to be only a *modicum,* and hence no final answer to 'the dimensions theology must recognize in the reality of prophetic suffering.' The particular problem seems to be 'the remainders,' which escape power control, *ibid.*

[212] This comes very close to the Sufi-informed Seyyid Hossein Nasr's opinion that: 'Both Christ and the Prophet, one of whom refrained from all matters of the world and the other immersed himself in it in order to transform it, were divine possibilities that had to be realized and were therefore realized by God and that both exemplars do in fact com from Him leading to two different perspectives on the relation between spiritual and temporal authority,' Nasr 1998, 224. See also Bijlefeld 1998, 215, who draws the attention to this coincidence. In addition to this complementary model, Nasr is also inclined to the Sufi-characteristic model of 'esoteric ecumenism' proposed by the Muslim convert Frithjof Schuon where differences on the 'formal

(rhetorical[213]) question:

> Perhaps it is the vocation of Islam among the religions to
> represent the indispensability of the power dimension in
> human affairs and in the will, however precarious, to subdue
> those affairs to the authority which is God's alone (254).

Thus stated, one sees that although there is a significantly more positive acknowledgement of Hijrah in Cragg's later writings,[214] there is also a fundamental reiteration of core ideas of his authorship. One might possibly conceive this as a move towards greater proximity to Islam, yet in continuity with his earlier writings, because the conflict remains between Muhammad's *Sirah* (the biography of the Prophet) and the power and perspective of the Cross.[215] In the meantime, some of the problems attached to his previous position may have received a better solution.[216]

5.6 The Question of Common Muslim-Christian Prayer: Parts, Potentiality and God's 'Nameability'

A quite different issue which may clarify how Cragg develops systematic-theological relations between his Christian self-understanding and Islam can be obtained by examining one practical interreligious issue between Christian and Muslims: his elaborations on common prayer between

---

theological level' may be solved on 'the metaphysical and esoteric level,' *ibid.* 220f. At this place it is easy to agree with Shabbir Akhtar's criticism of formulations by Nasr (and Schuon) that sometimes 'encourage both a departure from the norms of logic and a liberty to use exalted phrases of unclear meaning,' Akhtar 1990a, 218, n 25.

[213] It lacks a question mark, which may contribute to this interpretation.

[214] Yet this view still presupposes that *Hijrah* is seen as vindication. This view has however been disputed by Muslims, see e.g. Qureshi 1984, 234: 'The Hijrah did not offer vindication, it offered sacrifice—no gain, no booty, no security, was in prospect—nothing was certain except their growing faith.'

[215] Cf. *MC*, 52.

[216] Christopher Lamb asks 'how Cragg's position differs from pacifism,' and 'whether he confuses the issue by identifying the political expression of faith almost exclusively with violence and forcible coercion,' Lamb 1997, 92. An answer to these questions is implied in what has been quoted above. I disagree however with Lamb that this raises the questions about Cragg's understanding of the relation of the New Testament to the Old, *ibid.* 91. Given a Lutheran terminology, his earlier view raises the question about the relation between God who relates to the world as (continuous) Creator (that is, by the Law) on the one hand, and God who intervenes as Saviour (that is, the Gospel) on the other. Cragg's later position comes close to a Lutheran distinction, which maintains a qualitative difference yet interdependency between the two, be it in the Old or New Testament, or in creation and history.

people of the Christian and Islamic tradition. This issue is most suggestive and applies his major theological ideas to a concrete problem. This issue is of particular interest, not only because it has obvious theological implications, but also because it leads the interreligious discussion into one of its most vulnerable and intimate 'spheres.'[217] In its 'content' it resembles the issues of association, sacramentality and worship, as mentioned above in this chapter).

In *To Meet and to Greet (MG)*, 1992, the theme of common prayer is elucidated within a well-chosen structure which relates to the metaphor of one's making a journey in order 'to meet,' from remoteness to finally 'greeting' one another where 'eyes really meet.'[218] This journey, imaginatively and tellingly entitled, starts in 'Cosmopolis,' and having left 'Adamant square' and 'Cavil Row,' passes through 'Common Honesty' and 'Active Penitence' and finds 'Mutual Discovery' and 'Joint Liabilities.' Before coming 'Home,' one of the stations appears as 'Precincts of Prayer,' which rephrases the whole issue of common prayer. Between these 'Precincts' and the 'Home,' there is only one station: the 'Self in Question.' One might conclude that the matter of joint prayer is thus to be seen as an issue very far from separatedness, and very close to the place where 'eyes really meet'; a developed stage of interreligious co-existence. To examine this, let us first have a closer look at what kind of prayer Cragg thinks of here, and most important: how he substantiates the practice theologically.

Whereas *MG* reflects the general approach to common prayer, including diverse religious traditions, the 'Muslim-Christian spiritual anthology,' that is, *Common Prayer,* from 1999 (partly 1970),[219] is concerned with the specific Muslim-Christian issues relating to joint prayer.

---

[217] This is particularly evident in relation to the previous chapter, where it really 'burns' between Islam and Christianity. Whereas Cragg in the question of the different patterns of Muhammad and Jesus attained a more proximate relation by a new acknowledgement of Hijrah, he excludes the inclusion of the biographies of Jesus and Muhammad in his elaboration of common prayer, cf. below.

[218] This might sound somewhat sentimental but is in effect not. Cragg's point is an 'urgent realism' in contrast to some faith dialogues that have seemed to develop 'an air of self-congratulation, if not complacence,' *MG,* 1. In this respect Cragg requires paramount penitence in respect of 'the histories that accuse us all' and not only interreligious 'conversing.'

[219] *CP* is a revised version of *AG*. Parenthetical remarks refer to this anthology. Beside the highly interesting collection of prayers and citations found in Muslim, Christian and 'non-believing' sources under the themes: 'praise,' 'penitence' and 'petition,' the preface ('A part of common prayer discovered'), and particularly the postscript ('A part of common prayer discussed') of *CP* are of especial interest for our concern. These binding 'scripts,' the preface and postscript, are however noticeably abridged and revised from *AG,* which comprised an introductory essay of 55 pages. Below *AG* is not considered unless for distinctive differences compared to *CP*.

Cragg's point of departure is what he regards as a 'certain kinship',[220] 'feasible fellowship' and 'common territory' (1, 120). As much as these notions are joined by a language of commonality, Cragg also use a vague approach, particularly expressed by a distinction in respect of aim of common prayer between 'something understood' and 'someone understood' (3). His drive is 'empathy,' as a remedy for exclusivism (121). The commonality-approach is feasible, Cragg argues, as long as one admits the legitimacy of doing a 'part,' not 'the whole.' If so, and if they are able to be justified, these parts must in turn be tested as to whether they refer to the 'whole faith-identity' of each religion. One will see below that these distinctions prove to be central to his whole approach to common prayer.

Yet, it is important to have clear in mind what Cragg intends practically by common prayer: It is not the formal and ritual worship, that is, liturgy, *salat*. Instead he opts for the Islamic *du'a'* which he equates with Christian 'personal devotion' (2).[221] Cragg's vision is not to merge 'those formal aptitudes which will always remain distinctive' but search for a less formal use of 'parts' of Muslim-Christian spiritual heritage that can serve in 'school assemblies, civic groups, or where people meet in—otherwise—only mental dialogue' *(ibid.)*. Though not wholly consistent, it seems that he prefers the private and meditative instead of the corporate and liturgical (126).

In the collection Cragg includes in *CP* there is no *Tasliyah* (the invocation of God's blessing of the Prophet), nor the Christian, threefold

---

[220] A very good example here is the way he sees a *convergence* between surah *al-Fatihah* (surah 1, 'The Opener') on the one hand, and *Te Deum* on the other, particularly by the use of the emphatic (antepositioned!) pronouns (Arab. *iyyaka* and Lat. *Te* respectively), *ibid.* 120.

[221] *Du'a'* is derived from the verb *da'a* (vd'w) which in its verbal noun (*du'a'*) means a prayer, supplicaton, call, shout, or petition, *CQ,* 358, or an appeal or invocation, or simply: personal prayer (of request) addressed to God, *EI,* 2:617 (article signed L. Gardet). This can be done on behalf of oneself or another, or against someone, *EI, ibid.* In both cases is entailed an (Semitic) understanding of the effective value of the spoken word. *EI* notices a variety of kind of prayers to be submitted to *du'a'*. It also relates the meaning to the Hebrew *berakah,* its distinction from *salat,* and kin terms: *dhikr, hizb* and *wird.* Although exposed to various discussions in classical Islamic philosophy (*falsafa*) and theology (*kalam,* e.g., made a problem by the Mu'tazila because of it being derogatory to the pure divine transcendence, but also seen as a problem by the Ash'ari theologians because of its tension with absolute divine predetermination and immutable decree), for the pious Muslim 'by and large' *du'a'* 'effects a relationship between the man at prayer and not the celestial spheres, but God, integrating and often sublimating the familiar conception of the power of the name (*ism*) over the one named (*musamma*),' *ibid.* 618. As will be recognized below, this fits very well to Cragg's 'project,' and it seems that Cragg is more interested in this popular use and its theological implications than the traditional discussions and reservations.

Name of God ('in the name of the Father, the Son and the Holy Spirit'). In Cragg's view this is, however, feasible as a means of allowing the faiths in a plural world to 'find at least some modest communion' (118). A peculiar argument from Cragg is that if it is possible to utilize the same kind of technology across religious traditions in order to control and guide within the modern world, it should also be possible to request similar moral and spiritual liabilities, referring to 'religious frames of reference' (119). Common responsibility implies a common spiritual liability! The acute question, that Cragg raises himself, is whether this leads to religious compromise or 'fantasy of shared devotion'.

The theological justification for common prayer is related to the matter of part versus whole mentioned above, particularly denoted by the terms: 'partial common prayer' (129) and 'potential prayer' (122). The Christian theological question Cragg here seems to ponder is whether it is possible to use a kind of prayer in which vague or non-specific wording, at least compared to explicit Christian or other language, can be integrated into a specific Christian wording. That is, in Cragg's words, is it possible to find an 'elastic language of the Name of God [that] carries us both' (122)? With his distinctive language, Cragg sees this eventually as a matter of self-abnegation,[222] mediation, and placing 'the things of the Spirit' before dogma. In short, the possibility of seeing 'the mind of Christ' *potentially* in the common prayer.

Cragg's theological clue is found in what he calls the nameability of God (123).[223] Based on the *du'a* and the use of God's name in *Bismillah*,[224] Cragg explores the use of God's names in the Islamic tradition as entailing, in a 'vital sense', a divine-human relation.[225] This relation is not first established by the invocation of the name, but is already there in the very name. The point is that God is by his names describable—and addressable. If not, the implication for prayer will be severe: all worship

---

[222] In *AG*, 25, where the issue is whether to use Christ's name or not in common prayer, Cragg refers again to the issue of *kenosis* and the Phil. 2.5-11. By the example of Christ's 'self-expenditure', 'seeking men', and not 'securing' God as the 'very heart of the Christian faith about the nature of love and of God,' Christians should also be able to participate in common prayer with people of the 'adjacent faith' of Islam who believe in 'the same God' in respect of theological subject, albeit not in respect of theological predicates, without using the name of Christ for, for example, intercession, *ibid.* and 1 and 14f.

[223] This term is a *novum* in *CP* compared to *AG*. The matter of the concept is also more developed in *CP*. Cf. *AG*, 22f and 36f. Other issues, however, have been treated in a more condensed form in *CP*.

[224] The central invocation of *Al-Rahman al-Rahim* ('the merciful Lord of mercy') found in the beginning of the qur'anic surahs.

[225] See also *MC*, 103f.

and prayer are annulled, as is also all faith and theology, and Islam has come to its end. This nameability is common to Islam and Christianity, Cragg contends, while yet knowing how problematic it is to state it thus in the light of certain strands of Islamic theology. To state these commonalities, Cragg uses characteristic incarnational language: 'God, in His grace, *condescends*[226] to the realm of human language and—doing so—underwrites a theology in the very context of enjoining and evoking worship' (124, my emphasis). Consequently, he asks, based on his understanding of the divine Names of Allah in Islam: 'How near, then, by these lights, to 'the Word made flesh' to 'dwell among us that we might behold his glory'?' Hence, the development of a systematic concept that holds the Incarnation together with Allah's Names by Christology as the 'Self-naming of God presented in human history as 'truth through personality" *(ibid.)*. This, he asserts, must be 'a sufficient rationale' for a Christian taking part in common prayer with Muslims, thus seeing God's nameability as a potentiality of integrating not only *Bismillah* into Christology, but putting 'the whole significance of ... Christology' in the 'space' of Bismillah (125). Hence, 'Christian abstention from *Tasliya* can appreciate its Muslim intention only too well' (130).

This would be all very well were it not for an additional moment which has to be brought in to complete the picture. This regards how Cragg's omission of the strand of Muslim notions of repentance that are 'overly couched in 'fear of the Fire' and minatory 'frowns" and finds it 'better' to concentrate on the inwardness and sincerity of self-reproach. This is not to be understood as an entirely Christian theme, and Cragg directs attention to the rich Sufi tradition. Yet, it becomes obvious how his selection ultimately is governed by his christological concerns, and the anthropological implications embedded therein. In this emphasis one should probably read an attempt to justify the Christian participation in a common Muslim-Christian prayer on a less concrete level than when Christian and Muslim prayers are prayed separately, using the threefold Name of God or the blessing of Muhammad.

Thus the matter of extensification should be clearly enough outlined. Yet, one may ask whether any kind of intensification is entailed in this as well. This is obviously not the main point of Cragg's elaboration. However, the experience of coming to a common territory where one has not been before, where one can share praise, penitence and petition with Muslims, is conceptually already expanding the Christian self-understanding, because the range of fellow 'devotees' is enhanced. Cragg

---

[226] Cragg sees the succession of *Al-Rahman al-Rahim* as representing a progression from 'who Allah is' to 'how Allah relates', or in Cragg's language of economy (*and* status): 'being-in doing', 125.

speaks, however, not very explicitly about the issue of intensification. This is the more present in an article from 1953 where an identical proposal of 'spiritual togetherness' based on *du'a'* is put forward:

> Surely the atmosphere generated by such mutuality will be the likeliest setting for growth into awareness of those aspects of the faith of Christ which could not at first be articulated within it [the *du'a'*]. . . leading inward from peripheral subjects towards central sanctuaries of belief.[227]

Yet, with regards to *CP,* there is in his intimate language of space/ inhabitation also a paraphrasing of μετανοια by 'room to turn in', which is most interesting. Using this notion he aims to assert what 'parties to common prayer' may afford to one another (131). My contention is that Cragg in this, and if he is to resemble the New Testament use as well as to avoid sentimental usage, must think of a mutual change of mind and heart, including conversion, regret and repentance.

Possible evidence for this can be found in his notion of the reciprocity of 'meeting' and 'meaning', mentioned above (128). In his reading of the Qur'an, Cragg finds something participatory, yet as human and not only Islamic. Hence, by 'meeting' and 'participation,' there is also implied a meaning. But also the reverse: that shared meaning fuses relationship. Nevertheless, this seems to be human more than specifically Islamic, which again resembles what I considered as the vaguely stated 'religious criterion' in the previous chapter the human existence, which in particular includes 'unresolved issues of integrity,' to which mutual patience and a meeting of minds may contribute (129). As such Cragg's approach to common prayer can be characterized as leaving aside conventional controversies in order to hope for their solution (131), which is certainly consistent with a major tendency in his authorship.

5.7 Conclusion

In my exploration of Cragg's Christian interpretation of Islam I have found a significant consistency of approach and ideas. The reason for this may be found in his own autobiographic testimony that a major 'sifting of mind' occurred during the preceding years (Lebanon, 1939-1947) of the beginning of his writing. This is possibly the reason why it is difficult to

---

[227] Cragg 1953, 128f. This article is tellingly entitled: 'The Somehow may be This-How: A Plead for Constructive Muslim-Christian Theological Relations Today'.

discover how in detail his self-understanding has been changed throughout his writing. However, if one asks more generally about a theological intensification on behalf of Cragg, it is possible to see his whole authorship as an extensive endeavour to reinterpret and expand his self-understanding in order to relate to major Islamic concerns. This can also be stated thus: his Islam interpretation has equipped him with a perspective by which he has been enable to gain a renewed understanding of the Christian faith.

The consistency in his writings is already apparent in his earlier works, such as *ITC* and *CM,* since major Christian-Muslim themes which recur later in his authorship have already their distinctive shapes and explanations (Jesus Christ, suffering/death of Jesus, the understanding of God, church and power). I have also drawn attention to the contrasted patterns of Muhammad and Jesus as shown in their biographical succession after having experienced rejection and suffering because of their teaching. The way all these themes are addressed reflects both a concern for making the Christian faith relevant for Muslims, as also preparing Christians for a renewed formulation of their own self-understanding. A predominant way of doing this is to look for religious areas and ideas common to Muslims and Christians, which by further scrutiny may end up as 'contrasted idioms.' These are mainly: the creation of God as sacramental, human wronging and forgiveness, the understanding of God's relationality and revelation, prophethood as an activity on behalf of God, and common prayer. In his elaboration of these, central Islamic and Christian matters are simultaneously addressed. In short, one may say that all his elaboration revolves round his intention to reformulate the Islamic and Qur'anic notion of God's sovereignty (*takbir*), based on Qur'anic reasons for doing so, but always in the direction of a Christian understanding of the Incarnation, suffering, death and Resurrection of Jesus Christ.

In a chapter on the relation between the manner in which God expresses Himself to humans, and how He is experienced by these, I have shown how Cragg uses creation as a common area of Muslim-Christian relation. Creation, which includes everything from human beings and activity to prophethood, represents, according to Cragg, a capacity for revelation. That is, God is on the one hand able to express Himself and His intention for the world by using mundane vehicles, and, on the other, humans may experience God in nature as well as in the life of other persons. Hence creation is regarded as sacramental. This fact is, however, distorted by human wrongdoing, not least religiously motivated. By addressing how this involves God, Cragg reveals a contrasted understanding of forgiveness in Islam and Christianity. Whereas forgiveness is effortless in Islam, Christianity requires that evil is borne (personally) in order to bear it away. Relation and revelation have thus to be related to redemption. Yet, these contrasted approaches to a common theme, uncover different interpretations of God's 'expressionality'.

The understanding of God's relationality is particularly addressed in a chapter on 'association' and 'dissociation', in particular related to the qur'anic/Islamic concepts of *shirk* and *tanzil*. Cragg maintains firstly that the qur'anic doctrine of the dissociation of God from the human realm (anti-*shirk*) is inconsistent with his relation (association, *shirk*) to humans in the creation, as witnessed also by the Qur'an. If one opts for a God outside of relations, one runs the danger of deism and even atheism, neither of which Cragg perceives Islam to adopt. Secondly, this has also bearing for his reinterpretation of the sending of the Qur'an *(tanzil)* and revelation *(wahy)*. Whereas the traditional Islamic view is that Muhammad functioned mechanically as a mouthpiece by the reception of the Qur'an, Cragg maintains that it is impossible to hold this together with the view of a relational God who is dependent upon and involves the personality of his messengers. Nevertheless, Cragg opts for a Christian acknowledgement of Muhammad as a prophet of God, bringing an important contribution to the doctrine of the unity of God.

The themes of evil and its necessary consequence of suffering become crucial when Cragg engages in the encounter of Islamic and Hebrew-Christian prophethood. How is God to be interpreted and what is the proper divine agency when His messengers experience rejection, ignorance and suffering? Cragg establishes at this point a preliminary common ground for seeing Muhammad in Mecca and Jesus in Gethsemane as experiencing personal, prophetic suffering caused by their messages. Cragg sees this as suffering on behalf of God. Yet, the continuation of their lives by either the way of *Hijrah* (power, rescue) or Gethsemane (long-suffering as bearing away the evil by which the suffering was caused) reveals two different ways to understand the messengers, and consequently God. Whereas Islamic prophethood is self-sufficient, Hebrew prophethood requires something 'beyond,' which Cragg sees in the filiality of God the Son, vicariously (on behalf of God and the people) bearing away evil. Cragg sees the latter as exceeding Muslim understanding of God as sovereign, because God's sovereignty appears as love and thus shows itself able to cope with evil in a more convincing way. These two differing patterns are, however, seen in a complementary perspective in his last works.

Lastly, I have seen how Cragg's theological perception of God's relationality has bearing for the concrete issue of Muslim-Christian joint prayer given his view that certain strands of qur'anic theology (the 'nameability' of God) have a potential for Christian meaning. He recommends a common prayer 'in parts', that is, by excluding *Tasliyah* (blessing of Muhammad) and the name of the Triune God from the common precincts. This is according to Cragg possible as long as such a prayer on a lower level of identification can be integrated into a Christian theology at full length and identification.

We will now turn to two chapters which seek to use the previous examinations of Smith and Cragg with respect to two different approaches to the problem of the study: In Chapter 6 I will present and use Andreas Grünschloß' complex model of interreligious perception in order to characterize the positions of Smith and Cragg more precisely, as well as, based on these characterizations, to develop some hypotheses which relate to the problem of our study. In Chapter 7 I will critically appraise especially Smith, but also Cragg, in order to develop their positions towards what I present as my own contribution to a comparative theology.

6

EXTENSIFICATION AND INTENSIFICATION

6.1 Introduction

The purpose of this chapter is a) to characterize the interreligious relations of Smith and Cragg more specifically, which *inter alia* will include a hermeneutical clarification of their approaches, and b) by this to prepare the theological discussion and interpretation in the next chapter (Chapter 7). As a helpful resource for this I have chosen the studies of interreligious perception given by Andreas Grünschloß.[1] Because this is a rather complex model, I will expound it as it is induced and developed. I will present a diagram of it, which is primarily a translation of the German one found in Grünschloß' own study.

6.2 Andreas Grünschloß' Model for Interreligious Perception
6.2.1 INTRODUCTION

The *Habilitationsschrift* of Andreas Grünschloß, *Der eigene und der fremde Glaube,* aims at developing a formal heuristic model for 'alien-perception'.[2] This model is developed in order to enable one to develop comprehensive and specified classifications of interreligious encounters (7). The other objective he delineates, is to examine whether it is possible to discover a religious 'xenology' (Gr. ξενος, strange, alien, foreign, unusual, novel) which might include a certain tolerance of ambiguity as well as a reservation in terms of insecurity and ultimate assessments, or whether

---

[1] Grünschloss 1999. Subsequent parenthetical remarks in the text refer to this study.
[2] It is rather difficult to translate the German term 'Fremdwahrnehmung'. It seems that 'Wahrnehmung' in Grünschloss' vocabulary includes several aspects: a. Perceiving (the Other), b. evaluating (the Other), and c. accepting the Other as Other, particularly by being aware of its otherness (cf. 'Ambiguitätstoleranz' as an important descriptive as well as normative term, see 10, 261ff, 292, 312f). Instead of the more passive term of 'awareness' I choose to use 'perception', which is more active and which is also open to an evaluative element. This is also the term Grünschloss himself uses in his English Summary, 316-18.

that which is religiously alien and strange has to be perceived and reconstructed in terms of a mode of deficiency (10).[3]

It is important for our study, however, that Grünschloß, with his distinctive system-theoretically informed language, sees his classificatory effort as enabling new insights for the specific constitution of the identity of religious systems (8).[4] Thus, his model and theory is fundamentally developed in connection to the relation between identity and alterity (10). This becomes evident as he on the one hand stresses the element of self-reference in every interreligious relation (31ff), whereas he on the other hand claims that the relation between identity and alterity is to be understood in terms of a process of interpenetration, where

> one's own religious identity is always crystallized and constituted anew in dependency on the system-internal reflection on the religiously alien, which can be mostly oriented either deductively or inductively (10).

Consequently, this self-referential interreligious process will continuously provide us new representations of identity and alterity (10). His hypothesis is therefore that interreligious relations are

> not only a product of system-specific or context-dependent openness towards a differentiated perception of the 'alien' but as much an openness toward self-relativizing strategies towards oneself, even from the 'alien' (32).[5]

Stated thus, it makes sense to distinguish between self-relating and self-change. I find it therefore potentially helpful to utilize Grünschloß' heuristic model for the clarification and reconstruction of the systematic interreligious relations of Smith and Cragg, yet on an abstract and formal level. This will provide us with more refined results to discuss when I turn

---

[3] Which, in fact, is one of the conclusions of his analyses of the instances of the Qur'an, Bhagavad-Gita and the Pali-Canon, see his ch. 5, 231ff.

[4] Whereas Grünschloss' material consists of 'xenological' patterns found in the Qur'an, Bhagavad-Gita and the Pali-canon, our material is Christian theologians who attempt to make similar contributions across the borders of religious traditions. However, I do not see any compelling reason why that which he applies to his study should not in principle apply to mine. See more on this below.

[5] This hypothesis refers at this place to 'hierarchisch-inklusive oder harmonisierende Verhaltnisbestimmungen' and is thus not a general hypothesis. For my study, however, the reference is presumably wide enough to comprise both Smith and Cragg.

to examine their contributions in relation to a normative theological context in the next chapter.

In the following I will explain the most important features and corollaries of his model step by step, yet leaving out certain elements that I do not regard to be highly relevant or even applicable to the material. Some aspects of it are also too detailed to highlight here but will be explained and referred to as I subsequently use and need them in the subsequent analyses. What follows is therefore an attempt to translate Grünschloß' model into English, which has not been done yet. I have also included my translation and representation of its graphic version (82f) below (p. 296).

6.2.2 FORMAL ANALYSIS OF INTERRELIGIOUS RELATIONS: THE ADDITION OF *EXOTISM* (INFERIORITY) AND *MODALITY* TO THE TRADITIONAL TRIPARTITE SCHEME

Grünschloß' first step is to expand the traditional tripartite scheme within theology of religions (exclusivism, inclusivism, pluralism) because he finds this to be neither comprehensive nor logical.[6] Based on a formal analysis of the relation between one religion (R_1) and other religions (R_n) he depicts the fundamental categories of relating to be those of 'superiority' $(R_1 > R_n)$, 'parity' $(R_1 = R_n)$ and 'inferiority' (exotism) $(R_1 < R_n)$. Combined with the former scheme and the difference between 'distance', 'hierarchy' and

---

[6] Grünschloss' work can be seen as a *micro*-reaction, a reaction at the level of details, based on N. Luhman's social theory of systems, against the *macro*-classification of the traditional tripartite scheme in theology of religions (15), particularly in the formal logical shape and defence of Perry Schmidt-Leukel, see the preface (vi) and the very encounter (16-30). His argument against Schmidt-Leukel's claims of comprehensiveness and inevitability/definiteness is as stark as the conclusion: 'Schmidt-Leukels totalisierende Fassung der tripolaren Klassifikation [bleibt] ... hinter dem in der Forschung bereits etablierten Differenzierungsgrad zurück' (30). This is particularly due to the formal logical deficiency as well as the inadequacy for comparative religion and the study of interreligious relations. A major argument by Grünschloss is that particular religions, theologians, and so forth, can be exclusivist, inclusivist and pluralist *simultaneously,* e.g. as shown in his demonstration of this in the cases of P. Tillich and the Qur'an (25). This is particularly to be expected from religious systems where various principles of construction live side by side, and very often in opposition to each other (29).
It should also be mentioned that Schmidt-Leukel, based on formal arguments, opts for four positions, the fourth being atheism. Needless to say, within the perspective of interreligious relations, if atheism is taken as 'non-religiousness', this is not a relevant position.

'harmony', Grünschloß ends up with four main[7] categories for interreligious relating:

    a) distancing[8] (exclusivism),

    b) hierarchizing superiority (inclusivism),

    c) hierarchizing inferiority (exotism) and

    d) harmonizing (pluralism)

The crucial point here is that the possibility of exotism allows for positions that estimate the positions of other, foreign religious systems or persons to be of a (partly) better status because they possess something that may contribute to one's own situation/system. This can be as simple as if the Other represents a position that may rescue one's own tradition from undesirable consequences of the future.

    Another point, which Grünschloß has borrowed from Schubert Ogden, is the importance of modality in the depiction of interreligious positions and relations (38f). The point here is to open up, from the point of one's own perspective, to positions where the possibility, but also the ambivalence and contingence of religiously alien events of 'truth' and 'salvation' are emphasized, that is, To make it possible to maintain a view of what might happen in other religions, represented in elements or in their totalities, without asserting that it necessarily occurs. One might, however, object that this option[9] embodies the epistemological problem

---

[7] On his way to these main categories Grünschloß works in a more differentiated way, most notably with additional *sub-models,* particularly in the area *between* a 'flat-rate' (*pauschal*) superiority ('exclusivism') and a 'flat-rate' parity ('pluralism'), that is, various kinds of *inclusive superiority* (36): a. (1.2) an inclusive superiority of *discontinuity* that comes very close to a 'flat-rate' superiority ($R1>Rn$; $R1=[1]$, $Rn=[\leq 0,5$ or similar]), b. (1.3) an inclusive superiority of *continuity* ($R1>Rn$; $R1=[1]$, $Rn=[0...<1]$), c. (1.4) a *self-relativizing* superiority of continuity and inclusivism ($R1>Rn$; $R1=[0,6...1]$, $Rn=[0...<1]$), and finally, crossing the 'border' to 'parity,' d. (2.3) *parity with certain differentiations* ($R1\geq Rn$; $R1=[1]$, $Rn=[0...1]$).

For an analysis of Smith and Cragg it is particularly important to have these specified sub-modes of parity and superiority in mind because it is reasonable to locate their positions here, at least in respect of the *main* features of their positions. These sub-categories are however not included in the graphic model Grünschloß develops, nor in my reproduction of it below.

[8] My use of these verbal nouns may seem somewhat awkward. My intention however has been to preserve their *verbal* character as provided by the original German use, see also note 15 below.

[9] I use 'option' because this matter should rather be thought of as a *possibility* of any position and not a position in itself, e.g. 'possible superiority', 'possible parity', and 'possible inferiority', *ibid.* 39. The aim is to establish a category that enables one to depict a horizon of relations characterized by uncertainty and ambivalence, *ibid.* The 'classic' example is of course the difference between asking whether salvation outside Christianity is possible and stating that it actually occurs.

of discerning the presupposed definition of 'truth' or 'salvation' (39). On the other hand, this position is important because it allows for vagueness and hesitation about making statements about other religions that are more sweeping that one really feels able to substantiate.[10] Throughout Grünschloß' study this holds an important place wherever he discusses diverse ways of relating to the Other. Yet, it is not represented in the graphic representation of his model.[11]

6.2.3 THE RECEPTION AND MODIFICATION OF ULRICH BERNER'S STUDIES IN SYNCRETISM

Contrasting Pairs of Concepts
As mentioned above, the main source of the classificatory scheme that Grünschloß develops is Ulrich Berner's study in syncretism, which he describes as a 'model.' In brief, one may first characterize his reception of this model as an explication and simplification of what he perceives as too condensed (47). Secondly, Grünschloß also modifies some of the elements of Berner's model (51, 64ff). Nevertheless, Grünschloß sees the model as plausible, particularly in respect of its descriptive clarifying and contrasting pairs of concepts, shown below, which serve a high degree of differentiation (47, 52). These are:

internal rationalization 1 external systematization

reversible 1 irreversible

real new creation (invention)[12] 1 recombination of the existing

delimitation, distinguishing 1 resolving, overcoming distinction[13]

level of system 1 level of elements

These need certainly some explanation. Firstly, one should recognize that the first and last pairs of concepts represent the 'bottom' and 'top' and are thus deliberately placed by Grünschloß. In Berner's model, namely, there is a fundamental discernment between a level of elements and a level of system (44f). Whereas the former represents the 'content and

---

[10] See for example how D. Tracy rather frankly admits that he has not yet reached a position where he is able to make final judgements on interreligious issues, see Tracy 1990, 97. This position of modality, it will be shown below, is particularly relevant for the characterization of Cragg's position. Smith, however, tends to make explicit affirmative statements about truth and salvation in religious traditions other than his own.

[11] *Ibid.* 82f

[12] 'Tatsächliche Neuschöpfung.'

[13] 'Aufhebung, Überwindung von Grenzen.'

material' of interreligious relations, the latter represents the conceptualization and systematization. In addition to these levels, Berner places on the 'top' a general distinction between rationalization, as caused by system-internal challenges on the one hand, and systematization as caused by system-external challenges on the other. Given his emphasis on processes of change one may identify developments both in respect of intra-religious matters as well as in inter-religious matters. Finally, Berner maintains that one should start at the top (internal-external processes) and then go down to the levels of system and of elements. On this Grünschloß does not agree with Berner. Neither does he see that Berner's categories of rationalization and systematization should remain the overriding categories,[14] nor does he want to go from the top to the bottom. On the contrary, he opts to go the other way around.

How the other pairs of contrasting concepts play into this may be best observed by looking at how Berner develops his categories on the two levels of system and elements. For practical reasons I choose to combine the presentation of Berner with attention to how Grünschloß develops and modifies his insights and categories. It may be helpful for the purpose of further comprehension of this to have an eye on the diagram below (p. 247) in order to place successively the various elements that are being added to the model throughout.

Systemic Level: Relations and Syncretism

According to Grünschloß, the two most important concepts in Berner's model are 'syncretism' and 'relating'[15] (48f). The main difference between these is that whereas the former resolves and overcomes the differences between the familiar and the alien system, the latter preserves clear distinctions between the two (*Grenzüberwindung* vs. *Grenzziehung*).

Most important here is the possibility of a meta-system level. This is for example the case when existing systems assimilate into a new 'combination.' This has to be distinguished from a syncretism on the systemic (conceptual) level, which only entails a fusion of still different

---

[14] These notions do not necessarily convey the meanings of these as found in 'common' use and should as far as I am concerned be replaced by 'intensification' and 'extensification', cf. how Grünschloß adopts these notions from A. Feldkeller below. In the meantime I will use 'rationalization' and 'systematization', as Grünschloss also does.

[15] Originally 'Relationierung.' In order to preserve the constructive aspect of this and other terms I prefer to use the verbal form and not the more 'ontological' nouns, e.g. 'relation,' 'hierarchy,' 'harmony,' and so on. One will, however, see that this rule is not sustained without exceptions, e.g. 'syncretism.' In those instances, I follow Grünschloß' (and Berner's) choices of form.

systems. Interestingly, Grünschloß denotes certain pluralist approaches (Cantwell Smith, Hick, Knitter) as inclusivism on a meta-system level (277-282). The point is that the new normativa are displaced from particular religious traditions by gaining 'recourse to a new last theological resort at a superior level.'[16]

Nevertheless, the most differentiated concept is that of relating. Within this concept it is possible to discern sub-forms reaching from 'harmonizing', via 'hierarchizing' to 'distancing' types. Concerning these, one may use them partly or in totality in order to conceive the religiously alien. That is, for example, to perceive something as partly distanced from oneself, or as totally distanced from oneself, which of course makes a difference. Concerning the hierarchizing/superiority category, Berner introduces further differentiations within these. One could probably speak here of different aspects within this category, for example in respect of: evaluation, epistemology, material and spatial inclusion, and lastly regarding genesis and temporal matters (67f). Grünschloß finds that this, which is a combined result of Berner's and his own efforts, provides further precision, and asserts that it should not only be used for the superiority type, but also for distancing and harmonizing kinds of relating. Seen together, he sees the possibility of attaining a distinctive picture (68) of how multidimensional motives and processes develop interreligious relations.

One should also notice that while these relations are conceived primarily as normative (assessments about other traditions/positions), Grünschloß suggests using a supplementing descriptive range relating to the degree of analogy both in structural and historical respect, ranging from '(radically) different', via 'similar' to 'identical' (71f). Grünschloß' suggestion is that such a descriptive perception of the degree of similarity can be discerned as quite independent from the normative developments of relations (distance, hierarchy and harmony).[17] Most interestingly, Grünschloß sees in this a heuristic possibility to gain insight into the dynamic intertwining of cognitions in the service of self-reference.[18]

---

[16] Grünschloß 1999, 278: ' ... *Rekurs auf ein neues theologisches Letztprinzip* auf einer übergeordneten Ebene,' emphasis original.

[17] E.g. a distancing relation of a religious system towards another is possible in spite of 'recognition' of degrees of similarity or identity between the two, 71. The example at this place is the Jewish-Christian relationship, which is certainly adequate.

[18] That is, to see a) which elements of 'knowledge' about oneself and the religious environment are held together in a descriptive way, b). what historical or structural role these have played in nurturing one's own identity, and c) how these have been activated and (re-)interpreted as self-referential matters of function [*Funktionalisierungen*] in order to develop explicit relations, 72.

Moreover, regarding the matters of syncretism and relating, both are determined as mostly reversible, either in the fashion of (re-)combination of already existing elements or as systematic new ordering of heterogeneous elements. It is, however, also possible to discern irreversible processes resulting in distinctively new elements. Grünschloß denotes these as evolution and synthesis respectively. Whereas the former (evolution) is defined as a system-internal process (rationalization) of originating new elements with a constitutive function for that particular system, the latter (synthesis) refers to the interreligious encounter (systematization) where alien elements come into being in a way that, in difference to syncretism, they are no longer able to be derived immediately from the other competing system but have become inseparable from the new system.

However, Grünschloß extends Berner's model somewhat on this level of system (51). In particular, these extensions are twofold: a) In correlation to the above discussion of exotism/inferiority, he makes a further distinction within the hierarchizing/superiority way of 'relating', namely between superiority and inferiority. b) He also attempts to develop differentiations within 'internal rationalization', namely as 'system-immanent changes of the self-reference.' According to Grünschloß, it might be possible to conceive a similar differentiation as within relating and syncretism. Reasonable categories range from 'preserving the 'old'' (repristination) to 'creation of something 'new'' (evolution). Between these extremes various categories are possible: recombination, shift of accentuation, reinterpretation, reformation.[19]

Regarding the logical comprehensiveness, Grünschloß also considers the possible categories elimination/extinction (decline of a religious system) on the one hand, and conversion (changing of system) on the other (72f). These can be seen as extremes on either side of intensification (decay of one's position, for example) and extensification (moving/changing to another system).

In addition to Berner's emphasis on self-referential change, Grünschloß finds it also pertinent to make self-referential constancy a

---

[19] Although this is an explicit expansion of Berner's model (51, 64) Grünschloss is not as precise or exhaustive in his definition of these categories as he is in his comprehension of the 'relating'-categories: Whereas he defines 'recombination' and 'reinterpretation' as 'combinatory reordering' and 'shifting of accent' respectively, 'reformation' refers to 'the elimination of certain 'old' elements in favour of innovative elements', 64. Hence his thesis that change *within* a system will imply either a *shift of accent* or a *differentiation (Ausdifferenzierung) of a new sub-tradition of the system*. This is a significant insight in respect of a 'sifting' of Smith and Cragg's positions. I will need to develop further these and similar concepts below.

theme (65f). This he does in connection to the categories of 'repristination' and 'orthodoxy' referring to the (reactive) stabilizing of the 'identity' and 'continuity' of the particular religious system. Also here he finds it possible to make a certain differentiation, for example from 'constant reproduction' to 'repristining extrapolation' (of internal heresy/heretics). Most interestingly, Grünschloß finds it unavoidable to make this a theme because

> the plain perception of religiously alien systems or elements is directed immediately by such internal cognition, as 'anticipating schemes' that operate systematically and selectively, and which produce certain effects of expectation (65).

Consequently, what he conceives as an interreligious hermeneutic 'level of perception,' or the anticipating schemes, must be recognized as *prior* to 'the use of information [*Informationsverarbeitung*] for conceptual relating.' At this point the relation to Gadamer (and Jauss: horizon of expectation, cf. Chapter 4.4.5) is obvious. One might thus speak of three stages in the hermeneutic process: a) anticipation, b) relating/ systematization/use of information, and c) internal rationalization. If perceived as a hermeneutic circle, however, the latter (c) may simultaneously have the role of anticipation (a) in the next 'round.'

Elemental Level: Some Additional Differentiations

At the level of elements Grünschloß purports in principle to use the same classifications as at the level of system. This is particularly the case for the matter of internal rationalization and relating, but also for syncretism. This is also basically true of Berner, although Grünschloß also lets his own supplements at the level of system have relevance at the level of elements.

Regarding syncretism, however, it seems that Berner's differentiation is more complex at the level of elements than at the level of system (54). On the elemental level, syncretism is differentiated into several sub-forms: absorbing, addition, agglomeration, and equivalation. Some of these are even further differentiated (agglomeration = identification, transformation, functional change, substitution).[20] It should also be mentioned that Grünschloß, regarding 'syncretism' at both the level of

---

[20] At this point the differentiation becomes almost too complex. Grünschloss is obviously aware of this (69: 'die Handhabbarkeit des Modell in der Praxis gefährden könnte') and makes some remarks about Berner's choice of concepts. Regarding the relation between 'agglomerate substitution' and 'equivalation', the only difference Berner notes between them relates to the function of the former as an

Rewarding Encounters

system and of elements, prefers the vocabulary of inclusion although he applauds Berner's dynamic concept of syncretism (77ff).[21] The distinction between the elemental and systemic level can be viewed indirectly when he at one point clarifies the difference between syncretism at the level of elements, understood as 'the actual reception and material appropriation of alien elements' (material inclusion), from 'inclusivism' at the level of system, understood as 'the conceptual-argumentative 'inclusive' determinations of the relations to the alien' (hierarchical-conceptual, 80). This difference is thus conceived as being between, on the one hand, relating conceptually in an inclusive way, which must not imply any kind of material inclusion, and, on the other hand, appropriating materially in a syncretist manner, which does not necessarily require a conceptual 'inclusion'.

A third differentiation of levels occurs, however, in connection with certain of Berner's sub-categories (biomorph, sociomorph, technomorph) at the level of elements, which Grünschloß suggests should be placed on a deeper level (that is, the lowest) (66). Consequently, he introduces a level of (possibilities of) expression [*Ausdrucksmöglichkeiten*, 68]. This level should comprise expressions as different as: performative acts, images, symbols and linguistic performance (74). The difference between the level of elements and the level of expression shall moreover be understood as the difference between 'material', quite formally understood, on the one hand, and 'phenomena of expression and details' on the other.[22] At this point Grünschloß is dependent upon the studies of 'linguistic content-regarding processes of transformation'[23] within C. Colpe's and K. Berger's writings on the religious-cultural environment of the New Testament (68).

'explicitly distancing replacement of the other religious system', which is not the case of the latter. Regarding the relation between 'functional change' and 'absorption', Grünschloss maintains that the difference between these has to be suggested, namely as the possibility of 'absorbing' without change of function, yet in a new context of function. Needless to say, at this point the activity of classification has become rather demanding.

For the sub-forms on the elemental level, see also Colpe 1987 who uses similar, yet not identical terms and categories. Colpe's article on 'syncretism' in *EncRel (E)* is a most interesting attempt to advance the consensus in the state of scholarship when written, a consensus that was developed from 1970 onwards, Colpe 1987, 219.

[21] This is explicitly a matter of communication, given the polemic context of its original use.

[22] The argument for this third level is that it may contain elements, distinguished from the elemental level, which are less formal, less necessary and more dependent upon particular points of view (*Anschauungsbezogen*, 66).

[23] 'Sprachlich-inhaltliche Transformationsprozesse.' For the works of Colpe/Berger,

To sum up, Grünschloß has thus established three levels within which further corresponding differentiations occur. Seen together, this makes his model extremely complex. This certainly runs the risk of becoming confusing, but may also be seen as advantageous as far as it enables one to decompose the interreligious relations and interpenetrations in order to contribute to a 'characteristic picture', especially where the tensions between and within different levels might be observed (81). Moreover, it is his thesis that the number of main types of relations are limited,[24] as are also the possibilities for expanding his model because he contends that the fundamental structures are given by it (84). Nevertheless, the model may sharpen the view of interreligious relations (85) and be utilized in as different disciplines as philology, systematic theology (particularly theology of religions) and social science (84). This raises the question whether it may serve for the classification and characterization of our material as explored in Chapters 2-5. Before I discuss that I find it timely to include the Model (overleaf).

6.2.4 ON THE RELEVANCE OF GRÜNSCHLOSS' MODEL FOR THE PRESENT STUDY

Extensification and Intensification

One of those Grünschloß encounters in order to 'test' his model, is Andreas Feldkeller. His works on plurality and syncretism in the environment of the Early Christianity[25] have challenged the model of Berner, though Grünschloß tends to think they have more in common than Feldkeller likes to admit (54-63). At this place I will only make use of one of the pairs of concepts that Feldkeller uses in his alternative multi-perspective[26]

---

see e.g. C. Colpe, 'Nicht 'Theologie der Religionsheschichte' sondern 'Formalisierung religionsgeschichtlicher Kategorien zur Verwendung für theologische Aussagen,'' in idem, *Theologie, Ideologie, Religionswissenschaft: Demonstration ihrer Unterscheidung, TB* 68, München 1980; C. Colpe and K. Berger, ed., *Religionsgescgichtliches Textbuch zum Neuen Testament, TNT* 1, Göttingen 1987.

[24] See his ch. 5, where he traces *typical* relations from within his analyses of the instances of the Qur'an, Bhagavad-Gita and Pali.

[25] Particularly 'Der Synkretismus-Begriff im Rahmen einer Theorie von Verhältnisbestimmungen zwischen Religionen,' *EvTh* 52 (1992), 224-245; *Identitätssuche des syrischen Urchristentums. Mission, Inkulturation und Pluralität im ältesten Heidenchristentum.* NTOA 25. Göttingen/Freiburg (Switzerland) 1993; *Im Reich des syrischen Göttin. Eine religiös plurale Kultur als Umwelt des frühen Christentums.* SVFR 8. Gütersloh 1994.

[26] 'Mehr-perspektivische'. Feldkeller's argument is that Berner's model lacks a sense of the various perspectives included in the perception of 'other' religions. These perspectives are based on a system-theoretical distinction between *social* and *psychical* systems on the one hand, and between a *synchronic* mode of relating to

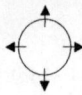

Rationalization
- perfecting
- stabilizing
- reacting

Systematization
- progressive
- stabilizing
- vertical (bottom→ top)

Heuristic model for interreligious perception and hermeneutics,
cf. Grünschloß 1999, 82f

Intensification | Extensification

Evolution ↔ Synthesis — irreversible new creation — SYSTEMIC LEVEL

new — reversible recombination

"systemic determination of relations"

Reformation | Relating (aLS) ↔ Syncretism "systemic inclusion"

Reinterpretation | Analogical relations — delimitations ← overcoming limitations

Recombination — *similar* — at level of system

↓ — at meta-level of system

old

distancing | hierarchizing | harmonizing

superiority | inferiority

Repristination

| evaluative epistemological temporal genetic quantitative-spatial | evaluative epistemological temporal genetic quantitative-spatial "inclusive" | evaluative epistemological temporal genetic quantitative-spatial | evaluative epistemological temporal genetic quantitative-spatial |

Conversion

Extinction

["exclusivism"] | ["inclusivism"] | ["exotism"] | ["pluralism"]

Evolution — ELEMENTAL LEVEL

new — "elemental determination of relations"

Reformation | Relating (aLE) — "material inclusion"

Reinterpretation | Analogical relations | Syncretism level of elements

Recombination — *similar*

old

distancing | hierarchizing | harmonizing

superiority | inferiority

Repristination

| evaluative epistemological temporal genetic quantitative-spatial | evaluative epistemological temporal genetic quantitative-spatial "inclusive" | evaluative epistemological temporal genetic quantitative-spatial | evaluative epistemological temporal genetic quantitative-spatial |

Extinction

absorption
addition
agglomeration
 identification
 transformation
 functional change
 substitution
equivalation

"symbolic and performative forms of expression" — EXPRESSIONS

Symbolic relations | pictorial and linguistic forms of expression | performative forms of expression

Biomorph, anthropomorph, technomorph, sociomorph

near-distant, bright-dark, foreground-background, pure-impure

iconographical theocrasy, quotation, topical presence *(analogue)*

conversion talk, apologetics, missionary sermon, 'dialogue', etc.

quotation, allusion, borrowing, topic, imitation, implicit antithesis, alienation, etc. (→ Colpe/Berger)

coexistence, symbiosis, synoecism, legal positioning, etc.

'Holy War', religious tolerance, demarcation, cultic community, commensality, connubiality, etc.

296

approach to religious diversity, of which also Grünschloß draws attention to. This is the distinction between intensification and extensification (60).[27]

As I see it, this pair expresses very well the concern of our study, as already developed, and mentioned, in the introductory chapter. I also find that these terms convey the meaning of 'rationalization' and 'systematization' better than the originals and will replace the latter two with them.

Religious System Versus Christian Students of Islam

Grünschloß' model aims to comprehend the perception of religiously unfamiliar elements from the perspective of religious systems. Yet, whereas he himself has analysed how the Qur'an, the Gita and the Pali-canon (Grünschloß) perceive 'alien(s)', my material compares two Christian theologians and students of religion who attempt to interpret another religious tradition, namely Islam. Should this imply any kind of problems? I cannot see that it should.

Most interestingly at this point, Berner's study itself uses for its exemplary part the self-understanding of Origen. The main points of Grünschloß' study can therefore be perceived as, with the terminology of our study, the relation between self-understanding and understanding of the Other, or as he puts it: the process of alien-perception of self-referential systems. As my material consists of two theologians who belong to and represent the Christian tradition, yet in different ways, the perspective of religious systems is represented as well. More important, however, is that they each present a distinctive self-understanding that aims to relate conceptually to other religious traditions in general, and Islam in particular.

---

other religions and a *diachronic* mode in which one uses the cultural and religious heritage of one's own on the other, 57. Grünschloss assents to the comprehensiveness of these distinctions of perspective but does not think they are cogent from a systematic religious point of view ('im Kontext religiöse Systeme'), 58.

[27] The particular place in Feldkeller's elaborations where this pair occurs is his description of the perspective of 'religious biography', as the *personal and diachronic* form of religious perception of the religiously 'Other'. With Grünschloss I do not see any reason for reserving this distinction to the area of biography. Also at a systematic as well as at a synchronic level this distinction might be utilized easily as a heuristic tool.

To represent Feldkeller's position satisfactory, it must be said that the distinction between intensification and extensification occurs as pair of opposites *within* the development of 'new convictions,' whereas the 'old convictions' persist by either a considerable *integration* or *rejection*. In addition to this, corresponding to the act of rejection and dismissal on the 'old remaining' side, on the 'new developing' side Feldkeller chooses the categories of inversion and conversion, *ibid.*

An Over-Complex Differentiation?

One may ask, is the model as developed by Grünschloß too complex for the purpose of analysing and characterizing the interreligious approaches of Smith and Cragg? On the one hand this is certainly right: it is not relevant to relate them to every part of the model as presented above. This contributes to the point that it should be used carefully, without forcing the material into the heuristic categories.

On the other hand, with a complex model the analytical grid is so developed that it is possible to use what is relevant to establish a 'characteristic picture' of the various positions, and even: of various parts and emphases within these positions. Utilizing the range of extensification and intensification, as in Grünschloß' model, it is possible to discern features of an approach that would not have been easily discernable otherwise. This is particular the case in respect of the differentiation between levels (system, elements, expressions), but also the differentiation within extensification (syncretism, relating) and of intensification (from repristination, recombination ... evolution).

Object-Language and Meta-Language

It is particularly reasonable at this place to make and reiterate some comments from the introductory chapter on the relation between the language of the primary material (object-language) of the present study and its various kinds and levels of analytical language (meta-language). Within the study, there may be discerned at least two levels of meta-language: a) The first level applies to my reconstruction of Smith and Cragg's writings as related to the problem of the relation between self-understanding and Islam-interpretation. This matter has already been addressed in the Introduction. b) The next level is now present as I aim to utilize the heuristic model of Grünschloß for the further determination of the results of the first examination of their studies. At this level the theoretical reconstruction will be stronger and more formal as the analytical resources are reinforced by more precise tools, yet without concealing the fact that this 'manoeuvre' is still a part of the process of determination of which the primary material makes the point of departure. c) A further stage in this process will occur in Chapter 7 as I intend to interpret and integrate theologically the theoretical results of the two former reconstructions (a. and b.). The progress of the study can thus be seen as one of merging the material from Smith and Cragg with increasingly theoretical perspectives and determination.

Heuristic Indispensability or Post-Interpretation?
A core idea of Grünschloß' model is that it should be used heuristically, that is, as a set of categories by which to analyse the material. Important here is his criticism of Feldkeller, whose model he recognizes in several respects to be 'a later/additional interpretation of the findings' and not 'an indispensable heuristic presupposition' (59). The pertinent question to pose is whether it is possible to use Grünschloß' model after the first analysis, the reconstruction of the primary material. Or, alternatively, should it precede any investigation of the material concerned? If the latter, the presentation and use of his classificatory scheme should be displaced to the Introduction in order to support and guide the analysis from the very beginning.

As I see it, there are at least three clues to a viable answer: Firstly, Grünschloß himself establishes a certain distance between the language of objects and the meta-objectival language which in itself indicates a certain distance between theory and material. Secondly, and most important, the 'profile' of Grünschloß' model is already integrated in the approach of the present study, as outlined in the introductory chapter (self-understanding and self-change). As I use Grünschloß model explicitly in this second lap of analysis, this does not mean that it is disregarded as 'a methodological presupposition' (63). Rather the contrary: the objective of preserving the object-character of the material, as well as using analytical tools in a way that restrains oneself and keeps the categories manageable and transparent (59), may be more easily executed in a *successive* way. Finally, our study is not primarily an attempt to invent new analytical tools, but to use a specific model for a specific purpose, which I maintain as justified from within the framework of Grünschloß' model.

6.3 'Extensification' in the Works of Smith and Cragg

I will now see how Smith and Cragg's endeavours to relate to Islam can be characterized and 'decomposed' by the apparatus given in Grünschloß' heuristic model. As I proceed, I find it reasonable to discern between the aspect of extensification (self-relating) and intensification (self-change) respectively. The levels of expressions, elements and system will be addressed successively within each subchapter.

6.3.1 SMITH

Before we see how extensification can be thought of at an elemental level in Smith's work, it may prove rewarding to just to present how Smith coped with the interreligious coexistence at the various places he taught, which indeed were designed for such *convivencia*. To a large extent this corresponds to what Grünschloß calls the level of expression.

At McGill (see the Biography) we note that he established as a prerequisite that half of the graduate-degree students should be Muslims, which also applied to the teaching staff. Moreover, the students should also spend a significant time in a Muslim-dominated country overseas in advance of graduation. This attempt at coexistence and 'co-study' may be characterized as being together in diversity, yet with the aim of learning from each other and becoming critically self-conscious of the world one jointly participates in. It seems that there was at no time any coercion toward fusing of the particular traditions.

This became quite visible at one event after having become Director of the newly established Center for the Study of World Religions at Harvard. At the top of a new building there was located an 'inter-faith chapel' only decorated with a skylight in the ceiling (the only assumed common symbol!). Nevertheless, Smith turned this chapel into a colourful library, which subsequently was expanded into a common room. Originally, having met the needs for diverse as well as common religious practice, Smith responded that religious practice was not to be shared at the Center but undertaken separately: in the Church, the temples and mosques. Religious experience, however, should be shared and his idea with the room was thus that each should return after devotion and 'become friends, as we studied together, ... lived together, talked together.'[28] With his notion of corporate critical self-consciousness in mind, this is probably as close as one might get to a physical expression of it. In sum, Smith opts for a combination of separation at the level of expression where distinctive religious practice is maintained and realized separately, whereas the experience of it is brought to and used for a fellowship across dividing borders. This solution seems to presuppose 'the enrichment of all without transfer of allegiance.'[29] Yet, the crucial question is what occurs when the differentiated practice of separation and *convivencia* is interpreted at the levels of elements and system.

This can be seen in the Islamic instance, as shown in Chapter 3, where Smith's studies of *islam, iman,* and correlating concepts in the Qur'an and in the Islamic tradition and philosophy, show that what distinguishes Islam and Muslims from, for example Christians, is not as important as what makes people of the two diverse traditions converge, namely the common humane capacity of *faith*. The question is whether or

---

[28] Smith 1992b, 55f.
[29] *CR,* 48.

not in the end the colourful common room in the library at Harvard is far more important than the church or mosque outside. Yet, how is his approach to be characterized if this is the case? A first and most important issue to decide is how Smith relates to the distinction between relating and syncretism. The question may be raised thus: Is his interreligious hermeneutics a matter of overcoming distinctions between religious traditions, or not?

On the one hand, one may be inclined to say that his view of personal faith has in fact overcome any distinction, being a genetic quality and potentiality of all human beings. His stress on 'corporate,' 'new world order,' despite all the differences between religious traditions, as a primary feature of the demands of 'our time' may also point in a syncretist direction, especially when melded (!) with a 'world theology.'[30] Yet, the problem is that Smith never depicts this faith as one, particular thing. On the contrary, he is rather allergic towards an ontological description of faith. He uses instead the notions of (personal) 'quality' and 'potentiality', and describes the results it may create in those who have it. At this place the interdependency between faith, on the one hand, and belief and particular traditions, on the other, also plays a significant role. Smith's position is that faith is nurtured by the particular beliefs of diverse traditions. It seems therefore more likely to locate him within the harmonizing position than within a syncretist position, although syncretist features belong to his approach. On the other hand, as he hesitates to make any significant distinction between different levels and kinds of faith, he does not fit into the hierarchizing positions.

However, it might be possible to describe his position even more precisely. Given Grünschloß' discernment between flat-rate parity and

---

[30] See Martin 2000, 277. Luther H. Martin's assertion that Smith is a syncretist is part of his major thesis that 'comparative religion as exemplified by Smith ... but also as it has been practiced in the academy generally, is largely indistinguishable from the historical syncretisms of religious practice,' 279. This thesis seems to be based on a close link between 'study' and 'worship'/'religious practice,' notably elucidated by a reference to Russell McCutcheon about a 'dominant and virtually unaltered presupposition' of comparativists namely, that they: 'like the people they study, are also 'worshippers' on their own spiritual quests,' *ibid.* It must however be said that Martin's concept of syncretism is too loose, particularly because it lacks an awareness of adjacent alternatives. This becomes paradoxical when he quotes a person like Andreas Grünschloß as a representative for a Smith-like 'world community' tradition (from F. Max Müller, via R. Otto and Radhakrishnan, to Ross Reat, Edmund Perry and Ursula King). It becomes also clear when he describes positions which maintain 'alternative manifestations of some postulated essentialism' as 'a form of religious syncretism.' Given Grünschloß distinction between syncretism and harmony, this cannot be regarded a *decisive* criteria, although it may be included as a *non-decisive* characteristic.

parity with certain differentiations[31] I think it is possible to proceed a step further. As I see it, Smith makes several important differentiations within his theory and theology of 'the comparative history of religion.' For instance: that diverse religious traditions are really different. They do not converge *per se*. However, noting the distinction between faith and belief it is possible to attain a convergence at the level of faith, although not in the form of an essential identity. This allows him also to speak of different kinds of faith, although he disallows the use of its plural: 'faiths.' Consequently, I regard 'parity with certain differentiation' as a quite precise description of Smith's approach so far, that is, as an incipient characterization.

I state it thus because I find it inadequate to end the examination there. His approach conveys namely certain features that might modify this verdict. Firstly, one might ask whether he actually addresses 'other religions' from the point of a particular religion, or whether he establishes an over-view from which he comprehends any religion in respect of their relations, not in particular to each other, but even more to the ultimate reality: to transcendence. In short, is Smith's approach to be seen more as 'transcendentological' (cf. his self-description of it as 'transcendentology') than relational? Yet, any answer to this is certainly dependent upon what level one operates and which vantage point one chooses. According to Grünschloß, the classic pluralist theologians (in particular Smith, Hick, Knitter) should be denoted as inclusivists on a meta-systemic level.[32] This makes sense and becomes evident if one, from this point of view, examines Smith's assessment of traditional Christian exclusivism, which he renounces resolutely. This also makes sense as far as such 'inclusivists on a meta-systemic level' have crossed the threshold to theocentric (or soteriocentric in the case of Knitter) theological 'universes.'

The question, however, is whether Smith's approach in this respect also conveys certain exclusivist features. I think here in particular

---

[31] See n 7 above, p. 288, for these sub-forms. This resembles both Schmidt-Leukel's distinction between 'radikal' and 'gemäßig' pluralism, see Schmidt-Leukel 1993, 168, and K. Ward's differentiation within the pluralist position, between 'hard' and 'soft' pluralism, see Ward 1994, 317. K. Ward, for example, defines the 'hard' version by an affirmation of the statement 'all great traditions are equally authentic manifestations of ultimate truth,' which he regards as incoherent, whereas the 'soft' pluralism, which represents his own position, is related to the idea that 'the Real can manifest in many traditions and humans can respond to it appropriately in them.' Nevertheless, the terminological likeness is not the most important thing at this place, but the utility of the concepts in identifying characteristics in the positions of concern. In that respect Ward's definitions correspond to the differentiation Grünschloß makes.

[32] Grünschloß 1999, 281.

of his criticism of Christian theological approaches that do not share his global view of something 'new.' One might object that this is not a matter of perceiving other people's religiousness, but certain strands within his own, Christian tradition. However, this will apply equally to exclusivist or fundamentalist positions within other traditions. What counts against this 'distancing' assessment by Smith, is his appreciation of his father's Calvinist, exclusivist, faith. This points subsequently in a harmonizing direction where differences in the end are neutralized. One might therefore conclude that there is certain ambivalence in Smith's harmonizing position at this point, so that it may be more properly characterized as an over-view.

This becomes even clearer when we examine Smith's position in the light of the analytical dimension of epistemology. According to Smith, his approach is determined by his access to the Christian channel of faith. In this respect one might speak of informational privilege. This channel, however, albeit particular, is not exclusive as means of attaining faith. As far as epistemology is concerned, one may therefore speak of a cluster of particular accesses to a proper way (faith) of relating, in reciprocity[33], to a single reality (transcendence). Hence, the differences between Christ and the Qur'an, between Islam and Christianity, between forgiveness in Islam and redemption in Christian theology, between prophethood in Islam and sonship in Christianity, are insignificant in functional regards, that is, with regard to faith.

6.3.2 CRAGG

As with Smith, some anecdotes may illustrate the expressional level of Cragg's interreligious efforts. The first is already mentioned in relation to the genesis of *CM*. This classic grew first out of relationship with a group of Christians in New York who had been ministering in Muslim-dominated parts of the world. As a contribution to the reflection they did retrospectively, Cragg's study was helpful as an intra-Christian source of reflection on Christian-Muslim relations. In effect this and subsequent studies drew the 'mind of the Qur'an' (cf. *MQ*) closer to Christian minds. Also his time as (co)editor of the *Muslim World* served in many ways this same purpose, and thus represented what was almost a revolution in the Christian way of relating to Muslims. In all this Islam also became a challenge for his self-understanding.[34]

---

[33] A central (Protestant) point for Smith is that faith is both a human capacity and at the same time given by God.

[34] See Lamb 1981, 16.

Another story relates to his non-writing encounters with Muslims. One of these meetings took place in Nigeria. In 1958 (two years after the launch of *CM!*) there was a conference of the African churches where Cragg addressed the issue of Christian relation to Muslims. Yet, as most of the reporters on the conference were Muslims, it happened that they met Cragg after his address, which they were not allowed to attend. Edwin Robertson, the press-officer of the conference, then tells about a sympathetic Cragg seeking understanding, and in whom the journalist found a Christian who 'understood them better than themselves.'[35] That day Cragg became their *imam,* which probably more than anything makes overt the impact of the personality of Cragg.[36] Similar stories exist from his travel to other places in 'the Muslim world.'[37]

The last matter I want to mention here is already mentioned in the previous chapter. This concerns the issue of common prayer. If there is one place in Cragg's authorship that the suspicion of syncretism should be raised, it is to his suggestion of a partial and potential common prayer. Yet, although he suggest a common devotion between Muslims and Christians based on leaving out certain features of their domestic worship, which weights for a syncretistic description, the whole proposal seems to be part of a 'superiority-hierarchizing' concept where a prayer or praise without the exclusively Muslim or Christian features can be integrated within a Christian Christology. This is also squarely the case when Cragg reverses the issue and says that the notion of Name (nameability) in Islam leaves open a space for the whole significance of a Christian Christology. His proposal of common prayer belongs therefore finally within a characteristic superiority-hierarchizing approach. At this place it is also impossible to divide the level of expression from the elemental and systemic level.

If we are to consider further how Cragg's interreligious hermeneutics are to be characterized, we may proceed to his elaboration of certain elements. Here too it may be hard, if not impossible, to distinguish properly between what belongs to a level of elements and what belongs to a systemic (conceptual) level. This is of course due to the decisive role of the elements on both Christian and Islamic side: prophethood vs. 'more than' prophethood (Muhammad, Jesus), central issues in the Qur'an

---

[35] Robertson 1976, 46.

[36] See for example how Jørgen S. Nielsen describes the way Cragg's 'personality and his unique style of speaking and writing ... spoke as strongly as what he actually said,' Cragg became 'almost a *guru* of Christian engaging in dialogue with people of other faiths, especially Islam,' Nielsen 1997, vii.

[37] I refer at this place to a talk I had with Christopher Lamb 23 May 2000 where he told me about a similar episode in one of his visits to India.

(creation, idolatry, revelation, human-divine association). What seems to be a feature of Cragg's elemental comprehensions is that the kind of interreligious perception he develops depends upon what matter he addresses. Another way of saying this is that Cragg's strategy moves from a markedly harmonic approach to some matters (for example God's relation to humans through his creation), to a quite distancing stance in regards of others (the role of power in the accomplishments of the vocations of Muhammad and Jesus). If this is right, it justifies the use of Grünschloß' model because these differences are significant in order to develop a more complete, and complex, picture of his position.

The harmonizing approach relates primarily to his exploration of creation and its corresponding sign-features. Regarding these, Cragg develops far-reaching commonalities between the Qur'anic world of meaning and the Jewish-Christian tradition. This commonality is primarily given by his view of God as entering into relation with humans. In a sum, both traditions employ a theistic, in opposition to a deistic, view of God: a common Semitic understanding of religion.

This harmonic fellowship of ideas almost breaks down as he addresses the issue of anthropology in the Qur'an. This is so because Cragg's view of humans as finally not capable of being guided onto the 'right path'. On the contrary, they deliberately choose to go astray from and object to the law of God. The remedy as proposed in the Qur'an is therefore not appropriate or far-reaching enough. Cragg finds the only pertinent answer to this human crisis in the vicarious suffering of Jesus, on behalf of humans and God, which 'by bearing' bears sin and evil away. With regards to such suffering, continuity is to be found to a larger degree between the personal sufferings of Old Testament prophets and the culmination in the passion of Jesus, and to a lesser degree between them and the pre-Hijrah rejection and toils Muhammad experienced in Mecca. Yet, this gains a quite hard assessment which almost leaves the interreligious realm of 'less-more' in favour of an 'either-or'-approach, because the differences between Muhammad's and Jesus' ways of dealing with evil diverge so diametrically. However, in his latest writings the complementarity between their uses of power is pointed out.

If we return to the subcategories of 'relating' in the model of Grünschloß (evaluative, epistemological, temporal, genetic, quantitative-spatial) we may first note that Cragg does not pay decisive attention to the categories of time and space in this respect. According to Cragg it is on the contrary important to estimate the qur'anic 'mind' independently of its place after the Hebrew-Christian history. That does not mean that he maintains a view of qur'anic isolation from Jewish-Christian influence, by for example a full-miraculous explanation of the genesis of the Qur'an.

However, it implies that the critical difference between the completion of the missions of Muhammad and Jesus can be compared on a synchronic level as a difference in respect of use of power for the success of one's divinely induced vocation. Neither is it of any importance that the event of the Qur'an occurred in the Arabian Peninsula and not in Palestine. The continuity of Old Testament prophethood and Jesus is in the end a matter of coinciding pattern, and not of coinciding continuity of time or geography.

On a systemic level, however, it might be possible to note a modified view of this. This applies first of all to earlier parts of his authorship, particularly *ITC* and *CM,* where Cragg explicitly sees Western Christianity as apt to help Islam of the East in certain travesties with which it has been confronted in the twentieth century. This, however, is not to be seen in isolation but as a part of a 'movement of faith', that is, the way Islam and Muslims encounter the problems of modernity may have important contributions to their confidence in their own faith, or they may be moved 'Christwards'. One might conclude that this capacity to help Islam is not linked to a spatial privilege as such, but more because of a capacity that Western religion, *in casu* Christianity, has developed in order to cope with the aftermath of the Enlightenment, that is, this is temporally determined.

It is reasonable to see this rejection of time and space as having fundamental interreligious significance as dependent upon his notion of a common Semitic theism. This makes it firstly impossible to trace differences back to different gods, for example God/JHWH vs. Allah, where possibly the latter could represent a demonic quality. Secondly, this also entails a rejection of privileged information, that is, Islam is not a kind of Christian *jahiliyya* (time of ignorance) which, as it were, awaits the right information in order to break out of its lack of proper religious knowledge, but is another way of proceeding with the same kind of information.

However, this viewpoint should be adjusted by the role the suffering of Jesus plays as a pattern. Is this information to which Muslims have the same access as Christians? On the one hand, especially for the force of his (apologetic) argument, one may perceive Cragg's approach as having the passion of Jesus as the accomplishment—at the end—of an already existing pattern from the great Old Testament prophets. On the other hand, it is difficult to imagine that Cragg's emphasis on this pattern of bearing evil by long-suffering could be properly discovered without having a christological point of departure, and further: a particular (kenotic) christology. From a hermeneutical point of view it seems right to emphasize the latter in this respect, as a heuristic interreligious vehicle, or even, the central normative point of evaluation of Islam as, in this respect, deficient. Thus, we have again moved onto to the level of system. I will now draw attention to relevant issues at this level, which might hopefully enable one to sharpen the picture of Cragg's position somewhat.

The level of system is mostly represented by what I have called the general context of Cragg's interreligious hermeneutics, or simply, his interreligious hermeneutics (Chapter 4). Although one might see that chapter consisting of many 'elements,' for example the Holy Spirit and Christ, the perspective is that of Christianity relating to other religions. In that respect, therefore, the elements are connected to this general perspective. That does not mean, as we have seen, that for example Christ cannot be explored in his elemental relation to certain elements of Islam.

Concerning extensification (systematization) within Cragg's works, and given the model of Grünschloß and Berner, it might be reasonable first to clarify how Cragg relates to the fundamental difference between syncretism and relating. The keywords here are 'delimitation, distinguishing' vs. 'resolving, overcoming distinction'. As Cragg in many respects can be said to be an evangelical theologian and missionary, one would rather expect him to be inclined to an exclusivist position and thus draw a sharp distinction between his Christian faith and 'other religion'. This is, however, not the case. On the contrary, Cragg explicitly renounces exclusivism and its 'dread of syncretism,' and affirms a 'finer possibility' of non-immunity and mediation. Yet, there is no reason to call this a syncretism proper, although his position is directed more toward syncretism than the distancing position he calls 'paralysis with dogma.' There is no doubt that Cragg maintains his Christian faith as distinct from, for example, the faith of Muslims. Yet, on the other side we have seen how Cragg develops a view of commonalities, particularly regarding the human existence. This is, however, not done in a manner that proposes a syncretist framework. In other words: Cragg is a man of relations. The subsequent question must therefore be: what kind of relations does he aim to develop?

Cragg does not seem particularly inclined to a harmonizing position. Even when his approach to Islam must be said to be sympathetic, his conclusions in respect of difference and controversy are quite confrontational. And, although he may very often begin with commonalities and continuities between Islam and Christianity, in the end, and especially as seen together, the discontinuities and conflicts are as important as the affirmations and agreements. Hence flat-rate parity and parity with certain differentiations seem to be excluded as characterizations of Cragg's position.[38]

Based on his rather stark criticism of the custodian-minded exclusivists (e.g. Brunner, Barth, Tomko, Newman), most probably to be seen as a reaction against his own religious background, it is possible, as

---

[38] For these sub-forms, see note 7 above, p. 288.

aforementioned, to place him within a hierarchizing position, and then particularly within the superiority, inclusivist kind. I say 'particularly' because reasons may be given for the claim that Cragg actually sees the Christian view as 'the least one,' the minor powerless one, based on Gethsemane as his normative point of departure. To this, his rephrasing of the traditional 'extra ecclesiam nulla salus' by *infra ecclesiam salus est* correlates (*MG* 157). Thus, his perspective is from 'below.' This is also underlined by his attention to Christian self-criticism.[39] In this particular respect the sub-form of self-relativizing superiority might apply to Cragg.

Yet, there is no doubt that he employs a range where primarily Jesus as 'love who suffers' is given 'the highest score,' yet at the bottom, whereas 'prestige and power' are located as the distortion, yet at the apparent top (cf. the spatial location of Gethsemane and the Dome of the Rock!). That this is the case becomes evident if we ask whether Cragg at any point see any reason for converting from one faith to another. As the answer is Yes! as he commends conversion to Christ (not primarily Christianity), the alternative of inferiority/exotism seems in the end to be irrelevant to Cragg.

The reason for this is found if we ask how Cragg is to be characterized within a superiority-hierarchizing way of relating. Again the matter of Christic pattern seems to be most significant. There is as we have seen a characteristic differentiation within Cragg's interreligious hermeneutics. This differentiation is firstly represented by his emphasis on the common human existence that every human being has to ponder (identical human challenge), then further by his emphasis on the one God and unitary revelation (single ultimate reality), and finally to what extent various religions make a theme the interaction between God and human, particularly expressed by the pattern which correlates with God's kenosis in the creation, the Incarnation and by the Holy Spirit. It is particularly in relation to this latter pattern that the evaluative becomes so significant in respect of the extent to which this kenotic reality is received and perceived in the various religious traditions. Whereas the former two differentiations facilitate a certain unity between religions, the latter makes the difference in respect of fullness obvious, that is, a ranking with a certain element of discontinuity. Hence there is evidence for placing Cragg within a position both of inclusive superiority of continuity as well as within one of inclusive superiority of discontinuity.[40]

---

[39] One may ask whether the matter of self-criticism should not be made a theme under 'intensification' and not here. Cragg's point here is, however, that confronted with the Gospel, Christianity (as all religions) is 'evaluated.' The matter of self-criticism here is thus not primarily of interreligious character.

[40] See note 7 above, p. 288 for these sub-forms.

The major qualifying point in Cragg's approach is therefore evaluative and theological. To some extent one might say that Cragg is a-historical when he compares the Christic pattern in Christianity and Islam. His extensive use of the Qur'an and not the tradition and traditional exegesis also points in this direction. This pattern is shaped in a way which makes it possible to apply it to phenomena outside the Jewish-Christian traditions. Yet, this does not take into full account how Cragg presupposes the genesis of the pattern. My contention is that an adequate understanding of this pattern must recognize how it represents his general interpretation of who God is according to how he acts in history and how He has been testified in the Jewish-Christian Scriptures. Thus Muhammad is measured by a historical-Scriptural pattern.

Nevertheless, it bears the assets of a pattern, an idea. With Grünschloß one may well call this a reduction of complexity[41] as it sets out to reduce the complexity of Islam to a question of how Muhammad aligns to a Jewish-Christian pattern. The result is, however, that Cragg by this 'operation' is able to combine harmonizing affirmations (of Muhammad in Mecca) as well as with distancing criticism (of Muhammad after Hijrah). Yet, as this is seen within a unitary or common perspective, although not affirming any essential identity, it is more likely to produce a hierarchy of responses to this pattern, rather than either distancing or harmonizing responses. Nevertheless, at this point, which comes close to the core of how Cragg 'extensifies' his Christian faith on the systemic level, it is clear that a complex model of determining his interreligious perception is important for drawing an appropriate characteristic picture of it. Using traditional tri-partite language: Cragg is pluralist, exclusivist, and particularly inclusivist. Yet, the most important benefits of the use of the model are: firstly, the possibility of distinguishing Cragg's approach from adjacent positions, and secondly how it enables a differentiation within the traditional inclusivist position.

Another feature is also that Cragg appears as more harmonious at the level of system than on the elemental level. This might be seen as a result of the controversy he depicts between the 'personal history'-patterns of Jesus and Muhammad. It might also be connected to his reluctance to conclude explicitly on the theological assessment of other religions as seen in Chapter 4.4.4. This agnostic position, which is 'reinforced' throughout his authorship, leaves him inevitably with some rather harmonizing characteristics.

---

[41] Grünschloss 1999, 250.

6.3.3 COMPARISON

Despite my different placing of Smith and Cragg according to Grünschloß' model and various differentiations, there is much in common between the two. I find it important to take this as a point of departure for a comparison.

Significantly, both operate with a single transcendent reality. Whether this is called God, ultimate reality or the t/Transcendent, people of the world are not divided due to a plurality of gods or transcendences. This is also the case with their view of human beings where they operate with a set of commonalities. In short, the human condition is shared. The obvious result of this is that it is possible to operate within a considerable framework which people of diverse traditions share.

At the same time, the understanding of the limits of such commonalities is where Cragg leaves Smith. Whereas Smith sees the human capacity of faith as the most fundamental element of his theology of comparative religion, and thus as sufficient, Cragg maintains that this human capacity has to be qualified by the proper divine remedy for its inherent problem of evil (need for redemption), that is, it has to be qualified by Christ. Hence it is not only faith that is important, but also Christ who defines what we can have faith in, or in the cases where Christ is not properly known, how Christ may fulfil what seems to be directed Christwards.

Again, I think it is possible to talk about a reduction of complexity in Cragg's writing at this point. In Cragg's case the Christic pattern, 'love who suffers,' works as a guiding principle and criteria for his perception of how his Christian faith may relate, and in fact relates, to foreign religiousness. This is simultaneously the place where there is another correlation with Smith. As we have seen, in Smith's case the distinction between 'faith' and externals, or particulars, is fundamental as a guiding principle. A reduction of complexity is inherent to both his general theory and theology of religiousness. The difference in respect of their approach to complexity-reducing ideas and patterns is, however, that Smith seems to have placed his emphasis on faith relative to Christology, but not necessarily dependent upon Christology, whereas the Christ-event and the stories of Jesus are determinative for the development of the Christic pattern according to Cragg. It seems to me that this has as a consequence that relations between Christian faith and Islam as conceived by Cragg gain more dynamic both in respect of discovery of commonalities and emphasis on contrasts, whereas relations in Smith's approach tend to delete such relations as they are aligned to the ultimate level of faith-convergence.

6.4 'Intensification' in the Works of Smith and Cragg
6.4.1 SMITH

I think it is quite reasonable to understand the faith-belief distinction in Smith's writing as equivalent to the elemental and systemic levels in Grünschloß' model. Although the pair itself is a matter of Smith's distinctive conceptualization, I find his distinction in this case, between external (beliefs, believing, religious complexes) and internal (faith) aspects of religiousness, to resemble the elemental-systemic levels as provided by Grünschloß. Given his differentiation of faith however, as especially shown in Grünschloß' dissertation on Smith, this is not that simple. We may therefore put it like this: the most important concept at the level of system: faith, is at the same time not excluded from playing a role at the elemental level.

Nevertheless, at the elemental level Smith's main point is that any religious tradition is part of the historical processes that intertwine diverse religious traditions. In these complex processes Smith has shown quite convincingly how certain beliefs may change throughout history, especially as the contact with other traditions is extensive and sustained. In this flux, the main characteristic is simply change, which of course also applies to Christian ways of having faith.

Yet, from within such a perspective of historical processes Smith proposes a qualitative difference between particularity and generality. For his own part, his studies of certain Islamic elements, in particular the meanings of *islam*, *iman*, 'Scripture/Qur'an', *Shahadah*, and *arkan*, induce his general distinction between faith and belief and in turn lead him to a new understanding of the foundations of his own faith. This new understanding is that faith should be perceived as a generic human quality and thus a part of the universal history of salvation, and not a faith confined to a particular (for example Christian) tradition. Stating it thus, in effect he operates on a systemic level.

Yet, this obvious self-change, which implies a radical departure from a christocentric theology, deserves closer attention. Given the fundamental role and priority of personal faith over cumulative tradition and beliefs, there is a certain stability within the whole 'quality' of faith. Change of beliefs may thus not necessarily imply alteration of one's faith, although it is likely that we should think of an inescapable dynamic of change within faith also (Smith: 'any one man's faith is different any given morning from what it was the preceding afternoon'[42]). This is,

---

[42] *ME*, 190.

however, not to be regarded as an evolution of faith, but as a growing and living (with)in faith.

Smith is eager to maintain that what he is proposing is a vision that is in continuity with certain strands of the past. One might venture to call it a pretentious 'neoclassicism,' which is at the same time, in Smith's terms, global, humanist and religious. His language in this respect is that of reformation, not primarily in terms of 'the elimination of certain 'old' elements in favour of innovative elements,'[43] but to bring the present expression of Christian faith, that is, of faith, back to what it was previously. Structurally, therefore, one might thus discern a similarity between him and the (Protestant) Reformers. Anyway, Smith does not hesitate to see himself as, in many ways, a reformer.

Yet, there is another feature of this rhetoric that moves in a revolutionary direction, and this may very well correspond with the fact that any determination of intensification in Smith's case depends on which vantage point one chooses to use. If one chooses to use what may loosely be called a traditional Christology or a christocentric theology, Smith can be said to cross the threshold to evolution. Smith would probably agree with this as he untiringly announces that 'something new' is about to come, and, normatively, has to come. What he would not agree with, however, is that this excludes his view from being Christian, although only *inter alia*. As we have noticed, his assertion is that his view of faith is channelled through Christ, as is also his view of others' faith. Yet, this view is not in the end held as a particular view, but as a 'God's eye view.' Hence, Smith steps up to a higher-level vantage point. The question is whether S. Mark Heim is right in, more generally, characterizing the position of the pluralist 'fathers' J. Hick, P.F. Knitter and Smith this way: That they develop new religious positions.[44] I see this as corresponding to what Grünschloß calls inclusivism at a meta-systemic level,[45] which, most interestingly, seems to include certain exclusivist assets once having established this kind of position.[46] I therefore find it reasonable to characterize the intensification in Smith's interreligious hermeneutics as evolution in relation to the old-new axis, and as something that at the same time appears to be far less and far more than a theology defined by Christology, that is, Smith appreciates Christian faith, but disallows any talk about *the* Christian faith. The question is whether Smith does two things at once: a) Extinction of a christocentric theology and b) evolution into another religion: transcendentology, which includes a shift of level

---

[43] Cf. Grünschloß' definition, note 19 above.
[44] Heim 1995, 129f. See also my article Mæland 2000, 296.
[45] Grünschloß 1999, 281.
[46] Heim 1995,

from a level where relations are important to a level where the (converging) 'essential' religiousness of people plays down any 'accidental' religious difference. Using his own language: It seems that the so-called religiousness in the world has been 'Platonized' corporatively by Smith, whereas all 'externals,' including 'the Christian faith', have been 'Aristotelianized'.[47] The question is whether interreligious relations remain meaningful when their importance is diminished as a result of his prioritizing of faith over belief.

The argument against this negative assessment is that he still only speaks of divergence vs. convergence, and not, regarding the latter, of ultimate identity. Nevertheless, given his emphasis on this as a human quality, potential, and so on, it seems likely that we should see faith as only a distinctive version of a human *existential,* eventually entailing a kind of humanist mysticism where relations in the end are subordinated to the unitary universal: faith.

6.4.2 CRAGG

If we turn our attention to Cragg, there is little doubt that there is an element of intensification in his writing. As I have shown, this can be traced back to his dissertation from 1950, and is in fact most prominently expressed there, a work which in many ways is an elaboration on his experiences of the world which he met when he served in Beirut in the 40s. Since then his theology has been a 'negotiated' theology, cf. *FLN*. I will now give some clues to how intensification in the case of Cragg can be depicted in the light of Grünschloß' model.

In one way the matter is as simple as this: Cragg is energetically wanting to communicate the Gospel to Muslims. Yet the Gospel as traditionally presented to Muslims is to a large extent misunderstood. This was at his bitter experience in Lebanon. In order to be understood properly Cragg therefore returns to central Christian truths, which he reconsiders and to some extent rephrases with the qur'anic world of meaning in mind.

At the systemic level Cragg has been forced to work out how his Christian theology and faith can be developed, having been confronted with the challenge of Islam. In his theological autobiography (*FLN*) this is seen as a negotiation between life and faith. This seems particularly to have been realized through his elaboration on what he calls the 'open

---

[47] Cf. *ME* where he characterizes people who idealize only their own position: 'This is to look for essences; to Platonize one's own faith and to Aristotelianize other Peoples,' 57.

faith' and the 'omni-active' Spirit. This is moreover present in his dissertation where he speaks of Christianity as thrown uniquely back upon its most distinctive truths and its most ultimate reserves of the Spirit by Islam. This means that the challenge of Islam demands an elucidation of the Christian faith, not only on the surface but in its depths. It seems however that Cragg is quite reluctant to admit any kind of agnostic 'interludes.'[48] The degree of intensification is therefore rather to be understood as clarification as well as an activating of larger parts of the Christian faith, which would otherwise not have occurred. In *FLN* this view is confirmed:

> What Blackpool held for me in boyhood is still where my
> conclusion has arrived, knowing it the larger and the deeper
> for what it has traversed (256).

The intensification may thus not only be seen as a matter of innovative reformulation, but also rather of reactivating and uncovering of elements already existent in his Christian faith and theology. My suggestion is that Grünschloß' scheme should be enhanced at this point, although I affirm the validity of his foundational alternatives: a) 'shift of accent' (recombination, reinterpretation, etc.) and b) 'differentiation of a new sub-tradition of the system' (reformation).[49] I think the former of these options suits Cragg better as a characterization than the latter (which fits Smith far better). Whether it suffices to speak of these on a scale between 'old' and 'new' is debatable. My suggestion is that one should also think of intensification in quantitative-spatial terms: of 'more' vs. 'less' (fullness/size), 'deep' vs. 'shallow' (depth), and so on, that is, to what extent one's self-understanding is expanded, supplemented, on the one hand, or diminished or threatened by the challenge of other religions, on the other. The latter element would thus in its extreme resemble the possibility of extinction in Grünschloß' model. Cragg's notion of a 'sanctuary of incorporation' also contributes to my suggestion that intensification in the case of Cragg is as much a matter of incorporative expansion as, for example, revision vs. repristination in 'innovative' terms.

---

[48] Cf. my interview of him 21 May 2000, Cragg 2000d. See also note 51 below. There, Cragg explicitly rejected more radical notions like 'reformation', 'evolution', but also 'rediscovery', all for the reason that they presupposed an interim period of agnosticism which had never been his case. In another interview, Cragg 2000c, he deliberately used the term 'reconsideration' to describe the response to the 'force of rejection.' Yet, such a reconsideration is in his case to be 'of what you always have said.'

[49] For these alternatives, see note 19 above, p. 292.

Finally, one should also give due recognition to how the drive and power of Cragg's interreligious hermeneutics is ultimately linked to his Pneumatology. The continuous 'proceeding' of the Holy Spirit from God into the world, rules out any rationalization understood as 'self-possession.' The divine kenosis in the Incarnation and the Holy Spirit can similarly only be realized as self-expenditure. I think it is pertinent to see in this continuous movement also a steady request for a certain development of what one has to 'commend,' and thus some degree of self-change, albeit not in very radical sense. Cragg's way of having this is that mission is always education of the content of one's own faith.[50]

If we proceed from his engagement with general interreligious hermeneutics to his particular encounter with Islamic 'elements,' the matter of intensification is probably less obvious. One may indeed ask: is there any sign of change in his Christian self-understanding throughout his comprehension of Muslim 'faith-ing'? An answer to this can be proposed from different angles. One is to see Cragg's emphasis on the open, self-expending faith and the work of the Holy Spirit as reaction against what he perceives as the rather static and exclusive system of Islam. Reading his personal article on 'Being Christian and being Muslim' from 1980 may contribute to this view, as may also the way he perceives the 'Tribunal of Islam' in *FLN*.

A negative way of stating a conclusion would be to say that it is unlikely that his self-understanding has not been reinforced by his encounter with Islam. If so, this is to maintain that there is a movement from 'old' to 'new' in respect of emphasizing the element of flexibility, openness and willingness to reformulate. However, what I positively have discerned in both his general hermeneutics and his interpretation of Islam is a reaction against 'orthodoxy' and 'dullness' respectively. These labels apply both to Christian closed-mindedness in general, and to cowardly and unimaginative attempts to relate Christian faith to Muslims.

Yet, there is nothing to bear out an assertion that something quite new results from this reaction. Hence there is no 'reformation,' not to say 'evolution,' implied. I do not even think there is a rediscovery in all this, only a movement in reaction against the 'custodian minds' of both Christians and Muslims, and towards a more creative expression of the Christian faith, which hopefully turns out to be more accessible and perceptive for Muslims. This corresponds to his own careful gentleman's way of having it: refinement, elucidation and purification.[51] This, however,

---

[50] Cragg 2000c.

[51] 'Refinement' is the term Cragg himself preferred to use when I interviewed him 21 May 2000 and asked him to characterize how his encounter with Islam has had any impact upon his Christian theology, Cragg 2000d. Cf. also his letter to me dated 29

comes very close to Gadamer's idea of the 'interior word' (cf. Chapter 4) as the hermeneutic universal. 'Refinement' is also a useful description of the conversation structure of hermeneutics as viewed by Gadamer. As such there is a movement within Cragg's horizon, a self-converse, which also includes elements of self-interrogation and self-criticism.

This view of 'movement-within' is reinforced by the fact that despite Cragg's Christian faith being inherently creative and self-giving, there is no way of overcoming its identity (with God in Christ and in the Holy Spirit) by being risky and elastic. It is all included in its inducement and authentic origin, that is, its decisive precedents in the Old and New Testament. Given this identity, one might subsequently say that the alternatives that really matter for Cragg are those of the closed mind versus the perceptive mind. His proposal is that the threshold to the latter has to be risked if one is to respond properly to the gospel as well as to one's addressees. In short, but differently put, the intensified Cragg is not so much a reformer or reviser as he is the perceptive theological poet who refines the original and unsurpassable story and doctrine of Christ for the Muslim mind.

6.4.3 COMPARISON

Andreas Grünschloß refers at one place in his book on interreligious perception to N. Luhmann who contends that a necessary prerequisite for evolution is that the 'self-reproduction' (intensification) happens 'on the basis of unstable elements.'[52] This point may prove helpful for a brief comparison of Smith and Cragg.

As we noted in relation to Cragg, his writings seem in the end to lack unstable and unsettled elements. He also confirms this regarding the coincidence of his boyhood faith and his faith as an 81-year-old-man (*FLN*, at the time it was written). His moving away from an 'orthodox' (closed-minded) faith to a more imaginative and risk-taking one may thus be seen as a movement within his settled horizon. On the other hand, however, we noticed an agnostic feature in his theology of religions in general. If taken as a symptom of a lack of fixedness of his position in

---

May 2000, Cragg 2000e: 'Open listening [to Islam] proved enriching because it demanded a refining (not abandoning) of what was always held ... The Muslim perception—if heeded—had the potential to elucidate and hopefully purify one's commendation of the meaning ... Hermeneutics, thus, is not only 'domestic' attention to the text but also existing in interfaith discourse in hope of inner honesty.'

[52] Grünschloß 1999, 289. This refers to N. Luhmann, *Soziale Systeme: Grundriß einer allgemeinen Theorie,* Frankfurt 1984/1987, 502f.

relation to other religious traditions, one might at least admit an unsettled element here. This unsettledness is to be awaited from a position that aims to develop an open theology that is perceptive and hospitable, yet determined by decisive particular 'precedents.' This unsettledness seems, however, to be 'settled' or served by the wide-ranging kenotic shape of his theology.

If we consider Smith's writings there is not only a readiness but also a demand to shift from a christocentric view to a theocentric organization (or pistocentric or transcendentocentric). My contention is that because of the radicality of the shift it should be called evolution. I think this is so even if he himself tends to be attracted to a 'reformatory' description of his theory and theology, especially because he sees his view as an expression found in older times and theology. Nevertheless, Smith's own implicit argument for this kind of change is primarily induced by his assertion that a christocentric (not to say ecclesiocentric) view is unstable in the 20th century global environment, and thus in need of being replaced by a grander view: a world theology.

What seems to be an interesting common feature of both Smith and Cragg, however, is that both achieved settled views during and shortly after their dissertations. Since then there are only minor developments, many of which can be most easily foreseen provided by what they previously had proposed and produced. Yet I do not think it is right to say that this stabilization occurs by necessity.[53] On the other hand, I regard it possible to explain it hermeneutically. This is demonstrated in one of the hypotheses which follows.

6.5 Hypotheses

One of the questions that my study raises is whether there can be located any correlation between extensification and intensification. Is it, for example, possible to induce any general hypotheses from the material I have examined and classified so far? I think so, although these will have

---

[53] Cf. P.F. Knitter who first moved to a theocentric position, cf. Knitter, and then to a soteriocentric (a theology of religions informed heavily by theology of liberation). Another comparable example that people who for a long time have sustained a position eventually move to another can be seen in G. D'Costa's latest writing, cf. D'Costa 2000. From being one of the most prominent spokesmen for the Rahnerian inclusivist position, cf. D'Costa 1985 and 1990b, he has now moved in direction of a quite exclusivist position, cf. D'Costa 2000, informed by e.g. J. Milbank, A. McIntyre, and also, I was told in a conversation with him 30 March 2000, by some of his evangelical post-graduate students.

to be reinforced with or criticized by additional material if they are to gain further validity.

To me it seems first of all clear in the case of Smith and Cragg that *their Christian self-understanding and their attempts to interpret the Islamic tradition are mutually interdependent.* By this I mean that it is possible to discover a line between central features of their Christian self-understanding and what they emphasize in Islam. That these are 'interdependent' means that there is a connection between the two without saying that this can be definitely traced back to either extensification (by means of prejudices, fore-meanings) or intensification (as a matter of Islamic influence).

I think, however, that it is reasonable to maintain that *the kind and degree of intensification is dependent upon the degree of extensification.* By this I will assert that the ways in which Smith and Cragg attempt to relate their normative Christian self-understanding to Islam affect how their Christian self-understandings are developed or changed in these encounters. In Smith's case an inclusive relation to Islam on a meta-level, that is, on a level higher than that of the Christian tradition, entails a demand of an evolution of a christocentric theology towards a transcendentological or pistocentric theology.

In this respect I will add another suggestion, namely that in the case of Smith, *where the kind of extensification is about to overcome the distinction between the normative self-understanding of a religious tradition and the self-understanding of other traditions, the intensification tends to go towards an evolution to a new religious position.* This runs, however, the danger of undervaluing the difference between religious traditions, particularly by establishing a meta-perspective which makes the elemental differences between religions relative to a superior unitary perspective, as in Smith's case.

Cragg, on the other hand, has been characterized as superiority-hierarchizing, and has been seen as recruiting as much as possible of his Christian faith, which he perceives as an open-faith. Intensification is thus nothing but a movement within his always held Christian theological fundamentals. However, it seems as if in Cragg's case, a *working out of the Christian faith as open, one is also able to refine and uncover existing elements within it in a way that seems to expand it without altering its fundamental features.*

Based on this there is no reason to say that much extensification, whatsoever that should mean, implies much intensification. My point here is that the kind and degree of extensification colours the intensification. In hermeneutic terms this is nothing but a statement about the significance and impact of pre-commitments, fore-meanings, horizons, etc. Or in Grünschloß' words: Interreligious perception is self-referential.

On the other hand, one might possibly make a prognosis that *absence of intensification presupposes a closed faith.* This is at least the whole backdrop for understanding Cragg's attempt to avoid this fate, which was a clear enough option provided by his distinctive evangelical background. This applies also to Smith, albeit his openness conveys other features, which I will address in the next chapter (Chapter 7).

Nevertheless, if we see interreligious perception as a continuously returning of 'forth' and 'back,' of extensification and intensification, I will maintain that in every 'next lap' of the interreligious understanding of the Other, if I may use such vague notions, the intensified faith becomes the point of departure for extensification. Put very simply, the intensified faith becomes the extensified faith, the faith that is to be related. Seen in this *continuous hermeneutic perspective,* I will suggest that *throughout interreligious hermeneutical processes of perception one might expect an increasing degree of stabilization of the self-understanding because the intensified faith becomes integrated in the extensified faith as far as the latter is dependent upon the initial intensification.* My contention is that the case-studies of Smith and Cragg support this suggestion.

This process towards stabilization may lastly be seen as, conscious or unconscious, *a desire to reduce the complexity of the Other by developing patterns and ideas that function as simplified measures for the various interreligious relations.* This can be seen as a two-fold activity. First, one may aim to simplify ones own self-understanding in order to communicate better or more easily with the Other. Second, in order to grasp the Other in all its complexity and nuances, one will similarly attempt to develop concepts and patterns by which the Other is dealt with in an easier and complexity-reduced way. How these attempts can be justified and/or criticized belongs to the next chapter.

6.6 Conclusion

After presenting the heuristic model for interreligious perception of Andreas Grünschloß, I have in this chapter made an attempt to figure out how Smith and Cragg's attempts to develop systematic relations between their Christian self-understandings and their understanding of Islam can be determined more precisely. These 'characteristic pictures', which are the outcomes of this, reveal that Smith and Cragg represent quite different interreligious approaches both in terms of extensification (self-relating, systematization) and intensification (self-change, rationalization).

In Smith's case, what seems to depict his self-relating best is either a harmonizing position with certain differentiations, or alternatively, inclusivism at a meta-systemic level. The latter is preferred because his Christian self-understanding seems to differentiate out a new sub-tradition based on his interpretation of 'faith' and 'transcendence', which causes his self-understanding to evolve into a new religious position if contrasted to a christocentric theology. This fits well with his self-description as reformer.

Cragg, on the other hand, represents in respect of extensification/ self-relating, on the whole, an inclusive approach (superiority-hierarchizing), which also includes distancing and harmonizing features. At one place (common prayer) we may on one level recognize syncretistic features, whereas on an integrative level this still belongs to a partly harmonizing and partly superiority-hierarchizing mode of relation. This approach is facilitated both by an emphasis on commonalities (creation, human condition) as well as on contrasts (prophetic success versus prophetic and filial suffering). As regards intensification/self-change, Cragg cannot be seen as very radical in terms of revision, reformation, and so forth. The way his encounter with Islam has impacted upon his Christian self-understanding is by means of refining and elucidating his always-held Christian faith in the Incarnation and vicarious redemption of Jesus for human sin and evil.

In two comparisons of the two I have emphasized what they have in common as well as what they disagree about. Central issues of divergence are: first, the role of complexity-reducing patterns and ideas and their relation to history, generative events, and the Other, and second, the kind, degree and solution of unstable or unsettled elements of one's self-understanding.

Lastly, I have developed some hypotheses that suggest a mutual dependency between self-relating (extensification) and self-change (intensification), where also stabilization and the need for reduction of complexity are pointed up.

My concern in the next chapter will be to interpret how these options and hypotheses may be justified or criticized from my own preferred theological point of view. One will find that this point of assessment is already anticipated in my characterization of Smith's position as a new religious position, and my sympathy for Cragg shown in Chapter 4 and 5. Based on these assessments I will constructively develop what I see as fundamental features of a comparative theology.

7
TOWARDS A CHRISTIAN COMPARATIVE THEOLOGY

7.1. Introduction

In this last chapter I will aim at a theological interpretation and integration of theory as developed and induced so far in the study. For the structure of this chapter I will use the two different meanings of 'understanding' employed in the study: a) understanding something alien/other, b) doing this as Christian theologian. Whereas the former will emphasize the method and process of such understanding, the latter will focus on the Trinitarian substantiation of it. In what follows I will also seek to demonstrate how the two interrelate.

7.2. Comparative Theology as Hermeneutic Enterprise
7.2.1. INTRODUCTION

Utilizing hermeneutical theory I have shown how Smith and Cragg's positions can be viewed as interreligious attempts to perceive religious traditions more generally, and Islam in particular. My purpose here is to relate this view to certain premises that have been proposed by David Tracy, and which I also in turn will modify and criticize.

In his development of a 'shared method for comparative theology'[1] across otherwise sharp differences, David Tracy has presented three[2] premises that he sees as important and hopefully affirmative for anyone attempting to work within the field of comparative theology. These are:

1. Comparative theology must be a reinterpretation of the central symbols of a particular religious tradition for the contemporary religiously pluralistic world.

---

[1] Tracy 1987, 452.
[2] Tracy includes also a fourth, which he maintains follows from the three first ones: 'That contemporary theologians must engage in two complementary kinds of interpretation of a tradition—those now known as 'hermeneutics of retrieval' and the 'hermeneutics of critique and suspicion.'

2. A new paradigm for comparative theology must be so formulated that the interpretations of a tradition can no longer be grounded in older, classicist, bases but must rely on new foundations that incorporate both past tradition and the present religious pluralism.

3. In keeping with the demands of an emerging globalism and a pluralistic world, theologians of all traditions must risk addressing the question of religious pluralism on explicitly theological grounds.

I will try to address these 'premises' by engaging with what I perceive to be the central commonalities and differences in Smith and Cragg. My contention is that it might prove rewarding to view the approaches of Smith and Cragg from Tracy's vantage point as a first hermeneutic assessment of their contributions. Though Trinitarian concerns will be entailed to some extent in my examination below, a more thorough Trinitarian discussion of their positions belongs to the next subsection.

7.2.2 RELATION, PARTICIPATION AND SELF-REFERENCE

One major common feature of the approaches of Smith and Cragg is their emphases on participation. As seen from within their theological and theoretical frameworks, participation correlates to central matters within these, such as, most notably, 'faith' and 'corporate critical self-consciousness' (Smith) and the 'creative and risking mind' (Cragg). This common feature can easily be overlooked but should be seen as

> an *epistemological alternative* to the prevailing positivistic ways of understanding anything different; alternative in that it [does] not presume a detached 'objectivity' but rather demand[s] some form of participation in a mode of understanding more akin to faith than to knowledge, as generally understood.[3]

Despite its loose formulation, I think this way of seeing things connects Smith and Cragg's interreligious approaches to Tracy's item 1 ('reinterpretation ... for the contemporary religiously pluralistic world') and 2 ('incorporate ... the present religious pluralism') above. Moreover, Smith's 'corporate critical self-consciousness', 'personalist programme', and 'world community', and Cragg's 'creative and risking mind', seek

---

[3] David E. Burrell, CSC, about the famous Catholic Islamicist Louis Massignon, Burrell 1998, 272, my emphasis.

explicitly to relate one's self-understanding to that of the Other. Thus, understanding implies interpretation, which again implies participation.[4] This is evident in their distinctive ways, when the *de facto* religious pluralism, or better, the *de facto* religious plurality, is closely linked to the development of their respective comparative theologies, their 'new paradigms' (cf. Tracy's item 2), which seek to integrate religious plurality within their normative frameworks. Thus, the Other is a resource for the development of their self-understandings. Transferred into hermeneutic language, one might describe this as the *interpretandum* becoming bound together with the *interpretans*.[5] Nevertheless, interreligious hermeneutics will always be heterogeneous, that is, understanding the Other cannot occur as a mere depiction of what the Other is per se, but will always be bound to the conditions of both Oneself and of the Other. There remains a hiatus between Oneself and the Other, in spite of all talk about participation.[6] In this, comparison is not merely to be thought of as a supplement to one's self-understanding. In effect, to be comparative must include a concession of plurality,[7] and the prejudgments of one's own self-understanding are risked through the encounter with the Other,[8] as particularly and legitimately stressed by Cragg.

However, I will contend that there is still a significant difference between Smith and Cragg to be considered in this respect. This can be briefly put thus: whereas the difference between 'Christian' and 'the Other' is obviously present in Cragg's case, it runs the risk of dissolving in Smith's preference for 'faith' over 'belief' and 'religion'. The question is whether his meta-inclusivism[9] undermines the possibility to relating to the Other simply because faith bridges any difference between Oneself

---

[4] Cf. Schweiker 1992, 264: '[My basic guiding assumption is that] understanding is achieved through interpretation. The attitude and perspective of the interpreter is that of the participant rather than the objectifying perspective of the observer concerned with propositional statements about events and facts.' This citation resonates clearly with the one of Burrell immediately above.

[5] Watson 1992, 148f. This runs quite counter to both (neo-)classicist (*focus imaginarius*) and modern historicist, objectivist and/or positivist hermeneutics. See also Straub 1999, 73f: 'Die Bildung, Reproduktion und Umbildung von Personaler Identität ist kein monologischer Akt der Selbsterzeugung. Sie ist notwendigerweise an die dialogisch strukturierte, praktische Anerkennug durch andere gebunden.' For this statement Straub is dependent upon Charles Taylor.

[6] Cf. Ratschow 1979, 123, and Tillich 1963a, 141.

[7] Cf. Pye 1997, 5: 'Any attempts to view religions *in their plurality,* in a conceptual frame of reference, involves the intellectual act of comparison,' emphasis original.

[8] Cf. also Bernstein 1992, 309, who relates this particular understanding of the encounter with the Other to Gadamer. See also Ratschow: 'Wer eine Gottesverehrung ein-sieht, der verehrt diesen Gott und hängt ihm an,' Ratschow op.cit., 123.

[9] Cf. Grünschloß, Chapter 6.4.1 (= 'inclusivism at a meta-systemic level').

and the Other and consequently erodes the point of departure for any ability to relate. Thus, Smith seems not to aim at understanding the Other in its otherness, but rather at 'recognizing the essential identity of another person's self-understanding with one's own.'[10]

The premise I use for this appraisal is that 'relatability' requires a certain distance, gap, or difference, between Oneself and the Other.[11] I see this request for difference and distance as, in many ways, coinciding with Tracy's demand that the 'new paradigm ... must rely on new foundations that incorporate both *past tradition* and the *present religious pluralism*' (item 2, my emphasis), where 'past' and 'present' correlate partly to, without equating with, 'identity' and 'alterity'.

If this interpretation is acknowledged, I still find it necessary to advance the perception of the problem somewhat, mainly because I find Tracy's premise too loosely formulated if interreligious hermeneutics is not only to be viewed as relationally concerned, but also as sustaining a critical potential. The crucial point here is first how 'relations' and 'relationality' should be understood. In a theological context, Colin Gunton has developed a view of human relationality based on his doctrine of creation and *imago Dei*. Gunton contrasts relationality with human capacity for fixed qualities, in a way that I find rewarding:

> Human being in the image of God is to be understood relationally rather than in terms of the possession of fixed characteristics such as reason and will, as has been the almost universal tendency of the tradition ... To be in the image of God is to subsist in *relations of mutual constitutiveness* with other human beings.[12]

The benefit of Gunton's view is, firstly, that it is possible to maintain a mutual relationality between humans, which of course opens up to hermeneutic perceptions. Secondly, according to Gunton, this makes it possible to keep both 'a confidence in its truth [i.e. the truth of the Christian

---

[10] Gualtieri 1973, 16.

[11] Cf. T.W. Adorno's suggestion of 'a distanced nearness' (i.e. *Minima Moralia,* transl. E.F.N. Jephcott, London: Verso, 1974, 89), which Kenneth Surin sees as an alternative to the approaches of Smith and Hick. This notion can be seen as relating 'self' to the 'other' while preserving his/her 'otherness', Surin 1990a, 125.

[12] Gunton 1993/1998, 3, my emphasis. This is his second (of three) point in his doctrine of *creation.* Nevertheless, I find it reasonable to extend this to apply also to my subject, not least given his interest for 'true plurality and diversity' (i.e. the doctrine of the creation) and the scope of his book: *The One, the Three and the Many* (i.e. the title).

faith] and an openness to the reception of criticism and truth from whatever quarter.'[13] Hence, 'relation-in-openness' goes hand in hand with 'otherness in relation,'[14] and thus holds particularities, relatedness and otherness, together in tension.[15] Consequently, this enables one to maintain one's particular beliefs, authorities, and practices, without excluding the Other from playing a part in the constitution of Oneself. The alternatives to this view of mutuality and relationality would either be to regard commonalities, consensus, and cores, as fundamental, or, on the other hand, to retain fragmentation and isolation, which is what Gunton primarily aims to remedy.

This view conveys a critical potential towards Smith's approach. First, I will suggest that the retreat from relations in Smith's general and particular (Islam) interreligious approach, to a unitary and converging human capacity/potential (faith), is reductionist both in respect of 'identity' and 'alterity'. Given Smith's position, there are left no tensions between the Christian and Muslim view of, for example, Christ, between the Christian and Muslim view of God's sovereignty, because all function as channels for the faith of each. It is difficult to see that his approach in the end is an extension of a Christian 'self'.[16]

This relates intimately to the fact that Smith presupposes that there is nothing like 'a religion' or 'religions.' However, this view has been severely criticized by both Christian and Muslim parties.[17] In this regard it

---

[13] *Ibid.* 7.

[14] *Ibid.* 229 and 7.

[15] *Ibid.* 6: 'Only where relatedness is held in tension with genuine otherness can things, both human and divine, all be given their due.'

[16] For the use of 'extension of the self', which resonates with Grünschloß' terminology, see Barnes 1989, 131. Interestingly, Michael Barnes, based on his 'dialogical theory of relationships' and 'interpenetration,' sees 'inclusivism' as 'little more than an extension of the self.' Barnes, on the other hand, applauds Smith's position, which he implicitly relates to 'synthesis', *ibid.* 126. This is also one of Smith's own description of his corporate critical self-consciousness: that it should make one, synthesized and converging apprehension (*WT*, 66). Yet, 'synthesis' is not qualified in any pretentious way here, nor when it is used in order to characterize one feature of Smith's alternative historical approach (against 'analytical').

[17] See e.g. Edwards 2000. Mark Edwards makes three philological criticisms against Smith's treatment of 'religion' in *ME*: a) Smith's claim that the ancients did not think of 'a religion' is hard to verify because of the lack of an indefinite article in either Greek or Latin, b) Smith ignores some uses of *religio* which may suggest an earlier and more widespread distinction between particular communities than he allows, and c) Smith does not consider a variety of Greek terms such as *ethnos, nomos* and *hairesis,* which are used to express a competition of religions either within a community or between communities. These are particularly important since Greek dominated Christian thought in the two first centuries.
A Muslim counterpart of this criticism can be found in Ismail Raji al-Faruqi, who claims: 'That 'Islam' means submission and personal piety does not preclude it

is telling that Smith's view of interpenetration is put on the level of intertwinement of religious traditions. In Smith's structure of ideas this implies that the aspect of relation is reserved to the level of beliefs and externals, not the level of faith. This latter, ultimate and real level is, on the other hand, reserved for convergence, if not unity, which enables him to neutralize the dissonances into a grand view.

Nevertheless, Smith sees this as required by the present[18] globalization. I think Smith is right by posing the demands for unity that our situation requires, for example realized in *some* kind of a world community, if one is to avoid on the one hand violent expressions of religious disagreements, and, on the other, 'a *de facto* syncretism of resurgent religions all claiming universality.'[19] Yet, I think he achieves a false solution to the problem. My main objection is that one should not, and cannot, neutralize those things which form people's identities and to which people find themselves committed. Pursuing Smith's path, one thereby risks disengaging oneself from a point of self-reference, which in the end will make it impossible to speak of any perspective and position at all. Any system or tradition, either open or closed to its surroundings, needs a reference to which major features of its perspective adhere, and from which any openness towards its surroundings has to take its starting point. In short, no relating without a theologically distinctive 'self'.[20] And in this, 'self' should not to be regionally confined, nor should the awareness of and relation to the Other lead into self-forgetfulness.[21]

---

from meaning a religious system of ideas and imperatives. If this I contended, the Muslim's understanding across the centuries is conclusive,' Faruqi 1998, 7. Cf. also note 37 below. See Smith 1961a, 231, to view the contrast to Smith: 'In Heaven, I personally believe, as do devout Muslims, there is God. On earth, there is Islamic history. Between them, I see no intermediary fixed system.'

[18] For Smith, this was a new overwhelming challenge already in the 50's!

[19] Khodr 1971/1981, 37.

[20] Since this regards relations, this must apply equally to the 'self' of Muslims. I think, therefore, that Richard M. Frank is right in asserting that: 'If Christians and Muslims were to accept Smith's theories as a basis on which to establish communication, they would find that they had nothing significant to talk about,' Frank 1986 (review of *UI*), 321, col. 1. Frank maintains further that: 'Without intentional coherence with its normative foundations there is no control against the caprice of imagination on the one hand or against rationalizing reductionism on the other,' *ibid.* 320, col. 2.

[21] Cf. Gregersen 1991, 22, who maintains the following about theology as science: 'Theology is an independent science open to its surroundings, where independency is different from regionalism, and openness to the surroundings is different from self-forgetfulness,' my translation (Da. original: 'Teologien er en selvstændig omverdensåpen videnskab, men selvstændighet er ikke det same [som] regionalitet, og omverdensåpenhet er ikke det samme som selvforglemmelse'). A comparable statement about Christian theology can be found in Paul Tillich, e.g. Tillich

My proposal at this point is to encourage and develop attitudes that are honest and realistic about the desire, the demand for, and the duty to extend and commend one's self-understanding and self-commitment. In this, one's beliefs cannot but play a significant role. Such proactive attitudes could very well be stimulated in order to participate with people of different faiths, including to learn, to be corrected and to strengthen one's self-understanding. Thus I think syncretism can be avoided, as can the further undesired consequence of reactive resurgence, and a unity may appear on another level than a level of universals or mysticism. My proposal is that this encounter should rather appear at the level of mutual understanding, where 'mutual' comprises both extensification and intensification for all parties. In this, I will claim that Cragg's 'cross-reference' theology is viable whereas Smith's pistocentric theology is not.[22] I will therefore suggest that:

Participation as an epistemological alternative is to be acknowledged because it enables one to integrate religious plurality with one's own conviction and commitment. If such integration is to succeed it requires a certain distance between Oneself and the Other. Otherwise the potential for mutual formation is undermined, and relations will erode due to neutralization or even extinction of necessary tensions between identity and alterity on a level of universals (or mysticism). The alternative, which should be aimed at, is a hermeneutic 'synopsis' on the level of mutual understanding where both sincere extensification and

---

1963b, 320: 'Christianity has in its very nature an openness in all directions.' This openness, including the readiness to accept judgement from outside, was, according to Tillich, lost by the hierarchical and polemical development of Christianity. Thus it retreated from itself being a 'center of crystallization for all positive religious elements after they have been subjected to the criteria implied in this center.'

[22] See also Rajashekar 1988. In this article it is J. Paul Rajashekar aims to ponder the correlation (cf. Tillich and D. Tracy; cf. also Tracy's premises above) between an assessment of 'the theological significance of religious plurality in our midst' ('situation') and 'the significance of our faith commitments in that situation' ('self-understanding'), *ibid.* 14. In this, Rajashekar affirms Smith's claim that every theology is inescapably a self-theology, but criticizes his claim that faith is a category common to all religious traditions, *ibid.* 15 (cf. *WT*). On the other hand, Cragg's 'cross-reference' theology is praised as a viable theological example of 'mutual interaction,' *ibid.* 17f. For his own, Rajashekar claims that: 'To provide effective responses, our traditional theological self-interpretations may need to be revised, reconceived, and reconceptualized,' *ibid.* 18. Interestingly enough, Rajashekar presupposes a coherence view of truth (cf. Rescher's criteria below, Chapter 7.2.3) in his approach, see e.g. p. 19: 'Christians, by being attentive to the truth claims of others and especially to the questionings that give rise to different answers in other faiths, are compelled to incorporate those questions and answers in articulating their distinctive claim.'

intensification are preserved and encouraged. Distinctive self-references will be required for this to succeed, which will also entail the risk of changing one's self-understanding.

7.2.3 CHANGE BETWEEN INNOVATION AND EXPANSION

The title of this subchapter relates both to 'self-change' in the title of this study, and Tracy's first premise (cf above): the issue of reinterpretation. The following question will be pursued: to what extent and in what way is it possible to reinterpret the Christian tradition in order to reflect, 'take into account,' or even incorporate current religious plurality?

First of all, it seems that Tracy has put the emphasis on innovation when he has made comparative theology a theme. One reason for this request for comparative theology to entail something genuinely new may be the general request for justification of any new theological 'label' (*in casu,* 'comparative'). To some degree I find this to be a pertinent requirement. Theological sub-disciplines or sub-activities should not be constructed without having, or having the potential to gain, fresh knowledge to put across. Yet, on the other hand, Tracy's demand for 'new foundations' seems to be a too radical demand for both hermeneutical, historical and religious/doctrinal reasons.

Hermeneutically, as seen in Cragg's work, intensification may not only be seen as 'innovation,' 'evolution,' and so forth, but also as expansion in the meaning of 'discovery' of past tradition, 'refinement' of existing doctrines, and 'precision' of what always was held to be true. Historically, one might further contend that 'any and all religious practices are historical formations,'[23] of which religious concepts are to be included. Yet this does not necessarily imply that that which has been formed (at a later stage) is a 'new foundation.' Given the (perceived) authority and integrity of the past, this is unlikely to be the case very often, and should at least not be put forward as a prerequisite for a comparative theology. On normative religious/theological grounds 'new foundation' will be too radical for religious representatives who find themselves loyal to either Scripture, church or tradition. And why should these commitments be suspended for comparative purposes? The question may on the contrary be inverted: Can normative theological foundations (Scripture, church, tradition, etc.) be overcome at all? Seen together, I will claim with J. Paul Rajashekar (from a Lutheran perspective), that

---

[23] Martin 2000, 281.

the hermeneutical character of our theological task
necessarily raises questions of theological continuity with
the tradition.[24]

A way out of this impasse is to replace the alternatives old/new
foundations with degrees of interpretation of new experiential data.[25] One
obvious 'new experimental datum' in this study is 'religious plurality'. If
this view is adopted (degrees of interpretation ...), there is included a
distinctive relation to the 'past' of the tradition, but also a rethinking of
the tradition in the light of 'present'. Instead of old foundations, I will
speak of decisive elements of the past. And, instead of new foundations
I will propose rather to think of how these decisive elements appear to be
persuasive in a different context than that within which they originated.
Given more of such decisive elements from various traditions, one may
speak of a *competition* between perspectives, each aiming to maintain
truth in a present situation. Viewed thus, doctrines may develop and
change in the way they are used, interpreted, expanded and innovated in
the encounter with other religious traditions. My contention is that such
a modification should be made in order to make Tracy's position more
precise and adequate (cf. his item 2).

It is also possible to see religious change as an expression of a
desire for unity, integrity and continuity.[26] This is clearly the case with

---

[24] Rajashekar 1988, 20.

[25] For degrees of truth, see e.g. Rescher 1973, 197-200. This relates also to his
modification of the Laws of Bivalence and of Excluded Middle, caused by his preference
for the coherence theory, see *ibid.* 44, point 6, and especially p. 199 where he makes
the following claim for a classical theory of coherence, related to a *precriterial*
'relative completeness' *sub judice*: 'The possibility of new truths based on new data
will always be open.' Yet, such truths have to be *tested* before they can be announced
as truths from a *postcriterial* view of truth. Note that Rescher follows a *criterial*
approach to truth, not a definitional, *ibid.* 1. Wolfhart Pannenberg's Christian
approach to new experimental data comes close to Rescher's position, cf. my
examination of Pannenberg in Mæland 1999, especially pp. 178-181.

[26] Light 2000, 180. One of Timothy Light's suggestions is that of 'a human capacity
to simultaneously mix cultural material and to claim that cultures are unitary.' This
is seen as equally applicable to groups as to individuals, 165. This is, according to
Light, true of all human knowledge and all human behaviour, 183. 'The Principle
of Religious Change,' therefore, is seen as inseparable from 'The Principle of
Cognitive Integrity.' Hence 'today's orthodoxy is the result of yesterday's mixing,
and it has never been otherwise,' 185. One might accuse Light for ignoring the
possibility of e.g. conversion, but also of extinction. His clue is however that
radical change may occur from without, but is still interpreted as continuity from
within. Though this is probably the case of most instances, I will still maintain that
it does not comprise all possibilities (e.g. of a subjective view that a radical change
happened when changing religious affiliation).

Cragg when he 'negotiates' and 'sifts' his always held Christian faith in Muslim soil—before the Tribunal of Islam, as he calls it,[27] yet without any radical change but a 'ripening consistency.'[28] This is also present in Smith's claim to be continuous with certain (classic and mystic) strands of the past, despite his overt claim to being reformatory. This way of seeing religious change, as an attempt to re-establish continuity and integrity with the past, coincides with the induced suggestions of stabilization and complexity-reducing strategies that were suggested at the end of the last chapter.

One way of expressing the same issue can be, as Smith has claimed, to require that if something is claimed to be true, it should relate to all that is true. This relates certainly to what I called 'degrees of interpretation of new experiential data' immediately above, but also to Gadamer's view of a hermeneutic totality: a totality of meaning as well as an extension of the 'tradition,' rather than a shift. This can be seen in a study of Gadamer's hermeneutic where Mary Ann Stenger attempts to show how his hermeneutics can be applied to and adopted by cross-cultural philosophy of religion.[29] Her interpretation of Gadamer with regard to his concept of (fusion of) horizons implies that, given that one's own horizon is open towards others' horizons, and one's own horizon is contingent,[30] it follows that an expansion of it, rather than a shift, is likely to occur when one approaches others' horizons. Finally, because language is 'the record of finitude,'[31] Gadamer sees each word related to an imagined totality of meaning and every interpretation functioning as an extension of the 'tradition.' If seen this way, extensification and intensification become two sides of the same coin, which correlates with what several of the induced hypotheses in Chapter 6 seemed to require, including the hypotheses about stabilization.

Having arrived here, it seems natural to adopt a *coherence* theory of truth. According to Nicholas Rescher, this kind of truth-theory should entail the following features 'integral to the traditions of the subject,' that is, the traditional ways of understanding a coherence theory of truth:[32]

    1. The truth of a proposition[33] is to be assessed in terms of its

---

[27] Cf. the title of ch. 8 in *FLN*.

[28] His self-description in a letter to the author, 21 May 2000, Cragg 2000e.

[29] Stenger 1995.

[30] *Ibid.* 159.

[31] *Ibid.* 160.

[32] See Rescher 1973, 43f.

[33] Dependent on Rescher's use of 'proposition', Rescher 1973 *passim,* I use it in the following sense here: 'a claim that something is true, real, a matter of fact, etc'. Hence, a coherence theory of truth should not be seen as competing with a correspondence theory of truth, *ibid.*, 10.

'coherence' with others; its relationships of compatibility or conflict with others.

2. The truth of a proposition is therefore a contextual matter; one cannot in general determine whether or not a proposition is true by inspecting it in isolation, but only in the setting of other propositions.

3. Thus, the truth of propositions depends crucially on matters of systematization of the logical linkages of propositions with other propositions together with which they form a connected network.

4. This system of truths must therefore be consistent and the propositions must be connected; they must form a cohesive unit, whose very cohesiveness acts to exclude other possibilities.

5. The systematic unit must also be sufficiently large to embrace the domain of real fact; it must exhibit a certain completeness—nothing can be omitted without due warrant.

6. Hence the systematic facets—consistency, comprehensiveness, and cohesively unitary—must be predominant in the coherence determination of truth.

Interestingly, both Smith and Cragg aim to fulfil these requirements. This could have been demonstrated extensively with regard to compatibility/conflict, contextuality, systematization, consistency/ connectedness and comprehensiveness (cf. above). However, do these features bear any potential for a critical appraisal of the positions of Cragg and Smith?

Regarding Smith, I will argue that there is a lack of consistency in his position, and if so, it is incoherent. My argument runs as follows: his concept of faith does not esteem 'decisive elements of the past'. This relates both to matters of Scripture/Canon and ecumenical understanding of the church and its relation to non-Christian tradition. On the contrary, the person and work of Christ and the mission of the church are downplayed, neutralized and subordinated to his single, formal definition of humane religiousness; faith. It is therefore impossible to acknowledge that Smith takes the Incarnation, suffering, death and resurrection of Jesus, as well as the mission of the church, as seriously as the Scriptures witness about these things themselves, or as seriously as Christian writers both ancient and modern have written about it. Consequently, since Smith's approach is not able to integrate decisive Christian elements it cannot reach the completeness and hence the degree of coherence one should require of an approach entitled 'Christian'.[34] In short: Smith is not able to integrate major Christian concepts within his concept of faith.

---

[34] Most interestingly, the criterion for consistency and coherence at this place coincides with one of Smith's own criteria in 2.6.3[3].

The coherence theory of truth orients itself inwardly; to sift the true from the false within a body of gathered information, consisting of a set of inconsistent elements. In this, the challenge will be to transform incoherence into coherence, disorder into system, *prima facie* truths into qualified truths, etc. Based on this, Smith certainly leaves the disorder and incoherence on the level of 'beliefs' and departs to the level of convergence in order to safeguard faith. In principle this would be possible were it not that he does not succeed in keeping with common interpretations of Christology and the church. What he offers is a consensus beyond the particulars, beyond what has traditionally counted, beyond what has been understood as Christian. In short, Smith is primarily concerned with faith as form (response), not its content. This fits very well with the fact that Smith allows for contradictions in respect of such issues (cf. his use of an Indian view of truth, Chapter 2), while coherence is reserved to the level of morality, personal and mutual understanding, including the aim of a world community. Hence the coherence he aims at is not comprehensive enough to include central Christian data.

It is exactly at this point that Cragg's approach appears to be stronger than Smith's. For Cragg it is precisely the central events and elements of God's work with humans through Christ that structure his approach. I will therefore maintain that his comparative theological approach succeeds in integrating decisive features of the ecumenical Christian tradition.

Yet, his approach does not stop there. It also aims to integrating elements of importance from other religious traditions. One may however ask: Is Cragg comprehensive enough? Regarding his use of Islam, one may ask: does he consider Islam comprehensively? In this respect it is probably wise to listen to some strands of the criticism that have been raised against his approach, especially concerned with the question whether he 'christianizes' Islam. To put it in a general mode: does he in the end, draw Islam back into his own religious perspective?[35] In this, a 'hermeneutic of retrieval' should not achieve a total priority over a 'hermeneutic of critique and suspicion'.[36] In the case of Cragg, for example, I have shown how several critics have claimed that he is not sufficiently self-critical in the way he relates Islam to his Christian self-understanding. In interreligious hermeneutics this is a crucial matter as far as balance,

---

[35] Cf. the following statement of Michael Pye about 'the German religion and religions' school (Schleiermacher, Otto, Söderblom, Wach, and Ratschow), which he distinguish from the 'history of religions' school (including comparative religion): 'in the end, they draw everything back into their own religious perspective,' Pye 1997, 4.

[36] Cf. Tracy's fourth premise, note 2 above, p. 321.

mutuality and 'otherness' are concerned. In the case of Islam interpretation, any criticism of Islam should also entail an explicit readiness to criticize also one's own Christian position or matters that relate to a Christian position. This seems to be somewhat underdeveloped by Cragg and this has been particularly revealed in parts of the Muslim reception of his writings. This also applies, at least partly, to Smith.[37]

However, this view of coherence does not mean that a comparative theology should be all-embracing in order to be comprehensive. With Rescher, it is too much to say that an aim for coherence should entail coherence with everything. On the other hand, it is too little to aim for coherence with something.[38] Most interestingly, Rescher maintains that the coherence theory should never serve as a

> primary truth-originative standard, but only as one that is secondary and truth expansive.[39]

The criterion of coherence in the appraisal of Smith and Cragg is therefore a criterion of their ability to expand their Christian tradition. In Smith's case the coherence (related to the Christian tradition) is too small. In Cragg's case the coherence is limited to a target domain (Islam) of which some elements have not been addressed extensively (*Shar'iah,* eschatology, historic Islam, etc). I will therefore assert that

Smith's approach, as far as it claims to be Christian, is unable to relate to, cohere with, and extend towards Islam because his point of departure differs from what may commonly be seen as a Christian point of view, at least in a wider ecumenical sense.

Cragg's approach, on the other hand, is consistent and coherent[40] but could have reached a greater degree of completeness by having addressed further issues within the Islamic tradition. Cragg's strength, however, is that with his connection to and consistency with decisive events of the Christian 'past', he has shown how new formulations and greater precision are both possible and required if one is to avoid a slow

---

[37] See e.g. Faruqi's criticism of Smith's renouncement of an Islamic essence, Faruqi 1998, 4ff. See also how Smith was branded as 'the great enemy of Islam' in the Pakistan journal *Al-Islam* (April 1958, 129), Tibawi 1963, 299, n45.

[38] Rescher 1973, 49.

[39] *Ibid.* 50.

[40] I therefore agree with Christopher Lamb, Lamb 1997, 172: '[Cragg's] missionary concepts are thoroughly theological, not merely pragmatic, and offer, with the qualifications already noted, a coherent and biblically-grounded Christian theology of interfaith relations.'

death of Christian communication, that is, without some kind of innovation or expansion, barren repetition and eventually extinction takes over.[41]

Some kind of reinterpretation is inescapable as far as interpretation of Oneself and the Other is concerned. This should not only be seen as innovation in temporal terms, but also as expansion and development in terms of amount and awareness of content. A coherence view of truth may illuminate how this may be both possible and required. In such a view connection, consistency and comprehensiveness are seen as necessary features. If innovation is executed at the expense of connection, consistency and comprehensiveness, it cannot appear as more coherent than positions that do maintain such.

The question that remains is how awareness and acknowledgement of religious change can be interpreted from a Christian, point of view, which is both my own, Smith's and Cragg's point of departure. Hence, is it possible to hold together Christian identity (self-reference), the necessity and ability to relate (self-relating), and innovation and/or expansion (self-change)?

7.3 Comparative Theology as Christian Enterprise

Within the confinements of the questions just raised, this chapter is an attempt to 'address the question of religious pluralism on explicitly theological grounds,' as Tracy's third premise reads (cf. above). These 'explicit theological grounds' follow a Trinitarian approach.

7.3.1 UNIVERSALS, PARTICULARS AND THE DOCTRINE OF CREATION

I choose to start with the role commonalities/universals and differences/ particulars play in Smith and Cragg. From a normative theological perspective the relation between commonalities and particularities becomes

---

[41] Cf. Basil Mitchell who maintains that: 'A system of belief dogmatically adhered to will simply ossify, and will not undergo those modifications which are necessary, in changing circumstances, to maintaining its identity,' Mitchell 1994, 30. This openness to modification should, however, with direct correlation to my evaluation of Smith, be distinguished from 'complete open-mindedness' because 'the putative system will be subject to so many fluctuations as not to develop a coherent identity at all,' *ibid.* Mitchell seems to fit into both Cragg's terminology and the theoretical perspective we have adopted here.

acute, as the subsequent cluster of questions address: are that which is perceived as differences interchangeable, as is maintained by Smith? Can the various 'answers' given by the religious traditions, scriptures, rituals, and so forth, be reduced to play only a secondary role in relation to the universal point of convergence; faith? Why commit oneself to a religious community if its distinctive features do not matter in the end? And how are we to develop religious identity when externals are downplayed? Furthermore, if externals are given lower priority, why not work for a syncretistic community where differences are kept within a superior framework? Or would this be a contradiction in terms, that externals matter in the end?

From a particularist position within comparative theology, most notably represented by the Catholic theologians Joseph A. DiNoia and Gavin D'Costa, it has been claimed strongly that differences matter. Such particularists hold that the paradox of pluralist and theocentric positions is that they can be viewed as representatives of non-Christian positions. This is so because the way in which they have dissolved a particular Christian point of departure in order to facilitate a comparative theology can be integrated within another religious 'system.' Thus, for example, DiNoia asks, based on Smith's use of 'idolatry',[42] and his preference for 'personal faith' over historical identities, whether this is simply a 'Muslim theology of religions.'[43] The following general statement of the philosopher Nicholas Rescher can also be seen in this line of argument, namely that

> a combination-standpoint [i.e. synthesis(m)[44]] will also—
> in so far as it is possible at all—be just one more possible
> standpoint, just one more alternative in the overall
> spectrum.[45]

---

[42] See Smith 1987a.

[43] DiNoia 1992, 183.

[44] Nicholas Rescher distinguishes between synthesis (*combination* of position) and syncretism (*conjunction* of positions): 'A syncretist *conjunction* of positions is not a *synthesis*. Synthesis is the construction of a combining standpoint that mixes a piece of one position with some different piece of another ... The synthesist seeks somehow to co-ordinate dissonant positions in grand all-embracing synthesis,' Rescher 1993/1996, 94, emphases original. Synthesis is also seen as: 'resorting to the 'interpretative' qualifications or emendations that reconcile discordant views via distinctions,' *ibid.*, 92, emphasis original.

[45] Rescher 1993/1996, 94. It seems that this description answers the question Langdon Gilkey poses to Smith, Gilkey 1981, 304, col. 1: 'If such a principle [Smith's interpretation of God, humanity, of history, and of destiny] does not come either from a given religious tradition or from a given secular culture, from where does it arise?'

It seems that such a position has already stepped beyond a syncretist[46] position. Yet, can this be justifiably applied to Smith's view of faith and corporate critical self-consciousness?

It is, no doubt, Smith's sincere aim to 'enlarge one's vision of truth without losing loyalty to one's own, however finite [vision of truth]' (*WT*, 89). I will however, with my previous characterization and discussion of his position still in mind (Chapter 6), argue that his enlargement of his view of truth, most notably seen in his concepts of 'faith' and 'corporate critical self-consciousness', makes it a problem to keep steadfastly to a Christian vision of truth.[47] This is not to disallow Smith from asserting that his vision of truth takes its point of departure from his Christian conviction. No doubt, Smith's comparative theology has been inspired by the life and example of Jesus. What I doubt, however, is whether there can be found for biblical warrants his truth claims.[48] His approach also runs the risk of becoming hermeneutically and methodologically odd as pointed out above, and which has brought about the following response from Wolfhart Pannenberg[49]

> It is not always clear whether Smith is himself conscious of starting (not only personally but methodologically) from the Christian knowledge of God and going on to an awareness of the same God in all human history of religion—'seeing Christ's face in all human persons' [Smith

---

[46] Cf. note 44 above for a distinction between 'synthesism' and 'syncretism'. Rescher describes syncretism as that which adopts one position and conjoins it with alternative positions, certainly enabled by leaving out the non-contradiction principle, yet running the risk of self-defeat because one cannot avoid seeing the alternatives to oneself as equally valid. In this way, *affirmare* implies *negare*. If so, symphony is illusory and is replaced by cacophony—beyond the façade of openness and liberality.

[47] See also Coward 1985, 33.

[48] Let me just mention what I see as a non-synthesist statement *par excellence* in the New Testament: Matth. 28.18-20. The Great Commission is not an interpretation or emendation of dissonant elements of various religious traditions, but a handover of a divine aim, mediated by and embodied in the Son of Man who claims to represent universal authority: The One for the Many ('all nations'), cf. Isa. 53.11f. By this, *extension* becomes the direction of movement rather than synthesis. This does not rule out the viability of maintaining some synthesist features of a Christian theology, but it seems that this major extensification of the Gospel is downplayed in Smith: it merely functions as a means for Christians only, and not for people outside. This is of course not to say that Smith maintains that there is no interaction between different traditions, rather the contrary, only that it is not required for Christians to commend the Gospel to people of other traditions, because they have their own 'channels.'

[49] Pannenberg 1990/1995, 104, n7.

1987b, 66] ... or whether he claims a knowledge of the one
'transcendent reality' [Smith 1987b, 62] independent of the
different cumulative traditions. His assertion that 'at first'
he starts to interpret other cultures from his Western
Christian perspective, but 'less so in the end' [Smith 1987b,
63] remains ambiguous as to whether the comparative study
of religions ends up in providing a completely independent
evidence of the unity and sameness of the 'transcendent
reality' they point to or whether it merely confirms that God
of the Bible is also recognizable in other forms of 'faith.'
The second I could sympathize with, while the first seems
illusive, even if we postulate a 'universal, corporate, critical
self-consciousness' of human beings across the barriers of
cultural differences [*WT,* 60].

A similar response can be seen in Richard Swinburne's review of *Faith
and Belief* where he accuses Smith of ignoring the writings of modern
empiricists philosophers on knowledge and belief, especially related to
the connection between knowing a person and knowing that something
is the case:

> You cannot just know someone without having any
> knowledge or any rate true belief about them ... The same
> goes for God ... Man will never know God unless he has
> some true beliefs about what he is like, and also some true
> beliefs about how he is to be reached ... To suppose that no
> beliefs are necessary for religious advance is madness. You
> cannot get to London, let alone Heaven, without some true
> beliefs.[50]

The crucial point in Smith in this respect is precisely the relation between
faith and belief, or between universality and particularity, at least as Smith
himself understands these notions. My suggestion is that he confuses
those 'levels' as he gives priority to convergence/commonality. When,
for example, Smith asserts that all history is *Heilsgeschichte,* he
paradoxically empties history for events of divine revelation and salvation
while remaining immanentist and anthropocentric.[51] As Langdon Gilkey

---

[50] Swinburne 1980, 241f.

[51] Gilkey 1981, 303-304. Smith's sharp distinction between human/mundane truth
and cosmic truth supports undoubtedly this assessment.
An attempt to develop a view of redemption/salvation that is both general/ common,
that is, Christianity and other religions are placed together as the same kind of

has demonstrated, the (religious) participation of members of religious communities depends on the category and authority of a defining and definitive centre of the shaping tradition, although this may allow for an inclusive interpretation.[52]

It seems possible to see this confusion of levels as a shift from the level of salvation to that of creation and general history, because faith, in Smith's terms, can be seen as what Michael Barnes (who explicitly follows Smith and distinction between faith and belief) calls

> that fundamental acknowledgement of *creatureliness* in the face of whatever one takes to be the transcendent; it represents the human response to the transcendent dimension of religion.[53]

If faith is seen as a capacity of 'creatureliness,' a human potential for seeking, experiencing, feeling and thinking about something transcendent, Smith's position becomes far more attractive than if it is given the role of 'superdoctrine'[54] over particulars, as is the case of his concept of faith, which also conveys certain ideological features.[55] If one places faith on the level of creation, it will also come close to the anthropological features

---

religions, yet, as such, are antithetic to a specific salvation/revelation embodied in Christianity, is done by Carl Heinz Ratschow. In his second thesis with regards to the relationship between Christian theology and science of religion (*Religionswissenschaft*) he maintains: 'Das Christentum ist Religion wie der Hinduismus oder Buddhismus, insofern es seinen Gläubigen, wie es Religionen tun, das sinnverstellende Lebensleiden sowie den stetigen Bruch in das Sterben hinein zur sinnhaften Möglichkeit, verantwortlich zu leben, aufschließt und somit menschliches Dasein transzendiert. Alle Religion ist Erlösungsreligion,' Ratschow 1973, 423. In their 'dying' in order to 'live,' in reverence for g/God, the religions share the same destiny. Yet, this does in the case of Ratschow *not* mean that the issue of salvation is exhausted since it is *Deus absconditus* the religion's experience in this, not the word, work and person of Jesus Christ who illuminates the hidden god, Ratschow 1979, 122. Hence, in the end, Ratschow 'draws the line' and concludes that there is an ultimate antithesis between Christianity and other religions: Whereas human self-oblation (*mortificatio*) is consecutive of salvation (*vivificatio*) in Christianity, it is constitutive in the religions. See Knitter 1973, 46, for a description of Ratschow's approach at this place. This illustrates however my point immediately below that one should rather relate Smith's approach to a general but not all-decisive perspective (creation), than to an all-decisive level (salvation).

[52] *Ibid.*

[53] Barnes 1989, 127, my emphasis.

[54] Rescher 1993/1996, 92, although Smith is not regarded explicitly by this term in Rescher.

[55] Cf. Gavin D'Costa who follows theologians like Kenneth Surin, John Milbank and Gerard Loughlin, as well as the philosopher Alasdair MacIntyre and sees 'Christian pluralism' as a 'species of Enlightenment modernity,' which he sees as a 'particular

of what I have called Cragg's 'modest theory of religion' (cf. Chapter 4.5.2). Smith is probably aware of this possibility, and aims deliberately to conquer tenets from what can be called 'the traditional level of salvation,' for example the way in which he connects *sola fide* to his idiosyncratic perception of faith. For a theology based on insights from the Protestant Reformation, however, this sounds rather awkward: *Sola fide* remains inextricably connected to *solus Christus*.[56] In that respect, at the level of salvation, *solus* is not interchangeable with *inter alia*, and *sola fide* should be used accordingly, that is, *fides Christi* as the only redeeming *fides*. If not, the coherential request for internal consistency[57] (cf. above) seems not to have been met.

Yet, one should be careful while assessing Smith thus. First, there *is* a close relation between faith and belief in Smith's writings.[58] It is not Smith's view that faith is independent of belief. According to Smith there is no faith unless there are beliefs. Beliefs should not be seen as

---

shaping tradition' that fails to encourage 'openness, tolerance, and equality,' D'Costa 2000, 1f. Whereas D'Costa does not examine Smith's position, which he has done *implicitly* elsewhere, see D'Costa 1991 and 1993, it is likely that D'Costa's conclusions applies to Smith as well: 'The Enlightenment, in granting a type of equality to all religions, ended up denying public truth to any and all of them ... Their god is modernity's god,' *ibid.* 2. This is not to overstate the case as Smith may propose to use 'God' and 'reason' interchangeably, see *CR,* 58, note 48 (and Chapter 2.2 above), although he qualifies this proposal with 'or if the rationalist tradition is true.' For a 'materialist' critique of Smith, see Kenneth Surin who suggests with direct reference to Smith (and Hick) that 'it is no mere coincidence that 'global' theologies have appeared at the precise historical moment when capitalism has entered its global stage,' Surin 1990a, 120f. Surin sees in Smith 'a placeless and deculturated kind of way' that celebrates 'factitious unities and commonalities—by systematically overlooking ... the real asymmetries of power which exist between the 'First' and the 'Third' worlds,' Surin 1990b, 196f. Hence, Smith belongs to particular historical, political and social forces that provide the context of his approach, *ibid.* 192.

[56] Cf. Richard Swinburne who in his review of *FB* criticizes Smith for unclothing God for proprieties. In this Swinburne 'restores' St Thomas Aquinas whom Smith takes as a warrant for his view of *fides,* Swinburne 1980, 240.

[57] See also H. Küng's 'interreligious criteria' in regards of 'What is True Religion?' Küng 1994, 139f: 1. General *ethical* criterion: A religion is true/good if it is humane. 2. General *religious* criterion: A religion is good/true if it remains faithful to its origin and canon, faithful to its authentic nature, to the determining scripture or the most significant figure. 3. The specific *Christian* criterion: A religion is true/ good if it in theory as well as in practice gives room for the Spirit of Jesus Christ. I will assert that in Smith's case it is rather the second criteria that he fails to meet, references to 'the confessed center on which the evaluator stands while making his test,' but consequently also the third though this is the one that he explicitly affirms himself (Jesus as the impulse of his view).

[58] Cf. e.g. Chapter 2.2.

unnecessary 'clothing' which can be undressed if desired, but as necessary epistemological vehicles for gaining access to faith. Provided this view of faith and belief, crucial questions emerge however. Which one is the integrative of the two? Does not belief have an impact upon how faith is shaped? Or, is faith in the end formless, of which one gets the impression, because faith is never defined or 'shown' by him, only approached via its consequences, 'virtues' and 'fruits'?

I have elsewhere shown how Smith prefers to use 'transcendence', and the corresponding *finitum non capax infiniti* in order to emphasize the 'ineffability' of transcendence and its priority to 'immanence'. Such a preference conveys however certain paradoxes, as has been demonstrated by Peter Slater in his review of *FB,* which again backs up what has been said so far about Smith:

> The thought that God may be actively identified with the concrete particularities of history, that the expressions as well as the occasions of faith may be divinely rooted, seems alien to Smith's conception ... in practice [he] values transcendence over immanence. He is so eager to affirm such transcendence that he loosens ties to the Christ figure and risks disembodying the Christian faith completely. Ironically, this move reflects a more, not less, parochial[59] outlook on Christianity, enshrining a classical Protestant mistrust of sacramental religion. Despite the drift towards theology, Smith's weakness here is that he is not theological enough. For if we would do justice to our data, we must adopt a truly theological reading of history which acknowledges all the varieties of Christian expression, not only among medieval mystics but also among modern theologies of liberation.[60]

No wonder that Smith's 'vertical' view does not make the Incarnation a proper theme. Or better: the incarnational aspects of his approach have not explicitly shaped his approach.[61] According to Slater, neither does he make salvation so much a theme, a theme which Slater sees as the key to

---

[59] Slater describes Smith's own cultural background as 'self-negating Canadian internationalism.' See also Buckalew 1987, 55 ('marked internationalism').

[60] Slater 1982, 99. Buckalew has in his dissertation a very interesting discussion about the criticism of Gilkey (Gilkey 1981) at this point. Buckalew defends Smith to some extent by asserting that his position contains a christological kenotic motif, although it could have been more emphasized, Buckalew 1987, 108.

[61] See e.g. his notion of ideal relationship (*ME,* 150f) in the end of Chapter 2.4.4.

religion.[62] Against Smith's shift of levels, from salvation to creation, I will maintain the interrelation between salvation and creation. In other words: Because creation is a fallen creation it needs redemption, and because salvation is the salvation of creation it runs the risk of retreating from history if it is not properly based on a doctrine of creation. This interrelatedness between creation and salvation has also bearing for how we view relations.

Colin Gunton maintains that a Trinitarian theology, that is, a theology of the *economy* and *perichoresis* of the Father, Son and Holy Spirit, which conceives relatedness without absorption, may help us developing a theology of relations and of particularity.[63] By affirming the view of *recapitulatio* in Irenaeus, Gunton sees for example the distinctive work and mode of the Spirit as the perfection of creation, namely, by respecting and constituting otherness, particularity, distinctiveness, uniqueness, etc. Though this is not part of the context and concern of Gunton, this must apply as much to Muslims as to Christians. Hence, to improve creation through Christ is to perfect the difference and identity of particulars. Yet, because creation is fallen, it requires a completion through redemption. If thus religions are seen as part of creation, this may imply the following expression, as borrowed from a German-language article: 'Not all will remain what they are.'[64] Redemption presupposes creation, but entails transformation and completion.[65] If this view is adopted, the following statement is meaningful: 'all things cohere in Christ.'[66] If not, the importance of Christian salvific particulars (Christ's suffering, death and resurrection) can hardly be maintained with regards to universality and authenticity. But also the opposite, the adherents of diverse religious traditions, the religious creatures, will remain what they are: creatures, but also fallen creatures.

I will therefore suggest, that the role of Christian particulars is to be given a more prominent place than in the works of Smith. They are not

---

[62] *Ibid.* 100; with Patrick Burke.

[63] Gunton 1993/1998, 205f.

[64] Balz 1995. Ger. *Nicht alle werden bleiben, was sie sind.*

[65] It is Gunton's point to stress that Irenaeus' approach implies not only a 'return to the beginning,' but something *more* than what was in the beginning. On the opposite, he criticizes people like Pannenberg for dissolving the protology by an imbalanced preference for eschatology over protology.

[66] Gunton, op.cit., 178. I assume that he alludes to Eph. 1.10, where economy (οικονομοιαν) and coherence (ανακεφαλαιωσασθαι) are the themes, which they also are in Gunton's Bampton Lectures (see e.g. his ch. 6). He may possibly also bear Col 2.2f in mind ('that they may have the full riches of complete understanding, in order that they may know the mystery of God, namely, Christ, in whom are hidden all the treasures of wisdom and knowledge').

to be seen merely as means of attaining personal faith and a global view of humankind's religiousness but convey a decisive content that shapes faith in a distinctive way, against which non-Christian religious traditions are to be measured. Simultaneously, since Christian particulars relate to the world and history as a whole, particulars cannot be maintained without the whole as a perspective and environment. The otherness of, for example, Islam is therefore significant in terms of being within the relational field of a Christian field. The integrative force is, however, given by the decisive Christian particulars.

7.3.2 CHRISTOLOGY: BETWEEN EVENT AND PATTERNS OF EXCESS?

This view of decisive Christian particulars is easily discernable in Cragg's writings. His prime concern is to make Christian particulars relevant for the world's religious traditions, especially Islam. For this aim, not only is his making Christian theology relevant for non-Christians important, but also making non-Christian traditions and ideas understandable for Christians.

In such endeavours it remains a primary challenge how to proceed from the simple stories told about and by Jesus to an elaborate systematic account of the possibility of making these relevant and cogent for reception in different traditions. In short, this is the problem of translating the 'story of Jesus' into the 'story for reception.' My contention is that such systematic efforts will convey a theoretical element as far as they approach the meaning of the 'story.' This is obviously present in Cragg's attempt to see the story of Jesus within a continuous framework of 'suffering love on behalf of God,' which spans selected parts of the Old as well as the New Testament, but also in Smith's notion of an moral 'impulse' from Jesus, which he claims should permeate any Christian interreligious encounter. One may, however, ask: how can it be possible to discern between valid and invalid ways of utilizing the 'story of Jesus'?

Let me start with what I find to be an inescapable criterion: the link between the latter ('story for reception') and the former ('Jesus story') should be obvious. If we apply this criterion to Smith, it is possible to discover this in his *moral* of hermeneutics, which is certainly not a minor issue. In Smith there is an impulse for interreligious relations that is induced by the example of Christ. One illustration of this, which also relates directly to the issue we are addressing (theory/pattern), is how 'participation' may imply a (christological) kenotic motif. In his dissertation, Ronald W. Buckalew argues that in Smith 'participation' represents Christ as an 'implicit kenotic motif,' likewise with regards to 'humility'.[67]

However, it is difficult to see how this criterion can apply to the conceptual claims Smith makes elsewhere. In the latter case, that is, in relation to 'faith', his Christology is not only minimized,[68] but also subordinated to faith in a way that makes it no longer play any defining role for faith. One might argue with S. Mark Heim, that

> Smith's twin emphases on concrete history on one hand and on faith as an existential, contentless orientation are in tension.[69]

And, the more the distinction between internals (faith) and externals (belief) are insisted upon, 'the less plausible his claims to make the historian the arbiter of religious questions.'[70] This means that when faith is made contentless, while transcendence and cosmic salvation are left ineffable, it becomes difficult to maintain the significance of something historical. Hence, history does not contain anything of decisive significance.[71] Consequently, Smith's approach is nothing but a retreat to agnosticism, where mystery meets mystery.[72] This is a severe problem with Smith,[73] and I will claim that he does not fulfil John Henry Newman's first 'note' on what he calls a 'genuine development of an idea' within Christian doctrine: Preservation of its type, that is, 'that the parts and proportions of the developed form, however altered, correspond to those which belong to

---

[67] Buckalew 1987, 65ff. Buckalew maintains in his sensitive examination of the motif of *kenosis* that 'Christ as humble participant in human religious history is a significant theme which lies just below the surface, teasingly present, only occasionally breaking through to explicit expression in fragmented form in Smith's writings,' *ibid.* 66. Cf. e.g. *ME,* 9, where Smith talks about 'a transcendent and *concerned* reality,' my emphasis.

[68] Hughes 1985, 328.

[69] Heim 1995, 69.

[70] *Ibid.*

[71] Which Langdon Gilkey has accused him of maintaining, Gilkey 1981, 303, col. 2: 'There is here no category of 'special revelation,' a special point in history or in consciousness where a special and decisive (if not exclusive) manifestation of 'God' is affirmed to have taken place.'

[72] Heim 1995, 69. Cf. also Langdon Gilkey, Gilkey 1981, 304, col. 1, who describes Smith's theology *inter alia* thus: 'the elusiveness of the transcendent in these pages.' See also Ratschow 1979, 124, where Carl Heinz Ratschow describes one way (of two) of evading the 'hiatus' between religions: by talking about God as 'Mystery'. According to Ratschow, this implies that 'Aus-sage wird nichts-sagend.'

[73] Cf. the fourth 'systematic presupposition' of P. Tillich's 'Ablehnung der Orthodoxie' in respect of a consideration of the significance the history of religions may have for the systematic theologian, that is, 'die Annahme, daß ein zentrales Ereignis in der Geschichte der Religionen geben kann,' Tillich 1994, 52.

its rudiments.'[74] In short, it is difficult to see Smith's Christology as expressing the implications of biblical traditions.[75]

Having assessed Smith's approach thus, it remains to decide whether and how Cragg's approach can contribute to a valid way of making the 'Jesus story' relevant and cogent to a non-Christian reception. In other words, is Cragg's 'Christic pattern' and 'cross-reference' theology viable ways of translating the 'Jesus story' into a 'story for reception'?

Before reaching a more comprehensive evaluation of Cragg's approach, which will be done in the next chapter, one should keep in mind that his Christic pattern (and 'cross-reference' theology) is not only used in order to discover commonalities between Jesus and the Old Testament and Jesus and Islam (and other religious traditions), but is used in order to find 'dimensions mutually compatible and rigorously incompatible.'[76] Cragg's use of a Christic pattern is thus meant to meet the requirement of a proper theological *tertium comparationis*: that both similarities and differences are addressed in the light of it. This view seems, however, to presuppose certain premises. Firstly, that the Christic pattern is properly linked to (primarily but not exclusively) the Christ-event, that is, not only treated as a formal idea, but as the expression and implication of the history and event of Christ. Indeed, his claim of a Christic pattern presupposes 'a Messiahship we can identify within history.'[77] His examination of this in the Old Testament as well as the New Testament is persuasive. Secondly, a Christic pattern that is used in order to contrast or connect the Christian tradition with (particularly) Islam seems to require a certain excess on behalf of Christ, that is, Christ cannot be confined to the community of people who believe in Him. If, in the words of Cragg, a resonance of the Christian faith cannot be heard by recruiting, engaging and exciting 'what the other has,'[78] Christ and the Other become isolated and fragmented. If this cannot remain the Christian position, the question persists how Christ can recruit, engage and excite what the Other has.

Further examination of these premises belongs to the next chapter where Christology and Pneumatology are held together. However I find it

---

[74] Newman ²1878/1989, 171. See Macquarrie 1993, 174f for this reference. Cf. also Pannenberg

[75] See Pannenberg 1976, 344, cf. Chapter 2.6.2. Among four criteria which Pannenberg claims that should be met if 'theological hypotheses are to be judged as not substantiated,' the first reads: 'if and only if: 1. they are intended as hypotheses about the implications of the Israelite-Christian faith but cannot be shown to express implications of biblical traditions (even when changes in experience are allowed for).'

[76] Cragg 2000e.

[77] *COR,* 23. See Chapter 4.5.6.

[78] Cf. *CFs,* 13.

timely to draw the attention to the correlation of Cragg's Christic pattern (love who suffers in the procession of the Son, and the Spirit) and Gadamer's concept of the inner/interior word which neither diminish, nor alter, nor become exhausted by becoming external (cf. Chapter 4). In this there appears a coincidence between philosophical hermeneutics and Christian theology. If so, a strong substantiation of both 'self' and 'relating' is substantiated both hermeneutically (the being of the word by expression) and christologically (the being of Christ by self-expenditure). One might also think of this as a presupposition for self-change as far as 'self' has broken out of its own confinements and thus is 'risking itself' from the impact of 'the outside.'

Nevertheless, at this juncture I will only maintain that in a systematic effort to make the story of Jesus relevant for a religiously plural world, a certain theoretical endeavour should be permitted in order to merge the 'given past' and 'the mind of the receiver.' The use of concepts and ideas should, however, be continuously measured by their dependency upon the decisive story of Jesus and its successfulness of making Christ perceptive for a non-Christian audience. The justification of such theoretical activity should also address the issue of Christological 'excess'. In this there is a correlation between philosophical hermeneutics (Gadamer) and a kenotic view of the relevance of Christ outside the Christian community (Cragg) with especial regards to self-relating, but also self-change.

7.3.3 THE HOLY SPIRIT: 'MOVING CHRISTWARDS' BEYOND PERSONAL SALVATION?

The next doctrinal issue that arises from these theological elaborations is therefore the doctrine of the Spirit. Because I agree with Cragg that Pneumatology traditionally, at least in the Western Church, has been underdeveloped in some respects,[79] I will insist that our understanding of the Spirit should not deal exclusively with its role and work in the church since it is also 'active in the world'. The question, however, is how this activity should be conceived? In what follows I will maintain that the work of the Spirit 'before' and outside the church neither coincides with the work of the Spirit in the church after Pentecost, nor can it be seen as

---

[79] This point is also maintained by Smith, as part of his criticism against 'exclusivists' who he accuses of *de facto* having neglected the work of the Spirit and God as Creator, and thus have run the risk of becoming 'Unitarians of the Son,' Smith 1991a, 23. See also Pannenberg 1993, 123.

independent of this.[80] For that reason I do neither regard conclusive talk about the Spirit 'outside the church' as particularly successful, nor conclusive talk about the Spirit 'confined to the church.' Hence, either we are talking about the Spirit of the Father, of Christ, and in the church, or we are talking of none at all. This implies at the same time that a qualified talk of the Spirit *in* the world, that is, *inter alia* in the religious traditions, must be related to a Trinitarian theology. Whether this is to be seen as 'beyond Scriptures' (Cragg) will be addressed, and qualified, implicitly below. My argument with regards to this issue hinges on two premises: a) there is more to say about the Spirit in the Scriptures than what relates to the generation of Christian faith and the life in faith in the Christian community. b) The way in which the Spirit has been addressed in the Scriptures may open up for further doctrinal discussion.

I choose to start with Smith. In respect of Pneumatology the matter of identity is problematic in his account. Smith relates the Spirit primarily to its function and role of making scripture, that is, any religious Scripture, human. This means that the Spirit facilitates human faith despite 'the external visible forms through which the spiritual is mediated.'[81] This broad and vague notion of the Spirit can also be found in Cragg when he asserts the role of the Spirit in generating religiousness in various fashions (impulse, conception, expression, cf. Chapter 4), deliberately using language like 'unexpected' and 'disconcerting.' Yet, whereas in Smith this is seen as a completed work of the Spirit, in Cragg this is seen as a preparatory procession of the Spirit from God and the Son in order to 'take and open the things of Christ.' Nevertheless, since Cragg regards the work of the Spirit as inclusive, he suggests that non-Christian traditions may serve as 'school[s] of Christian faith, but far outside the prescripts of New Testament vocabulary and shape of mind.'

---

[80] See Lossky 1957/1991, 157. See also Regin Prenter who maintains that the Article 5 of *Confessio Augustana* (CA) 'does not exclude that the Spirit, without our ability to trace it, is present and active also where it is not given to humans, that is, before and after they have *received* it ... For the Scripture obviously distinguishes between the work of the Spirit before Pentecost and the outpouring of the Spirit over the people of God at the first Pentecost after the death and resurrection of Jesus. This 'before' and 'after' is not to be understood exclusively chronologically as an historical 'preceding' and 'proceeding' of the death and resurrection of Jesus Christ,' Prenter 1982, 25. That is also why I have bracketed 'before' above. I approve of this inclusive understanding of CA 5, which certainly resonates with Cragg's understanding of the Spirit's place' and time-inclusiveness, cf. note 91 below. Prenter also suggests that CA 7 and 8 should be read inclusively, though in another sense, that is, 'church' should be understood as 'the people of God', also including the chosen people of the old covenant. Thus, the Spirit was at work 'in the church' also in the Old Testament.

[81] Smith 1992b, 56.

As we see, the 'centres of gravity' are different for Smith and Cragg. This becomes clear if we see *how* they opt to *relativize* different parts in their traditions. In Smith's case the externals are optional and mutually interchangeable between different traditions. Faith is the unitary, *sine qua non* point of convergence between different traditions, whereas doctrines, beliefs, liturgies, and scriptures are made supportive, albeit relative. In Cragg's case it is the Old Testament that is interchangeable, whereas the 'finality of the Gospel of Christ' is made the central criterion, *sine qua non.* Since Smith has already been criticized on this issue, I find it necessary to pursue Cragg's view of a *preparatio evangelica* outside the Old Testament. I therefore ask: is it viable to conceive a 'school of Christian faith ... far outside the New Testament vocabulary and shape of mind'?

Cragg's position approximates the position of the seminal Lebanese Greek-Orthodox Metropolitan Georges Khodr who has maintained:

> Within God's plan, the great religions constitute training
> schools of the Divine mercy.[82]

This correlates further to his suggestion that one should shift away from a preoccupation with salvation history to a rediscovery of the *oikonomia*[83] of Christ, which 'is unintelligible without the economy of the Spirit.'[84] According to Khodr, this should not impair the meditorial role of the church, but does on the other hand not confine preparation and mediation to the church. On the other hand, the supreme task for the church is to

> identify all the Christic values in other religions, to show
> them Christ as the bond which unites them and His love as
> their fulfilment [by naming] Him whom others have already
> recognized as the Beloved.[85]

---

[82] Khodr 1971/1981, 47.

[83] *Ibid.* 43.

[84] *Ibid.* 46. The purpose of placing the Spirit between 'the history of Christ' and 'our history' is obviously to make the *how* of Christ's presence in the world a theme, as well as avoiding a position where ecclesial structures are made a 'conditio sine qua non for the presence of the Crucified and Risen in history,' Aagaard 1973, 276. On the contrary, 'it is the sending [Da. *sendelse*] of Pentecost that is the *sine qua non* for the Christ-event, in order to achieve history in the world,' *ibid.* 277. Aagaard continues to affirm Khodr's notion of the relation between Christ and the Spirit, but she asserts against his 'a-historical understanding of the economy of the Holy Sprit' that also the economy of the Spirit has a historical dimension, that is, the triune God acts historically and creates history, *ibid.*

[85] *Ibid.* 48f.

The pith of all this comes very close to Cragg's position.[86] A keyword here, which also may advance the argument, is the doctrine of the *kenosis* of the Spirit.[87] In short this refers to the Eastern way of speaking of the Spirit, that is, never of 'the Spirit alone' but of 'the Spirit *and* the deified person.'[88] The Spirit is thus seen as present in human persons in a hidden way.[89] In this, persons are made consubstantial with 'God's own life and being' by 'the acts of grace of the Spirit.'[90] According to Anna Marie Aagaard, this way of speaking of the *kenosis* of the Spirit is used in order to hold revelation, salvation, charismata, history and hiddenness together. By the *kenosis,* she claims, persons with the 'charismata' of 'love, joy, peace, forbearance, mildness, goodness and faithfulness' may represent the epiphany *(φανερωσις)* of the presence of God the Spirit.[91] This seems

---

[86] Cf. for example Cragg's concept of Christ as present in the religions primarily by the *prepossession* of Him in 'their own meanings.'

[87] Khodr explicitly adheres to a *kenotic* understanding of God's economy from creation onwards, *ibid.* 43. Most interestingly, Khodr sees his theology of mission and of the Spirit realized by the Nestorian Church (e.g. the Persian Church in Mesopotamia in relation to Islam). Moreover, not surprisingly, the Greek-Orthodox Khodr sees the *apophatic method* ('all concepts of God are idols') as most apt for a Christian estimation of talking about God in the 'scriptures of the non-Christian religions,' 48. This may at the first glance seem to resemble Smith's position. To some extent this is also true, in particular in Khodr and Smith's common inclination to mysticism. On the other hand, in Khodr, it is clear that 'all the other signs [i.e. of the non-Christian religions]' should be read by means of 'the mystery of which it [i.e. the Church] is the sign,' thereby '[revealing] to the world of the religions the God who is hidden within it, in anticipation of the final concrete unfolding and manifestation of the Mystery.' Hence Khodr's concept of mystery does not represent a *retreat* from the revelation in Christ, but makes it possible to relate the 'centrality and ontological uniqueness of Christ' (42), the economy of God, to the life of the religions of the world.

[88] Aagaard 1973, 238. English quotations are either original from her English Summary (pp. 281-285), or are translated by me from the Danish original.

[89] Cf. John 3.8: 'blows where it wills.' See also P. Evdokimov's statement cited in Aagaard 1973, 284: 'The more God is present, the more He is hidden even in his Revelation.' Vladimir Lossky sees the hiddenness of the Spirit as a consequence of it being 'the only one [of the Trinity] not having His image in another Person.' Therefore, 'the Holy Spirit, as Person, remains unmanifested, hidden, concealing Himself in His very appearing,' and thus 'concealed by the deity which He reveals to us, by the gift which He imparts,' Lossky 1957/1991, 160 and 162. Most interestingly, this combination of God's presence *and* hiddenness is also seen as the core of the Luther's view of God as 'hidden', Jenson 2000, 5f. His metaphysical distance, on the other hand, 'could only attenuate His visibility,' *ibid.* 5. For a suggestion to combine the Eastern, apophatic way of thinking about God as incomprehensible, and Luther's notion of *Deus absconditus,* see Prenter 1974, 92f.

[90] Aagaard op.cit., 238f. See also Khodr, op. cit. 43.

[91] Aagaard, op. cit. 239. 'Charismata' is here *not* understood as ' the equipment of a

to resonate with, for example, St. Basil of Caesarea who both maintained that there is 'no gift conferred upon creature in which the Holy Spirit is not present,'[92] and that the Spirit is 'wholly present to everyone and wholly everywhere at the same time.'[93]

My contention is that systematic theology should use the 'window of opportunity' that is available by the fact that the New Testament, in particular, does not exhaust what can be thought of the Spirit.[94] This is, however, not a sufficient reason itself to employ a kenotic Pneumatology. I will rather suggest that what is explicitly stated about the Spirit makes it possible to perceive its work in the world as hidden, especially how the Old Testament witnesses about the Spirit of creation and nature,[95] which I see

---

congregation for service, mission,' but as '*another kind of* charismata ... where not specific services and duties within the congregation are concerned, but where distinctive human phenomena become $\phi\alpha\nu\epsilon\rho\omega\sigma\iota\varsigma$ of the presence of the Holy Spirit in the world as the Spirit, which *gives the Kingdom of God history* after Cross and Resurrection,' *ibid.* 259, emphases mine. Aagaard sees this as part of the Pauline witness about the $\phi\alpha\nu\epsilon\rho\omega\sigma\iota\varsigma$ of the Spirit, cf. Gal. 5.22, Rom. 12-15, 1 Cor. 12-13. These charismata have in common that they are 'the history of love in the world,' and, as such, divine and not generated by humans. With regards to her use of 'charismata', I do *not* find it adequate, that is, as an implication of biblical witnesses, to see it as the 'history' of the Kingdom of God *after* Cross and Resurrection if viewed in a diachronic perspective. Yet, it would be possible to see them as anticipatory providential gifts, anticipating and resonating (Cragg) the life in the Kingdom, also at the same time as the life of the Kingdom is lived out otherwise (synchronically). This comes close to Cragg's notions of the Spirit's place- and time-inclusiveness. See also note 80 above. My qualification here correlates implicitly with Prenter's critique of Aagaard's combination of Trinitarian theology and 'secular theology,' including a 'neo-marxist' concept of history, Prenter *op.cit, passim.* The unfolding of my position belongs to what follows in this chapter.

[92] This is at least Lossky's rendering of *De Spiritu Sancto* XVI, 37, *PG*, XXXII, 133 C, Lossky 1957/1991, 163.

[93] *De Spiritu Sancto* IX, 22-23, McGrath 1995, 98, cited after C.F.J. Johnston, ed., *The Book of Saint Basil the Great on the Holy Spirit,* Oxford: Clarendon Press, 1892, pp. 51-54.

[94] Cf. in this respect Keith Ward who makes a list of things that require further 'reflective exploration' because their 'lack of doctrinal specificity' and in contrast to what is 'fixed,' 'unchangeable' and 'unrevisably true,' Ward 1994, 32f. Among these are most interestingly, with regards to that which follows below, the relation between Christ and the Spirit to God. This question is 'not resolved by the New Testament witness to Christ,' but, if Christ is 'the clue to the mystery of all human existence,' it has to be asked whether not 'Christians shall only truly understand Christ when they can see him in the context of that totality?' ibid 33. Such 'knowledge of the wider context in which it [i.e. the Christian faith] exists' may therefore deepen one's own Christian self-understanding, *ibid.* 325.

[95] See especially Pannenberg 1993 below. Pannenberg represents a Pneumatology 'beyond personal salvation,' as in the title of this chapter, taking his point of departure from the $\pi\nu\epsilon\upsilon\mu\alpha$ $\zeta\omega\omega\pi\omega\iota\omega\nu$ (cf. the Nicene Creed) which he sees as

as presupposed by the first Christians.[96]

My suggestion is to see the work of the Spirit dialectically in terms of referring to life-sustaining gifts, and of its 'moving people Christwards.' If so, it might be possible to find a coincidence, or at least a complementarity, between Cragg and Smith. In Smith, faith is described by its (differing) qualities and virtues: large, rich, strong, serene, generous, courageous, compassionate, patient, noble, creative. In Cragg the emphasis is on how people of other religions may be driven from within their own structures towards Christ. How can this be thought of? I will maintain that this seems to imply both an acknowledgement of divine gifts and of the hidden presence of the Spirit in non-Christian religions, as well as that these gifts and the hidden presence of the Spirit point towards their completion in Christ. It is, however, necessary to elaborate both of these a bit further. The issues of concern will possibly receive some light from my discussion of 'moving Christwards'.

Regarding 'moving Christwards', which is a distinctive Cragg-idiom,[97] I will propose both a differentiation of it and some substantiation for it. In short, this will relate to: a) the idea found in Paul of the goodness of God that leads to repentance (Rom. 2.4), which seems to adjoin both what Regin Prenter calls the 'gospel of Creation' (that is, God's providence), and, b) the Lutheran notion of *usus legis spiritualis* (*was Christum treiben*), that is, the Law will partly function in a way that makes the human consciousness fear 'sin, death and devil' so much that it flees to Christ in order to be rescued. If these are held together, I will maintain that there is both a positive and negative moving Christwards, one caused by attraction and providence, and one caused by emergency. These aspects will be treated explicitly (*ad* a.) as well as implicitly (*ad* b.) in what follows.

The Danish theologian Regin Prenter has in his magisterial dogmatics *Skabelse og genløsning (Creation and Redemption)*[98] an

---

an expression of the Old Testament view of the Spirit, for a long time forgotten by the Latin Church, but rediscovered by the Reformers (as explored by for example Prenter), *ibid.* 123 and 126. In this, Pannenberg draws on Eastern Pneumatology.

[96] I agree with Prenter that the sending of the Spirit at Pentecost does not exclude its 'previous' work as conceived in e.g. Ps. 104.30, that is, at work as hidden in *creatio continua,* Prenter 1974,

[97] Interestingly, a parallel to this is touched upon by Smith's proposal to see God as al-*Hudi* in Islam (the Guide; of humans towards God) as a close parallel to the Spirit in Christianity. The remaining difference is again that in Smith's case this is a moving 'Godwards' ('bring men to obedience and hence communion with Him', cf. Chapter 3.9), whereas in Cragg the Spirit provides a moving 'Christwards'. See also Smith 1992b, 56, where this connection seems to be implicit: 'The Word of God comes to us *through* the Bible, if in reading it we are guided by the Holy Spirit,' emphasis original.

[98] = Prenter 1962.

intriguing section on 'The gospel of Creation,'[99] following right after a section on 'The law of Creation.' Prenter's point is that God's providence may bridge His will of creation and His will of redemption in Jesus Christ.[100] In this respect, providence can be understood as, for example, 'any bracingness, any meal, any good night's sleep, any healthy laughter, any good piece of music' (219). He asserts therefore that

> God's providence is the unalterable direction of the act of
> creation towards the act of redemption, its conformity with
> the death and resurrection of Jesus Christ and mankind's
> death and resurrection in Him (216).

Yet, there is no immediate access to this knowledge by reason. That would either make providence responsible for evil and destruction, or evil would be interpreted as something unessential (217).[101] The gospel of Creation is hidden, and Prenter holds that seeing providence as serving the final victory of God's redemptive will requires the ambiguity of the human condition to be interpreted in the light of the death and resurrection of Jesus Christ (216). In that light providence bears witness that "the Father of the lights' (James 1.17) ... employs all means in order to raise the whole human being to eternal life and to tear off the powers of death' (219). Yet, on the other hand, the gospel of Creation is still effective even in the fall to the ground of a sparrow (221, cf. Matt. 10.29). Thus, the Cross is present in Creation (216).

From within this perspective, considering religious plurality, it is possible to see Christ as present in the world's religions as far as these are part of God's continuous creation.[102] Yet, this presence can only be anticipated and touched, whereas the proper interpretation of the ambiguity of the human condition, and comparably the divine providence and wrath, can only be sought in the light of the death and resurrection of Jesus Christ.

A pertinent question to raise here is how Cragg's 'Christic pattern' should be interpreted against this backdrop. As far as I can see, a clue can be found in the difference between presence (of Christ) and identification (of providence as 'the death and resurrection of Christ in

---

[99] *Ibid.* pp. 216-220. Subsequent parenthetical remarks refer to Prenter 1962.

[100] Cf. also how Cragg relates Christ to creation by his distinction between 'law of creation' and 'love of creation', Cragg 1982b, 30. See Chapter 5.5.4.

[101] Cf. also Jenson 2000, 6, where R.W. Jenson refers to Luther's famous dictum in *De Servo Arbitrio* with regards to God: *aut malum aut nullum esse Deum, WA* 18: 784.

[102] Given criteria like 'preservation of life', 'development and sustenance of cultural integrity and identity', etc., I find this to be a reasonable interpretation of the relation between Creation and religious traditions.

Creation'). A possible advance of Prenter's view can be found in his own study of Luther's view of the Holy Spirit as *Spiritus Creator*.[103] Here, Prenter sees a distinction within Luther's view of Christ, as a) a pattern, idea, and b) as Christ Himself (*Christus ipse*). Most interestingly, this difference is only discernable as far as the persons of the Trinity are distinguished and seen together. This means that whereas the former refers to the Christ in the law (the idea and pattern of Christ), the latter refers to 'Christ as redeeming reality.'[104] To bridge between the two, which cannot be separated, is seen as the work of the Spirit. And, since *fides Christi* is faith in *Christus ipse,* 'it is the Spirit alone which makes the all-decisive difference.'[105] To take advantage of Cragg's terminology, this implies that we must distinguish between 'Christic patterns', on the one hand, and 'a Christian faith' and 'Christ Himself' on the other. Whereas the former patterns are present in the world religions, they cannot be theologically identified except in the light of the suffering, dead and risen Jesus Christ *ipse*. Yet, 'to move Christwards,' from the Christic pattern to *Christus ipse,* is entirely the work of the Spirit, albeit it is felt like 'a negative/emergent moving Christwards' (*usus legis spiritualis,* cf. above).

This work of the Spirit generates eventually *fides Christi,* which is salvific and consequently all-decisively different. Interpreted thus, Cragg's view of 'moving Christwards' as 'a valid theory of development and change'[106] becomes theologically meaningful. In this, the Spirit who makes the all-decisive difference is the 'origin of all life' who *prepares* all humanity for the arrival of the Son,[107] and who, in the new life of *fides Christi,* has the power of sustaining and finally overcoming the absurdities of the present world.[108] Thus, the fragmentary presence and manifestation of the Spirit in time and space, and in the history of religious traditions, has been conquered by the actualisation of the criterion for the new kind of life in Christ.[109]

A criticism of Smith may gain fuel from this view because Smith's *fides* is, as was mentioned already in this chapter, unlikely to be identified with *fides Christi*. Whereas the former is a human faculty, the latter presupposes the *theologia crucis* and the Spirit as *donum*. As in Cragg,

---

[103] Prenter 1953.
[104] *Ibid.*, 182.
[105] *Ibid.*
[106] See Chapter 4.2.1.
[107] Pannenberg sees this as the merit of Irenaeus, paraphrasing his view thus: 'the spirit of God 'from the very beginning' assisted people in adjusting themselves to the actions of God by announcing the future, reporting the past, and interpreting the present. Thus the spirit, according to Irenaeus, was the first to reveal God to humanity,' Pannenberg 1993, 126.
[108] Pannenberg 1993, pp. 123 and 137.
[109] Cf. Tillich 1963a, 140f and 144.

the Gospel fulfils by contrast rather than by similarity.[110] *Fides Christi* relates therefore to what Cragg calls a 'lifting of the whole level of relationship.'[111] Yet, an extenuating circumstance is that Smith sees faith, as also Luther, as a given miracle, a new-creation, a divine act, etc. At best, one may say that there are features of a pistology that sees the salvific faith as passively originated, by divine grace. The problem, however, is that this faith in principle is separated from the work of Christ and the Spirit (in this respect). In the end, Christ's suffering, death and resurrection are not necessary for 'the nations', but helpful means for the Christian in order to get in touch with T/transcendence (the Father of Christ?). One may therefore conclude that Christ's function in Smith aligns to the way other channels function in other traditions, but there is nothing like an all-decisive *fides Christi*. Put differently: there is no criterion for spiritual presence. Consequently, Smith's *fides* remains fragmentary and ambiguous. This becomes certainly all the more acute as Islam is addressed, especially since the 'how God' question is unsatisfactory answered, which in the end reduces the importance of this distinctively Trinitarian issue. In other words: Smith neutralizes the 'radicalization of monotheism',[112] as found in Christian theology.

As one may have noted throughout my examination of the role of the Spirit, I have been addressing Creation and Christ as well. The reason for this is their interrelatedness and *perichoresis,* as conceived in Trinitarian theologies.[113] As aforementioned, I have been reluctant to address the issue of 'the Spirit and the religions' as a matter of the Spirit outside the church. The reason for this should be obvious at this point: the Spirit belongs to the Trinity, and since the Trinity is present both in the church (visibly in the word and the sacraments) and outside it (as hidden), the Spirit in the religions cannot be separated from the Spirit in the church. This means also that the Trinity, including the economy of the Son and the Spirit, is to be thought of as primary to the church.[114] This view rests on two premises.

Firstly, the Spirit is the *Spritus creator* and thus the Spirit of the *creatio continua* in which the people and institutions of any religious tradition and community are included as *loci* for 'God's transcendent and active presence at the heart of creation.'[115]

---

[110] See Chapter 4.2.3.

[111] *MC,* 129, see Chapter 5.5.4.

[112] Michel 2000, 8.

[113] For this, see e.g. D'Costa 2000, 164, and Gunton 1993/1998, 163-166.

[114] In this, I approve Cragg's theological interrogation into 1 Tim. 3.15, Chapter 4.5.5. Consequently, my contention is that the 'pillar and ground of truth' is ultimately God the Father, Son and Holy Spirit, though, on the other hand, this truth is efficiently available and shown in its fullness in the church.

[115] Michel 2000, 7.

Secondly, if one perceives some kind of *praeparatio* or resonance of the Christ-event outside the Jesus-story and 'Jesus-community' (the church), the Spirit cannot be disconnected from the Son either. In this, the work of the Spirit may resemble Jesus' promises about he that will come and 'convict the world of guilt in regard to sin and righteousness and judgement,' as well as he who will actualise the truth of the Son, and consequently of the Father (John 16.8-15).

This means also, that if the Father, Son, and Spirit are present, anticipated or resonated in some way in the religions, the religions cannot be entirely disconnected from the church either, though it remains a theological difference between living in the hidden presence of the triune God on the one hand, and worshipping the Father, Son and Holy Spirit in communion, and in their identified and overt relatedness. This difference is primarily related to the given and promised communion with God as connected with fides Christi.[116] In this, the Holy Spirit will cease to be external to us, and become internal[117] in us, in what the Eastern Church denotes 'divine life.' Thus, the Spirit liberates us and helps us cry 'Abba, Father,' testifying that we are God's children (Rom. 8.15f). Finally, in this, and relating this Pneumatology with Cragg's Christology, we are also co-heirs of Christ, sharing his sufferings—and glory

To sum up, the God of the church is the God of the religions, though felt, seen, interpreted and celebrated differently. My contention is that this is also the deepest substantiation for any relation between Christian theology and Islam. This may also be seen as the substantiation for possible self-changes in respect of the doctrine of the Spirit since we discover new bearings of the Spirit in its activity in the religions. Such discoveries may thus entail a deeper penetration of the Christian faith and a better expression of it, as well as better equipment for relating to the Other. This is divine 'excess' expressed in a Trinitarian language.

I therefore suggest that the Spirit is, as the Spirit of the Father and the Son, actively present as hidden in the world's religions in the sustenance of life and in the preparation of faith in Christ. This is a presence of the Trinity, because of their interrelatedness and perichoresis. Consequently, the religions can neither be disconnected from the church, nor do they coincide with the church. It remains a difference whether one encounters the Spirit as hidden, or in the promised communion with the identified and worshipped Triune God. Nevertheless, this theology of divine 'excess' enables Christian theology both to relate to other religions as well as become itself more deeply penetrated and better understood.

---

[116] For the emphasis on 'promise', see Pannenberg 1990/1995, 104.
[117] Lossky 1957/1991.

BIOGRAPHY AND REFERENCES

Outline of the Life and Work of Kenneth Cragg and Wilfred Cantwell Smith

In order to support the reading of the various texts of Smith and Cragg within their historical contexts, I offer this brief outline of their *curricula vitae* with regards to their education, as well as the positions and offices which they have been given, and occupied, during their careers.[1]

(ALBERT) KENNETH CRAGG

1913	Born in England, 8 March.
1931-34	Undergraduate studies in Modern History, Jesus College, Oxford
1934	Ordination training and theological studies, Tyndale Hall (Bible Churchmen's Missionary Society's College, Clifton, Bristol, later Trinity College.)
1936	Ordained. Deacon, 1936. Priest, 1937.
1936-39	Curate at St Catherine's, Higher Tranmere, Birkenhead, Diocese of Chester.
1937	Ellerton Theological Prize, Oxford University ('The Place of Authority in Matters of Religious Belief')
1939-47	Missionary service in Lebanon for the British Syria Mission at Lebanon Bible Institute. Also Chaplain, All Saints' Church, Beirut, Lebanon, for the Bishop of Jerusalem. 1940: Married to Theodora Melita in Beirut. 1941: Stay in Gaza because of an evacuation of civilians from Lebanon. 1942-47: Warden, St Justin's House for Palestinian students (closed in 1948 because of the Arab/Israeli war). Taught English classes first, and then

---

[1] The biographical information about Cragg is found in Jones 1988, 39ff, Lamb 1981, 15, idem 1997, ch. 1, and in the CD-Rom *Who's Who 1897-1996: One Hundred Years of Biography*, in addition to what can be read out of several articles and other publications by him and about him. Of particular value is his autobiography or 'Christian story-study' from 1994, which sheds light upon both the 'whole' of his life as well as its 'parts': *Faith and Life Negotiate. A Christian Story-Study (FLN)*. Where there are disagreements between the sources, I rely on *FLN*.

In Smith's case, cf. *The International Who's Who* 1994-95, 1450; Smith 1981, vf; Jones 1988, 39ff; Cragg, *TT*, 242ff; and especially Oxtoby 1976, viii-xv, and Grünschloß 1994, 27-66, particularly 64f. See also McCutcheon 1992.

	became Adjunct Professor of Philosophy, affiliated to the American University of Beirut.
1947	T H Green Moral Philosophy Prize, Oxford University ('Morality and Religion').
1947-51	Rector of Longworth Rectory, Berkshire, just outside Oxford. Doctoral studies in Modern Islam.
1948	Sheriff's Chaplain, Berks.
1950	D.Phil. presented to the Faculty of Theology, Oxford (Cragg 1950, *Islam in the Twentieth Century: The Relevance of Christian Theology and the Relation of the Christian Mission to its Problems*). Supervised by Ernest Payne. Examined by H A R Gibb and H Danby.
1951-56	Professor of Arabic and Islamics, Hartford Seminary Foundation, Connecticut. 1954: Extensive travel in the 'Muslim world,' for the first time outside the Middle East, provided by Rockefeller Foundation.
1952-60	Co-editor (with Edwin Calverly) and then editor of *The Muslim World* (Quarterly)
1956-62	Residentiary Canon of St George's Collegiate Church, Jerusalem. 1956-59: Operation Reach; study programme on Christian engagement with Islam throughout the Middle East.
1959-67	St Augustine's College, the Central College for the Anglican Communion, Canterbury. Fellow, 1959-60. Sub-Warden, 1960-61. Warden, 1961-67. The college was forced to close in 1967 by Archbishop Ramsey. Examining Chaplain to the Archbishop of Canterbury, 1961-67. Honorary Canon of Canterbury, 1961-80. Proctor in Convocation, Canterbury, 1965-68.
1961	Selected Preacher, Cambridge.
1962	Selected Preacher, Dublin.
1965-66	Visiting Professor, Union Theological Seminary, New York.
1966	Reader, Faculty of Divinity, Cambridge.
1967	Jordan Lecturer, School of Oriental and African Studies, University of London.
1968	Visiting Professor, University of Ibadan, Nigeria.
1969	Visiting Professor, Bangalore, June Term.
1969-74	By-Fellow, Gonville and Caius' College, Cambridge.
1970-73	Assistant Bishop in the Jerusalem Archbishopric (from 1975: the Province of Jerusalem and the Middle East of the Episcopal Church) for the Anglican communities in Egypt, residing in Cairo.
1973-78	Reader in Religious Studies, Sussex University. 1978: Retired.
1974	Select Preacher, Oxford.
1974-78	Honorary Assistant Bishop of Chichester.
1978-81	Vicar of Helme and Assistant Bishop, Wakefield Diocese.
1981-	Retired and became Assistant Bishop of Oxford Diocese. Lives in Oxford.

1984-85	Visiting Professor, Virginia Theological Seminary, Alexandria, Virginia, from which he also received an Honorary D.D.
1993	Honorary D.D., Leeds.
1999	Honorary Fellow of Jesus College, Oxford.

WILFRED CANTWELL SMITH

1916	Born in Toronto, Canada, 21 July. B.A. studies in Oriental studies, which included classical Semitic languages (Hebrew and Arabic) and Near Eastern history, at the University College, University of Toronto. At this time he also worked and had positions both in the Student Volunteer Movement for Foreign Missions and The Student Christian Movement. Thereafter, he went to Westminster College, Cambridge, England, where he continued Oriental languages and started his theological studies. His Arabic and Islamic Studies were done at St John's College, University of Cambridge, under Hamilton A R Gibb. Smith also studied at University of Madrid and American University of Cairo (at the age of seventeen, before he went to university.)
1941-49	Service in the interdenominational Canadian Overseas Missions Council at Forman Christian College, Univ. of Punjab, Lahore, India (now Pakistan). Here he taught Indian and Islamic History to Muslims during the War, from 1941 to 1945. He also lived in the Muslim part of the city. In 1943 he was ordained for interdenominational duties, and at the same time became recognized as minister in the Presbyterian Church of Canada.
1947	M.A. in Oriental Languages, Princeton University.
1948	Ph.D., Dept. of Oriental Languages and Literatures, Princeton University (Smith 1948, *The Azhar Journal: Survey and Critique*), supervised by Philip K Hitti.
1949-63	W M Birks Professor of Comparative Religion, Faculty of Divinity, and from 1951 Director of Institute of Islamic Studies (until 1963), both McGill University, Montreal, Canada. As a curiosity, the Institute of Islamic Studies required that half its graduate-degree candidates and half its teaching staff should be Muslims. In 1961 his ordination was transferred from the Presbyterians to the United Church of Canada (Methodists, Congregationalists and 'half' of the Presbyterians).
1960	Visiting Professor, London University.
1964-73	Professor of Worlds Religions and Director of Center for the Study of World Religions, Divinity School, Harvard University
1965	Visiting Professor, Princeton University
1966	Strong Lectures, Australia
1966-69	President of the American Society for the Study of Religion
1968	Visiting Professor, University of Toronto

1972	Cadbury Lectures, Birmingham
1973-78	McCulloch Professor and Chairman, Department of Religion, Dalhousie University, Halifax, Nova Scotia, Canada
1974	Iqbal Lectures, Panjab. Chauveau Medal, and Fellow of Royal Society of Canada.
1975	Richards Lectures, Virginia
1977-78	President of Middle East Studies Association of North America
1978	Visiting Professor, University of Washington
1978-84	Professor in Comparative History of Religion and Chairman, Committee on the Study of Religion, Harvard University
1979-80	President of Canadian Theological Society
1982-83	President of American Academy of Religion
1984-	Retired, professor emeritus, Harvard
1984-86	Visiting Professor at Trinity College, University of Toronto, and Sr. Killam Research Fellow
2000	Died 7 February, Toronto.

Abbreviations

WORKS OF CRAGG

AC	*The Arab Christian.* 1991b
AG	*Alive to God.* 1970
CCI	*Counsels in contemporary Islam.* 1965
CFs	*The Christ and the faiths.* 1986
CI	*The Christian and Islam.* 1957a
CM	*The call of the minaret.* 1956c/1964
COR	*The Christian and other religion.* 1977a
CP	*Common prayer.* 1999a
CWP	*Christianity in world perspective.* 1968a
DC	*What decided Christianity.* 1989
DF	*Defending (the) faith.* 1997b
DR	*The Dome and the Rock.* 1964
ECF	*The education of Christian faith.* 2000a
EQ	*The event of the Qur'an.* 1994c
FLN	*Faith and life negotiate.* 1994a
GHT	*With God in human trust.* 1999c
HI	*The house of Islam.* 1969a
IAS	*Islam among the spires.* 2000f
ITC	*Islam in the twentieth century.* D.Phil. diss. 1950
IW	*Islam from within.* With R. Marston Speight. 1980c
JM	*Jesus and the Muslim.*
LC	*The lively credentials of God.* 1995a
MC	*Muhammad and the Christian.* 1984
MG	*To meet and to greet.* 1992c
MQ	*The mind of the Qur'an.* 1973

PAL	*Palestine: The Prize and Price of Zion.* 1997a
PF	*The pen and the faith.* 1985b.
PM	*The privilege of man.* 1968b
PP	*Paul and Peter.* 1980
PWC	*Poetry of the Word at Christmas.* 1996
RMH	*Returning to Mount Hira'.* 1994b
RQ	*Readings in the Qur'an.* 1999b
SEG	*The secular experience of God.* 1998a
SM	*Sandals at the mosque.* 1959c
TT	*Troubled by truth.* 1992a
TYJ	*This year in Jerusalem.* 1982
WSuf	*Wisdom of the Sufis.* 1976
WWd	*The weight in the word.* 1999d

WORKS OF SMITH

BH	*Belief and history.* 1977
CR	Comparative religion: Whither and why? 1959/1966
CS	The comparative study of religion. Reflections on the possibility and purpose of a religious science. 1950.
FB	*Faith and belief.* 1979a
FOM	*The faith of other men.* 1962/1965
IH	*Islam in modern history.* 1957a
ME	*The meaning and end of religion.* 1963
MI	*Modern Islam in India.* 1946
QT	*Questions of religious truth.* 1967b.
RD	*Religious diversity*, ed. Williard G. Oxtoby. 1976
UI	*On understanding Islam.* (19XX/)1981a-p
WS	*What is scripture?* 1993
WT	*Towards a world theology.* 1981

OTHER

Abbreviations in the text should be first checked against the listings above. If not found there, they may be found in *IATG²* (*Internationales Abkürzungsverzeichnis für Quellenwerke mit bibliographischen Angaben*, zusammengestellt von Siegfried M Schwertner, 2. überarb. und erw. Auflage. Berlin: Walter de Gruyter, 1992). All other abbreviations are taken from *IATG²* except the following:

CDPh	*The Cambridge dictionary of philosophy*, gen. ed. Robert Audi.
CEIsl	*The concise encyclopaedia of Islam*, ed. Cyril Glassé.
CQur	Kassis, Hanna E: *A concordance of the Qur'an.*

ICMR   *Islam and Christian-Muslim relations* (1990-)
IJST   *International Journal of Systematic Theology* (1999-)
JIMMA   *Journal of the Institute of Muslim Minority Affairs* (1980-)
Q   *The Qur'an*
MJR   *Marburg Journal of Religion* (1996-)
MTSR   *Method & theory in the study of religion: Journal of the North American Association for the Study of Religion* (1989-)

Reference Works and Text Editions

The Book of Common Prayer. With amendments made by the Measures of the Church Assembly in 1964, 1965, and 1969. Oxford: Oxford University Press.

The Cambridge dictionary of philosophy [CDPh]. 1995. Gen. ed. Robert Audi. Cambridge: Cambridge University Press.

The concise encyclopaedia of Islam [CEIsl]. Ed. Cyril Glassé. London: Stacey International.

Denzinger. 1991. *Enchiridion symbolorum definitionum et declarationum de rebus fidei et morum/ Kompendium der Glaubensbekenntnisse und kirchlichen Lehrentscheidungen,* 37th edn. Ed. Peter Hünermann (by assistance of Helmut Hoping). Freiburg i.B., Basel, Rom and Wien: Herder.

The encyclopaedia of Islam [EI]. 1960-1999 (so far, series not accomplished). New edn. Ed. and prepared by various leading orientalists. Vols. I-X (hitherto). Leiden, New York et al.: E J Brill.

The encyclopedia of religion [EncRel(E)]. 1987. Ed. Mircea Eliade. New York: Macmillan, and London: Collier Macmillan, vols. 1-16.

Handwörterbuch des Islam [HIsl]. 1941. Ed. A J Wensick and J H Kramers. Leiden: E J Brill.

The Holy Bible: New International Version (NIV). Colorado Springs, CO: International Bible Society, and London et al: Hodder & Stoughton.

IATG²: Internationales Abkürzungsverzeichnis für Quellenwerke mit bibliographischen Angaben (International glossary of abbreviations for theology and related subjects). 1992. Siegfried M Schwertner. 2. überarb. und erw. Auflage. Berlin: Walter de Gruyter.

The International Who's Who, 1994-95. 58th edn. London.

Kassis, Hanna E. *A concordance of the Qur'an* [CQur]. Foreword by Fazlur Rahman. Berkely, Los Angeles and London: University of California Press. 1983.

The Koran Interpreted. Translated with a new introduction by Arthur J Arberry. Oxford: Oxford University Press 1964/1982.

The Koran. Translated with notes by N J Dawood. London et al.: Penguin Books 1999 (¹1956).

Koranen. Norwegian translation of the Qur'an by Einar Berg, bilingual. Oslo 1989.

Biography and References

Lampe, G W H, ed. 1968 (1961). *A patristic Greek lexicon.* Oxford: Oxford
University Press.
Lewis, Charlton T and Charles Short. 1887/1955. *A Latin dictionary.* Revised
and enlarged, and in great part rewritten. Oxford: The Clarendon
Press.
Novum testamentum graece, 26. Aufl., Stuttgart 1898/1979.
Shorter encyclopaedia of Islam [SEI]. 1953. Ed. H A R Gibb and J H Kramers.
Leiden: E J Brill.

Main Works of Wilfred Cantwell Smith and Kenneth Cragg

KENNETH CRAGG

1950   Islam in the twentieth century: The relevance of Christian
            theology and the relation of the Christian mission to its
            problems. (Part I: i-xii + 1-563, part II: 1-280). D.Phil. diss.,
            University of Oxford.
1953   'The somehow may be this-how': A plea for constructive
            Muslim-Christian theological relations today. *MW* 43:2 (Apr.),
            118-129.
1956a   The Qur'an and the Christian reader. I. *MW* 46: 61-68.
1956b   ['Abd al-Tafahum (pseud.)], 'City of Wrong', *MW* 46: 132-143
            (I) and 224-236 (II).
1956c/1964 *The call of the minaret.* New York: Oxford University Press/
            Galaxy.
1957a   *The Christian and Islam* [CI]. Beirut: Near East School of
            Theology.
1957b   'Hearing by the Word of God'. *IRM* 46, 241-251.
1959a   The divine word in human trust. *SW* 52: 376-384.
1959b   ['Abd al-Tafahum (pseud.)], The Qur'an and the Holy
            Communion. In *MW* 49:3 (Jul.), 239-248.
1959c   *Sandals at the mosque: Christian presence amid Islam* [SM].
            London: SCM Press.
1961   The Encounter of Christianity and Islam. *SW* 54: 126-136.
1962   Review of Norman Daniel, *Islam and the West.* In *MW* 52:1
            (Jan), 59-61.
1964a   Encounter with non-Christian faiths. *USQR* 19: 299-309.
1964b   *The Dome and the Rock: Jerusalem studies in Islam* [DR].
            London: SPCK.
1965   *Counsels in contemporary Islam* [CCI]. Islamic Surveys, no. 3
            [condensed and up-dated version of ITC]. Edinburgh: Edinburgh
            University Press.
1966a   This cruciform world: A study in Christian universality. *USQR*
            21: 103-115.
1968a   *Christianity in world perspective* [CWP]. London.

361

1968b   *The privilege of man: A theme in Judaism, Islam and Christianity*
         [PM]. Jordan lectures in comparative religion, no. 8 [School of
         Oriental and African Studies (SOAS), London]. London: Athlone
         Press.

1969a   *The house of Islam* [HI]. Belmont, CA.

1969b   'The Tempter said . . .': Reflections on Christian theology and
         development. *IRM* 58 (Oct), 379-389.

1969c   Dialogue with other faiths: Essays written for the Lambeth
         Conference 1968. In *Lambeth Essays on Faith,* ed. the
         Archbishop of Canterbury, 32-39. London: SPCK.

1970   *Alive to God: Muslim and Christian prayer.* [Compiled with an
         introductory essay by Cragg.] London, New York, Toronto:
         Oxford University Press, 1970.

1971   The cross in the Qur'àn. *BTF* 3: 11-19.

1973   *The mind of the Qur'an: Chapters in reflection* [MQ]. London:
         Allen and Unwin.

1974   Islam and Incarnation. In *Truth and dialogue: The relationship
         between world religions,* ed. John Hick, 126-139. London.

1976   *Wisdom of the Sufis* [WSuf]. London: Sheldon Press.

1977a   *The Christian and other religion: The measure of Christ* [COR].
         Oxford.

1977b   Us and ours. *IRM* 66: 169-175.

1980a   Being Christian and being Muslim: A personal debate. *Religion*
         10: 196-208.

1980b   Christianity as a world religion. *ThRev* 3, no. 2: 10-19.

1980c   Together with R Marston Speight: *Islam from within. Anthology
         of a religion* [IW], Chs. 1,2,6-8 written by Cragg. The religious
         life of man series, ed. Frederick J. Streng. Belmont, CA:
         Wadsworth Publishing Company.

1980d   *Paul and Peter: Meeting in Jerusalem* [PP]. Bible Reading
         Fellowship, Book Club, no. 7. London: Bible Reading
         Fellowship

1981a   'Greater is God.' Contemporary *Takbir*: Muslim and Christian.
         MW 71: 27-39.

1981b   Temple Gairdner's legacy. *IBMR* 5, no. 4: 164-167.

1982a   *This year in Jerusalem: Israel in experience* [TYJ]. London:
         Darton, Longman and Todd.

1982b   Doing the New Testament right: Synoptic reflections of a
         layperson. In *Christological perspectives: Essays in honour of
         Harvey K. McArthur,* ed. Robert F. Berkey/ Sarah A. Edwards,
         24-41. New York.

1984   *Muhammad and the Christian: A question of response* [MC].
         London/ New York.

1985a   *Jesus and the Muslim. An exploration* [JM]. London. Reprinted
         1999.

1985b   *The pen and the faith: Eight modern Muslim writers and the*

	Qur'an [PF]. [= Ian Douglas Memorial Lectures, Henry Martin Institute of Islamic Studies, Hyderabad, India.] London.
1986	*The Christ and the faiths* [CFs]. Philadelphia, Pennsylvania.
1989	*What decided Christianity* [DC]. Worthing: Churchman.
1990	Holding faith and conceding pluralism: A Christian position. In *Christian mission and interreligious dialogue,* ed. Paul Mojzes/ Leonard Swidler, 174-186. Lewiston/ Qeenston/ Lampeter
1991a	Comment on Shabbir Akhtar: Faust and the new idolaters: Reflections on shirk (Akhtar 1990b). *ICMR* 2: 124-126.
1991b	*The Arab Christian. A history in the Middle East* [AC]. Westminster and Louisville, KY: John Knox Press.
1992a	*Troubled by truth: Life-studies in inter-faith concern* [TT]. Edinburgh/ Cambridge/ Durham.
1992b	Peace, pacificism and religious faith. *JIMMA* 13, no. 1 (January): 215-221.
1992c	*To meet and to greet: Faith with faith* [MG]. London: Epworth.
1993a	Prepositions and salvation. *IBMR* 17: 2-3.
1993b	The riddle of man and the silence of God: A Christian perception of Muslim response. *IBMR* 17: 160-163.
1993c	The singer and the song: Christology in the context of world religions. In *Christology in Dialogue,* ed. Robert F Berkey and Sarah A Edwards, 185-200. Cleveland, OH: The Pilgrim Press.
1994a	*Faith and life negotiate: A Christian story-study* [FLN]. Norwich: The Canterbury Press.
1994b	*Returning to Mount Hira': Islam in contemporary terms* [RMH]. London: Bellow Publishing.
1994c	*The event of the Qur'an. Islam in its scripture* [EQ]. Republishing with new additional preface (first published 1971). Oxford: Oneworld Publications.
1995a	*The lively credentials of God* [LC]. London: Darton, Longman and Todd.
1996	*Poetry of the Word at Christmas* [PWC]. 2nd rev. and expanded edn. (¹1987.) London: New Millennium.
1997a	*Palestine. The prize and price of Zion* [PAL]. London and Herndon, VA: Cassell.
1997b	*Defending (the) faith: The matter of the article* [DF]. London: New Millennium.
1998a	*The secular experience of God* [SEG]. Harrisburg, PA/ Herefordshire.
1998b	'My tears into thy bottle': Prophethood and God. *MW* 88:3-4, 238-255.
1999a	*Common prayer. A Muslim-Christian spiritual anthology* [CP]. Rev. and abr. version of *AG*.
1999b	*Readings in the Qur'an* [RQ]. Selected and translated by K C Republishing (first published 1988). Brighton/ Portland, Or: Sussex Academic Press.

1999c   *With God in human trust. Christian faith and contemporary humanism. A meeting of minds* [GHT]. Brighton/ Portland, Or: Sussex Academic Press.

1999d   *The weight in the word. Prophethood: Biblical and Quranic* [WWd]. Brighton, Portland, Or: Sussex Academic Press.

2000a   *The education of Christian faith: Critical and literary encounters with the New Testament* [ECF]. Brighton, Portland, Or: Sussex Academic Press.

2000b   Sermon delivered on Easter Vigil, Christ Church Cathedral, Oxford, 22 Apr. Author's memory and notes.

2000c-d   Interviews with Cragg by author 29 February (c) and 21 May 2000 (d). Author's notes.

2000e   Letter from Cragg to author, 29 May 2000. Possessed by author.

2000f   *Islam among the spires: An Oxford reverie.* London: Melisende.

2001   *Muhammad in the Qur'an. The task and the text.* London: Melisende

2002   *Am I not Your Lord? Human meaning in divine question.* London: Melisende

WILFRED CANTWELL SMITH

1946   *Modern Islam in India: A social analysis* [MI]. Second revised edn., [¹1943], reprint of 1985. New Delhi: Usha Publications.

1948   The Azhar Journal: Survey and critique. Ph.D. diss., Princeton University.

1950   The comparative study of religion. Reflections on the possibility and purpose of a religious science. [Inaugural Lecture, McGill University, Faculty of Divinity, 8 Dec 1949.] McGill University: Montreal.

1954   *Pakistan as an Islamic state.* [Revised version as Ch. 5 in *IH*]

1957a   *Islam in modern history.* Princeton, N J: Princeton University Press.

1957b   Review of *CM* (Cragg). *JR* 37, 201-202.

1959/1966 Comparative religion: Whither and why? In *The History of Religions: Essays in Methodology,* ed. Mircea Eliade/Joseph M Kitagawa, 31-58. 6th imprint (1st: 1959). Chicago/London: The University of Chicago Press.

1961a   The comparative study of religion in general and the study of Islam as a religion in particular. *Colloque sur la Sociologie Musulmane,* Actes 11-14 (Septembre): 217-231.

1961b   The Christian in a religiously plural world, in *FOM*, part II, 105-128. Also reprinted in an abridged version in *RD,* 3-21, with preface by W.G. Oxtoby. [First held as an address in the Canadian Theological Society, 1961.]

1962/1965 *The faith of other men* [FOM]. A Mentor Book, New York: The

New American Library and London: The New English Library
Limited, first printing. [Reprinted as *Patterns of faith around the
world.* Oxford: Oneworld Publications, 1998. The first part
originally held as popular radio talks, 'The University of the
Air', Canadian Broadcasting Corporation, 1962.]

1963   *The meaning and end of religion* [ME]. Minneapolis: Fortress
Press, 1962/1963/1991.

1964   Mankind's religiously divided history approaches self-
consciousness. [Inaugural Lecture, Center for the Study of World
Religions, Divinity School, Harvard University, 1964] *HDB* 29,
no. 1: 1-17.

1967a   The mission of the Church and the future of missions. In *The
Church in the modern world: Essays in honour of James
Sutherland Thomson,* ed. George Johnston and Wolfgang Roth,
154-170. Toronto: The Ryerson Press.

1967b   *Questions of religious truth* [QT]. London: Victor Golliancz.

1969a   Participation: The changing Christian role in other cultures.
OBMRL 20, no. 4 (April): 1-13. [Also published in *RS* 18, no. 1
(1970): 56-74, and as abridged form in *RD*, 117-137.]

1973b   On dialogue and 'faith': A rejoinder. *Journal of Religion and
Religions* 3 (Autumn): 106-114.

1974a   A human view of truth. In *Truth and dialogue: The relationship
between world religions,* ed. John Hick. London. [Reprinted in
Smith 1997.]

1974b   Conflicting truth-claims. In *Truth and dialogue: The relationship
between world religions,* ed. John Hick. London.

1976   *Religious diversity* [RD], ed. and introduction by Williard G
Oxtoby. New York: Crossroad.

1976a   The study of religion and the study of the Bible. In *RD*, 41-56,
with preface by W G Oxtoby. [Reprinted with minor alterations
from *JAAR* 39 (1971), 131-140.]

1976b   Objectivity and the humane sciences. In *RD*, 158-190. [Abridged
version of an address to the Royal Society of Canada, 4 June
1974, Transactions of the Royal Society of Canada, Ottawa:
Royal Society of Canada, 1975, 81-102.]

1977   *Belief and history* [BH]. [Reprinted as *Believing: An historical
perspective.* Oxford: Oneworld Publications, 1998.]

1979a   *Faith and belief* [FB]. Princeton, N J: Princeton University
Press.

1979b   Thinking about persons. *Hum(P)* 15: 147-152.

1980a   The true meaning of scripture: An empirical historian's
nonreductionist interpretation of the Qur'an. *IJMES,* 11: 487-
505. Reprinted in *WS.*

1981   *Towards a world theology: Faith and the comparative history of
religion.* Hampshire/London: Macmillan.

1981b   The Shahadah as symbolic representation of Muslim's faith. In

UI, 26-37. [First published as 'Muslims' in *FOM*.]

1958/1981c The historical development in Islam of the concept of islam as an historical development. In *UI*, 41-77. [First presented to a conference on Muslim historiography, 1958, the School of Oriental and African Studies, University of London.]

1960/1981e Islamic law: *Shari'ah* and *Shar'*. In *UI*, 87-109. [First read to the Islamics section of the International Congress of Orientalists' quadrennial meeting, Moscow 1960, Smith's first visit to the Soviet Union. First published in a *Festschrift* to his teacher, Sir Hamilton Gibb.]

1974/1981f Faith, in the Qur'an: And its relation to belief. In *UI*, 110-134. [First delivered as the first lecture of two (the second = Smith 1974/1981o) of the Iqbal Memorial Lectures at the University of the Punjab, Lahore, 1974.]

1971/1981g Faith, in later Islamic history; the meaning of ta√dïq. In *UI*, 135-161.

1974/1981h Faith, in later Islamic history; the meaning of arkan. In *UI*, 1162-173. [First published in 1974 in a Festschrift in honour of Niyazis Berkes, colleague at the Islamic Institute, McGill.]

1959/1981m Some similarities and some differences between Christianity and Islam. In *UI*, 233-246. [First written for and published in *The World of Islam: Studies in Honour of Philip K. Hitti,* ed. James Kritzeck and R. Bayly, London: MacMillan, and New York: St Martin's, 1959, 47-59.]

1974/1981o Muslim and Christian: Faith convergence, belief divergence. In *UI*, 265-281. [First delivered as the second lecture of two (the first = Smith 1974/1981f) of the Iqbal Memorial Lectures at the University of the Punjab, Lahore, 1974.]

1967/1981p Is the Qur'an the word of God? In *UI*, 282-300. [First published in *QT*, 1967, 39-64.]

1984 The world Church and the world history of religion: The theological issue. *PCTSA* 39, 52-68.

1987a Idolatry: In comparative perspective. In *The Myth of Christian Uniqueness,* ed. John Hick/ Paul F. Knitter, 53-68. New York: Maryknoll, Orbis.

1987b Theology and the world's religious history. In *Toward a Universal Theology of Religion,* ed. Leonard Swidler, 2nd printing, 51-72. New York: Maryknoll, Orbis.

1987c Taking goodness seriously. *University of Toronto Bulletin,* 29 June, 13. [Address given at the Convocation for the School of Graduate Studies, 8 June.]

1987d Theology and the academic study of religion. *IliffRev* 44, no. 3: 9-18.

1988a Mission, dialogue, and God's will for us. *IRM* 77, no. 307 (July): 360-374.

1988b Transcendence. [Ingersoll Lecture, 10 March, 1988.] *HDB* 18: 10-15.

1991a   Christian-Muslim relations: The theological dimension. *Studies in Interreligious Dialogue* 1:1, 8-24.

1991b   A note on the Qur'an from a comparativist perspective. In *Islamic studies presented to Charles J Adams,* ed. Wael B Hallaq and Donald P Little, 183-192. Leiden: E.J. Brill, 1991.

1992   Can believers share the Qur'an and the bible as word of God. In *On sharing religious experience: Possibilities of interfaith mutuality,* ed. Jerald D Gort et al., 55-63. Amsterdam: Rodopi and Grand Rapids, MI: Eerdmans.

1993   *What is scripture? A comparative approach* [WS]. London: SCM Press.

Classified Reference List[2]

WITH DIRECT REFERENCE TO CRAGG

Akhtar, Shabbir. 1990a. *A faith for all seasons: Islam and Western modernity.* London: Bellew Publishing.

_____ . 1990b. Faust and the new idolaters: Reflections on shirk. *ICMR* 1, 252-260.

_____ . 1991. An Islamic model of revelation. *ICMR* 2, 95-105.

Ayoub, Mahmoud M. 1987. Review of *JM. JES* 24:3 (Sum), 449.

Berentsen, Jan-Martin. 1994. *Det moderne Areopagos. Røster fra den religionsteologiske debatten i vårt århundre* [Moderen Areopagus: Voices in theology of religions in our century]. Stavanger: Misjonshøgskolens forlag.

Bijlefeld, Willem A. 1967. The danger of 'christianizing' our partners in the dialogue. *MW* 57:3, 171-177.

Cox, Harvey. 1990. World religions, politics aside. [Review of *CFs.*] *CrossCur* 40 (Spr), 120-124.

Cracknell, Kenneth. 1988. Review of *CFs. Theol.* 91 (Mar), 162-163.

D'Costa, Gavin. 1987. Review of *CFs. ET* 98:9 (Je), 284-285.

*D'Souza, Andreas. 1980. The origin of Islam as interpreted by W. Montgomery Watt and A. Kenneth Cragg: An analysis and evaluation. M.A. diss., McGill University, Canada.

---

[2] In order to include as many of the dissertations on Smith and Cragg as possible, particularly because of their interest for the current status of research (cf. the Introduction) I have decided to present also those that I have not consulted myself. These are marked with an asterisk (*) immediately in front of the entry of the work of concern. However, as quite good abstracts of most of these are available in various databases, it has indeed been possible to attain a certain overview of this part of the secondary literature.

I would also like to mention that *some* of the reviews of Smith and Cragg's various studies are not referred to in the text, but have been included in order to show the attention paid to these studies in different reviews.

_____ . 1992. Christian approaches to the study of Islam: An analysis of the writings of Watt and Cragg. *BHMI* 11 (July-Dec): 33-80.

Gabriel, Theodore. 1988. Review of *CFs. MoTh* 4 (Ja), 220-221.

Griffith, Sidney H. 1994. Kenneth Cragg on Christians and the call to Islam. *RStR* 20:1, 29-34.

Grunebaum, G.E. von. 1970. Approaching Islam: A digression. *MES* 6: 127-149.

*Hambrick-Stowe, Elizabeth A. 1972. Inter-faith dialogue: The work of Kenneth Cragg. M.A. diss., Pacific School of Theology.

Khan, Abrahim H. 1986. Metatheological reflections on recent Christian acknowledgement of Muhammad as prophet: Inter-faith dialogue and the academic study of religion. *TJT* 2: 188-203.

Lamb, Christopher. 1981. The editorials of The Muslim World, 1911-1968. In *MW* 71: 3-26.

_____ . 1997. *Retrieval to Islam: Kenneth Cragg's Christian vocation to Islam.* London. [Submitted as Ph.D., Birmingham University, 1987.]

*McCulloch, Laurence R. 1962. The Christian approach to Islam in the writings of Samuel Zwemer and Kenneth Cragg. S.T.B thesis, Biblical Seminary, New York.

Mosser, David N. 1990. Review of *CFs. LuthQ* 4:1 (Spr), 76f.

Newbigin, Lesslie. 1987. Review of *CFs. JThS* 38 (Oct), 585-588.

Nielsen, Jørgen S. 1997. 'Foreword' in Lamb 1997, viif.

Parrinder, Geoffrey. 1984. Review of *MC. ET* 96 (Dec), 90.

Race, Alan. 1984. Review of *MC. Theol.* 87 (Nov), 466-467.

Rahbar, Muhammad Daud. 1958. Review of *CM*. In *MW* 48 (Ja), 40-51.

*Richards, N. 1993. Muslim Christology: With particular reference to continuing Muslim/Christian debate. M.Phil. diss., University of Nottingham.

Robertson, Edwin. 1976. Kenneth Cragg: A Christian iman. In *idem*, *Breakthrough*. Belfast: Christian Journals.

Qureshi, Jamil. 1984. 'Alongsidedness – in good faith?' An essay on Kenneth Cragg. In Asaf Hussain, Robert Olson, Jamil Qureshi, ed., *Orientalism, Islam, and Islamists,* 203-258. Brattleboro, Vt, 1984.

Scherer, James. 1960. Review of *SM. LuthQ* 12 (Nov), 356.

Schimmel, Annemarie. 1962. Zum christlich-muslimischen Dialog. *Kairos* 4:1, 56f.

_____ . 1985. Review of *MC. JES* 22:4, 784f.

Scott, David A. 1989. Review of *CFs. SJTh* 42, 445-447.

Slomp, Jan. 1990. Kenneth Cragg and the Qur'an. In Ludwig Hagemann and Ernst Pulfort, ed., *'Ihr alle seid Brüder': Festschrift für Adel Theodor Khoury zum 60. Geburtstag.* Würzburg, Altenberge.

Smart, Ninian. 1970. Review of *PM. MCM* 13, 214f.

*Tebbe, J A 1998. Christian scriptures in Muslim culture in the work of Kenneth Cragg. Ph.D., Open University, U.K.

*Virgint, John Edward. 1970. The 'frontier' theologies of Kenneth Cragg and
        Arend van Leeuwen: With special reference to the contemporary
        Christian-Muslim encounter. M.A. diss., Hartford Seminary
        Foundation, 1970.

Waugh, Earle H. 1993. Review of *AC. JR* 73:4, 651-652.

Watt, W Montgomery. 1957. Review of *CM. JThS* 8:2, 405-407.

_____. 1970. Review of *PM.* In *JSSt* 15 (Aut), 273.

*Wilson, Harry Kurz, III. 1995. The stigma of baptism in the evangelization of
        Muslims: An historical and critical evaluation. Ph.D. diss.,
        Southwestern Baptist Theological Seminary.

Wood, Nicholas J. 1996. Confessing Christ in a plural world: A missiological
        approach to inter-faith relations with particular reference to
        Lesslie Newbigin and Kenneth Cragg. D.Phil. diss., University of
        Oxford.

WITH DIRECT REFERENCE TO SMITH

Almond, Philip C. 1983. Wilfred Cantwell Smith as theologian of religions.
        HThR 76:3, 335-42.

*Anderson, Brian David. 1991. The locus and effect of divine revelation among
        non-Christian religions: A critical analysis of the views of Karl
        Barth, Karl Rahner and Wilfred Cantwell Smith. Ph.D. diss.,
        Southwestern Baptist Theological Seminary.

*Bae, Kuk-Won. 1998. Homo fidei: A critical understanding of faith in the
        writings of Wilfred Cantwell Smith and its implications for the
        study of religion. Ph.D. diss., Harvard University.

Berthrong, John. 1989. The theological necessity of pluralism: The
        contribution of Wilfred Cantwell Smith. *TJT* 5: 188-205.

*Bollinger, Gary Allen. 1981. Personal faith and interfaith encounter. Ph.D.,
        The Claremont Graduate School.

*Brown, Douglas George. 1997. An examination of alienating trends in religious
        education. E.D.D. diss., University of Toronto.

Buckalew, Ronald William. 1987. A return of the Servant: Kenotic Christ and
        religious pluralism in the thought of Raimundo Panikkar and
        Wilfred Cantwell Smith. Ph.D. diss., Union Theological
        Seminary, Virginia.

Burrell, David, C S C. 1983. Faith and religious convictions: Studies in
        comparative epistemology [Review of *BH, FB* and *WT*]. *JR* 63,
        64-73.

*Cameron, Roberta Llewellyn. 1997. The making of Wilfred Cantwell Smith's
        'World Theology'. Ph.D. diss., Concordia University, Canada.

*Christiano, George. 1986. An analytical assessment of the faith development
        theory of J W Fowler, an approach to moral education. E.D.D.
        diss., Rutgers State University of New Jersey.

Cracknell, Kenneth. 2001. *Wilfred Cantwell Smith: A Reader.* Oxford:

Rewarding Encounters

Oneworld.

D'Costa, Gavin. 1994. Review of *WS. Theol.* 97, 301-302.

*Doyle, D M. 1984. The distinction between faith and belief and the question of religious truth: The contribution of Wilfred Cantwell Smith. Ph.D. diss., Catholic University of America.

Droge, A J. 1996. Review of *WS. JR* 76:3, 519-520.

Edwards, Mark. 2000. Religion and religions in Antiquity: Is Cantwell Smith right? Paper delivered to the Patristics Seminar, Trinity Term, Univ. of Oxford.

al-Faruqi, Ismail Raji. 1998. *Islam and other faiths.* Ed. Ataullah Siddiqui. Leicester: The Islamic Foundation, The International Institute of Islamic Thought.

*Fellows, Ward J. 1988. The dilemma of univeralism and particularism in four Christian theological views if the relation of Christianity to other religions (Tillich, Rahner, Smith, Hick). Ph.D. diss., Union Theological Seminary.

*Fernhout, Johan Harry. 1986. Moral autonomy and faith commitment: Conflict or integrality. A critical assessment of competing perspectives in foundational issues in moral education. Ph.D. diss., University of Toronto.

Frank, Richard M. 1986. Ambiguities of understanding [Review of *UI*]. *JAOS* 106, 313-321.

*Gardner, Laurie Beth. 1989. Viktor Frankl and Wilfred Cantwell Smith: A study of a psychiatrist's contribution to world theology. A.B. thesis, Harvard University.

Gilkey, Langdon. 1981. A theological voyage with Wilfred Cantwell Smith. *RStR* 7, no. 4: 298-306.

Grünschloß, Andreas. 1994a. *Religionswissenschaft als Welt-Theologie. Wilfred Cantwell Smiths interreligiöse Hermeneutik.* FSÖTh 71, ed. Wolfhart Pannenberg/ Reinhard Slenczka. [Delivered as diss., University of Heidelberg, 1991/92.] Göttingen: Vandenhoeck & Ruprecht.

_____. 1994b. Der eigene und der fremde Glaube: Probleme und Perspektiven gegenwärtiger Religionstheologie. *EvErz* 46, 287-299.

*Gualtieri, Antonio R. 1969. Theological evaluations of Christians of the religious faith of non-Christians. Ph.D. diss., McGill University, Dept. of Divinity.

_____. 1973. Can we know the religious faith of others? Some light from Wilfred Cantwell-Smith. *Religion and Society* 20, no. 3, 6-17.

Heim, S Mark. 1995. *Salvations: Truth and difference in religion.* New York: Maryknoll, Orbis.

Hick, John. 1992. On Wilfred Cantwell Smith: His place in the study of religion. *MTSR* 4, no. 1-2: 5-20.

Hughes, Edward J. 1985. The global philosophy of Wilfred Cantwell Smith: An experiment in intercultural thought. Ph.D. diss., Claremont

Graduate School.

_____ . 1992. Wilfred Cantwell Smith and the Perennial philosophy. *MTSR* 4:1-2, 27-46.

Küng, Hans. 1986. Introduction: The debate on the word 'religion'. *Conc(GB)* 22:1 (Christianity and world religions, ed. Hans Küng and Jürgen Moltmann), xi-xv.

Loughlin, Gerard. 1992. Review of *WT*. *The Heythrop Journal* 33, 209-212.

Meynell, Hugo. 1985. The idea of a world theology. *Modern Theology* 1:2, 149-161.

McCutcheon, Richard T. 1992. Wilfred Cantwell Smith: A chronological bibliography. In Despland, Michael and Gérard Vallée, ed., *Religion in history: The word, the idea, the reality. EdSR* 13, 243-252. Canada: Canadian Corporation for Studies in Religion/ Corporation Canadienne des Sciences Religieuses and Wilfrid Laurier University Press.

*Mitchell, Robert G. 1994. Cumulative tradition and faith: The comparative methodology of Wilfred Cantwell Smith. M.A. diss., California State University.

Newbigin, Lesslie. 1979. Review of *ME. Theol.* 82, 294-296.

*Nicholson, W. I. 1978. Toward a theology of comparative religion: A study in the thought of Hendrik Kraemer and Wilfred Cantwell Smith. Ph.D. diss., Southern Baptist Theological Seminary.

*Van Orman, Kimberly. 1994. Pragmatic and comparative perspective on the experience of faith: A study of William James and Wilfred Cantwell Smith. M.A. diss., Kent State University.

Oxtoby, Williard G. 1976. Editor's introduction. In *RD*, ed. and introduction by Williard G Oxtoby. New York: Crossroad

Pruett, Gordon E. 1990. World theology and world community. The vision of Wilfred Cantwell Smith. *SR* 19: 397-412.

*Psychas, Paul Joseph. 1986. A critique of modern Western secularism: The global perspective of Wilfred Cantwell Smith. A.B. thesis, Harvard University.

*Rasiah, Iswaradevan. 1984. The contribution of Wilfred Cantwell Smith to inter-faith understanding. Th.D., Boston University School of Theology.

*Rokhsefat, Seyed Mostafa. 1994. Wilfred Cantwell Smith's contribution to the study of Islam. M.A. diss., McGill University, Canada.

Sharpe, Eric. 1973. Dialogue and faith. *Journal of Religion and Religions* 3 (Autumn): 89-105.

*Shawver, D J 1974. Wilfred Cantwell Smith's conceptions of religious truth. M.A. diss., McGill University, Dept. of Religious Studies.

Slater, Peter. 1982. Review essay: Three views of Christianity. *JAAR* L:1, 97-109

Smart, Ninian. 1992. W C Smith and complementarity. *MTSR* 4, no. 1-2: 21-26.

*Stetson, Bradley Leon. 1993. Religious belief and religious pluralism. Ph.D. diss., University of Southern California.

*Stephens, Robert J. 1998. The 'meaning' but not the 'end of religion':
Humanity, transcendence and scripture according to Wilfred
Cantwell Smith. M.A. diss., University of Kansas, Religious
Studies.

Stevens, P.T. 1986. Wilfred Cantwell Smith's concept of faith: A critical study
of his approach to Islam and Christianity. M.A. diss., University
of Durham.

Surin, Kenneth. 1990a. Towards a materialistic critique of 'religious pluralism'.
An examination of the discourse of John Hick and Wilfred
Cantwell Smith. In *Religious pluralism and unbelief. Studies
critical and comparative,* ed. Ian Hamnett, 114-129. London/
New York: Routledge.

_____. 1990b. A 'politics of speech'. In *Christian Uniqueness
Reconsidered: The Myth of a Pluralistic Theology of Religions,*
ed. Gavin D'Costa, 192-212. New York: Maryknoll, Orbis.

Swinburne, Richard. 1980. Review of *FB. RelSt* 16, 239-242.

Tadsen, Rose, O.S.U. 1985. Jesus Christ in the world theology of Wilfred
Cantwell Smith. Ph.D. diss., Faculty of Theology, University of
St Michael's College, Toronto, Ontario.

Waardenburg, Jacques. 1981. Preface. In *UI,* v-viii.

WITH DIRECT REFERENCE TO BOTH CRAGG AND SMITH

Aydin, Mahmut. 1998. Modern western Christian theological understandings
of Muslims since the Second Vatican Council. Ph.D. diss.,
University of Birmingham.

Bijlefeld, Willem A. 1969. A prophet and more than a prophet? Some
observations on the Qur'anic use of the terms 'prophet' and
'apostle'. *MW* 59:1, 1-28.

Ipema, Peter. 1971. The Islam interpretations of Duncan B Macdonald, Samuel
M Zwemer, A Kenneth Cragg and Wilfred C Smith: An analytical
comparison and evaluation. Ph.D. diss., Hartford Seminary
Foundation.

Jones, Richard J. 1988. Wilfred Cantwell Smith and Kenneth Cragg on Islam:
Their contrasting implications for a theology of religion and a
theology of mission. Ph.D. diss., Toronto School of Theology,
Department of Theology.

_____. 1992. Wilfred Cantwell Smith and Kenneth Cragg on Islam as a
Way of Salvation. *IBMR* 16: 105-10.

Hock, Klaus. 1986. Der Islam im Spiegel westlicher Theologie: Aspekte
christlich-theologischer Beurteilung des Islams im 20.
Jahrhundert. Diss., University of Hamburg, Fachbereich
Evangelische Theologie.

*Milne, James William. 1975. How the approaches of Wilfred Cantwell Smith
and Kenneth Cragg as Christians to Islam compare with special

references to the subjects of revelation and knowledge of God.
M.A. diss., Concordia University, Canada.

Newbigin. 1989. The Christian faith and the world religions. In Geoffrey
Wainwright, ed., *Keeping the faith. Essays to mark the centenary
of Lux Mundi,* 310-340. London: SPCK.

Rajashekar, J. Paul. 1988. The challenge of religious pluralism to Christian
theological reflection. In *LWF.R* 23-24. Geneva: Lutheran World
Federation.

Tibawi, A L. 1963. English-speaking Orientalists: A critique of their approach
to Islam and Arab nationalism. *MW* 53, 185-204 (I) and 298-313
(II).

*Wallace, Ronald. 1994. Inter-faith dialogue as a method for the scientific study
of religion. Ph.D. diss., University of Toronto.

GENERAL REFERENCES

Aagaard, Anna Marie. 1973. *Helligånden sendt til verden* [The Holy Spirit sent
into the world]. [Diss. Århus University 1972. With English
Summary, 281-285] Aarhus: Aros.

Balz, Heinrich. 1995. Nicht alle werden bleiben, was sie sind. Die Religionen in
evangelischer Perspektive. *ThBeitr* 26:3, 128-135.

Barnes, Michael, S.J. 1989. *Religions in conversation: Christian identity and
religious pluralism.* London: SPCK.

Bernstein, Richard J. 1992. Reconciliation and rupture: The challenge and
threat of otherness. In Reynolds and Tracy 1992, 295-314.

Bijlefeld, Willem A. 1959. *De Islam als na-christelikje Religie.* Leiden.

_____ . 1998. Introduction [guest editorial, special issue of *MW* on
Muslim-Christian relations]. *MW* 88:3-4, 213-217.

Burrell, David E., C.S.C. 1998. Mind and heart at the service of Muslim-
Christian understanding: Louis Massignon as trailblazer. *MW*
88:3-4, 268-278.

Chadwick, Owen. 1970. *The Victorian Church.* [An ecclesiastical history of
England, vol. VIII, gen. ed., J C Dickinson.] Part II. London:
Adam & Charles Black.

Colpe, Carsten. 1987. Syncretism. In *EncRel(E),* vol. 14, 218-227.

Congregation for the doctrine of faith. 2000. *Dominus Iesus: On the unicity and
salvific universality of Jesus Christ and the Church.* Rome/ http:/
/www.marianland.com/vatican001.html

Coward, Harold. 1985. *Pluralism: Challenge to world religions.* New York:
Maryknoll, Orbis.

Cracknell, Kenneth. 1995. *Justice, courtesy and love: Theologians and
missionaries encountering world religions, 1846-1914.* London:
Epworth.

D'Costa, Gavin. 1985. Karl Rahner's anonymous Christian—a reappraisal.
MoTh 1:2, 131-148.

_____ . 1986a. *Theology and religious pluralism: The challenge of other religions.* Basil Blackwell: Oxford.

_____ . 1990b. 'Extra ecclesiam nulla salus' revisited. In *Religious Pluralism and Unbelief. Studies Critical and Comparative,* ed. Ian Hamnett, 130-147. London and New York: Routledge.

_____ . 1990c/1995. Ed. *Christian uniqueness reconsidered: The myth of a pluralistic theology of religions.* New York: Maryknoll, Orbis.

_____ . 1990d. Taking other religions seriously: Some ironies in the current debate on a Christian theology of religions. *Thom.* 54:3, 519-530.

_____ . 1991. A Christian reflection on some problems with discerning 'God' in the world religions. *Dialogue & Alliance* 5:1, 4-17.

_____ . 1993. Whose objectivity? Which neutrality? The doomed quest for a neutral vantage point from which to judge religions. *RelSt* 29, 79-95.

_____ . 2000. *The meeting of religions and the Trinity.* [Faith meets faiths series, ed. P.F. Knitter.] New York: Maryknoll, Orbis.

Dean, Thomas. 1995. Ed. *Religious pluralism and truth: Essays on cross-cultural philosophy of religion.* SUNY Series in Religious Studies, ed. Harold Coward. Albany, NY: State University of New York.

DiNoia, J A. 1992. *The diversity of religions: A Christian perspective.* Washington, D.C.: The Catholic University of America Press.

Gadamer, Hans-Georg. 1975[E]. *Truth and method.* New York: Seabury Press.

_____ . 1990[G]. *Wahrheit und Methode: Grundzüge einer philosophischen Hermeneutik* ([1]1960). 6. durchges. Aufl. *Gesammelte Werke,* Bd. 1. Tübingen: Mohr Siebeck.

_____ . 1994. 'Foreword' to Grondin 1994, ix-xi.

Gasché, Rodolphe. 1999. *Of minimal things. Studies on the notion of relation.* Stanford, CA: Stanford University Press.

Gore, Charles, ed. 1890a. *Lux Mundi: A series of studies in the religion of the Incarnation.* 7th edn. ([1]1889). London: John Murray.

_____ . 1890b. The Holy Spirit and inspiration. In idem 1890a, 315-362. [With a minor rewriting compared to the original print of 1889 in order to obviate further misunderstanding due to a partly very critical reception when first issued.]

Gregersen, Niels Henrik. 1991. Kulturen i teologien og teologien i kulturen. *Teologi og kultur: Foredrag fra veiledningsseminar for forskerrekrutter i teologi/kristendomskunnskap,* 1-24. Bergen: Samarbeidsutvalget for forskerutdanning i teologi/kristendomskunnskap.

Griffiths, Paul J. 1997. Comparative philosophy of religion. In *A companion to philosophy of religion,* ed. Philip L. Quinn and Charles Talliaferro, 615-620. Oxford/ Malden, MA: Blackwell.

Grondin, Jean. 1994. *Introduction to philosophical hermeneutics.* New Haven and London: Yale University Press.

Grünschloß, Andreas. 1999. *Der eigene und der fremde Glaube. Studien zum interreligiösen Fremdwahrnehmung in Islam, Hinduismus,*

Buddhismus und Christentum. HUTh 37, hrsg. H.D. Betz et. al. Tübingen: Mohr Siebeck.

Gunton, Colin E. 1993/1998. *The one, the three and the many. God, creation and the culture of modernity. The 1992 Bampton lectures.* Cambridge: Cambridge University Press.

Haddad, Wadi Z. 1987. Article on 'Taftazani, al-' in *ER*, Vol. 14, 244.

Hammerschmidt, Anette C. 1997. *Fremdverstehen: Interkulturelle Hermeneutik zwischen Eigenem und Fremdem* [diss. at Universität Hamburg, 1993.] München: Iudicium.

Harvey, Van A. 1987. Hermeneutics. In *EncRel(E)*, 6:279-287.

Hick, John. 1973/1988. *God and the universe of faiths.* Houndmills/ London.

Jenson, Robert W. 2000. The hidden and triune God. *IJST* 2:1 (Mar), 5-12.

Kerr, David. 1981. The problem of Christianity in Muslim perspective: Implications for Christian mission. *IBMR* 5, no. 4: 152-162.

Khodr, Georges. 1971/1981. The economy of the Holy Spirit. In Gerald H Anderson and Thomas F Stransky, C.S.P., ed., *Faith meets faith,* 36-49. [Mission Trends, no. 5, first printed in *Ecumenical Review,* 1971]. New York/ Ramsey/ Toronto: Paulist Press, and Grand Rapids: Eerdmans.

Knitter, Paul F. 1973. What is German Protestant theology saying about the non-Christian religions? *NZSTh* 15, 38-64.

Kraemer, Hendrik. 1960. Islamic culture and missionary adequacy. *MW* 50, 244-251.

Küng, Hans. 1991 ([1]1990, Ger.). *Global responsibility: In search of a new world ethic.* London: SCM Press.

Lapidus, Ira M. 1988/1995. *A history of Islamic societies.* Reprinted 1995 ([1]1988). Cambridge/New York: Cambridge University Press.

Leuze, Reinhard. 1978. Möglichkeit und Grenzen einer Theologie der Religionsgeschichte. *KuD* 24, 230-243.

_____. 1994. *Christentum und Islam.* Tübingen: J C B Mohr.

Light, Timothy. 2000. Orthosyncretism: An account of melding in religion. *MTSR* 12, 162-186.

Lossky, Vladimir. 1957/1991. *The mystical theology of the Eastern Church.* Cambridge: James Clarke & Co.

Macquarrie, John. 1993. Doctrinal development: Searching for criteria. In Coakley, Sarah and Pailin, David A, ed. 1993. *The making and remaking of Christian doctrine: Essays in honour of Maurice Wiles,* 161-176. Oxford: Oxford University Press.

Martin, Luther H. 2000. Of religious syncretism, comparative religion and spiritual quests. *MTSR* 12, 277-286.

McGrath, Alister E. 1995. Ed. *The Christian theology reader.* Oxford/ Cambridge, MA: Blackwell.

McIntyre, John. 1987. *Faith, theology and imagination.* Edinburgh: Handsel Press.

Michel, Thomas, SJ. 2000. God's unity and trinity: The Islamic-Christian debate. [= D'Arcy Memorial Lectures 2000, *Paul of Antioch and*

Ibn Taymiyya: The modern relevance of a medieval polemic,
lecture no. 4, delivered 24 Feb, Campion Hall, University of
Oxford.] 8pp, n.p.

Mitchell, Basil. 1994. *Faith and criticism*. [The Sarum Lectures 1992.] Oxford:
Oxford University Press.

Mæland, Bård. 1997a. Religionene som systematisk-teologisk problemfelt
[Eng. The religions as a systematic theological problem]. *NTM*
51:2, 109-128.

_____. 1997b. Åpenhet, identitet og (selv)kritikk: Til forholdet mellom
interreligiøs dialog og religionsteologi [Eng. Openness, identity
and (self-)criticism: The relation between dialogue and theology
of religions]. *Religion og livssyn* 9:3, 11-15.

_____. 1999. Tradisjon og nydannelse. En drøfting av 'invensjon' innenfor
dogmatisk teoridannelse [Eng. Tradition and new formulations:
'Invention' within doctrinal theory]. *TTK* 70:3, 174-192.

_____. 2000. Religious plurality: A discussion of the theories of John Hick
and S Mark Heim [= English summary]. *SMT* 88:2, (267)291-
297.

Nagel, Tilman. 1990. Theologie und Ideologie im modernen Islam. In *Der
Islam,* ed. Munir Ahmed et al., Bd. III [Vol 25,3 of *Die
Religionen der Menschheit*, ed. Peter Antes et al.], Stuttgart/
Berlin/ Köln: W. Kohlhammer.

Nasr, Seyyed Hossein. 1998. Islamic-Christian dialogue: Problems and
obstacles to be pondered and overcome. *MW* 88:3-4, 218-237.

Newman, John H [2]1878/1989. *An essay on the development of Christian
doctrine.* Foreword by Ian Ker. Notre Dame, IN: Univ. of Notre
Dame Press.

Panikkar, Raimundo. 1978. *The intrareligious dialogue.* New York, NY/
Ramsey, NJ: Paulist Press.

Pannenberg, Wolfhart. 1976. *Theology and the philosophy of science,* London:
Darton, Longman and Todd.

_____. 1988. *Systematische Theologie, Bd. 1.* Göttingen: Vandenhoeck &
Ruprecht

_____. 1990/1995. Religious pluralism and conflicting truth claims. In
Gavin D'Costa 1990c/ 1995, 96-106.

_____. 1993. The doctrine of the Spirit and the task of a theology of
nature. In idem, *Toward a theology of nature: Essays on science
and faith,* 123-137. Ed. Ted Peters. Louisville, Ky: Westminster/
John Knox Press.

Pontifical Council for Interreligious Dialogue. 1981/1990. *Guidelines for
dialogue between Christians and Muslims.* Interreligious
documents, No. 1. Prepared by Maurice Borrmans. French
original ed. 1981. New York/Mahwah, N J: Paulist Press.

Power, Daniel N 1989. The Holy Spirit: Scripture, tradition, and
interpretation. In Geoffrey Wainwright, ed., *Keeping the faith.
Essays to mark the centenary of Lux Mundi.* London: SPCK.

Prenter, Regin. 1953. *Spiritus creator: Luther's concept of the Holy Spirit.* [Da. original: *Spiritus creator: Studier i Luthers theologi av Regin Prenter,* København 1946.] Philadelphia: Muhlenberg Press.

_____. 1962. *Skabelse og genløsning [Creation and redemption].* 3rd ed. København: G E C Gads forlag.

_____. 1974. 'Helligånden sendt til verden.' ['The Holy Spirit sent into the world' = opponent's criticism at the defence of Anna Marie Aagaard's thesis, Aagaard 1973] *TTK* 45:2, 81-102.

_____. 1982. Den Hellige Ånds gjerning i kirken [The work of the Holy Spirit in the church]. *In* Lars Østnor, ed., *Jeg tror på Den Hellige Ånd: Vår lutherske kirke i møte med den karismatiske utfordring.* Oslo: Gyldendal.

Pye, Michael. 1997. Reflecting on the plurality of religions. MJR 2:1, 1-6. http://www.uni-marburg.de/fb03/religionswissenschaft/journal/ mjr/oxford.html

Race, Alan. 1983. *Christians and religious pluralism. Patterns in the Christian theology of religions.* Maryknoll, New York: Orbis.

Rahman, Fazlur. 1979. *Islam.* 2nd edn. Chicago and London: University of Chicago Press.

Ratschow, Carl Heinz. 1973. Systematische Theologie. In Ulrich Mann, ed., *Theologie und Religionswissenschaft: Der gegenwärtige Stand ihrer Forschungsergebnisse und Aufgaben im Hinblick auf ihr gegenseitiges Verhältnis,* 413-424. Darmstadt: WBG.

_____. 1979. *Die Religionen.* Handbuch Systematischer Theologie, Bd. 16. Gütersloh: Mohn.

Rescher, Nicholas. 1973. *The coherence theory of truth.* Oxford: Oxford University Press.

_____. 1993/1996. *Pluralism: Against the demand for consensus.* Oxford: Oxford University Press.

Reynolds, Frank and Tracy, David. 1992. *Discourse and practice.* (SUNY series, *Toward a comparative philosophy of religions,* ed. Frank Reynolds and David Tracy). Albany, N Y: State University of New York Press.

Said, Edward W. 1978/1995. *Orientalism: Western conceptions of the Orient.* Reprinted with a new Afterword. London et. al.: Penguin Books.

Schmidt-Leukel, Perry. 1993. Zur Klassifikation religionstheologischer Modelle. *Cath(M)* 47, 163-183.

Schweiker, William. 1992. The drama of interpretation and the philosophy of religions: An essay on understanding in comparative religious ethics. In Reynolds and Tracy 1992, 263-294.

da Silva, António Barbosa. 1986. *Can religions be compared? Methodological issues in inter-religious discursive dialogue with special regard to the contributions of the phenomenology and philosophy of religion.* Uppsala: The Theological Faculty.

Straub, Jürgen. 1999. *Verstehen, Kritik, Anerkennung. Das Eigene und das Fremde in der Erkenntnisbildung interpretativer Wissenschaften.*

Rewarding Encounters

Essener Kulturwissenschaftliche Vorträge, Bd. 4. Göttingen: Wallstein Verlag.

Stenger, Mary Ann. 1995. Gadamer's hermeneutics as a model for cross-cultural understanding and truth in religion. In Dean 1995, 151-168.

Sundermeier, Theo. 1996. *Den Fremden verstehen: Eine praktische Hermeneutik.* Göttingen: Vandenhoeck & Ruprecht.

Thiselton, Anthony C. 1992. *New horizons in hermeneutics: The theory and practice of transforming biblical reading.* Grand Rapids, Mi: Zondervan.

Tillich, Paul. 1963a. *Systematic theology.* Vol. 3. Chicago: The University of Chicago Press. Reprinted by Xpress Reprints, SCM Press: London, 1997.

_____ . 1963b. Christianity and the encounter of the world religions. In *Paul Tillich: Main Works/ Hauptwerke,* ed. C H Ratschow, Vol. 5, ed. R P Scharlemann, 291-325. Berlin/ New York.

_____ . 1994. Die Bedeutung der Religionsgeschichte für den systematischen Theologen. In *Christentum und nichtchristliche Religionen: Theologische Modelle im 20. Jahrhundert,* ed. Karl-Josef Kuschel, 51-64. Darmstadt.

Tomko, Jozef. 1990. Missionary challenges to the theology of salvation. In Christian mission and interreligious dialogue, ed. Paul Mojzes/ Leonard Swidler, 12-32. Lewiston/ Qeenston / Lampeter.

Tracy, David. 1987. Comparative theology. *EncRel(E)* 14:446-455.

_____ . 1990. *Dialogue with the other: The inter-religious dialogue.* (Louvain theologial & pastoral monographs, No. 1.) Louvain: Peters Press and Grand Rapids, MI: Eerdmans.

Ward, Keith. 1994. *Religion and revelation.* Oxford: Oxford Univ. Press.

_____ . 2000. *Religion and community.* Oxford: Oxford Univ. Press.

Watson, Stephen H. 1992. *Extensions: Essays on interpretation, rationality, and the closure of modernism.* [SUNY Series in Contemporary Continental Philosophy, ed. Dennis J. Schmidt.] New York: State University of New York Press.

Weinandy, Thomas G. 2000. *Does God suffer?* Edinburgh: T&T Clark.

Welker, M. 1988. 'Einheit der Religionsgeschichte' und 'universales Selbstbewusstsein' – Zur gegenwärtigen Suche nach Leitbegriffen im Dialog zwischen Theologie und Religionswissenschaft. *EvTh* 48, 3-18.

Welsby, Paul A. 1984. *A history of the Church of England 1945-1980.* Oxford: Oxford University Press.

Wetlesen, Jon. 1983. Samtaler med tekster i lys av Gadamers hermeneutikk [Conversations with texts in the light of Gadamer's hermeneutics]. *NFT* 18, 219-244.

Williams, Rowan. 2000. *On Christian theology.* Oxford: Blackwell.

INDEX

re-interpretation 52, 155, 218, 292
Real, the 47
reality, gradations of 24
recapitulation 270, 341
reciprocity 9, 16, 153ff, 199, 246,
281, 303
recombination 289
reconceptualization 28, 32
reconciliation 12, 27, 32, 83, 230
reconstruction 9, 11, 17, 131, 149,
260, 286ff, 298ff
Redeemer 229, 233
redefining 155
redemption 159, 174, 230, 232, 234,
247, 269, 283, 303, 310, 341
refinement 87, 315, 328
reflexive relation 6
Reformation, Protestant 79, 131,
339
reformer 14, 40, 312
reformulation 13, 50, 96, 165, 246,
314
reification 37ff
reification-hypothesis 94
relatio 5, 156
relationality 192, 235, 238, 244, 268,
273, 324
relativism 59, 63, 170
relativist 59
reordering 292
repristination 293, 298
Rescher, Nicholas 329, 330, 335f,
338
resonance 204, 344, 354
Resurrection 83, 196, 228, 270
revelation, general 82, 191
special 82, 343
Robert, Hans Jauss 181
Roman Catholic Church 52, 170, 193

S

sacrament 67, 84, 111, 169, 196,
238, 265
sacramentality 234ff
sahha 118
Said, Edward W 4
salat 238, 277f
salvation 41, 80ff, 164 *passim*
history of 56
human/mundane 137
language of 113

personal 137
social 137
salvific 89, 213, 224, 341, 352
sanctorum communionem 172
Sanctuary of Incorporation 166, 174,
180, 314
scheme, tripartite 287
Schleiermacher 38, 163, 332
Schmidt-Leukel, Perry 287, 302
School of Oriental and African
Studies 91
Scotus, Duns 6
scriptural energies 171
scripture, general theory of 125
self-change 3ff
self-communication 154, 226
self-consciousness 57, 69
critical 69
critical corporate 58, 67ff
disciplined 28
historical 57
planetary 28
self-constitutive 6
self-expenditure 181, 315, 345
self-expression 154f, 184, 235, 247
self-giving 166ff, 180ff
self-oblation 173, 181, 338
self-reference 3, 30, 217, 291, 328
self-referential 3, 6, 286, 292
self-relating 3ff
self-relativizing 286, 288, 308
self-renewal 7
self-theologies 76
servant, Lord's 263
Servant's Song 229
Shahadah 99, 102ff, 250, 311
Al-Shahrashtani 252
shari'ah 70, 136, 237ff, 333
Sharpe, Eric 16
Shi'ah 229
shirk 103, 111f, 241, 248ff
shubbiha lahum 267
sidq 118
Sikhism 38
simul justus et peccator 80
sincerity, activist 114ff, 122
Sirah 276
Slater, Peter 1, 340
Slomp, Jan 146, 160, 193, 237, 252
Smart, Ninian 15, 250
social theory of systems 287